The Expositor's Bible
The Book of Ezekiel
By John J. Skinner
Edited by Anthony Uyl

Devoted Publishing
Woodstock, Ontario, 2017

The Expositor's Bible: The Book of Ezekiel
The Expositor's Bible: The Book of Ezekiel
By John J. Skinner (?-1925)
Professor of Old Testament Exegesis, Presbyterian College, London
This edition Edited by Anthony Uyl
Originally Edited by Sir William Robertson Nicoll (1851-1923)

Originally Published by:
London; Hodder And Stoughton 1895

The text of the Expositor's Bible: The Book of Ezekiel is all in the Public Domain. The layout and Devoted Publishing logo are Copyright ©2017 Devoted Publishing. This edition is published by Devoted Publishing a division of 2165467 Ontario Inc.

**What kind of philosophies do you have?
Let us know!**

Visit our online store: www.devotedpublishing.com
Contact us at: devotedpub@hotmail.com
Visit us on Facebook: @DevotedPublishing

Published in Woodstock, Ontario, Canada 2017

For bulk educational rates, please contact us at the above email address.

ISBN: 978-1-77356-100-4

Table of Contents

Preface 5
Part I - The Preparation And Call Of The Prophet 6
   Chapter I - Decline And Fall Of The Jewish State.. 6
      Footnotes:.. 9
   Chapter II - Jeremiah And Ezekiel 10
      Footnotes:.. 14
   Chapter III - The Vision Of The Glory Of God. Chapter i 15
      Footnotes:.. 20
   Chapter IV - Ezekiel's Prophetic Commission. Chapters ii., iii 21
      Footnotes:.. 25
Part II - Prophecies Relating Mainly To The Destruction Of Jerusalem 26
   Chapter V - The End Foretold. Chapters iv.-vii 26
      Footnotes:.. 32
   Chapter VI - Your House Is Left Unto You Desolate. Chapters viii.-xi 33
      Footnotes:.. 39
   Chapter VII - The End Of The Monarchy. Chapters xii. 1-15, xvii., xix 40
      Footnotes:.. 45
   Chapter VIII - Prophecy And Its Abuses. Chapters xii. 21-xiv. 11 46
      Footnotes:.. 50
   Chapter IX - Jerusalem--An Ideal History. Chapter xvi. 51
      Footnotes:.. 56
   Chapter X - The Religion Of The Individual. Chapter xviii 57
      Footnotes:.. 61
   Chapter XI - The Sword Unsheathed. Chapter xxi 63
      Footnotes:.. 67
   Chapter XII - Jehovah's Controversy With Israel. Chapter xx 68
      Footnotes:.. 72
   Chapter XIII - Ohola And Oholibah. Chapter xxiii 74
      Footnotes:.. 76
   Chapter XIV - Final Oracles Against Jerusalem. Chapters xxii., xxiv 77
      Footnotes:.. 81
Part III - Prophecies Against Foreign Nations 82
   Chapter XV - Ammon, Moab, Edom, And Philistia. Chapter xxv 82
      Footnotes:.. 87
   Chapter XVI - Tyre. Chapters xxvi., xxix. 17-21 88
      Footnotes:.. 93
   Chapter XVII - Tyre (Continued): Sidon. Chapters xxvii., xxviii 94
      Footnotes:.. 98
   Chapter XVIII - Egypt. Chapters xxix.-xxxii 100

The Expositor's Bible: The Book of Ezekiel
    Footnotes:.. 106
Part IV - The Formation Of The New Israel 108
    Chapter XIX - The Prophet A Watchman. Chapter xxxiii 108
        Footnotes:.. 113
    Chapter XX - The Messianic Kingdom. Chapter xxxiv 114
        Footnotes:.. 119
    Chapter XXI - Jehovah's Land. Chapters xxxv., xxxvi 120
        Footnotes:.. 126
    Chapter XXII - Life From The Dead. Chapter xxxvii 127
        Footnotes:.. 131
    Chapter XXIII - The Conversion Of Israel 132
        Footnotes:.. 135
    Chapter XXIV - Jehovah's Final Victory. Chapters xxxviii., xxxix 136
        Footnotes:.. 140
Part V - The Ideal Theocracy 141
    Chapter XXV - The Import Of The Vision 141
        Footnotes:.. 147
    Chapter XXVI - The Sanctuary. Chapters xl.-xliii 148
        Footnotes:.. 153
    Chapter XXVII - The Priesthood. Chapter xliv 155
        Footnotes:.. 161
    Chapter XXVIII - Prince And People. Chapters xliv.-xlvi. passim 163
        Footnotes:.. 167
    Chapter XXIX - The Ritual. Chapters xlv., xlvi 169
        Footnotes:.. 176
    Chapter XXX - Renewal And Allotment Of The Land. Chapters xlvii., xlviii 177
        Footnotes:.. 181

John J. Skinner

Preface

In this volume I have endeavoured to present the substance of Ezekiel's prophecies in a form intelligible to students of the English Bible. I have tried to make the exposition a fairly adequate guide to the sense of the text, and to supply such information as seemed necessary to elucidate the historical importance of the prophet's teaching. Where I have departed from the received text I have usually indicated in a note the nature of the change introduced. Whilst I have sought to exercise an independent judgment on all the questions touched upon, the book has no pretensions to rank as a contribution to Old Testament scholarship.

The works on Ezekiel to which I am chiefly indebted are: Ewald's Propheten des Alten Bundes (vol. ii.); Smend's Der Prophet Ezechiel erklärt (Kurzgefasstes Exegetisches Handbuch zum A. T.); Cornill's Das Buch des Proph. Ezechiel; and, above all, Dr. A. B. Davidson's commentary in the Cambridge Bible for Schools, my obligations to which are almost continuous. In a less degree I have been helped by the commentaries of Hävernick and Orelli, by Valeton's Viertal Voorlezingen (iii.), and by Gautier's La Mission du Prophète Ezechiel. Amongst works of a more general character special acknowledgment is due to The Old Testament in the Jewish Church and The Religion of the Semites by the late Dr. Robertson Smith.

I wish also to express my gratitude to two friends--the Rev. A. Alexander, Dundee, and the Rev. G. Steven, Edinburgh--who have read most of the work in manuscript or in proof, and made many valuable suggestions.

Part I – The Preparation And Call Of The Prophet

Chapter I - Decline And Fall Of The Jewish State

Ezekiel is a prophet of the Exile. He was one of the priests who went into captivity with King Jehoiachin in the year 597, and the whole of his prophetic career falls after that event. Of his previous life and circumstances we have no direct information, beyond the facts that he was a priest and that his father's name was Buzi. One or two inferences, however, may be regarded as reasonably certain. We know that that first deportation of Judæans to Babylon was confined to the nobility, the men of war, and the craftsmen (2 Kings xxiv. 14-16); and since Ezekiel was neither a soldier nor an artisan, his place in the train of captives must have been due to his social position. He must have belonged to the upper ranks of the priesthood, who formed part of the aristocracy of Jerusalem. He was thus a member of the house of Zadok; and his familiarity with the details of the Temple ritual makes it probable that he had actually officiated as a priest in the national sanctuary. Moreover, a careful study of the book gives the impression that he was no longer a young man at the time when he received his call to the prophetic office. He appears as one whose views of life are already matured, who has outlived the buoyancy and enthusiasm of youth, and learned to estimate the moral possibilities of life with the sobriety that comes through experience. This impression is confirmed by the fact that he was married and had a house of his own from the commencement of his work, and probably at the time of his captivity. But the most important fact of all is that Ezekiel had lived through a period of unprecedented public calamity, and one fraught with the most momentous consequences for the future of religion. Moving in the highest circles of society, in the centre of the national life, he must have been fully cognisant of the grave events in which no thoughtful observer could fail to recognise the tokens of the approaching dissolution of the Hebrew state. Amongst the influences that prepared him for his prophetic mission, a leading place must therefore be assigned to the teaching of history; and we cannot commence our study of his prophecies better than by a brief survey of the course of events that led up to the turning-point of his own career, and at the same time helped to form his conception of God's providential dealings with His people Israel.

At the time of the prophet's birth the kingdom of Judah was still a nominal dependency of the great Assyrian empire. From about the middle of the seventh century, however, the power of Nineveh had been on the wane. Her energies had been exhausted in the suppression of a determined revolt in Babylonia. Media and Egypt had recovered their independence, and there were many signs that a new crisis in the affairs of nations was at hand.

The first historic event which has left discernible traces in the writings of Ezekiel is an irruption of Scythian barbarians, which took place in the reign of Josiah (c. 626). Strangely enough, the historical books of the Old Testament contain no record of this remarkable invasion, although its effects on the political situation of Judah were important and far-reaching. According to Herodotus, Assyria was already hard pressed by the Medes, when suddenly the Scythians burst through the passes of the Caucasus, defeated the Medes, and committed extensive ravages throughout Western Asia for a period of twenty-eight years. They are said to have contemplated the invasion of Egypt, and to have actually reached the Philistine territory, when by some means they were induced to withdraw. [1] Judah therefore was in imminent danger, and the terror inspired by these destructive hordes is reflected in the prophecies of Zephaniah and Jeremiah, who saw in the northern invaders the heralds of the great day of Jehovah. The force of the storm, however, was probably spent before it reached Palestine, and it seems to have swept past along the coast, leaving the mountain land of Israel untouched. Although Ezekiel was not old enough to have remembered the panic caused by these movements, the report of them would be one of the earliest memories of his childhood, and it made a lasting impression on his mind. One of his later prophecies, that against Gog, is coloured by such reminiscences, the last judgment on the heathen being represented under forms suggested by a Scythian invasion (chs. xxxviii., xxxix.). We may note also that in ch. xxxii. the names of Meshech and Tubal occur in the list of conquering nations who have already gone down to the under-world. These northern peoples formed the kernel of the army of Gog, and the only occasion on which they can be supposed to have played the part of great conquerors in the past is in connection with the Scythian devastations, in which they probably had a share.

The withdrawal of the Scythians from the neighbourhood of Palestine was followed by the great reformation which made the eighteenth year of Josiah an epoch in the history of Israel. The conscience of the nation had been quickened by its escape from so great a peril, and the time was favourable for carrying out the changes which were necessary in order to bring the religious practice of the country into conformity with the requirements of the Law. The outstanding feature of the movement was the discovery of the book of Deuteronomy in the Temple, and the ratification of a solemn league and covenant, by which the king, princes, and people pledged themselves to carry out its demands. This took place in the year 621, somewhere near the time of Ezekiel's birth. [2] The prophet's youth was therefore spent in the wake of the reformation; and although the first hopes cherished by its promoters may have died away before he was able to appreciate its tendencies, we may be sure that he received from it impulses which continued with him to the end of his life. We may perhaps allow ourselves to conjecture that his father belonged to that section of the priesthood which, under Hilkiah its head, co-operated with the king in the task of reform, and desired to see a pure worship established in the Temple. If so, we can readily understand how the reforming spirit passed into the very fibre of Ezekiel's mind. To how great an extent his thinking was influenced by the ideas of Deuteronomy appears from almost every page of his prophecies.

There was yet another way in which the Scythian invasion influenced the prospects of the Hebrew kingdom. Although the Scythians appear to have rendered an immediate service to Assyria by saving Nineveh from the first attack of the Medes, there is little doubt that their ravages throughout the northern and western parts of the empire prepared the way for its ultimate collapse, and weakened its hold on the outlying provinces. Accordingly we find that Josiah, in pursuance of his scheme of reformation, exercised a freedom of action beyond the boundaries of his own land which would not have been tolerated if Assyria had retained her old vigour. Patriotic visions of an independent Hebrew monarchy seem to have combined with new-born zeal for a pure national religion to make the latter part of Josiah's reign the short "Indian summer" of Israel's national existence.

The period of partial independence was brought to an end about 607 by the fall of Nineveh before the united forces of the Medes and the Babylonians. In itself this event was of less consequence to the history of Judah than might be supposed. The Assyrian empire vanished from the earth with a completeness which is one of the surprises of history; but its place was taken by the new Babylonian empire, which inherited its policy, its administration, and the best part of its provinces. The seat of empire was transferred from Nineveh to Babylon; but any other change which was felt at Jerusalem was due solely to the exceptional vigour and ability of its first monarch, Nebuchadnezzar.

The real turning-point in the destinies of Israel came a year or two earlier with the defeat and death of Josiah at Megiddo. About the year 608, while the fate of Nineveh still hung in the balance, Pharaoh Necho prepared an expedition to the Euphrates, with the object of securing himself in the possession of Syria. It was assuredly no feeling of loyalty to his Assyrian suzerain which prompted Josiah to throw himself across Necho's path. He acted as an independent monarch, and his motives were no doubt the loftiest that ever urged a king to a dangerous, not to say foolhardy, enterprise. The zeal with which the crusade against idolatry and false worship had been prosecuted seems to have begotten a confidence on the part of the king's advisers that the hand of Jehovah was with them, and that His help might be reckoned on in any undertaking entered upon in His name. One would like to know what the prophet Jeremiah said about the venture; but probably the defence of Jehovah's land seemed so obvious a duty of the Davidic king that he was not even consulted. It was the determination to maintain the inviolability of the land which was Jehovah's sanctuary that encouraged Josiah in defiance of every prudential consideration to endeavour by force to intercept the passage of the Egyptian army. The disaster that followed gave the death-blow to this illusion and the shallow optimism which sprang from it. There was an end of idealism in politics; and the ruling class in Jerusalem fell back on the old policy of vacillation between Egypt and her eastern rival which had always been the snare of Jewish statesmanship. And with Josiah's political ideal the faith on which it was based also gave way. It seemed that the experiment of exclusive reliance on Jehovah as the guardian of the nation's interests had been tried and had failed, and so the death of the last good king of Judah was a signal for a great outburst of idolatry, in which every divine power was invoked and every form of worship sedulously practised in order to sustain the courage of men who were resolved to fight to the death for their national existence.

The Expositor's Bible: The Book of Ezekiel

By the time of Josiah's death Ezekiel was able to take an intelligent interest in public affairs. He lived through the troubled period that ensued in the full consciousness of its disastrous import for the fortunes of his people, and occasional references to it are to be found in his writings. He remembers and commiserates the sad fate of Jehoahaz, the king of the people's choice, who was dethroned and imprisoned by Pharaoh Necho during the short interval of Egyptian supremacy. The next king, Jehoiakim, received the throne as a vassal of Egypt, on the condition of paying a heavy annual tribute. After the battle of Carchemish, in which Necho was defeated by Nebuchadnezzar and driven out of Syria, Jehoiakim transferred his allegiance to the Babylonian monarch; but after three years' service he revolted, encouraged no doubt by the usual promises of support from Egypt. The incursions of marauding bands of Chaldæans, Syrians, Moabites, and Ammonites, instigated doubtless from Babylon, kept him in play until Nebuchadnezzar was free to devote his attention to the western part of his empire. Before that time arrived, however, Jehoiakim had died, and was followed by his son Jehoiachin. This prince was hardly seated on the throne, when a Babylonian army, with Nebuchadnezzar at its head, appeared before the gates of Jerusalem. The siege ended in a capitulation, and the king, the queen-mother, the army and nobility, a section of the priests and the prophets, and all the skilled artisans were transported to Babylonia (597).

With this event the history of Ezekiel may be said to begin. But in order to understand the conditions under which his ministry was exercised, we must try to realise the situation created by this first removal of Judæan captives. From this time to the final capture of Jerusalem, a period of eleven years, the national life was broken into two streams, which ran in parallel channels, one in Judah and the other in Babylon. The object of the captivity was of course to deprive the nation of its natural leaders, its head and its hands, and leave it incapable of organised resistance to the Chaldæans. In this respect Nebuchadnezzar simply adopted the traditional policy of the later Assyrian kings, only he applied it with much less rigour than they were accustomed to display. Instead of making nearly a clean sweep of the conquered population, and filling the gap by colonists from a distant part of his empire, as had been done in the case of Samaria, he contented himself with removing the more dangerous elements of the state, and making a native prince responsible for the government of the country. The result showed how greatly he had underrated the fierce and fanatical determination which was already a part of the Jewish character. Nothing in the whole story is more wonderful than the rapidity with which the enfeebled remnant in Jerusalem recovered their military efficiency, and prepared a more resolute defence than the unbroken nation had been able to offer.

The exiles, on the other hand, succeeded in preserving most of their national peculiarities under the very eyes of their conquerors. Of their temporal condition very little is known beyond the fact that they found themselves in tolerably easy circumstances, with the opportunity to acquire property and amass wealth. The advice which Jeremiah sent them from Jerusalem, that they should identify themselves with the interests of Babylon, and live settled and orderly lives in peaceful industry and domestic happiness (Jer. xxix. 5-7), shows that they were not treated as prisoners or as slaves. They appear to have been distributed in villages in the fertile territory of Babylon, and to have formed themselves into separate communities under the elders, who were the natural authorities in a simple Semitic society. The colony in which Ezekiel lived was located in Tel Abib, near the Nahr (river or canal) Kebar, but neither the river nor the settlement can now be identified. The Kebar, if not the name of an arm of the Euphrates itself, was probably one of the numerous irrigating canals which intersected in all parts the great alluvial plain of the Euphrates and Tigris. [3] In this settlement the prophet had his own house, where the people were free to visit him, and social life in all probability differed little from that in a small provincial town in Palestine. That, to be sure, was a great change for the quondam aristocrats of Jerusalem, but it was not a change to which they could not readily adapt themselves.

Of much greater importance, however, is the state of mind which prevailed amongst these exiles. And here again the remarkable thing is their intense preoccupation with matters national and Israelitic. A lively intercourse with the mother country was kept up, and the exiles were perfectly informed of all that was going on in Jerusalem. There were, no doubt, personal and selfish reasons for their keen interest in the doings of their countrymen at home. The antipathy which existed between the two branches of the Jewish people was extreme. The exiles had left their children behind them (Ezek. xxiv. 21, 25) to suffer under the reproach of their fathers' misfortunes. They appear also to have been compelled to sell their estates hurriedly on the eve of their departure, and such transactions, necessarily turning to the advantage of the purchasers, left a deep grudge in the breasts of the sellers. Those who remained in the land exulted in the calamity which had brought so much profit to themselves, and thought themselves perfectly secure in so doing because they regarded their brethren as men driven out for their sins from Jehovah's heritage. The exiles on their part affected the utmost contempt for the pretensions of the upstart plebeians who were carrying things with a high hand in Jerusalem. Like the French Émigrés in the time of the Revolution, they

John J. Skinner

no doubt felt that their country was being ruined for want of proper guidance and experienced statesmanship. Nor was it altogether patrician prejudice that gave them this feeling of their own superiority. Both Jeremiah and Ezekiel regard the exiles as the better part of the nation, and the nucleus of the Messianic community of the future. For the present, indeed, there does not seem to have been much to choose, in point of religious belief and practice, between the two sections of the people. In both places the majority were steeped in idolatrous and superstitious notions; some appear even to have entertained the purpose of assimilating themselves to the heathen around, and only a small minority were steadfast in their allegiance to the national religion. Yet the exiles could not, any more than the remnant in Judah, abandon the hope that Jehovah would save His sanctuary from desecration. The Temple was "the excellency of their strength, the desire of their eyes, and that which their soul pitied" (Ezek. xxiv. 21). False prophets appeared in Babylon to prophesy smooth things, and assure the exiles of a speedy restoration to their place in the people of God. It was not till Jerusalem was laid in ruins, and the Jewish state had disappeared from the earth, that the Israelites were in a mood to understand the meaning of God's judgment, or to learn the lessons which the prophecy of nearly two centuries had vainly striven to inculcate.

We have now reached the point at which the Book of Ezekiel opens, and what remains to be told of the history of the time will be given in connection with the prophecies on which it is fitted to throw light. But before proceeding to consider his entrance on the prophetic office, it will be useful to dwell for a little on what was probably the most fruitful influence of Ezekiel's youth, the personal influence of his contemporary and predecessor Jeremiah. This will form the subject of the next chapter.

Footnotes:

1. Herodotus, i. 103-106.

2. If the "thirtieth year" of ch. i. 1 could refer to the prophet's age at the time of his call, his birth would fall in the very year in which the Law Book was found. Although that interpretation is extremely improbable, he can hardly have been much more, or less, than thirty years old at the time.

3. The opinion, once prevalent, that it was the Chaboras in Northern Mesopotamia, where colonies of Northern Israelites had been settled a century and a half before, has nothing to justify it, and is now universally abandoned.

Chapter II - Jeremiah And Ezekiel

Each of the communities described in the last chapter was the theatre of the activity of a great prophet. When Ezekiel began to prophesy at Tel Abib, Jeremiah was approaching the end of his great and tragic career. For five-and-thirty years he had been known as a prophet, and during the latter part of that time had been the most prominent figure in Jerusalem. For the next five years their ministries were contemporaneous, and it is somewhat remarkable that they ignore each other in their writings so completely as they do. We would give a good deal to have some reference by Ezekiel to Jeremiah or by Jeremiah to Ezekiel, but we find none. Scripture does not often favour us with those cross-lights which prove so instructive in the hands of a modern historian. While Jeremiah knows of the rise of false prophets in Babylonia, and Ezekiel denounces those he had left behind in Jerusalem, neither of these great men betrays the slightest consciousness of the existence of the other. This silence is specially noticeable on Ezekiel's part, because his frequent descriptions of the state of society in Jerusalem give him abundant opportunity to express his sympathy with the position of Jeremiah. When we read in the twenty-second chapter that there was not found a man to make up the fence and stand in the breach before God, we might be tempted to conclude that he really was not aware of Jeremiah's noble stand for righteousness in the corrupt and doomed city. And yet the points of contact between the two prophets are so numerous and so obvious that they cannot fairly be explained by the common operation of the Spirit of God on the minds of both. There is nothing in the nature of prophecy to forbid the view that one prophet learned from another, and built on the foundation which his predecessors had laid; and when we find a parallelism so close as that between Jeremiah and Ezekiel we are driven to the conclusion that the influence was unusually direct, and that the whole thinking of the younger writer had been moulded by the teaching and example of the older.

In what way this influence was communicated is a question on which some difference of opinion may exist. Some writers, such as Kuenen, think that the indebtedness of Ezekiel to Jeremiah was mainly literary. That is to say, they hold that it must be accounted for by prolonged study on Ezekiel's part of the written prophecies of him who was his teacher. Kuenen surmises that this happened after the destruction of Jerusalem, when some friends of Jeremiah arrived in Babylon, bringing with them the completed volume of his prophecies. Before Ezekiel proceeded to write his own prophecies, his mind is supposed to have been so saturated with the ideas and language of Jeremiah that every part of his book bears the impress and betrays the influence of his predecessor. In this fact, of course, Kuenen finds an argument for the view that Ezekiel's prophecies were written at a comparatively late period of his life. It is difficult to speak with confidence on some of the points raised by this hypothesis. That the influence of Jeremiah can be traced in all parts of the book of Ezekiel is undoubtedly true; but it is not so clear that it can be assigned equally to all periods of Jeremiah's activity. Many of the prophecies of Jeremiah cannot be referred to a definite date; and we do not know what means Ezekiel had of obtaining copies of those which belong to the period after the two prophets were separated. We know, however, that a great part of the book of Jeremiah was in writing several years before Ezekiel was carried away to Babylon; and we may safely assume that amongst the treasures which he took with him into exile was the roll written by Baruch to the dictation of Jeremiah in the fourth year of Jehoiakim (Jer. xxxvi.). Even later oracles may have reached Ezekiel either before or during his prophetic career through the active correspondence maintained between the exiles and Jerusalem. It is possible, therefore, that even the literary dependence of Ezekiel on Jeremiah may belong to a much earlier time than the final issue of the book of Ezekiel; and if it should be found that ideas in the earlier part of the book suggest acquaintance with a later utterance of Jeremiah, the fact need not surprise us. It is certainly no sufficient reason for concluding that the whole substance of Ezekiel's prophecy had been recast under the influence of a late perusal of the work of Jeremiah.

But, setting aside verbal coincidences and other phenomena which suggest literary dependence, there remains an affinity of a much deeper kind between the teaching of the two prophets, which can only be explained, if it is to be explained at all, by the personal influence of the older upon the younger. And it is these more fundamental resemblances which are of most interest for our present purpose, because they may enable us to understand something of the settled convictions with which Ezekiel entered on the prophet's calling. Moreover, a comparison of the two prophets will bring out more clearly than anything else certain aspects of the character of Ezekiel which it is important to bear in mind. Both are men of strongly marked individuality, and no conception of the age in which they lived can safely be formed from the writings of either, taken alone.

It has been already remarked that Jeremiah was the most conspicuous public character of his day. If it be the case that he threw his spell over the youthful mind of Ezekiel, the fact is the most striking tribute to his influence that could be conceived. No two men could differ more widely in natural temperament and character. Jeremiah is the prophet of a dying nation, and the agony of Judah's prolonged death-struggle is reproduced with tenfold intensity in the inward conflict which rends the heart of the prophet. Inexorable in his prediction of the coming doom, he confesses that this is because he is over-mastered by the Divine power which urges him into a path from which his nature recoiled. He deplores the isolation which is forced upon him, the alienation of friends and kinsmen, and the constant strife of which he is the reluctant cause. He feels as if he could gladly shake off the burden of prophetic responsibility and become a man amongst common men. His human sympathies go forth towards his unhappy country, and his heart bleeds for the misery which he sees hanging over the misguided people, for whom he is forbidden even to pray. The tragic conflict of his life reaches its height in those expostulations with Jehovah which are amongst the most remarkable passages of the Old Testament. They express the shrinking of a sensitive nature from the inward necessity in which he was compelled to recognise the higher truth; and the wrestling of an earnest spirit for the assurance of his personal standing with God, when all the outward institutions of religion were being dissolved.

To such mental conflicts Ezekiel was a stranger, or if he ever passed through them the traces of them have almost vanished from his written words. He can hardly be said to be more severe than Jeremiah; but his severity seems more a part of himself, and more in keeping with the bent of his disposition. He is wholly on the side of the divine sovereignty; there is no reaction of the human sympathies against the imperative dictates of the prophetic inspiration; he is one in whom every thought seems brought into captivity to the word of Jehovah. It is possible that the completeness with which Ezekiel surrendered himself to the judicial aspect of his message may be partly due to the fact that he had been familiar with its leading conceptions from the teaching of Jeremiah; but it must also be due to a certain austerity natural to him. Less emotional than Jeremiah, his mind was more readily taken possession of by the convictions that formed the substance of his prophetic message. He was evidently a man of profoundly ethical habits of thought, stern and uncompromising in his judgments, both on himself and other men, and gifted with a strong sense of human responsibility. As his captivity cut him off from living contact with the national life, and enabled him to survey his country's condition with something of the dispassionate scrutiny of a spectator, so his natural disposition enabled him to realise in his own person that breach with the past which was essential to the purification of religion. He had the qualities which marked him out for the prophet of the new order that was to be, as clearly as Jeremiah had those which fitted him to be the prophet of a nation's dissolution. In social standing, also, and professional training, the men were far removed from each other. Both were priests, but Ezekiel belonged to the house of Zadok, who officiated in the central sanctuary, while Jeremiah's family may have been attached to one of the provincial sanctuaries. [4] The interests of the two classes of priests came into sharp collision as a consequence of Josiah's reformation. The law provided that the rural priesthood should be admitted to the service of the Temple on equal terms with their brethren of the sons of Zadok; but we are expressly informed that the Temple priests successfully resisted this encroachment on their peculiar privileges. It has been adduced by several expositors as a proof of Ezekiel's freedom from caste prejudice, that he was willing to learn from a man who was socially his inferior, and who belonged to an order which he himself was to declare unworthy of full priestly rights in the restored theocracy. But it must be said that there was little in Jeremiah's public work to call attention to the fact that he was by birth a priest. In the profound spiritual sense of the Epistle to the Hebrews we may indeed say that he was at heart a priest, "having compassion on the ignorant and them that are out of the way, forasmuch as he himself was compassed with infirmity." But this quality of spiritual sympathy sprang from his calling as a prophet rather than from his priestly training. One of the contrasts between him and Ezekiel lies just in the respective estimates of the worth of ritual which underlie their teaching. Jeremiah is distinguished even among the prophets by his indifference to the outward institutions and symbols of religion which it is the priest's function to conserve. He stands in the succession of Amos and Isaiah as an upholder of the purely ethical character of the service of God. Ritual forms no essential element of Jehovah's covenant with Israel, and it is doubtful if his prophecies of the future contain any reference to a priestly class or priestly ordinances. [5] In the present he repudiates the actual popular worship as offensive to Jehovah, and, except in so far as he may have given his support to Josiah's reforms, he does not concern himself to put anything better in its place. To Ezekiel, on the contrary, a pure worship is a primary condition of Israel's enjoyment of the fellowship of Jehovah. All through his teaching we detect his deep sense of the religious value of priestly ceremonies, and in the concluding vision that underlying thought comes out clearly as a fundamental principle of the new religious constitution. Here again we can see how each prophet was providentially fitted for the special work assigned him to do. To Jeremiah it was given, amidst the wreck of all the material embodiments in which faith had clothed itself in the past, to realise the essential truth of religion as personal communion with God, and so to rise to the conception of a purely spiritual religion, in which the will of God should be written in the heart of every believer. To Ezekiel was committed the different, but not less necessary, task of organising the religion of the immediate future, and providing the forms which were to enshrine the truths of revelation until the coming of Christ. And that task could not, humanly speaking, have been performed but by one whose training and inclination taught him to appreciate the value of those rules of ceremonial sanctity which were the tradition of the Hebrew priesthood.

Very closely connected with this is the attitude of the two prophets to what we may call the legal aspect of religion. Jeremiah seems to have become convinced at a very early date of the insufficiency and shallowness of the revival of religion which was expressed in the establishment of the national covenant in the reign of Josiah. He seems also to have discerned some of the evils which are inseparable from a religion of the letter, in which the claims of God are presented in the form of external laws and ordinances. And these convictions led him to the conception of a far higher manifestation of God's redeeming grace to be realised in the future, in the form of a new covenant, based on God's forgiving love, and operative through a personal knowledge of God, and the law written on the heart and mind of each member of the covenant people. That is to say, the living principle of religion must be implanted in the heart of each true Israelite, and his obedience must be what we call evangelical obedience, springing from the free impulse of a nature renewed by the knowledge of God. Ezekiel is also impressed by the failure of the Deuteronomic covenant and the need of a new heart before Israel is able to comply with the high requirements of the holy law of God. But he does not appear to have been led to connect the failure of the past with the inherent imperfection of a legal dispensation as such. Although his teaching is full of evangelical truths, amongst which the doctrine of regeneration holds a conspicuous place, we yet observe that with him a man's righteousness before God consists in acts of obedience to the objective precepts of the divine law. This of course does not mean that Ezekiel was concerned only about the outward act and indifferent to the spirit in which the law was observed. But it does mean that the end of God's dealings with His people was to bring them into a condition for fulfilling His law, and that the great aim of the new Israel was the faithful observance of the law which expressed the conditions on which they could remain in communion with God. Accordingly Ezekiel's final ideal is on a lower plane, and therefore more immediately practicable, than that of Jeremiah. Instead of a purely spiritual anticipation expressing the essential nature of the perfect relation between God and man, Ezekiel presents us with a definite, clearly conceived vision of a new theocracy--a state which is to be the outward embodiment of Jehovah's will and in which life is minutely regulated by His law.

If in spite of such wide differences of temperament, of education, and of religious experience, we find nevertheless a substantial agreement in the teaching of the two prophets, we must certainly recognise in this a striking evidence of the stability of that conception of God and His providence which was in the main a product of Hebrew prophecy. It is not necessary here to enumerate all the points of coincidence between Jeremiah and Ezekiel; but it will be of advantage to indicate a few salient features which they have in common. Of these one of the most important is their conception of the prophetic office. It can hardly be doubted that on this subject Ezekiel had learned much both from observation of Jeremiah's career and from the study of his writings. He knew something of what it meant to be a prophet to Israel before he himself received the prophet's commission; and after he had received it his experience ran closely parallel with that of his master. The idea of the prophet as a man standing alone for God amidst a hostile world, surrounded on every side by threats and opposition, was impressed on each of them from the outset of his ministry. To be a true prophet one must know how to confront men with an inflexibility equal to theirs, sustained only by a divine power which assures him of ultimate victory. He is cut off, not only from the currents of opinion which play around him, but from all share in common joys and sorrows, living a solitary life in sympathy with a God justly alienated from His people. This attitude of antagonism to the people, as Jeremiah well knew, had been the common fate of all true prophets. What is characteristic of him and Ezekiel is that they both enter on their work in the full consciousness of the stern and hopeless nature of their task. Isaiah knew from the day he became a prophet that the effect of his teaching would be to harden the people in unbelief; but he says nothing of personal enmity and persecution to be faced from the outset. But now the crisis of the people's fate has arrived, and the relations between the prophet and his age become more and more strained as the great controversy approaches its decision.

John J. Skinner

Another point of agreement which may be here mentioned is the estimate of Israel's sin. Ezekiel goes further than Jeremiah in the way of condemnation, regarding the whole history of Israel as an unbroken record of apostasy and rebellion, while Jeremiah at least looks back to the desert wandering as a time when the ideal relation between Israel and Jehovah was maintained. But on the whole, and especially with respect to the present state of the nation, their judgment is substantially one. The source of all the religious and moral disorders of the nation is infidelity to Jehovah, which is manifested in the worship of false gods and reliance on the help of foreign nations. Specially noteworthy is the frequent recurrence in Jeremiah and Ezekiel of the figure of "whoredom," an idea introduced into prophecy by Hosea to describe these two sins. The extension of the figure to the false worship of Jehovah by images and other idolatrous emblems can also be traced to Hosea; and in Ezekiel it is sometimes difficult to say which species of idolatry he has in view, whether it be the actual worship of other gods or the unlawful worship of the true God. His position is that an unspiritual worship implies an unspiritual deity, and that such service as was performed at the ordinary sanctuaries could by no possibility be regarded as rendered to the true God who spoke through the prophets. From this fountain-head of a corrupted religious sense proceed all those immoral practices which both prophets stigmatise as "abominations" and as a defilement of the land of Jehovah. Of these the most startling is the prevalent sacrifice of children to which they both bear witness, although, as we shall afterwards see, with a characteristic difference in their point of view.

The whole picture, indeed, which Jeremiah and Ezekiel present of contemporary society is appalling in the extreme. Making all allowance for the practical motive of the prophetic invective, which always aims at conviction of sin, we cannot doubt that the state of things was sufficiently serious to mark Judah as ripe for judgment. The very foundations of society were sapped by the spread of licence and high-handed violence through all classes of the community. The restraints of religion had been loosened by the feeling that Jehovah had forsaken the land, and nobles, priests, and prophets plunged into a career of wickedness and oppression which made salvation of the existing nation impossible. The guilt of Jerusalem is symbolised to both prophets in the innocent blood which stains her skirts and cries to heaven for vengeance. The tendencies which are uppermost are the evil legacy of the days of Manasseh, when, in the judgment of Jeremiah and the historian of the books of Kings, [6] the nation sinned beyond hope of mercy. In painting his lurid pictures of social degeneracy Ezekiel is no doubt drawing on his own memory and information; nevertheless the forms in which his indictment is cast show that even in this matter he has learned to look on things with the eyes of his great teacher.

It is scarcely necessary to add that both prophets anticipate a speedy downfall of the state and its restoration in a more glorious form after a short interval, fixed by Jeremiah at seventy years and by Ezekiel at forty years. The restoration is regarded as final, and as embracing both branches of the Hebrew nation, the kingdom of the ten tribes as well as the house of Judah. The Messianic hope in Ezekiel appears in a form similar to that in which it is presented by Jeremiah; in neither prophet is the figure of the ideal King so prominent as in the prophecies of Isaiah. The similarity between the two is all the more noteworthy as an evidence of dependence, because Ezekiel's final outlook is towards a state of things in which the Prince has a somewhat subordinate position assigned to Him. Both prophets, again following Hosea, regard the spiritual renewal of the people as the effect of chastisement in exile. Those parts of the nation which go first into banishment are the first to be brought under the salutary influences of God's providential discipline; and hence we find that Jeremiah adopts a more hopeful tone in speaking of Samaria and the captives of 597 than in his utterances to those who remained in the land. This conviction was shared by Ezekiel, in spite of his daily contact with abominations from which his whole nature revolted. It has been supposed that Ezekiel lived long enough to see that no such spiritual transformation was to be wrought by the mere fact of captivity, and that, despairing of a general and spontaneous conversion, he put his hand to the work of practical reform as if he would secure by legislation the results which he had once expected as fruits of repentance. If the prophet had ever expected that punishment of itself would work a change in the religious condition of his countrymen, there might have been room for such a disenchantment as is here assumed. But there is no evidence that he ever looked for anything else than a regeneration of the people in captivity by the supernatural working of the divine Spirit; and that the final vision is meant to help out the divine plan by human policy is a suggestion negatived by the whole scope of the book. It may be true that his practical activity in the present was directed to preparing individual men for the coming salvation; but that was no more than any spiritual teacher must have done in a time recognised as a period of transition. The vision of the restored theocracy presupposes a national resurrection and a national repentance. And on the face of it is such that man can take no step towards its accomplishment until God has prepared the way by creating the conditions of a perfect religious community, both the moral conditions in the mind of the people and the outward conditions in the miraculous transformation of the land in which they

The Expositor's Bible: The Book of Ezekiel
are to dwell.

Most of the points here touched upon will have to be more fully treated in the course of our exposition, and other affinities between the two great prophets will have to be noticed as we proceed. Enough has perhaps been said to show that Ezekiel's thinking has been profoundly influenced by Jeremiah, that the influence extends not only to the form but also to the substance of his teaching, and can therefore only be explained by early impressions received by the younger prophet in the days before the word of the Lord had come to him.

Footnotes:

4. This, however, is not certain. Although Jeremiah's property and residence were in Anathoth, his official connection may have been with the Temple in Jerusalem.

5. The passage xxxiii. 14-26 is wanting in the LXX., and may possibly be a later insertion. Even if genuine it would hardly alter the general estimate of the prophet's teaching expressed above.

6. Jer. xv. 4; 2 Kings xxiii. 26.

John J. Skinner

Chapter III - The Vision Of The Glory Of God. Chapter i

It might be hazardous to attempt, from the general considerations advanced in the last two chapters, to form a conception of Ezekiel's state of mind during the first few years of his captivity. If, as we have found reason to believe, he had already come under the influence of Jeremiah, he must have been in some measure prepared for the blow which had descended on him. Torn from the duties of the office which he loved, and driven in upon himself, Ezekiel must no doubt have meditated deeply on the sin and the prospects of his people. From the first he must have stood aloof from his fellow-exiles, who, led by their false prophets, began to dream of the fall of Babylon and a speedy return to their own land. He knew that the calamity which had befallen them was but the first instalment of a sweeping judgment before which the old Israel must utterly perish. Those who remained in Jerusalem were reserved for a worse fate than those who had been carried away; but so long as the latter remained impenitent there was no hope even for them of an alleviation of the bitterness of their lot. Such thoughts, working in a mind naturally severe in its judgments, may have already produced that attitude of alienation from the whole life of his companions in misfortune which dominates the first period of his prophetic career. But these convictions did not make Ezekiel a prophet. He had as yet no independent message from God, no sure perception of the issue of events, or the path which Israel must follow in order to reach the blessedness of the future. It was not till the fifth year of his captivity [7] that the inward change took place which brought him into Jehovah's counsel, and disclosed to him the outlines of all his future work, and endowed him with the courage to stand forth amongst his people as the spokesman of Jehovah.

Like other great prophets whose personal experience is recorded, Ezekiel became conscious of his prophetic vocation through a vision of God. The form in which Jehovah first appeared to him is described with great minuteness of detail in the first chapter of his book. It would seem that in some hour of solitary meditation by the river Kebar his attention was attracted to a storm-cloud forming in the north and advancing toward him across the plain. The cloud may have been an actual phenomenon, the natural basis of the theophany which follows. Falling into a state of ecstasy, the prophet sees the cloud grow luminous with an unearthly splendour. From the midst of it there shines a brightness which he compares to the lustre of electron. [8] Looking more closely, he discerns four living creatures, of strange composite form,--human in general appearance, but winged; and each having four heads combining the highest types of animal life--man, lion, ox, and eagle. These are afterwards identified with the cherubim of the Temple symbolism (ch. x. 20); but some features of the conception may have been suggested by the composite animal figures of Babylonian art, with which the prophet must have been already familiar. The interior space is occupied by a hearth of glowing coals, from which lightning-flashes constantly dart to and fro between the cherubim. Beside each cherub is a wheel, formed apparently of two wheels intersecting each other at right angles. The appearance of the wheels is like "chrysolite," and their rims are filled with eyes, denoting the intelligence by which their motions are directed. The wheels and the cherubim together embody the spontaneous energy by which the throne of God is transported whither He wills; although there is no mechanical connection between them, they are represented as animated by a common spirit, directing all their motions in perfect harmony. Over the heads and outstretched wings of the cherubim is a rigid pavement or "firmament," like crystal; and above this a sapphire stone [9] supporting the throne of Jehovah. The divine Being is seen in the likeness of a man; and around Him, as if to temper the fierceness of the light in which He dwells, is a radiance like that of the rainbow. It will be noticed that while Ezekiel's imagination dwells on what we must consider the accessories of the vision--the fire, the cherubim, the wheels--he hardly dares to lift his eyes to the person of Jehovah Himself. The full meaning of what he is passing through only dawns on him when he realises that he is in the presence of the Almighty. Then he falls on his face overpowered by the sense of his own insignificance.

There is no reason to doubt that what is thus described represents an actual experience on the part of the prophet. It is not to be regarded merely as a conscious clothing of spiritual truths in symbolic imagery. The description of a vision is of course a conscious exercise of literary faculty; and in all such cases it must be difficult to distinguish what a prophet actually saw and heard in the moment of inspiration from the details which he was compelled to add in order to convey an intelligible picture to the minds of his readers. It is probable that in the case of Ezekiel the element of free invention has a larger range than in the less elaborate descriptions which other prophets give of their visions. But this does not detract from the force of the prophet's own assertion that what he relates was based on a real and definite experience when in a state of prophetic ecstasy. This is expressed by the words "the hand of Jehovah was upon him" (ver. 3)--a phrase which is invariably used throughout the book to denote the prophet's peculiar mental condition when the communication of divine truth was accompanied by experiences of a visionary order. Moreover, the account given of the state in which this vision left him shows that his natural consciousness had been overpowered by the pressure of super-sensible realities on his spirit. He tells us that he went "in bitterness, in the heat of his spirit, the hand of the Lord being heavy upon him; and came to the exiles at Tel-abib, ... and sat there seven days stupefied in their midst" (ch. iii. 14, 15).

Now whatever be the ultimate nature of the prophetic vision, its significance for us would appear to lie in the untrammelled working of the prophet's imagination under the influence of spiritual perceptions which are too profound to be expressed as abstract ideas. The prophet's consciousness is not suspended, for he remembers his vision and reflects on its meaning afterwards; but his intercourse with the outer world through the senses is interrupted, so that his mind moves freely amongst images stored in his memory, and new combinations are formed which embody a truth not previously apprehended. The tableau of the vision is therefore always capable to some extent of a psychological explanation. The elements of which it is composed must have been already present in the mind of the prophet, and in so far as these can be traced to their sources we are enabled to understand their symbolic import in the novel combination in which they appear. But the real significance of the vision lies in the immediate impression left on the mind of the prophet by the divine realities which govern his life, and this is especially true of the vision of God Himself which accompanies the call to the prophetic office. Although no vision can express the whole of a prophet's conception of God, yet it represents to the imagination certain fundamental aspects of the divine nature and of God's relation to the world and to men; and through all his subsequent career the prophet will be influenced by the form in which he once beheld the great Being whose words come to him from time to time. To his later reflection the vision becomes a symbol of certain truths about God, although in the first instance the symbol was created for him by a mysterious operation of the divine Spirit in a process over which he had no control. In one respect Ezekiel's inaugural vision seems to possess a greater importance for his theology than is the case with any other prophet. With the other prophets the vision is a momentary experience, of which the spiritual meaning passes into the thinking of the prophet, but which does not recur again in the visionary form. With Ezekiel, on the other hand, the vision becomes a fixed and permanent symbol of Jehovah, appearing again and again in precisely the same form as often as the reality of God's presence is impressed on his mind.

The essential question, then, with regard to Ezekiel's vision is, What revelation of God or what ideas respecting God did it serve to impress on the mind of the prophet? It may help us to answer that question if we begin by considering certain affinities which it presents to the great vision which opened the ministry of Isaiah. It must be admitted that Ezekiel's experience is much less intelligible as well as less impressive than Isaiah's. In Isaiah's delineation we recognise the presence of qualities which belong to genius of the highest order. The perfect balance of form and idea, the reticence which suggests without exhausting the significance of what is seen, the fine artistic sense which makes every touch in the picture contribute to the rendering of the emotion which fills the prophet's soul, combine to make the sixth chapter of Isaiah one of the most sublime passages in literature. No sympathetic reader can fail to catch the impression which the passage is intended to convey of the awful majesty of the God of Israel, and the effect produced on a frail and sinful mortal ushered into that holy Presence. We are made to feel how inevitably such a vision gives birth to the prophetic impulse, and how both vision and impulse inform the mind of the seer with the clear and definite purpose which rules all his subsequent work.

The point in which Ezekiel's vision differs most strikingly from Isaiah's is the almost entire suppression of his subjectivity. This is so complete that it becomes difficult to apprehend the meaning of the vision in relation to his thought and activity. Spiritual realities are so overlaid with symbolism that the narrative almost fails to reflect the mental state in which he was consecrated for the work of his life. Isaiah's vision is a drama, Ezekiel's is a spectacle; in the one religious truth is expressed in a series of significant actions and words, in the other it is embodied in forms and splendours that appeal only to the eye. One fact may be noted in illustration of the diversity between the two representations. The scenery of Isaiah's vision is interpreted and spiritualised by the medium of language. The seraphs' hymn of adoration strikes the note which is the central thought of the vision, and the exclamation which breaks from the prophet's lips reveals the impact of that great truth on a human spirit. The whole scene is thus lifted out of the region of mere symbolism into that of pure religious ideas. Ezekiel's, on the other hand, is like a song without words. His cherubim are speechless. While the rustling of their wings and the thunder of the revolving wheels break on his ear like the sound of mighty waters, no articulate voice bears home to the mind the inner meaning of what he beholds. Probably he himself felt no need of it. The pictorial character of his thinking appears in many features of his work; and it is not surprising to find that the import of the revelation is expressed mainly in visual images.

Now these differences are in their own place very instructive, because they show how intimately the vision is related to the individuality of him who receives it, and how even in the most exalted moments of inspiration the mind displays the same tendencies which characterise its ordinary operations. Yet Ezekiel's vision represents a spiritual experience not less real than Isaiah's. His mental endowments are of a different order, of a lower order if you will, than those of Isaiah; but the essential fact that he too saw the glory of God and in that vision obtained the insight of the true prophet is not to be explained away by analysis of his literary talent or of the sources from which his images are derived. It is allowable to write worse Greek than Plato; and it is no disqualification for a Hebrew prophet to lack the grandeur of imagination and the mastery of style which are the notes of Isaiah's genius.

In spite of their obvious dissimilarities the two visions have enough in common to show that Ezekiel's thoughts concerning God had been largely influenced by the study of Isaiah. Truths that had perhaps long been latent in his mind now emerge into clear consciousness, clothed in forms which bear the impress of the mind in which they were first conceived. The fundamental idea is the same in each vision: the absolute and universal sovereignty of God. "Mine eyes have seen the King, Jehovah of hosts." Jehovah appears in human form, seated on a throne and attended by ministering creatures which serve to show forth some part of His glory. In the one case they are seraphim, in the other cherubim; and the functions imposed on them by the structure of the vision are very diverse in the two cases. But the points in which they agree are more significant than those in which they differ. They are the agents through whom Jehovah exercises His sovereign authority, beings full of life and intelligence and moving in swift response to His will. Although free from earthly imperfection they cover themselves with their wings before His majesty, in token of the reverence which is due from the creature in presence of the Creator. For the rest they are symbolic figures embodying in themselves certain attributes of the Deity, or certain aspects of His kingship. Nor can Ezekiel any more than Isaiah think of Jehovah as the King apart from the emblems associated with the worship of His earthly sanctuary. The cherubim themselves are borrowed from the imagery of the Temple, although their forms are different from those which stood in the Holy of holies. So again the altar, which was naturally suggested to Isaiah by the scene of his vision being laid in the Temple, appears in Ezekiel's vision in the form of the hearth of glowing coals which is under the divine throne. It is true that the fire symbolises destructive might rather than purifying energy (see ch. x. 2), but it can hardly be doubted that the origin of the symbol is the altar-hearth of the sanctuary and of Isaiah's vision. It is as if the essence of the Temple and its worship were transferred to the sphere of heavenly realities where Jehovah's glory is fully manifested. All this, therefore, is nothing more than the embodiment of the fundamental truth of the Old Testament religion--that Jehovah is the almighty King of heaven and earth, that He executes His sovereign purposes with irresistible power, and that it is the highest privilege of men on earth to render to Him the homage and adoration which the sight of His glory draws forth from heavenly beings.

The idea of Jehovah's kingship, however, is presented in the Old Testament under two aspects. On the one hand, it denotes the moral sovereignty of God over the people whom He had chosen as His own and to whom His will was continuously revealed as the guide of their national and social life. On the other hand, it denotes God's absolute dominion over the forces of nature and the events of history, in virtue of which all things are the unconscious instruments of His purposes. These two truths can never be separated, although the emphasis is laid sometimes on the one and sometimes on the other. Thus in Isaiah's vision the emphasis lies perhaps more on the doctrine of Jehovah's kingship over Israel. It is true that He is at the same time represented as One whose glory is the "fulness of the whole earth," and who therefore manifests His power and presence in every part of His world-wide dominions. But the fact that Jehovah's palace is the idealised Temple of Jerusalem suggests at once, what all the teaching of the prophet confirms, that the nation of Israel is the special sphere within which His kingly authority is to obtain practical recognition. While no man had a firmer grasp of the truth that God wields all natural forces and overrules the actions of men in carrying out His providential designs, yet the leading ideas of His ministry are those which spring from the thought of Jehovah's presence in the midst of His people and the obligation that lies on Israel to recognise His sovereignty. He is, to use Isaiah's own expression, the "Holy One of Israel."

This aspect of the divine kingship is undoubtedly represented in the vision of Ezekiel. We have remarked that the imagery of the vision is to some extent moulded on the idea of the sanctuary as the seat of Jehovah's government, and we shall find later on that the final resting-place of this emblem of His presence is a restored sanctuary in the land of Canaan. But the circumstances under which Ezekiel was called to be a prophet required that prominence should be given to the complementary truth that the kingship of Jehovah was independent of His special relation to Israel. For the present the tie between Jehovah and His land was dissolved. Israel had disowned her divine King, and was left to suffer the consequences of her disloyalty. Hence it is that the vision appears, not from the direction of Jerusalem, but "out of the north," in token that God has departed from His Temple and abandoned it to its enemies. In this way the vision granted to the exiled prophet on the plain of Babylonia embodied a truth opposed to the religious prejudices of his time, but reassuring to himself--that the fall of Israel leaves the essential sovereignty of Jehovah untouched; that He still lives and reigns, although His people are trodden underfoot by worshippers of other gods. But more than this, we can see that on the whole the tendency of Ezekiel's vision, as distinguished from that of Isaiah, is to emphasise the universality of Jehovah's relations to the world of nature and of mankind. His throne rests here on a sapphire stone, the symbol of heavenly purity, to signify that His true dwelling-place is above the firmament, in the heavens, which are equally near to every region of the earth. Moreover, it is mounted on a chariot, by which it is moved from place to place with a velocity which suggests ubiquity, and the chariot is borne by "living creatures" whose forms unite all that is symbolical of power and dignity in the living world. Further, the shape of the chariot, which is foursquare, and the disposition of the wheels and cherubim, which is such that there is no before or behind, but the same front presented to each of the four quarters of the globe, indicate that all parts of the universe are alike accessible to the presence of God. Finally, the wheels and the cherubim are covered with eyes, to denote that all things are open to the view of Him who sits on the throne. The attributes of God here symbolised are those which express His relations to created existence as a whole--omnipresence, omnipotence, omniscience. These ideas are obviously incapable of adequate representation by any sensuous image--they can only be suggested to the mind; and it is just the effort to suggest such transcendental attributes that imparts to the vision the character of obscurity which attaches to so many of its details.

Another point of comparison between Isaiah and Ezekiel is suggested by the name which the latter constantly uses for the appearance which he sees, or rather perhaps for that part of it which represents the personal appearance of God. He calls it the "glory of Jehovah," or "glory of the God of Israel." The word for glory (kabôd) is used in a variety of senses in the Old Testament. Etymologically it comes from a root expressing the idea of heaviness. When used, as here, concretely, it signifies that which is the outward manifestation of power or worth or dignity. In human affairs it may be used of a man's wealth, or the pomp and circumstance of military array, or the splendour and pageantry of a royal court, those things which oppress the minds of common men with a sense of magnificence. In like manner, when applied to God, it denotes some reflection in the outer world of His majesty, something that at once reveals and conceals His essential Godhead. Now we remember that the second line of the seraphs' hymn conveyed to Isaiah's mind this thought, that "that which fills the whole earth is His glory." What is this "filling of the whole earth" in which the prophet sees the effulgence of the divine glory? Is his feeling akin to Wordsworth's

> "sense sublime
> Of something far more deeply interfused,
> Whose dwelling is the light of setting suns,
> And the round ocean, and the living air,
> And the blue sky, and in the mind of man"?

At least the words must surely mean that all through nature Isaiah recognised that which declares the glory of God, and therefore in some sense reveals Him. Although they do not teach a doctrine of the divine immanence, they contain all that is religiously valuable in that doctrine. In Ezekiel, however, we find nothing that looks in this direction. It is characteristic of his thoughts about God that the very word "glory" which Isaiah uses of something diffused through the earth is here employed to express the concentration of all divine qualities in a single image of dazzling splendour, but belonging to heaven rather than to earth. Glory is here equivalent to brightness, as in the ancient conception of the bright cloud which led the people through the desert and that which filled the Temple with overpowering light when Jehovah took possession of it (2 Chron. vii. 1-3). In a striking passage of his last vision Ezekiel describes how this scene will be repeated when Jehovah returns to take up His abode amongst His people and the earth will be lighted up with His glory (ch. xliii. 2). But meanwhile it may seem to us that earth is left poorer by the loss of that aspect of nature in which Isaiah discovered a revelation of the divine.

Ezekiel is conscious that what he has seen is after all but an imperfect semblance of the essential glory of God on which no mortal eye can gaze. All that he describes is expressly said to be an "appearance" and a "likeness." When he comes to speak of the divine form in which the whole revelation culminates he can say no more than that it is the "appearance of the likeness of the glory of Jehovah." The prophet appears to realise his inability to penetrate behind the appearance to the reality which it shadows forth. The clearest vision of God which the mind of man can receive is an after-look like that which was vouchsafed to Moses when the divine presence had passed by (Exod. xxxiii. 23). So it was with Ezekiel. The true revelation that came to him was not in what he saw with his eyes in the moment of his initiation, but in the intuitive knowledge of God which from that hour he possessed, and which enabled him to interpret more fully than he could have done at the time the significance of his first memorable meeting with the God of Israel. What he retained in his waking hours was first of all a vivid sense of the reality of God's being, and then a mental picture suggesting those attributes which lay at the foundation of his prophetic ministry.

It is easy to see how this vision dominates all Ezekiel's thinking about the divine nature. The God whom he saw was in the form of a man, and so the God of his conscience is a moral person to whom he fearlessly ascribes the parts and even the passions of humanity. He speaks through the prophet in the language of royal authority, as a king who will brook no rival in the affections of his people. As King of Israel He asserts His determination to reign over them with a mighty hand, and by mingled goodness and severity to break their stubborn heart and bend them to His purpose. There are perhaps other and more subtle affinities between the symbol of the vision and the prophet's inner consciousness of God. Just as the vision gathers up all in nature that suggests divinity into one resplendent image, so it is also with the moral action of God as conceived by Ezekiel. His government of the world is self-centred; all the ends which He pursues in His providence lie within Himself. His dealings with the nations, and with Israel in particular, are dictated by regard for His own glory, or, as Ezekiel expresses it, by pity for His great name. "Not for your sake do I act, O house of Israel, but for My holy name, which ye have profaned among the heathen whither ye went" (ch. xxxvi. 22). The relations into which He enters with men are all subordinate to the supreme purpose of "sanctifying" Himself in the eyes of the world or manifesting Himself as He truly is. It is no doubt possible to exaggerate this feature of Ezekiel's theology in a way that would be unjust to the prophet. After all, Jehovah's desire to be known as He is implies a regard for His creatures which includes the ultimate intention to bless them. It is but an extreme expression in the form necessary for that time of the truth to which all the prophets bear witness, that the knowledge of God is the indispensable condition of true blessedness to men. Still, the difference is marked between the "not for your sake" of Ezekiel and the "human bands, the cords of love" of which Hosea speaks, the yearning and compassionate affection that binds Jehovah to His erring people.

In another respect the symbolism of the vision may be taken as an emblem of the Hebrew conception of the universe. The Bible has no scientific theory of God's relation to the world; but it is full of the practical conviction that all nature responds to His behests, that all occurrences are indications of His mind, the whole realm of nature and history being governed by one Will which works for moral ends. That conviction is as deeply rooted in the thinking of Ezekiel as in that of any other prophet, and, consciously or unconsciously, it is reflected in the structure of the merkaba, or heavenly chariot, which has no mechanical connection between its different parts, and yet is animated by one spirit and moves altogether at the impulse of Jehovah's will.

It will be seen that the general tendency of Ezekiel's conception of God is what might be described in modern language as "transcendental." In this, however, the prophet does not stand alone, and the difference between him and earlier prophets is not so great as is sometimes represented. Indeed, the contrast between transcendent and immanent is hardly applicable in the Old Testament religion. If by transcendence it is meant that God is a being distinct from the world, not losing Himself in the life of nature, but ruling over it and controlling it as His instrument, then all the inspired writers of the Old Testament are transcendentalists. But this does not mean that God is separated from the human spirit by a dead, mechanical universe which owes nothing to its Creator but its initial impulse and its governing laws. The idea that a world could come between man and God is one that would never have occurred to a prophet. Just because God is above the world He can reveal Himself directly to the spirit of man, speaking to His servants face to face as a man speaketh to his friend.

But frequently in the prophets the thought is expressed that Jehovah is "far off" or "comes from far" in the crises of His people's history. "Am I a God at hand, saith Jehovah, and not a God afar off?" is Jeremiah's question to the false prophets of his day; and the answer is, "Do not I fill heaven and earth? saith Jehovah." On this subject we may quote the suggestive remarks of a recent commentator on Isaiah: "The local deities, the gods of the tribal religions, are near; Jehovah is far, but at the same time everywhere present. The remoteness of Jehovah in space represented to the prophets better than our transcendental abstractions Jehovah's absolute ascendency. This far off is spoken with enthusiasm. Everywhere and nowhere, Jehovah comes when His hour is come." [10] That

The Expositor's Bible: The Book of Ezekiel

is the idea of Ezekiel's vision. God comes to him "from far," but He comes very near. Our difficulty may be to realise the nearness of God. Scientific discovery has so enlarged our view of the material universe that we feel the need of every consideration that can bring home to us a sense of the divine condescension and interest in man's earthly history and his spiritual welfare. But the difficulty which beset the ordinary Israelite even so late as the Exile was as nearly as possible the opposite of ours. His temptation was to think of God as only a God "at hand," a local deity, whose range of influence was limited to a particular spot, and whose power was measured by the fortunes of His own people. Above all things he needed to learn that God was "afar off," filling heaven and earth, that His power was exerted everywhere, and that there was no place where either a man could hide himself from God or God was hidden from man. When we bear in mind these circumstances we can see how needful was the revelation of the divine omnipresence as a step towards the perfect knowledge of God which comes to us through Jesus Christ.

Footnotes:

7. In the superscription of the book (ch. i. 1-3) a double date is given for this occurrence. In ver. 1 it is said to have taken place "in the thirtieth year"; but this expression has never been satisfactorily explained. The principal suggestions are: (1) that it is the year of Ezekiel's life; (2) that the reckoning is from the year of Josiah's reformation; and (3) that it is according to some Babylonian era. But none of these has much probability, unless, with Klostermann, we go further and assume that the explanation was given in an earlier part of the prophet's autobiography now lost--a view which is supported by no evidence and is contrary to all analogy. Cornill proposes to omit ver. 1 entirely, chiefly on the ground that the use of the first person before the writer's name has been mentioned is unnatural. That the superscription does not read smoothly as it stands has been felt by many critics; but the rejection of the verse is perhaps a too facile solution.

8. Not "amber," but a natural alloy of silver and gold, highly esteemed in antiquity.

9. Cf. Exod. xxiv. 10: "like the very heavens for pureness."

10. Duhm on Isa. xxx. 27.

John J. Skinner

Chapter IV - Ezekiel's Prophetic Commission. Chapters ii., iii

The call of a prophet and the vision of God which sometimes accompanied it are the two sides of one complex experience. The man who has truly seen God necessarily has a message to men. Not only are his spiritual perceptions quickened and all the powers of his being stirred to the highest activity, but there is laid on his conscience the burden of a sacred duty and a lifelong vocation to the service of God and man. The true prophet therefore is one who can say with Paul, "I was not disobedient to the heavenly vision," for that cannot be a real vision of God which does not demand obedience. And of the two elements the call is the one that is indispensable to the idea of a prophet. We can conceive a prophet without an ecstatic vision, but not without a consciousness of being chosen by God for a special work or a sense of moral responsibility for the faithful declaration of His truth. Whether, as with Isaiah and Ezekiel, the call springs out of the vision of God, or whether, as with Jeremiah, the call comes first and is supplemented by experiences of a visionary kind, the essential fact in the prophet's initiation always is the conviction that from a certain period in his life the word of Jehovah came to him, and along with it the feeling of personal obligation to God for the discharge of a mission entrusted to him. While the vision merely serves to impress on the imagination by means of symbols a certain conception of God's being, and may be dispensed with when symbols are no longer the necessary vehicle of spiritual truth, the call, as conveying a sense of one's true place in the kingdom of God, can never be wanting to any man who has a prophetic work to do for God amongst his fellow-men.

It has been already hinted that in the case of Ezekiel the connection between the call and the vision is less obvious than in that of Isaiah. The character of the narrative undergoes a change at the beginning of ch. ii. The first part is moulded, as we have seen, very largely on the inaugural vision of Isaiah; the second betrays with equal clearness the influence of Jeremiah. The appearance of a break between the first chapter and the second is partly due to the prophet's laborious manner of describing what he had passed through. It is altogether unfair to represent him as having first curiously inspected the mechanism of the merkaba, and then bethought himself that it was a fitting thing to fall on his face before it. The experience of an ecstasy is one thing, the relating of it is another. In much less time than it takes us to master the details of the picture, Ezekiel had seen and been overpowered by the glory of Jehovah, and had become aware of the purpose for which it had been revealed to him. He knew that God had come to him in order to send him as a prophet to his fellow-exiles. And just as the description of the vision draws out in detail those features which were significant of God's nature and attributes, so in what follows he becomes conscious step by step of certain aspects of the work to which he is called. In the form of a series of addresses of the Almighty there are presented to his mind the outlines of his prophetic career--its conditions, its hardships, its encouragements, and above all its binding and peremptory obligation. Some of the facts now set before him, such as the spiritual condition of his audience, had long been familiar to his thoughts--others were new; but now they all take their proper place in the scheme of his life; he is made to know their bearing on his work, and what attitude he is to adopt in face of them. All this takes place in the prophetic trance; but the ideas remain with him as the sustaining principles of his subsequent work.

1. Of the truths thus presented to the mind of Ezekiel the first, and the one that directly arises out of the impression which the vision made on him, is his personal insignificance. As he lies prostrate before the glory of Jehovah he hears for the first time the name which ever afterwards signalises his relation to the God who speaks through him. It hardly needs to be said that the term "son of man" in the book of Ezekiel is no title of honour or of distinction. It is precisely the opposite of this. It denotes the absence of distinction in the person of the prophet. It signifies no more than "member of the human race"; its sense might almost be conveyed if we were to render it by the word "mortal." It expresses the infinite contrast between the heavenly and the earthly, between the glorious Being who speaks from the throne and the frail creature who needs to be supernaturally strengthened before he can stand upright in the attitude of service (ch. ii. 1). He felt that there was no reason in himself for the choice which God made of him to be a prophet. He is conscious only of the attributes which he has in common with the race--of human weakness and

insignificance; all that distinguishes him from other men belongs to his office, and is conferred on him by God in the act of his consecration. There is no trace of the generous impulse that prompted Isaiah to offer himself as a servant of the great King as soon as he realised that there was work to be done. He is equally a stranger to the shrinking of Jeremiah's sensitive spirit from the responsibilities of the prophet's charge. To Ezekiel the divine Presence is so overpowering, the command is so definite and exacting, that no room is left for the play of personal feeling; the hand of the Lord is heavy on him, and he can do nothing but stand still and hear.

2. The next thought that occupies the attention of the prophet is the spiritual condition of those to whom he is sent. It is to be noted that his mission presents itself to him from the outset in two aspects. In the first place, he is a prophet to the whole house of Israel, including the lost kingdom of the ten tribes, as well as the two sections of the kingdom of Judah, those now in exile and those still remaining in their own land. This is his ideal audience; the sweep of his prophecy is to embrace the destinies of the nation as a whole, although but a small part be within the reach of his spoken words. But in literal fact he is to be the prophet of the exiles (ch. iii. 11); that is the sphere in which he has to make proof of his ministry. These two audiences are for the most part not distinguished in the mind of Ezekiel; he sees the ideal in the real, regarding the little colony in which he lives as an epitome of the national life. But in both aspects of his work the outlook is equally dispiriting. If he looks forward to an active career amongst his fellow-captives, he is given to know that "thorns and thistles" are with him and that his dwelling is among scorpions (ch. ii. 6). Petty persecution and rancorous opposition are the inevitable lot of a prophet there. And if he extends his thoughts to the idealised nation he has to think of a people whose character is revealed in a long history of rebellion and apostasy: they are "the rebels who have rebelled against Me, they and their fathers to this very day" (ch. ii. 3). The greatest difficulty he will have to contend with is the impenetrability of the minds of his hearers to the truths of his message. The barrier of a strange language suggests an illustration of the impossibility of communicating spiritual ideas to such men as he is sent to. But it is a far more hopeless barrier that separates him from his people. "Not to a people of deep speech and heavy tongue art thou sent; and not to many peoples whose language thou canst not understand: if I had sent thee to them, they would hear thee. But the house of Israel will refuse to hear thee; for they refuse to hear Me: for the whole house of Israel are hard of forehead and stout of heart" (ch. iii. 5-7). The meaning is that the incapacity of the people is not intellectual, but moral and spiritual. They can understand the prophet's words, but they will not hear them because they dislike the truth which he utters and have rebelled against the God who sent him. The hardening of the national conscience which Isaiah foresaw as the inevitable result of his own ministry is already accomplished, and Ezekiel traces it to its source in a defect of the will, an aversion to the truths which express the character of Jehovah.

This fixed judgment on his contemporaries with which Ezekiel enters on his work is condensed into one of those stereotyped expressions which abound in his writings: "house of disobedience" [11] --a phrase which is afterwards amplified in more than one elaborate review of the nation's past. It no doubt sums up the result of much previous meditation on the state of Israel and the possibility of a national reformation. If any hope had hitherto lingered in Ezekiel's mind that the exiles might now respond to a true word from Jehovah, it disappears in the clear insight which he obtains into the state of their hearts. He sees that the time has not yet come to win the people back to God by assurances of His compassion and the nearness of His salvation. The breach between Jehovah and Israel has not begun to be healed, and the prophet who stands on the side of God must look for no sympathy from men. In the very act of his consecration his mind is thus set in the attitude of uncompromising severity towards the obdurate house of Israel: "Behold, I make thy face hard like their faces, and thy forehead hard like theirs, like adamant harder than flint. Thou shalt not fear them nor be dismayed at their countenance, for a disobedient house are they" (ch. iii. 8, 9).

3. The significance of the transaction in which he takes part is still further impressed on the mind of the prophet by a symbolic act in which he is made to signify his acceptance of the commission entrusted to him (chs. ii. 8-iii. 3). He sees a hand extended to him holding the roll of a book, and when the roll is spread out before him it is found to be written on both sides with "lamentations and mourning and woe." In obedience to the divine command he opens his mouth and eats the scroll, and finds to his surprise that in spite of its contents its taste is "like honey for sweetness."

The meaning of this strange symbol appears to include two things. In the first place it denotes the removal of the inward hindrance of which every man must be conscious when he receives the call to be a prophet. Something similar occurs in the inaugural vision of Isaiah and Jeremiah. The impediment of which Isaiah was conscious was the uncleanness of his lips; and this being removed by the touch of the hot coal from the altar, he is filled with a new feeling of freedom and eagerness to engage in the service of God. In the case of Jeremiah the hindrance was a sense of his own weakness and unfitness for the arduous duties which were imposed on him; and this again was taken away by the consecrating touch of Jehovah's hand on his lips. The part of Ezekiel's experience with which we are dealing is obviously parallel to these, although it is not possible to say what feeling of incapacity was uppermost in his mind. Perhaps it was the dread lest in him there should lurk something of that rebellious spirit which was the characteristic of the race to which he belonged. He who had been led to form so hard a judgment of his people could not but look with a jealous eye on his own heart, and could not forget that he shared the same sinful nature which made their rebellion possible. Accordingly the book is presented to him in the first instance as a test of his obedience. "But thou, son of man, hear what I say to thee; Be not disobedient like the disobedient house: open thy mouth, and eat what I give thee" (ch. ii. 8). When the book proves sweet to his taste, he has the assurance that he has been endowed with such sympathy with the thoughts of God that things which to the natural mind are unwelcome become the source of a spiritual satisfaction. Jeremiah had expressed the same strange delight in his work in a striking passage which was doubtless familiar to Ezekiel: "When Thy words were found I did eat them; and Thy word was to me the joy and rejoicing of my heart: for I was called by Thy name, O Jehovah God of hosts" (Jer. xv. 16). We have a still higher illustration of the same fact in the life of our Lord, to whom it was meat and drink to do the will of His Father, and who experienced a joy in the doing of it which was peculiarly His own. It is the reward of the true service of God that amidst all the hardships and discouragements which have to be endured the heart is sustained by an inward joy springing from the consciousness of working in fellowship with God.

But in the second place the eating of the book undoubtedly signifies the bestowal on the prophet of the gift of inspiration--that is, the power to speak the words of Jehovah. "Son of man, eat this roll, and go speak to the children of Israel.... Go, get thee to the house of Israel, and speak with My words to them" (ch. iii. 1, 4). Now the call of a prophet does not mean that his mind is charged with a certain body of doctrine, which he is to deliver from time to time as circumstances require. All that can safely be said about the prophetic inspiration is that it implies the faculty of distinguishing the truth of God from the thoughts that naturally arise in the prophet's own mind. Nor is there anything in Ezekiel's experience which necessarily goes beyond this conception; although the incident of the book has been interpreted in ways that burden him with a very crude and mechanical theory of inspiration. Some critics have believed that the book which he swallowed is the book he was afterwards to write, as if he had reproduced in instalments what was delivered to him at this time. Others, without going so far as this, find it at least significant that one who was to be pre-eminently a literary prophet should conceive of the word of the Lord as communicated to him in the form of a book. When one writer speaks of "eigenthümliche Empfindungen im Schlunde" [12] as the basis of the figure, he seems to come perilously near to resolving inspiration into a nervous disease. All these representations go beyond a fair construction of the prophet's meaning. The act is purely symbolic. The book has nothing to do with the subject-matter of his prophecy, nor does the eating of it mean anything more than the self-surrender of the prophet to his vocation as a vehicle of the word of Jehovah. The idea that the word of God becomes a living power in the inner being of the prophet is also expressed by Jeremiah when he speaks of it as a "burning fire shut up in his bones" (Jer. xx. 9); and Ezekiel's conception is similar. Although he speaks as if he had once for all assimilated the word of God, although he was conscious of a new power working within him, there is no proof that he thought of the word of the Lord as dwelling in him otherwise than as a spiritual impulse to utter the truth revealed to him from time to time. That is the inspiration which all the prophets possess: "Jehovah God hath spoken, who can but prophesy?" (Amos iii. 8).

4. It was not to be expected that a prophet so practical in his aims as Ezekiel should be left altogether without some indication of the end to be accomplished by his work. The ordinary incentives to an arduous public career have indeed been denied to him. He knows that his mission contains no promise of a striking or an immediate success, that he will be misjudged and opposed by nearly all who hear him, and that he will have to pursue his course without appreciation or sympathy. It has been impressed on him that to declare God's message is an end in itself, a duty to be discharged with no regard to its issues, "whether men hear or whether they forbear." Like Paul he recognises that "necessity is laid upon him" to preach the word of God. But there is one word which reveals to him the way in which his ministry is to be made effective in the working out of Jehovah's purpose with Israel. "Whether they hear or whether they forbear, they shall know that a prophet hath been among them" (ii. 5). The reference is mainly to the destruction of the nation which Ezekiel well knew must form the chief burden of any true prophetic message delivered at that time. He will be approved as a prophet, and recognised as what he is, when his words are verified by the event. Does it seem a poor reward for years of incessant contention with prejudice and unbelief? It was at all events the only reward that was possible, but it was also to be the beginning of better days. For these words have a wider significance than their bearing on the prophet's personal position.

The Expositor's Bible: The Book of Ezekiel

It has been truly said that the preservation of the true religion after the downfall of the nation depended on the fact that the event had been clearly foretold. Two religions and two conceptions of God were then struggling for the mastery in Israel. One was the religion of the prophets, who set the moral holiness of Jehovah above every other consideration, and affirmed that His righteousness must be vindicated even at the cost of His people's destruction. The other was the popular religion which clung to the belief that Jehovah could not for any reason abandon His people without ceasing to be God. This conflict of principles reached its climax in the time of Ezekiel, and it also found its solution. The destruction of Jerusalem cleared the issues. It was then seen that the teaching of the prophets afforded the only possible explanation of the course of events. The Jehovah of the opposite religion was proved to be a figment of the popular imagination; and there was no alternative between accepting the prophetic interpretation of history and resigning all faith in the destiny of Israel. Hence the recognition of Ezekiel, the last of the old order of prophets, who had carried their threatenings on to the eve of their accomplishment, was really a great crisis of religion. It meant the triumph of the only conception of God on which the hope of a better future could be built. Although the people might still be far from the state of heart in which Jehovah could remove His chastening hand, the first condition of national repentance was given as soon as it was perceived that there had been prophets among them who had declared the purpose of Jehovah. The foundation was also laid for a more fruitful development of Ezekiel's activity. The word of the Lord had been in his hands a power "to pluck up and to break down and to destroy" the old Israel that would not know Jehovah; henceforward it was destined to "build and plant" a new Israel inspired by a new ideal of holiness and a whole-hearted repugnance to every form of idolatry.

5. These then are the chief elements which enter into the remarkable experience that made Ezekiel a prophet. Further disclosures of the nature of his office were, however, necessary before he could translate his vocation into a conscious plan of work. The departure of the theophany appears to have left him in a state of mental prostration.[13] In "bitterness and heat of spirit" he resumes his place amongst his fellow-captives at Tel-abib, and sits among them like a man bewildered for seven days. At the end of that time the effects of the ecstasy seem to pass away, and more light breaks on him with regard to his mission. He realises that it is to be largely a mission to individuals. He is appointed as a watchman to the house of Israel, to warn the wicked from his way; and as such he is held accountable for the fate of any soul that might miss the way of life through failure of duty on his part.

It has been supposed that this passage (ch. iii. 16-21) describes the character of a short period of public activity, in which Ezekiel endeavoured to act the part of a "reprover" (ver. 26) among the exiles. This is considered to have been his first attempt to act on his commission, and to have been continued until the prophet was convinced of its hopelessness and in obedience to the divine command shut himself up in his own house. But this view does not seem to be sufficiently borne out by the terms of the narrative. The words rather represent a point of view from which his whole ministry is surveyed, or an aspect of it which possessed peculiar importance from the circumstances in which he was placed. The idea of his position as a watchman responsible for individuals may have been present to the prophet's mind from the time of his call; but the practical development of that idea was not possible until the destruction of Jerusalem had prepared men's minds to give heed to his admonitions. Accordingly the second period of Ezekiel's work opens with a fuller statement of the principles indicated in this section (ch. xxxiii.). We shall therefore defer the consideration of these principles till we reach the stage of the prophet's ministry at which their practical significance emerges.

6. The last six verses of the third chapter may be regarded either as closing the account of Ezekiel's consecration or as the introduction to the first part of his ministry, that which preceded the fall of Jerusalem. They contain the description of a second trance, which appears to have happened seven days after the first. The prophet seemed to himself to be carried out in spirit to a certain plain near his residence in Tel-abib. There the glory of Jehovah appears to him precisely as he had seen it in his former vision by the river Kebar. He then receives the command to shut himself up within his house. He is to be like a man bound with ropes, unable to move about among his fellow-exiles. Moreover, the free use of speech is to be interdicted; his tongue will be made to cleave to his palate, so that he is as one "dumb." But as often as he receives a message from Jehovah his mouth will be opened that he may declare it to the rebellious house of Israel.

Now if we compare ver. 26 with xxiv. 27 and xxxiii. 22, we find that this state of intermittent dumbness continued till the day when the siege of Jerusalem began, and was not finally removed till tidings were brought of the capture of the city. The verses before us therefore throw light on the prophet's demeanour during the first half of his ministry. What they signify is his almost entire withdrawal from public life. Instead of being like his great predecessors, a man living full in the public view, and thrusting himself on men's notice when they least desired him, he is to lead an isolated and a solitary life, a sign to the people rather than a living voice.[14] From the sequel we gather that he excited sufficient interest to induce the elders and others to visit him in his house to inquire of Jehovah. We must also suppose that from time to time he emerged from his retirement with a message for the whole community. It cannot, indeed, be assumed that the chs. iv.-xxiv. contain an exact reproduction of the addresses delivered on these occasions. Few of them profess to have been uttered in public, and for the most part they give the impression of having been intended for patient study on the written page rather than for immediate oratorical effect. There is no reason to doubt that in the main they embody the results of Ezekiel's prophetic experiences during the period to which they are referred, although it may be impossible to determine how far they were actually spoken at the time, and how far they are merely written for the instruction of a wider audience.

The strong figures used here to describe this state of seclusion appear to reflect the prophet's consciousness of the restraints providentially imposed on the exercise of his office. These restraints, however, were moral, and not, as has sometimes been maintained, physical. The chief element was the pronounced hostility and incredulity of the people. This, combined with the sense of doom hanging over the nation, seems to have weighed on the spirit of Ezekiel, and in the ecstatic state the incubus lying upon him and paralysing his activity presents itself to his imagination as if he were bound with ropes and afflicted with dumbness. The representation finds a partial parallel in a later passage in the prophet's history. From ch. xxix. 21 (which is the latest prophecy in the whole book) we learn that the apparent non-fulfilment of his predictions against Tyre had caused a similar hindrance to his public work, depriving him of the boldness of speech characteristic of a prophet. And the opening of the mouth given to him on that occasion by the vindication of his words is clearly analogous to the removal of his silence by the news that Jerusalem had fallen. [15]

Footnotes:

11. Bêth mEri, or simply mErî, occurring about fifteen times in the first half of the book, but only once after ch. xxiv.

12. Klostermann.

13. In ch. iii. 12 read "As the glory of Jehovah arose from its place" instead of "Blessed be the glory," etc. (vrvm for vrvk).

14. A somewhat similar episode seems to have occurred in the life of Isaiah. See the commentaries on Isa. viii. 16-18.

15. These verses (ch. iii. 22-27) furnish one of the chief supports of Klostermann's peculiar theory of Ezekiel's condition during the first period of his career. Taking the word "dumb" in its literal sense, he considers that the prophet was afflicted with the malady known as alalia, that this was intermittent down to the date of ch. xxiv., and then became chronic till the fugitive arrived from Jerusalem (ch. xxxiii. 21), when it finally disappeared. This is connected with the remarkable series of symbolic actions related in ch. iv., which are regarded as exhibiting all the symptoms of catalepsy and hemiplegia. These facts, together with the prophet's liability to ecstatic visions, justify, in Klostermann's view, the hypothesis that for seven years Ezekiel laboured under serious nervous disorders. The partiality shown by a few writers to this view probably springs from a desire to maintain the literal accuracy of the prophet's descriptions. But in that aspect the theory breaks down. Even Klostermann admits that the binding with ropes had no existence save in Ezekiel's imagination. But if we are obliged to take into account what seemed to the prophet, it is better to explain the whole phenomena on the same principle. There can be no good grounds for taking the dumbness as real and the ropes as imaginary. Besides, it is surely a questionable expedient to vindicate a prophet's literalism at the expense of his sanity. In the hands of Klostermann and Orelli the hypothesis assumes a stupendous miracle; but it is obvious that a critic of another school might readily "wear his rue with a difference," and treat the whole of Ezekiel's prophetic experiences as hallucinations of a deranged intellect.

Part II - Prophecies Relating Mainly To The Destruction Of Jerusalem

Chapter V - The End Foretold. Chapters iv.-vii

With the fourth chapter we enter on the exposition of the first great division of Ezekiel's prophecies. The chs. iv.-xxiv. cover a period of about four and a half years, extending from the time of the prophet's call to the commencement of the siege of Jerusalem. During this time Ezekiel's thoughts revolved round one great theme--the approaching judgment on the city and the nation. Through contemplation of this fact there was disclosed to him the outline of a comprehensive theory of divine providence, in which the destruction of Israel was seen to be the necessary consequence of her past history and a necessary preliminary to her future restoration. The prophecies may be classified roughly under three heads. In the first class are those which exhibit the judgment itself in ways fitted to impress the prophet and his hearers with a conviction of its certainty; a second class is intended to demolish the illusions and false ideals which possessed the minds of the Israelites and made the announcement of disaster incredible; and a third and very important class expounds the moral principles which were illustrated by the judgment, and which show it to be a divine necessity. In the passage which forms the subject of the present lecture the bare fact and certainty of the judgment are set forth in word and symbol and with a minimum of commentary, although even here the conception which Ezekiel had formed of the moral situation is clearly discernible.

I

The certainty of the national judgment seems to have been first impressed on Ezekiel's mind in the form of a singular series of symbolic acts which he conceived himself to be commanded to perform. The peculiarity of these signs is that they represent simultaneously two distinct aspects of the nation's fate--on the one hand the horrors of the siege of Jerusalem, and on the other hand the state of exile which was to follow. [16]

That the destruction of Jerusalem should occupy the first place in the prophet's picture of national calamity requires no explanation. Jerusalem was the heart and brain of the nation, the centre of its life and its religion, and in the eyes of the prophets the fountain-head of its sin. The strength of her natural situation, the patriotic and religious associations which had gathered round her, and the smallness of her subject province gave to Jerusalem a unique position among the mother-cities of antiquity. And Ezekiel's hearers knew what he meant when he employed the picture of a beleaguered city to set forth the judgment that was to overtake them. That crowning horror of ancient warfare, the siege of a fortified town, meant in this case something more appalling to the imagination than the ravages of pestilence and famine and sword. The fate of Jerusalem represented the disappearance of everything that had constituted the glory and excellence of Israel's national existence. That the light of Israel should be extinguished amidst the anguish and bloodshed which must accompany an unsuccessful defence of the capital was the most terrible element in Ezekiel's message, and here he sets it in the forefront of his prophecy.

The manner in which the prophet seeks to impress this fact on his countrymen illustrates a peculiar vein of realism which runs through all his thinking (ch. iv. 1-3). Being at a distance from Jerusalem, he seems to feel the need of some visible emblem of the doomed city before he can adequately represent the import of his prediction. He is commanded to take a brick and portray upon it a walled city, surrounded by the towers, mounds, and battering-rams which marked the usual operations of a besieging army. Then he is to erect a plate of iron between him and the city, and from behind this, with menacing gestures, he is as it were to press on the siege. The meaning of the symbols is obvious. As the engines of destruction appear on Ezekiel's diagram, at the bidding of Jehovah, so in due time the Chaldæan army will be seen from the walls of Jerusalem, led by the same unseen Power which now controls the acts of the prophet. In the last act Ezekiel exhibits the attitude of Jehovah Himself, cut off from His people by the iron wall of an inexorable purpose which no prayer could penetrate.

Thus far the prophet's actions, however strange they may appear to us, have been simple and intelligible. But at this point a second sign is as it were superimposed on the first, in order to symbolise an entirely different set of facts--the hardship and duration of the Exile (vv. 4-8). While still engaged in prosecuting the siege of the city, the prophet is supposed to become at the same time the representative of the guilty people and the victim of the divine judgment. He is to "bear their iniquity"--that is, the punishment due to their sin. This is represented by his lying bound on his left side for a number of days equal to the years of Ephraim's banishment, and then on his right side for a time proportionate to the captivity of Judah. Now the time of Judah's exile is fixed at forty years, dating of course from the fall of the city. The captivity of North Israel exceeds that of Judah by the interval between the destruction of Samaria (722) and the fall of Jerusalem, a period which actually measured about a hundred and thirty-five years. In the Hebrew text, however, the length of Israel's captivity is given as three hundred and ninety years--that is, it must have lasted for three hundred and fifty years before that of Judah begins. This is obviously quite irreconcilable with the facts of history, and also with the prophet's intention. He cannot mean that the banishment of the northern tribes was to be protracted for two centuries after that of Judah had come to an end, for he uniformly speaks of the restoration of the two branches of the nation as simultaneous. The text of the Greek translation helps us past this difficulty. The Hebrew manuscript from which that version was made had the reading a "hundred and ninety" instead of "three hundred and ninety" in ver. 5. This alone yields a satisfactory sense, and the reading of the Septuagint is now generally accepted as representing what Ezekiel actually wrote. There is still a slight discrepancy between the hundred and thirty-five years of the actual history and the hundred and fifty years expressed by the symbol; but we must remember that Ezekiel is using round numbers throughout, and moreover he has not as yet fixed the precise date of the capture of Jerusalem when the last forty years are to commence.[17]

In the third symbol (vv. 9-17) the two aspects of the judgment are again presented in the closest possible combination. The prophet's food and drink during the days when he is imagined to be lying on his side represents on the one hand, by its being small in quantity and carefully weighed and measured, the rigours of famine in Jerusalem during the siege--"Behold, I will break the staff of bread in Jerusalem: and they shall eat bread by weight, and with anxiety; and drink water by measure, and with horror" (ver. 16); on the other hand, by its mixed ingredients and by the fuel used in its preparation, it typifies the unclean religious condition of the people when in exile--"Even so shall the children of Israel eat their food unclean among the heathen" (ver. 13). The meaning of this threat is best explained by a passage in the book of Hosea. Speaking of the Exile, Hosea says: "They shall not remain in the land of Jehovah; but the children of Ephraim shall return to Egypt, and shall eat unclean food in Assyria. They shall pour out no wine to Jehovah, nor shall they lay out their sacrifices for Him: like the food of mourners shall their food be; all that eat thereof shall be defiled: for their bread shall only satisfy their hunger; it shall not come into the house of Jehovah" (Hos. ix. 3, 4). The idea is that all food which has not been consecrated by being presented to Jehovah in the sanctuary is necessarily unclean, and those who eat of it contract ceremonial defilement. In the very act of satisfying his natural appetite a man forfeits his religious standing. This was the peculiar hardship of the state of exile, that a man must become unclean, he must eat unconsecrated food unless he renounced his religion and served the gods of the land in which he dwelt. Between the time of Hosea and Ezekiel these ideas may have been somewhat modified by the introduction of the Deuteronomic law, which expressly permits secular slaughter at a distance from the sanctuary. But this did not lessen the importance of a legal sanctuary for the common life of an Israelite. The whole of a man's flocks and herds, the whole produce of his fields, had to be sanctified by the presentation of firstlings and firstfruits at the Temple before he could enjoy the reward of his industry with the sense of standing in Jehovah's favour. Hence the destruction of the sanctuary or the permanent exclusion of the worshippers from it reduced the whole life of the people to a condition of uncleanness which was felt to be as great a calamity as was a papal interdict in the Middle Ages. This is the fact which is expressed in the part of Ezekiel's symbolism now before us. What it meant for his fellow-exiles was that the religious disability under which they laboured was to be continued for a generation. The whole life of Israel was to become unclean until its inward state was made worthy of the religious privileges now to be withdrawn. At the same time no one could have felt the penalty more severely than Ezekiel himself, in whom habits of ceremonial purity had become a second nature. The repugnance which he feels at the loathsome manner in which he was at first directed to prepare his food, and the profession of his own practice in exile, as well as the concession made to his scrupulous sense of propriety (vv. 14-16), are all characteristic of one whose priestly training had made a defect of ceremonial cleanness almost equivalent to a moral delinquency.

The last of the symbols (ch. v. 1-4) represents the fate of the population of Jerusalem when the city is taken. The shaving of the prophet's head and beard is a figure for the depopulation of the city and country. By a further series of acts, whose meaning is obvious, he shows how a third of the inhabitants shall die of famine and pestilence during the siege, a third shall be slain by the enemy when the city is captured, while the remaining third shall be dispersed among the nations. Even these shall be pursued by the sword of vengeance until but a few numbered individuals survive, and of them again a part passes through the fire. The passage reminds us of the last verse of the sixth chapter of Isaiah, which was perhaps in Ezekiel's mind when he wrote: "And if a tenth still remain in it [the land], it shall again pass through the fire: as a terebinth or an oak whose stump is left at their felling: a holy seed shall be the stock thereof" (Isa. vi. 13). At least the conception of a succession of sifting judgments, leaving only a remnant to inherit the promise of the future, is common to both prophets, and the symbol in Ezekiel is noteworthy as the first expression of his steadfast conviction that further punishments were in store for the exiles after the destruction of Jerusalem.

It is clear that these signs could never have been enacted, either in view of the people or in solitude, as they are here described. It may be doubted whether the whole description is not purely ideal, representing a process which passed through the prophet's mind, or was suggested to him in the visionary state but never actually performed. That will always remain a tenable view. An imaginary symbolic act is as legitimate a literary device as an imaginary conversation. It is absurd to mix up the question of the prophet's truthfulness with the question whether he did or did not actually do what he conceives himself as doing. The attempt to explain his action by catalepsy would take us but a little way, even if the arguments adduced in favour of it were stronger than they are. Since even a cataleptic patient could not have tied himself down on his side or prepared and eaten his food in that posture, it is necessary in any case to admit that there must be a considerable, though indeterminate, element of literary imagination in the account given of the symbols. It is not impossible that some symbolic representation of the siege of Jerusalem may have actually been the first act in Ezekiel's ministry. In the interpretation of the vision which immediately follows we shall find that no notice is taken of the features which refer to exile, but only of those which announce the siege of Jerusalem. It may therefore be the case that Ezekiel did some such action as is here described, pointing to the fall of Jerusalem, but that the whole was taken up afterwards in his imagination and made into an ideal representation of the two great facts which formed the burden of his earlier prophecy.

II

It is a relief to turn from this somewhat fantastic, though for its own purpose effective, exhibition of prophetic ideas to the impassioned oracles in which the doom of the city and the nation is pronounced. The first of these (ch. v. 5-17) is introduced here as the explanation of the signs that have been described, in so far as they bear on the fate of Jerusalem; but it has a unity of its own, and is a characteristic specimen of Ezekiel's oratorical style. It consists of two parts: the first (vv. 5-10) deals chiefly with the reasons for the judgment on Jerusalem, and the second (vv. 11-17) with the nature of the judgment itself. The chief thought of the passage is the unexampled severity of the punishment which is in store for Israel, as represented by the fate of the capital. A calamity so unprecedented demands an explanation as unique as itself. Ezekiel finds the ground of it in the signal honour conferred on Jerusalem in her being set in the midst of the nations, in the possession of a religion which expressed the will of the one God, and in the fact that she had proved herself unworthy of her distinction and privileges and tried to live as the nations around. "This is Jerusalem which I have set in the midst of the nations, with the lands round about her. But she rebelled against My judgments wickedly [18] more than the nations, and My statutes more than [other] lands round about her: for they rejected My judgments, and in My statutes they did not walk.... Therefore thus saith the Lord Jehovah: Behold, even I am against you; and I will execute in thy midst judgments before the nations, and will do in thy case what I have not done [heretofore], and what I shall not do the like of any more, according to all thy abominations" (vv. 5-9). The central position of Jerusalem is evidently no figure of speech in the mouth of Ezekiel. It means that she is so situated as to fulfil her destiny in the view of all the nations of the world, who can read in her wonderful history the character of the God who is above all gods. Nor can the prophet be fairly accused of provincialism in thus speaking of Jerusalem's unrivalled physical and moral advantages. The mountain ridge on which she stood lay almost across the great highways of communication between the East and the West, between the hoary seats of civilisation and the lands whither the course of empire took its way. Ezekiel knew that Tyre was the centre of the old world's commerce,[19] but he also knew that Jerusalem occupied a central situation in the civilised world, and in that fact he rightly saw a providential mark of the grandeur and universality of her religious mission. Her calamities, too, were probably such as no other city experienced. The terrible prediction of ver. 10, "Fathers shall eat sons in the midst of thee, and sons shall eat fathers," seems to have been literally fulfilled. "The hands of the pitiful women have sodden their own children:

they were their meat in the destruction of the daughter of My people" (Lam. iv. 10). It is likely enough that the annals of Assyrian conquest cover many a tale of woe which in point of mere physical suffering paralleled the atrocities of the siege of Jerusalem. But no other nation had a conscience so sensitive as Israel, or lost so much by its political annihilation. The humanising influences of a pure religion had made Israel susceptible of a kind of anguish which ruder communities were spared.

The sin of Jerusalem is represented after Ezekiel's manner as on the one hand transgression of the divine commandments, and on the other defilement of the Temple through false worship. These are ideas which we shall frequently meet in the course of the book, and they need not detain us here. The prophet proceeds (vv. 11-17) to describe in detail the relentless punishment which the divine vengeance is to inflict on the inhabitants and the city. The jealousy, the wrath, the indignation of Jehovah, which are represented as "satisfied" by the complete destruction of the people, belong to the limitations of the conception of God which Ezekiel had. It was impossible at that time to interpret such an event as the fall of Jerusalem in a religious sense otherwise than as a vehement outburst of Jehovah's anger, expressing the reaction of His holy nature against the sin of idolatry. There is indeed a great distance between the attitude of Ezekiel towards the hapless city and the yearning pity of Christ's lament over the sinful Jerusalem of His time. Yet the first was a step towards the second. Ezekiel realised intensely that part of God's character which it was needful to enforce in order to beget in his countrymen the deep horror at the sin of idolatry which characterised the later Judaism. The best commentary on the latter part of this chapter is found in those parts of the book of Lamentations which speak of the state of the city and the survivors after its overthrow. There we see how quickly the stern judgment produced a more chastened and beautiful type of piety than had ever been prevalent before. Those pathetic utterances, in which patriotism and religion are so finely blended, are like the timid and tentative advances of a child's heart towards a parent who has ceased to punish but has not begun to caress. This and much else that is true and ennobling in the later religion of Israel is rooted in the terrifying sense of the divine anger against sin so powerfully represented in the preaching of Ezekiel.

III

The next two chapters may be regarded as pendants to the theme which is dealt with in this opening section of the book of Ezekiel. In the fourth and fifth chapters the prophet had mainly the city in his eye as the focus of the nation's life; in the sixth he turns his eye to the land which had shared the sin, and must suffer the punishment, of the capital. It is, in its first part (vv. 2-10), an apostrophe to the mountain land of Israel, which seems to stand out before the exile's mind with its mountains and hills, its ravines and valleys, in contrast to the monotonous plain of Babylonia which stretched around him. But these mountains were familiar to the prophet as the seats of the rural idolatry in Israel. The word bamah, which means properly "the height," had come to be used as the name of an idolatrous sanctuary. These sanctuaries were probably Canaanitish in origin; and although by Israel they had been consecrated to the worship of Jehovah, yet He was worshipped there in ways which the prophets pronounced hateful to Him. They had been destroyed by Josiah, but must have been restored to their former use during the revival of heathenism which followed his death. It is a lurid picture which rises before the prophet's imagination as he contemplates the judgment of this provincial idolatry: the altars laid waste, the "sun-pillars" [20] broken, and the idols surrounded by the corpses of men who had fled to their shrines for protection and perished at their feet. This demonstration of the helplessness of the rustic divinities to save their sanctuaries and their worshippers will be the means of breaking the rebellious heart and the whorish eyes that had led Israel so far astray from her true Lord, and will produce in exile the self-loathing which Ezekiel always regards as the beginning of penitence.

But the prophet's passion rises to a higher pitch, and he hears the command "Clap thy hands, and stamp with thy foot, and say, Aha for the abominations of the house of Israel!" These are gestures and exclamations, not of indignation, but of contempt and triumphant scorn. The same feeling and even the same gestures are ascribed to Jehovah Himself in another passage of highly charged emotion (ch. xxi. 17). And it is only fair to remember that it is the anticipation of the victory of Jehovah's cause that fills the mind of the prophet at such moments and seems to deaden the sense of human sympathy within him. At the same time the victory of Jehovah was the victory of prophecy, and in so far Smend may be right in regarding the words as throwing light on the intensity of the antagonism in which prophecy and the popular religion then stood. The devastation of the land is to be effected by the same instruments as were at work in the destruction of the city: first the sword of the Chaldæans, then famine and pestilence among those who escape, until the whole of Israel's ancient territory lies desolate from the southern steppes to Riblah in the north. [21]

Ch. vii. is one of those singled out by Ewald as preserving most faithfully the spirit and language of Ezekiel's earlier utterances. Both in thought and expression it exhibits a freedom and animation seldom attained in Ezekiel's writings, and it is evident that it must have been composed under keen emotion. It is comparatively free from those stereotyped phrases which are elsewhere so common, and the style falls at times into the rhythm which is characteristic of Hebrew poetry. Ezekiel hardly perhaps attains to perfect mastery of poetic form, and even here we may be sensible of a lack of power to blend a series of impressions and images into an artistic unity. The vehemence of his feeling hurries him from one conception to another, without giving full expression to any, or indicating clearly the connection that leads from one to the other. This circumstance, and the corrupt condition of the text together, make the chapter in some parts unintelligible, and as a whole one of the most difficult in the book. In its present position it forms a fitting conclusion to the opening section of the book. All the elements of the judgment which have just been foretold are gathered up in one outburst of emotion, producing a song of triumph in which the prophet seems to stand in the uproar of the final catastrophe and exult amid the crash and wreck of the old order which is passing away.

The passage is divided into five stanzas, which may originally have been approximately equal in length, although the first is now nearly twice as long as any of the others. [22]

i. Vv. 2-9.--The first verse strikes the keynote of the whole poem; it is the inevitableness and the finality of the approaching dissolution. A striking phrase of Amos [23] is first taken up and expanded in accordance with the anticipations with which the previous chapters have now familiarised us: "An end is come, the end is come on the four skirts of the land." The poet already hears the tumult and confusion of the battle; the vintage songs of the Judæan peasant are silenced, and with the din and fury of war the day of the Lord draws near.

ii. Vv. 10-13.--The prophet's thoughts here revert to the present, and he notes the eager interest with which men both in Judah and Babylon are pursuing the ordinary business of life and the vain dreams of political greatness. "The diadem flourishes, the sceptre blossoms, arrogance shoots up." These expressions must refer to the efforts of the new rulers of Jerusalem to restore the fortunes of the nation and the glories of the old kingdom which had been so greatly tarnished by the recent captivity. Things are going bravely, they think; they are surprised at their own success; they hope that the day of small things will grow into the day of things greater than those which are past. The following verse is untranslatable; probably the original words, if we could recover them, would contain some pointed and scornful antithesis to these futile and vain-glorious anticipations. The allusion to "buyers and sellers" (ver. 12) may possibly be quite general, referring only to the absorbing interest which men continue to take in their possessions, heedless of the impending judgment. [24] But the facts that the advantage is assumed to be on the side of the buyer and that the seller expects to return to his heritage make it probable that the prophet is thinking of the forced sales by the expatriated nobles of their estates in Palestine, and to their deeply cherished resolve to right themselves when the time of their exile is over. All such ambitions, says the prophet, are vain--"the seller shall not return to what he sold, and a man shall not by wrong preserve his living." In any case Ezekiel evinces here, as elsewhere, a certain sympathy with the exiled aristocracy, in opposition to the pretensions of the new men who had succeeded to their honours.

iii. Vv. 14-18.--The next scene that rises before the prophet's vision is the collapse of Judah's military preparations in the hour of danger. Their army exists but on paper. There is much blowing of trumpets and much organising, but no men to go forth to battle. A blight rests on all their efforts; their hands are paralysed and their hearts unnerved by the sense that "wrath rests on all their pomp." Sword, famine, and pestilence, the ministers of Jehovah's vengeance, shall devour the inhabitants of the city and the country, until but a few survivors on the tops of the mountains remain to mourn over the universal desolation.

iv. Vv. 19-22.--At present the inhabitants of Jerusalem are proud of the ill-gotten and ill-used wealth stored up within her, and doubtless the exiles cast covetous eyes on the luxury which may still have prevailed amongst the upper classes in the capital. But of what avail will all this treasure be in the evil day now so near at hand? It will but add mockery to their sufferings to be surrounded by gold and silver which can do nothing to allay the pangs of hunger. It will be cast in the streets as refuse, for it cannot save them in the day of Jehovah's anger. Nay, more, it will become the prize of the most ruthless of the heathen (the Chaldæans); and when in the eagerness of their lust for gold they ransack the Temple treasury and so desecrate the Holy Place, Jehovah will avert His face and suffer them to work their will. The curse of Jehovah rests on the silver and gold of Jerusalem, which has been used for the making of idolatrous images, and now is made to them an unclean thing.

v. Vv. 23-27.--The closing strophe contains a powerful description of the dismay and despair that will seize all classes in the state as the day of wrath draws near. Calamity after calamity comes, rumour follows hard on rumour, and the heads of the nation are distracted and cease to exercise the functions of leadership. The recognised guides of the people--the prophets, the priests, and the wise men--have no word of counsel or direction to offer; the prophet's vision, the priest's traditional lore, and the wise man's sagacity are alike at fault. So the king and the grandees are filled with stupefaction; and the common people, deprived of their natural leaders, sit down in helpless dejection. Thus shall Jerusalem be recompensed according to her doings. "The land is full of bloodshed, and the city of violence"; and in the correspondence between desert and retribution men shall be made to acknowledge the operation of the divine righteousness. "They shall know that I am Jehovah."

IV

It may be useful at this point to note certain theological principles which already begin to appear in this earliest of Ezekiel's prophecies. Reflection on the nature and purpose of the divine dealings we have seen to be a characteristic of his work; and even those passages which we have considered, although chiefly devoted to an enforcement of the fact of judgment, present some features of the conception of Israel's history which had been formed in his mind.

1. We observe in the first place that the prophet lays great stress on the world-wide significance of the events which are to befall Israel. This thought is not as yet developed, but it is clearly present. The relation between Jehovah and Israel is so peculiar that He is known to the nations in the first instance only as Israel's God, and thus His being and character have to be learned from His dealings with His own people. And since Jehovah is the only true God and must be worshipped as such everywhere, the history of Israel has an interest for the world such as that of no other nation has. She was placed in the centre of the nations in order that the knowledge of God might radiate from her through all the world; and now that she has proved unfaithful to her mission, Jehovah must manifest His power and His character by an unexampled work of judgment. Even the destruction of Israel is a demonstration to the universal conscience of mankind of what true divinity is.

2. But the judgment has of course a purpose and a meaning for Israel herself, and both purposes are summed up in the recurring formula "Ye [they] shall know that I am Jehovah," or "that I, Jehovah, have spoken." These two phrases express precisely the same idea, although from slightly different starting-points. It is assumed that Jehovah's personality is to be identified by His word spoken through the prophets. He is known to men through the revelation of Himself in the prophets' utterances. "Ye shall know that I, Jehovah, have spoken" means therefore, Ye shall know that it is I, the God of Israel and the Ruler of the universe, who speak these things. In other words, the harmony between prophecy and providence guarantees the source of the prophet's message. The shorter phrase "Ye shall know that I am Jehovah" may mean Ye shall know that I who now speak am truly Jehovah, the God of Israel. The prejudices of the people would have led them to deny that the power which dictated Ezekiel's prophecy could be their God; but this denial, together with the false idea of Jehovah on which it rests, shall be destroyed for ever when the prophet's words come true.

There is of course no doubt that Ezekiel conceived Jehovah as endowed with the plenitude of deity, or that in his view the name expressed all that we mean by the word God. Nevertheless, historically the name Jehovah is a proper name, denoting the God who is the God of Israel. Renan has ventured on the assertion that a deity with a proper name is necessarily a false god. The statement perhaps measures the difference between the God of revealed religion and the god who is an abstraction, an expression of the order of the universe, who exists only in the mind of the man who names him. The God of revelation is a living person, with a character and will of His own, capable of being known by man. It is the distinction of revelation that it dares to regard God as an individual with an inner life and nature of His own, independent of the conception men may form of Him. Applied to such a Being, a personal name may be as true and significant as the name which expresses the character and individuality of a man. Only thus can we understand the historical process by which the God who was first manifested as the deity of a particular nation preserves His personal identity with the God who in Christ is at last revealed as the God of the spirits of all flesh. The knowledge of Jehovah of which Ezekiel speaks is therefore at once a knowledge of the character of the God whom Israel professed to serve, and a knowledge of that which constitutes true and essential divinity. [25]

3. The prophet, in ch. vi. 8-10, proceeds one step further in delineating the effect of the judgment on the minds of the survivors. The fascination of idolatry for the Israelites is conceived as produced by that radical perversion of the religious sense which the prophets call "whoredom"--a sensuous delight in the blessings of nature, and an indifference to the moral element which can alone preserve either religion or human love from corruption. The spell shall at last be broken in the new knowledge of Jehovah which is produced by calamity; and the heart of the people, purified from its delusions, shall turn to Him who has smitten them, as the only true God. "When your fugitives from the sword are among the nations, when they are scattered through the lands, then shall your fugitives remember Me amongst the nations whither they have been carried captive,

when I break their heart that goes awhoring from Me, and their whorish eyes which went after their idols." When the idolatrous propensity is thus eradicated, the conscience of Israel will turn inwards on itself, and in the light of its new knowledge of God will for the first time read its own history aright. The beginnings of a new spiritual life will be made in the bitter self-condemnation which is one side of the national repentance. "They shall loathe themselves for all the evil that they have committed in all their abominations."

Footnotes:

16. An ingenious attempt has been made by Professor Cornill to rearrange the verses so as to bring out two separate series of actions, one referring exclusively to the exile and the other to the siege. But the proposed reading requires a somewhat violent handling of the text, and does not seem to have met with much acceptance. The blending of diverse elements in a single image appears also in ch. xii. 3-16.

17. The correspondence would be almost exact if we date the commencement of the northern captivity from 734, when Tiglath-pileser carried away the inhabitants of the northern and eastern parts of the country. This is a possible view, although hardly necessary.

18. Or, with a different pointing, "She changed My judgments to wickedness."

19. See ch. xxvii.

20. Hammânim--a word of doubtful meaning, however. The word for idols, gillûlîm, is all but peculiar to Ezekiel. It is variously explained as block-gods or dung-gods--in any case an epithet of contempt. The asherah, or sacred pole, is never referred to by Ezekiel.

21. In ver. 14 the true sense has been lost by the corruption of the word Riblah into Diblah.

22. The reason may be that two different recensions of the text have been combined and mixed up. So Hitzig and Cornill.

23. Amos viii. 2.

24. Cf. Luke xvii. 26-30.

25. Ezekiel's use of the divine names would hardly be satisfactory to Renan. Outside of the prophecies addressed to heathen nations the generic name 'lhym is never used absolutely, except in the phrases "visions of God" (three times) and "spirit of God" (once, in ch. xi. 24, where the text may be doubtful). Elsewhere it is used only of God in His relation to men, as, e.g., in the expression "be to you for a God." 'l sdy occurs once (ch. x. 5) and 'l alone three times in ch. xxviii. (addressed to the prince of Tyre). The prophet's word, when he wishes to express absolute divinity, is just the "proper" name yhvh, in accordance no doubt with the interpretation given in Exod. iii. 13, 14.

John J. Skinner

Chapter VI - Your House Is Left Unto You Desolate. Chapters viii.-xi

One of the most instructive phases of religious belief among the Israelites of the seventh century was the superstitious regard in which the Temple at Jerusalem was held. Its prestige as the metropolitan sanctuary had no doubt steadily increased from the time when it was built. But it was in the crisis of the Assyrian invasion that the popular sentiment in favour of its peculiar sanctity was transmuted into a fanatical faith in its inherent inviolability. It is well known that during the whole course of this invasion the prophet Isaiah had consistently taught that the enemy should never set foot within the precincts of the Holy City--that, on the contrary, the attempt to seize it would prove to be the signal for his annihilation. The striking fulfilment of this prediction in the sudden destruction of Sennacherib's army had an immense effect on the religion of the time. It restored the faith in Jehovah's omnipotence which was already giving way, and it granted a new lease of life to the very errors which it ought to have extinguished. For here, as in so many other cases, what was a spiritual faith in one generation became a superstition in the next. Indifferent to the divine truths which gave meaning to Isaiah's prophecy, the people changed his sublime faith in the living God working in history into a crass confidence in the material symbol which had been the means of expressing it to their minds. Henceforth it became a fundamental tenet of the current creed that the Temple and the city which guarded it could never fall into the hands of an enemy; and any teaching which assailed that belief was felt to undermine confidence in the national deity. In the time of Jeremiah and Ezekiel this superstition existed in unabated vigour, and formed one of the greatest hindrances to the acceptance of their teaching. "The Temple of the Lord, the Temple of the Lord, the Temple of the Lord are these!" was the cry of the benighted worshippers as they thronged to its courts to seek the favour of Jehovah (Jer. vii. 4). The same state of feeling must have prevailed among Ezekiel's fellow-exiles. To the prophet himself, attached as he was to the worship of the Temple, it may have been a thought almost too hard to bear that Jehovah should abandon the only place of His legitimate worship. Amongst the rest of the captives the faith in its infallibility was one of the illusions which must be overthrown before their minds could perceive the true drift of his teaching. In his first prophecy the fact had just been touched on, but merely as an incident in the fall of Jerusalem. About a year later, however, he received a new revelation, in which he learned that the destruction of the Temple was no mere incidental consequence of the capture of the city, but a main object of the calamity. The time was come when judgment must begin at the house of God.

The weird vision in which this truth was conveyed to the prophet is said to have occurred during a visit of the elders to Ezekiel in his own house. In their presence he fell into a trance, in which the events now to be considered passed before him; and after the trance was removed he recounted the substance of the vision to the exiles. This statement has been somewhat needlessly called in question, on the ground that after so protracted an ecstasy the prophet would not be likely to find his visitors still in their places. But this matter-of-fact criticism overreaches itself. We have no means of determining how long it would take for this series of events to be realised. If we may trust anything to the analogy of dreams--and of all conditions to which ordinary men are subject the dream is surely the closest analogy to the prophetic ecstasy--the whole may have passed in an incredibly short space of time. If the statement were untrue, it is difficult to see what Ezekiel would have gained by making it. If the whole vision were a fiction, this must of course be fictitious too; but even so it seems a very superfluous piece of invention.

We prefer, therefore, to regard the vision as real, and the assigned situation as historical; and the fact that it is recorded suggests that there must be some connection between the object of the visit and the burden of the revelation which was then communicated. It is not difficult to imagine points of contact between them. Ewald has conjectured that the occasion of the visit may have been some recent tidings from Jerusalem which had opened the eyes of the "elders" to the real relation that existed between them and their brethren at home. If they had ever cherished any illusions on the point, they had certainly been disabused of them before Ezekiel had this vision. They were aware, whether the information was recent or not, that they were absolutely disowned by the new authorities in Jerusalem, and that it was impossible that they should ever come back peaceably to their old place in the state. This created a problem which they could not solve, and the fact that Ezekiel had announced the fall of Jerusalem may have formed a bond of sympathy between him and his brethren in exile which drew them to him in their perplexity. Some such hypothesis gives at all events a fuller significance to the closing part of the vision, where the attitude of the men in Jerusalem is described, and where the exiles are taught that the hope of Israel's future lies with them. It is the first time that Ezekiel has distinguished between the fates in store for the two sections of the people, and it would almost appear as if the promotion of the exiles to the first place in the true Israel was a new revelation to him. Twice during this vision he is moved to intercede for the "remnant of Israel," as if the only hope of a new people of God lay in sparing at least some of those who were left in the land. But the burden of the message that now comes to him is that in the spiritual sense the true remnant of Israel is not in Judæa, but among the exiles in Babylon. It was there that the new Israel was to be formed, and the land was to be the heritage, not of those who clung to it and exulted in the misfortunes of their banished brethren, but of those who under the discipline of exile were first prepared to use the land as Jehovah's holiness demanded.

The vision is interesting, in the first place, on account of the glimpse it affords of the state of mind prevailing in influential circles in Jerusalem at this time. There is no reason whatever to doubt that here in the form of a vision we have reliable information regarding the actual state of matters when Ezekiel wrote. It has been supposed by some critics that the description of the idolatries in the Temple does not refer to contemporary practices, but to abuses that had been rife in the days of Manasseh and had been put a stop to by Josiah's reformation. But the vision loses half its meaning if it is taken as merely an idealised representation of all the sins that had polluted the Temple in the course of its history. The names of those who are seen must be names of living men known to Ezekiel and his contemporaries, and the sentiments put in their mouth, especially in the latter part of the vision, are suitable only to the age in which he lived. It is very probable that the description in its general features would also apply to the days of Manasseh; but the revival of idolatry which followed the death of Josiah would naturally take the form of a restoration of the illegal cults which had flourished unchecked under his grandfather. Ezekiel's own experience before his captivity, and the steady intercourse which had been maintained since, would supply him with the material which in the ecstatic condition is wrought up into this powerful picture.

The thing that surprises us most is the prevailing conviction amongst the ruling classes that "Jehovah had forsaken the land." These men seem to have partly emancipated themselves, as politicians in Israel were apt to do, from the restraints and narrowness of the popular religion. To them it was a conceivable thing that Jehovah should abandon His people. And yet life was worth living and fighting for apart from Jehovah. It was of course a merely selfish life, not inspired by national ideals, but simply a clinging to place and power. The wish was father to the thought; men who so readily yielded to the belief in Jehovah's absence were very willing to be persuaded of its truth. The religion of Jehovah had always imposed a check on social and civic wrong, and men whose power rested on violence and oppression could not but rejoice to be rid of it. So they seem to have acquiesced readily enough in the conclusion to which so many circumstances seemed to point, that Jehovah had ceased to interest Himself either for good or evil in them and their affairs. Still, the wide acceptance of a belief like this, so repugnant to all the religious ideas of the ancient world, seems to require for its explanation some fact of contemporary history. It has been thought that it arose from the disappearance of the ark of Jehovah from the Temple. It seems from the third chapter of Jeremiah that the ark was no longer in existence in Josiah's reign, and that the want of it was felt as a grave religious loss. It is not improbable that this circumstance, in connection with the disasters which had marked the last days of the kingdom, led in many minds to the fear and in some to the hope that along with His most venerable symbol Jehovah Himself had vanished from their midst.

It should be noticed that the feeling described was only one of several currents that ran in the divided society of Jerusalem. It is quite a different point of view that is presented in the taunt quoted in ch. xi. 15, that the exiles were far from Jehovah, and had therefore lost their right to their possessions. But the religious despair is not only the most startling fact that we have to look at; it is also the one that is made most prominent in the vision. And the divine answer to it given through Ezekiel is that the conviction is true; Jehovah has forsaken the land. But in the first place the cause of His departure is found in those very practices for which it was made the excuse; and in the second, although He has ceased to dwell in the midst of His people, He has lost neither the power nor the will to punish their iniquities. To impress these truths first on his fellow-exiles and then on the whole nation is the chief object of the chapter before us.

Now we find that the general sense of God-forsakenness expressed itself principally in two directions. On the one hand it led to the multiplication of false objects of worship to supply the place of Him who was regarded as the proper tutelary Divinity of Israel; on the other hand it produced a reckless, devil-may-care spirit of resistance against any odds, such as was natural to men who had only material interests to fight for, and nothing to trust in but their own right hand. Syncretism in religion and fatalism in politics--these were the twin symptoms of the decay of faith among the upper classes in Jerusalem. But these belong to two different parts of the vision which we must now distinguish.

I

The first part deals with the departure of Jehovah as caused by religious offences perpetrated in the Temple, and with the return of Jehovah to destroy the city on account of these offences. The prophet is transported in "visions of God" to Jerusalem, and placed in the outer court near the northern gate, outside of which was the site where the "image of Jealousy" had stood in the time of Manasseh. Near him stands the appearance which he had learned to recognise as the glory of Jehovah, signifying that Jehovah has, for a purpose not yet disclosed, revisited His Temple. But first Ezekiel must be made to see the state of things which exists in this Temple which had once been the seat of God's presence. Looking through the gate to the north, he discovers that the image of Jealousy [26] has been restored to its old place. This is the first and apparently the least heinous of the abominations that defiled the sanctuary.

The second scene is the only one of the four which represents a secret cult. Partly perhaps for that reason it strikes our minds as the most repulsive of all; but that was obviously not Ezekiel's estimate of it. There are greater abominations to follow. It is difficult to understand the particulars of Ezekiel's description, especially in the Hebrew text (the LXX. is simpler); but it seems impossible to escape the impression that there was something obscene in a worship where idolatry appears as ashamed of itself. The essential fact, however, is that the very highest and most influential men in the land were addicted to a form of heathenism, whose objects of worship were pictures of "horrid creeping things, and cattle, and all the gods of the house of Israel." The name of one of these men, the leader in this superstition, is given, and is significant of the state of life in Jerusalem shortly before its fall. Jaazaniah was the son of Shaphan, who is probably identical with the chancellor of Josiah's reign whose sympathy with the prophetic teaching was evinced by his zeal in the cause of reform. We read of other members of the family who were faithful to the national religion, such as his son Ahikam, also a zealous reformer, and his grandson Gedaliah, Jeremiah's friend and patron, and the governor appointed over Judah by Nebuchadnezzar after the taking of the city. The family was thus divided both in religion and politics. While one branch was devoted to the worship of Jehovah and favoured submission to the king of Babylon, Jaazaniah belonged to the opposite party and was the ringleader in a peculiarly obnoxious form of idolatry.[27]

The third "abomination" is a form of idolatry widely diffused over Western Asia--the annual mourning for Tammuz. Tammuz was originally a Babylonian deity (Dumuzi), but his worship is specially identified with Phoenicia, whence under the name Adonis it was introduced into Greece. The mourning celebrates the death of the god, which is an emblem of the decay of the earth's productive powers, whether due to the scorching heat of the sun or to the cold of winter. It seems to have been a comparatively harmless rite of nature-religion, and its popularity among the women of Jerusalem at this time may be due to the prevailing mood of despondency which found vent in the sympathetic contemplation of that aspect of nature which most suggests decay and death.

The last and greatest of the abominations practised in and near the Temple is the worship of the sun. The peculiar enormity of this species of idolatry can hardly lie in the object of adoration; it is to be sought rather in the place where it was practised, and in the rank of those who took part in it, who were probably priests. Standing between the porch and the altar, with their backs to the Temple, these men unconsciously expressed the deliberate rejection of Jehovah which was involved in their idolatry. The worship of the heavenly bodies was probably imported into Israel from Assyria and Babylon, and its prevalence in the later years of the monarchy was due to political rather than religious influences. The gods of these imperial nations were esteemed more potent than those of the states which succumbed to their power, and hence men who were losing confidence in their national deity naturally sought to imitate the religions of the most powerful peoples known to them.[28]

In the arrangement of the four specimens of the religious practices which prevailed in Jerusalem, Ezekiel seems to proceed from the most familiar and explicable to the more outlandish defections from the purity of the national faith. At the same time his description shows how different classes of society were implicated in the sin of idolatry--the elders, the women, and the priests. During all this time the glory of Jehovah has stood in the court, and there is something very impressive in the picture of these infatuated men and women preoccupied with their unholy devotions and all unconscious of the presence of Him whom they deemed to have forsaken the land. To the open eye of the prophet the meaning of the vision must be already clear, but the sentence comes from the mouth of Jehovah Himself: "Hast thou seen, Son of man? Is it too small a thing for the house of Judah to practise the abominations which they have here practised, that they must also fill the land with violence, and [so] provoke Me again to anger? So will I act towards them in anger: My eye shall not pity, nor will I spare" (ch. viii. 17, 18).

***

The last words introduce the account of the punishment of Jerusalem, which is given of course in the symbolic form suggested by the scenery of the vision. Jehovah has meanwhile risen from His throne near the cherubim, and stands on the threshold of the Temple. There He summons to His side the destroyers who are to execute His purpose--six angels, each with a weapon of destruction in his hand. A seventh of higher rank clothed in linen appears with the implements of a scribe in his girdle. These stand "beside the brazen altar," and await the commands of Jehovah. The first act of the judgment is a massacre of the inhabitants of the city, without distinction of age or rank or sex. But, in accordance with his strict view of the divine righteousness, Ezekiel is led to conceive of this last judgment as discriminating carefully between the righteous and the wicked. All those who have inwardly separated themselves from the guilt of the city by hearty detestation of the iniquities perpetrated in its midst are distinguished by a mark on their foreheads before the work of slaughter begins. What became of this faithful remnant it does not belong to the vision to declare. Beginning with the twenty men before the porch, the destroying angels follow the man with the inkhorn through the streets of the city, and slay all on whom he has not set his mark. When the messengers have gone out on their dread errand, Ezekiel, realising the full horror of a scene which he dare not describe, falls prostrate before Jehovah, deprecating the outbreak of indignation which threatened to extinguish "the remnant of Israel." He is reassured by the declaration that the guilt of Judah and Israel demands no less a punishment than this, because the notion that Jehovah had forsaken the land had opened the floodgates of iniquity, and filled the land with bloodshed and the city with oppression. Then the man in the linen robes returns and announces, "It is done as Thou hast commanded."

The second act of the judgment is the destruction of Jerusalem by fire. This is symbolised by the scattering over the city of burning coals taken from the altar-hearth under the throne of God. The man with the linen garments is directed to step between the wheels and take out fire for this purpose. The description of the execution of this order is again carried no further than what actually takes place before the prophet's eyes: the man took the fire and went out. In the place where we might have expected to have an account of the destruction of the city, we have a second description of the appearance and motions of the merkaba, the purpose of which it is difficult to divine. Although it deviates slightly from the account in ch. i., the differences appear to have no significance, and indeed it is expressly said to be the same phenomenon. The whole passage is certainly superfluous, and might be omitted but for the difficulty of imagining any motive that would have tempted a scribe to insert it. We must keep in mind the possibility that this part of the book had been committed to writing before the final redaction of Ezekiel's prophecies, and the description in vv. 8-17 may have served a purpose there which is superseded by the fuller narrative which we now possess in ch. i.

In this way Ezekiel penetrates more deeply into the inner meaning of the judgment on city and people whose external form he had announced in his earlier prophecy. It must be admitted that Jehovah's strange work bears to our minds a more appalling aspect when thus presented in symbols than the actual calamity would bear when effected through the agency of second causes. Whether it had the same effect on the mind of a Hebrew, who hardly believed in second causes, is another question. In any case it gives no ground for the charge made against Ezekiel of dwelling with a malignant satisfaction on the most repulsive features of a terrible picture. He is indeed capable of a rigorous logic in exhibiting the incidence of the law of retribution which was to him the necessary expression of the divine righteousness. That it included the death of every sinner and the overthrow of a city that had become a scene of violence and cruelty was to him a self-evident truth, and more than this the vision does not teach. On the contrary, it contains traits which tend to moderate the inevitable harshness of the truth conveyed. With great reticence it allows the execution of the judgment to take place behind the scenes, giving only those details which were necessary to suggest its nature. Whilst it is being carried out the attention of the reader is engaged in the presence of Jehovah, or his mind is occupied with the principles which made the punishment a moral necessity. The prophet's expostulations with Jehovah show that he was not insensible to the miseries of his people, although he saw them to be inevitable. Further, this vision shows as clearly as any passage in his writings the injustice of the view which represents him as more concerned for petty details of ceremonial than for the great moral interests of a nation. If any feeling expressed in the vision is to be regarded as Ezekiel's own, then indignation against outrages on human life and liberty must be allowed to weigh more with him than offences against ritual purity. And, finally, it is clearly one object of the vision to show that in the destruction of Jerusalem no individual shall be involved who is not also implicated in the guilt which calls down wrath upon her.

II

The second part of the vision (ch. xi.) is but loosely connected with the first. Here Jerusalem still exists, and men are alive who must certainly have perished in the "visitation of the city" if the writer had still kept himself within the limits of his previous conception. But in truth the two have little in common, except the Temple, which is the scene of both, and the cherubim, whose movements mark the transition from the one to the other. The glory of Jehovah is already departing from the house when it is stayed at the entrance of the east gate to give the prophet his special message to the exiles.

Here we are introduced to the more political aspect of the situation in Jerusalem. The twenty-five men who are gathered in the east gate of the Temple are clearly the leading statesmen in the city; and two of them, whose names are given, are expressly designated as "princes of the people." They are apparently met in conclave to deliberate on public matters, and a word from Jehovah lays open to the prophet the nature of their projects. "These are the men that plan ruin, and hold evil counsel in this city." The evil counsel is undoubtedly the project of rebellion against the king of Babylon which must have been hatched at this time and which broke out into open revolt about three years later. The counsel was evil because directly opposed to that which Jeremiah was giving at the time in the name of Jehovah. But Ezekiel also throws invaluable light on the mood of the men who were urging the king along the path which led to ruin. "Are not the houses recently built?" [29] they say, congratulating themselves on their success in repairing the damage done to the city in the time of Jehoiachin. The image of the pot and the flesh is generally taken to express the feeling of easy security in the fortifications of Jerusalem with which these light-hearted politicians embarked on a contest with Nebuchadnezzar. But their mood must be a gloomier one than that if there is any appropriateness in the language they use. To stew in their own juice, and over a fire of their own kindling, could hardly seem a desirable policy to sane men, however strong the pot might be. These councillors are well aware of the dangers they incur, and of the misery which their purpose must necessarily bring on the people. But they are determined to hazard everything and endure everything on the chance that the city may prove strong enough to baffle the resources of the king of Babylon. Once the fire is kindled, it will certainly be better to be in the pot than in the fire; and so long as Jerusalem holds out they will remain behind her walls. The answer which is put into the prophet's mouth is that the issue will not be such as they hope for. The only "flesh" that will be left in the city will be the dead bodies of those who have been slain within her walls by the very men who hope that their lives will be given them for a prey. They themselves shall be dragged forth to meet their fate far away from Jerusalem on the "borders of Israel." It is not unlikely that these conspirators kept their word. Although the king and all the men of war fled from the city as soon as a breach was made, we read of certain high officials who allowed themselves to be taken in the city (Jer. lii. 7). Ezekiel's prophecy was in their case literally fulfilled; for these men and many others were brought to the king of Babylon at Riblah, "and he smote them and put them to death at Riblah in the land of Hamath."

While Ezekiel was uttering this prophecy one of the councillors, named Pelatiah, suddenly fell down dead. Whether a man of this name had suddenly died in Jerusalem under circumstances that had deeply impressed the prophet's mind, or whether the death belongs to the vision, it is impossible for us to tell. To Ezekiel the occurrence seemed an earnest of the complete destruction of the remnant of Israel by the wrath of God, and, as before, he fell on his face to intercede for them. It is then that he receives the message which seems to form the divine answer to the perplexities which haunted the minds of the exiles in Babylon.

In their attitude towards the exiles the new leaders in Jerusalem took up a position as highly privileged religious persons, quite at variance with the scepticism which governed their conduct at home. When they were following the bent of their natural inclinations by practising idolatry and perpetrating judicial murders in the city, their cry was, "Jehovah hath forsaken the land; Jehovah seeth it not." When they were eager to justify their claim to the places and possessions left vacant by their banished countrymen, they said, "They are far from Jehovah: to us the land is given in possession." They were probably equally sincere and equally insincere in both professions. They had simply learned the art which comes easily to men of the world of using religion as a cloak for greed, and throwing it off when greed could be best gratified without it. The idea which lay under their religious attitude was that the exiles had gone into captivity because their sins had incurred Jehovah's anger, and that now His wrath was exhausted and the blessing of His favour would rest on those who had been left in the land. There was sufficient plausibility in the taunt to make it peculiarly galling to the mind of the exiles, who had hoped to exercise some influence over the government in Jerusalem, and to find their places kept for them when they should be permitted to return. It may well have been the resentment produced by tidings of this hostility towards them in

Jerusalem that brought their elders to the house of Ezekiel to see if he had not some message from Jehovah to reassure them.

In the mind of Ezekiel, however, the problem took another form. To him a return to the old Jerusalem had no meaning; neither buyer nor seller should have cause to congratulate himself on his position. The possession of the land of Israel belonged to those in whom Jehovah's ideal of the new Israel was realised, and the only question of religious importance was, Where is the germ of this new Israel to be found? Amongst those who survive the judgment in the old land, or amongst those who have experienced it in the form of banishment? On this point the prophet receives an explicit revelation in answer to his intercession for "the remnant of Israel." "Son of man, thy brethren, thy brethren, thy fellow-captives, and the whole house of Israel of whom the inhabitants of Jerusalem have said, They are far from Jehovah: to us it is given--the land for an inheritance!... Because I have removed them far among the nations, and have scattered them among the lands, and have been to them but little of a sanctuary in the lands where they have gone, therefore say, Thus saith Jehovah, so will I gather you from the peoples, and bring you from the lands where ye have been scattered, and will give you the land of Israel." The difficult expression "I have been but little of a sanctuary" refers to the curtailment of religious privileges and means of access to Jehovah which was a necessary consequence of exile. It implies, however, that Israel in banishment had learned in some measure to preserve that separation from other peoples and that peculiar relation to Jehovah which constituted its national holiness. Religion perhaps perishes sooner from the overgrowth of ritual than from its deficiency. It is an historical fact that the very meagreness of the religion which could be practised in exile was the means of strengthening the more spiritual and permanent elements which constitute the essence of religion. The observances which could be maintained apart from the Temple acquired an importance which they never afterwards lost; and although some of these, such as circumcision, the Passover, the abstinence from forbidden food, were purely ceremonial, others, such as prayer, reading of the Scriptures, and the common worship of the synagogue, represent the purest and most indispensable forms in which communion with God can find expression. That Jehovah Himself became even in small measure what the word "sanctuary" denotes indicates an enrichment of the religious consciousness of which perhaps Ezekiel himself did not perceive the full import.

The great lesson which Ezekiel's message seeks to impress on his hearers is that the tenure of the land of Israel depends on religious conditions. The land is Jehovah's, and He bestows it on those who are prepared to use it as His holiness demands. A pure land inhabited by a pure people is the ideal that underlies all Ezekiel's visions of the future. It is evident that in such a conception of the relation between God and His people ceremonial conditions must occupy a conspicuous place. The sanctity of the land is necessarily of a ceremonial order, and so the sanctity of the people must consist partly in a scrupulous regard for ceremonial requirements. But after all the condition of the land with respect to purity or uncleanness only reflects the character of the nation whose home it is. The things that defile a land are such things as idols and other emblems of heathenism, innocent blood unavenged, and unnatural crimes of various kinds. These things derive their whole significance from the state of mind and heart which they embody; they are the plain and palpable emblems of human sin. It is conceivable that to some minds the outward emblems may have seemed the true seat of evil, and their removal an end in itself apart from the direction of the will by which it was brought about. But it would be a mistake to charge Ezekiel with any such obliquity of moral vision. Although he conceives sin as a defilement that leaves its mark on the material world, he clearly teaches that its essence lies in the opposition of the human will to the will of God. The ceremonial purity required of every Israelite is only the expression of certain aspects of Jehovah's holy nature, the bearing of which on man's spiritual life may have been obscure to the prophet, and is still more obscure to us. And the truly valuable element in compliance with such rules was the obedience to Jehovah's expressed will which flowed from a nature in sympathy with His. Hence in this chapter, while the first thing that the restored exiles have to do is to cleanse the land of its abominations, this act will be the expression of a nature radically changed, doing the will of God from the heart. As the emblems of idolatry that defile the land were the outcome of an irresistible national tendency to evil, so the new and sensitive spirit, taking on the impress of Jehovah's holiness through the law, shall lead to the purification of the land from those things that had provoked the eyes of His glory. "They shall come thither, and remove thence all its detestable things and all its abominations. And I will give them another heart, and put a new spirit within them. I will take away the stony heart from their flesh, and give them a heart of flesh: that they may walk in My statutes, and keep My judgments, and do them: and so shall they be My people, and I will be their God" (ch. xi. 18-20).

Thus in the mind of the prophet Jerusalem and its Temple are already virtually destroyed. He seemed to linger in the Temple court until he saw the chariot of Jehovah withdrawn from the city as a token that the glory had departed from Israel. Then the ecstasy passed away, and he found himself in the presence of the men to whom the hope of the future had been offered, but who were as yet unworthy to receive it.

Footnotes:

26. Of what nature this idolatrous symbol was we cannot certainly determine. The word used for "image" (semel) occurs in only two other passages. The writer of the books of Chronicles uses it of the asherah which was set up by Manasseh in the Temple, and it is possible that he means thus to identify that object with what Ezekiel saw (cf. 2 Chron. xxxiii. 7, and 2 Kings xxi. 7). This interpretation is as satisfactory as any that has been proposed.

27. The nature of the cults is best explained by Professor Robertson Smith, who supposes that they are a survival of aboriginal totemistic superstitions which had been preserved in secret circles till now, but suddenly assumed a new importance with the collapse of the national religion and the belief that Jehovah had left the land. Others, however, have thought that it is Egyptian rites which are referred to. This view might best explain its prevalence among the elders, but it has little positive support.

28. It has been supposed, however, that the sun-worship referred to here is of Persian origin, chiefly because of the obscure expression in ver. 17: "Behold they put the twig to their nose." This has been explained by a Persian custom of holding up a branch before the face, lest the breath of the worshipper should contaminate the purity of the deity. But Persia had not yet played any great part in history, and it is hardly credible that a distinctively Persian custom should have found its way into the ritual of Jerusalem. Moreover, the words do not occur in the description of the sun-worshippers, nor do they refer particularly to them.

29. Following the LXX.

Chapter VII - The End Of The Monarchy. Chapters xii. 1-15, xvii., xix

In spite of the interest excited by Ezekiel's prophetic appearances, the exiles still received his prediction of the fall of Jerusalem with the most stolid incredulity. It proved to be an impossible task to disabuse their minds of the prepossessions which made such an event absolutely incredible. True to their character as a disobedient house, they had "eyes to see, and saw not; and ears to hear, but heard not" (ch. xii. 2). They were intensely interested in the strange signs he performed, and listened with pleasure to his fervid oratory; but the inner meaning of it all never sank into their minds. Ezekiel was well aware that the cause of this obtuseness lay in the false ideals which nourished an overweening confidence in the destiny of their nation. And these ideals were the more difficult to destroy because they each contained an element of truth, so interwoven with the falsehood that to the mind of the people the true and the false stood and fell together. If the great vision of chs. viii.-xi. had accomplished its purpose, it would doubtless have taken away the main support of these delusive imaginations. But the belief in the indestructibility of the Temple was only one of a number of roots through which the vain confidence of the nation was fed; and so long as any of these remained the people's sense of security was likely to remain. These spurious ideals, therefore, Ezekiel sets himself with characteristic thoroughness to demolish one after another.

This appears to be in the main the purpose of the third subdivision of his prophecies on which we now enter. It extends from ch. xii. to ch. xix.; and in so far as it can be taken to represent a phase of his actual spoken ministry, it must be assigned to the fifth year before the capture of Jerusalem (August 591-August 590 b.c.). But since the passage is an exposition of ideas more than a narrative of experiences we may expect to find that chronological consistency has been even less observed than in the earlier part of the book. Each idea is presented in the completeness which it finally possessed in the prophet's mind, and his allusions may anticipate a state of things which had not actually arisen till a somewhat later date. Beginning with a description and interpretation of two symbolic actions intended to impress more vividly on the people the certainty of the impending catastrophe, the prophet proceeds in a series of set discourses to expose the hollowness of the illusions which his fellow-exiles cherished, such as disbelief in prophecies of evil, faith in the destiny of Israel, veneration for the Davidic kingdom, and reliance on the solidarity of the nation in sin and in judgment. These are the principal topics which the course of exposition will bring before us, and in dealing with them it will be convenient to depart from the order in which they stand in the book and adopt an arrangement according to subject. By so doing we run the risk of missing the order of the ideas as it presented itself to the prophet's mind, and of ignoring the remarkable skill with which the transition from one theme to another is frequently effected. But if we have rightly understood the scope of the passage as a whole, this will not prevent us from grasping the substance of his teaching or its bearing on the final message which he had to deliver. In the present chapter we shall accordingly group together three passages which deal with the fate of the monarchy, and especially of Zedekiah, the last king of Judah.

That reverence for the royal house would form an obstacle to the acceptance of such teaching as Ezekiel's was to be expected from all we know of the popular feeling on this subject. The fact that the few royal assassinations which stain the annals of Judah were sooner or later avenged by the people shows that the monarchy was regarded as a pillar of the state, and that great importance was attached to the possession of a dynasty which perpetuated the glories of David's reign. And there is one verse in the book of Lamentations which expresses the anguish which the fall of the kingdom caused to godly men in Israel, although its representative was so unworthy of his office as Zedekiah: "The breath of our nostrils, the anointed of Jehovah, was taken in their pits, of whom we said, Under his shadow shall we live among the nations" (Lam. iv. 20). So long therefore as a descendant of David sat on the throne of Jerusalem it would seem the duty of every patriotic Israelite to remain true to him. The continuance of the monarchy would seem to guarantee the existence of the state; the prestige of Zedekiah's position as the anointed of Jehovah, and the heir of David's covenant, would warrant the hope that even yet Jehovah would intervene to save an institution of His own creating. Indeed, we can see from Ezekiel's own pages that the historic monarchy in Israel was to him an object of the highest veneration and regard. He speaks of its dignity in terms whose very exaggeration shows how largely the fact bulked in his imagination. He compares it to the noblest of the wild beasts of the earth and the most lordly tree of the forest. But his contention is that this monarchy no longer exists. Except in one doubtful passage, he never applies the title king (melek) to Zedekiah. The kingdom came to an end with the deportation of Jehoiachin, the last king who ascended the throne in legitimate succession. The present holder of the office is in no sense king by divine right; he is a creature and vassal of Nebuchadnezzar, and has no rights against his suzerain. [30] His very name had been changed by the caprice of his master. As a religious symbol, therefore, the royal power is defunct; the glory has departed from it as surely as from the Temple. The makeshift administration organised under Zedekiah had a peaceful if inglorious future before it, if it were content to recognise facts and adapt itself to its humble position. But if it should attempt to raise its head and assert itself as an independent kingdom, it would only seal its own doom. And for men in Chaldæa to transfer to this shadow of kingly dignity the allegiance due to the heir of David's house was a waste of devotion as little demanded by patriotism as by prudence.

I

The first of the passages in which the fate of the monarchy is foretold requires little to be said by way of explanation. It is a symbolic action of the kind with which we are now familiar, exhibiting the certainty of the fate in store both for the people and the king. The prophet again becomes a "sign" or portent to the people--this time in a character which every one of his audience understood from recent experience. He is seen by daylight collecting "articles of captivity"--i.e., such necessary articles as a person going into exile would try to take with him--and bringing them out to the door of his house. Then at dusk he breaks through the wall with his goods on his shoulder; and, with face muffled, he removes "to another place." In this sign we have again two different facts indicated by a series of not entirely congruous actions. The mere act of carrying out his most necessary furniture and removing from one place to another suggests quite unambiguously the captivity that awaits the inhabitants of Jerusalem. But the accessories of the action, such as breaking through the wall, the muffling of the face, and the doing of all this by night, point to quite a different event--viz., Zedekiah's attempt to break through the Chaldæan lines by night, his capture, his blindness, and his imprisonment in Babylon. The most remarkable thing in the sign is the circumstantial manner in which the details of the king's flight and capture are anticipated so long before the event. Zedekiah, as we read in the second book of Kings, as soon as a breach was made in the walls by the Chaldæans, broke out with a small party of horsemen, and succeeded in reaching the plain of Jordan. There he was overtaken and caught, and sent before Nebuchadnezzar's presence at Riblah. The Babylonian king punished his perfidy with a cruelty common enough amongst the Assyrian kings: he caused his eyes to be put out, and sent him thus to end his days in prison at Babylon. All this is so clearly hinted at in the signs that the whole representation is often set aside as a prophecy after the event. That is hardly probable, because the sign does not bear the marks of having been originally conceived with the view of exhibiting the details of Zedekiah's punishment. But since we know that the book was written after the event, it is a perfectly fair question whether in the interpretation of the symbols Ezekiel may not have read into it a fuller meaning than was present to his own mind at the time. Thus the covering of his head does not necessarily suggest anything more than the king's attempt to disguise his person. [31] Possibly this was all that Ezekiel originally meant by it. When the event took place he perceived a further meaning in it as an allusion to the blindness inflicted on the king, and introduced this into the explanation given of the symbol. The point of it lies in the degradation of the king through his being reduced to such an ignominious method of securing his personal safety. "The prince that is among them shall bear upon his shoulder in the darkness, and shall go forth: they shall dig through the wall to carry out thereby: he shall cover his face, that he may not be seen by any eye, and he himself shall not see the earth" (ch. xii. 12).

II

In ch. xvii. the fate of the monarchy is dealt with at greater length under the form of an allegory. The kingdom of Judah is represented as a cedar in Lebanon--a comparison which shows how exalted were Ezekiel's conceptions of the dignity of the old regime which had now passed away. But the leading shoot of the tree has been cropped off by a great, broad-winged, speckled eagle, the king of Babylon, and carried away to a "land of traffic, a city of merchants." [32] The insignificance of Zedekiah's government is indicated by a harsh contrast which almost breaks the consistency of the figure. In place of the cedar which he has spoiled the eagle plants a low vine trailing on the ground, such as may be seen in Palestine at the present day. His intention was that "its branches should extend towards him and its roots be under him"--i.e., that the new principality should derive all its strength from Babylon and yield all its produce to the power which nourished it. For a time all went well. The vine answered the expectations of its owner, and prospered under the favourable conditions which he had provided for it. But another great eagle appeared on the scene, the king of Egypt, and the ungrateful vine began to send out its roots and turn its branches in his direction. The meaning is obvious: Zedekiah had sent presents to Egypt and sought its help, and by so doing had violated the conditions of his tenure of royal power. Such a policy could not prosper. "The bed where it was planted" was in possession of Nebuchadnezzar, and he could not tolerate there a state, however feeble, which employed the resources with which he had endowed it to further the interests of his rival, Hophra, the king of Egypt. Its destruction shall come from the quarter whence it derived its origin: "when the east wind smites it, it shall wither in the furrow where it grew."

Throughout this passage Ezekiel shows that he possessed in full measure that penetration and detachment from local prejudices which all the prophets exhibit when dealing with political affairs. The interpretation of the riddle contains a statement of Nebuchadnezzar's policy in his dealings with Judah, whose impartial accuracy could not be improved on by the most disinterested historian. The carrying away of the Judæan king and aristocracy was a heavy blow to religious susceptibilities which Ezekiel fully shared, and its severity was not mitigated by the arrogant assumptions by which it was explained in Jerusalem. Yet here he shows himself capable of contemplating it as a measure of Babylonian statesmanship and of doing absolute justice to the motives by which it was dictated. Nebuchadnezzar's purpose was to establish a petty state unable to raise itself to independence, and one on whose fidelity to his empire he could rely. Ezekiel lays great stress on the solemn formalities by which the great king had bound his vassal to his allegiance: "He took of the royal seed, and made a covenant with him, and brought him under a curse; and the strong ones of the land he took away: that it might be a lowly kingdom, not able to lift itself up, to keep his covenant that it might stand" (vv. 13, 14). In all this Nebuchadnezzar is conceived as acting within his rights; and here lay the difference between the clear vision of the prophet and the infatuated policy of his contemporaries. The politicians of Jerusalem were incapable of thus discerning the signs of the times. They fell back on the time-honoured plan of checkmating Babylon by means of an Egyptian alliance--a policy which had been disastrous when attempted against the ruthless tyrants of Assyria, and which was doubly imbecile when it brought down on them the wrath of a monarch who showed every desire to deal fairly with his subject provinces.

The period of intrigue with Egypt had already begun when this prophecy was written. We have no means of knowing how long the negotiations went on before the overt act of rebellion; and hence we cannot say with certainty that the appearance of the chapter in this part of the book is an anachronism. It is possible that Ezekiel may have known of a secret mission which was not discovered by the spies of the Babylonian court; and there is no difficulty in supposing that such a step may have been taken as early as two and a half years before the outbreak of hostilities. At whatever time it took place, Ezekiel saw that it sealed the doom of the nation. He knew that Nebuchadnezzar could not overlook such flagrant perfidy as Zedekiah and his councillors had been guilty of; he knew also that Egypt could render no effectual help to Jerusalem in her death-struggle. "Not with a strong army and a great host will Pharaoh act for him in the war, when mounds are thrown up, and the towers are built, to cut off many lives" (ver. 17). The writer of the Lamentations again shows us how sadly the prophet's anticipation was verified: "As for us, our eyes as yet failed for our vain help: in our watching we have watched for a nation that could not save us" (Lam. iv. 17).

But Ezekiel will not allow it to be supposed that the fate of Jerusalem is merely the result of a mistaken forecast of political probabilities. Such a mistake had been made by Zedekiah's advisers when they trusted to Egypt to deliver them from Babylon, and ordinary prudence might have warned them against it. But that was the most excusable part of their folly. The thing that branded their policy as infamous and put them absolutely in the wrong before God and man alike was their violation of the solemn oath by which they had bound themselves to serve the king of Babylon. The prophet seizes on this act of perjury as the determining fact of the situation, and charges it home on the king as the cause of the ruin that is to overtake him: "Thus saith Jehovah, As I live, surely My oath which he hath despised, and My covenant which he has broken, I will return on his head; and I will spread My net over him, and in My snare shall he be taken, ... and ye shall know that I Jehovah have spoken it" (vv. 19-21).

In the last three verses of the chapter the prophet returns to the allegory with which he commenced, and completes his oracle with a beautiful picture of the ideal monarchy of the future. The ideas on which the picture is framed are few and simple; but they are those which distinguish the Messianic hope as cherished by the prophets from the crude form which it assumed in the popular imagination. In contrast to Zedekiah's kingdom, which was a human institution without ideal significance, that of the Messianic age will be a fresh creation of Jehovah's power. A tender shoot shall be planted in the mountain land of Israel, where it shall flourish and increase until it overshadow the whole earth. Further, this shoot is taken from the "top of the cedar"--that is, the section of the royal house which had been carried away to Babylon--indicating that the hope of the future lay not with the king de facto Zedekiah, but with Jehoiachin and those who shared his banishment. The passage leaves no doubt that Ezekiel conceived the Israel of the future as a state with a monarch at its head, although it may be doubtful whether the shoot refers to a personal Messiah or to the aristocracy, who, along with the king, formed the governing body in an Eastern kingdom. This question, however, can be better considered when we have to deal with Ezekiel's Messianic conceptions in their fully developed form in ch. xxxiv.

III

Of the last four kings of Judah there were two whose melancholy fate seems to have excited a profound feeling of pity amongst their countrymen. Jehoahaz or Shallum, according to the Chronicler the youngest of Josiah's sons, appears to have been even during his father's lifetime a popular favourite. It was he who after the fatal day of Megiddo was raised to the throne by the "people of the land" at the age of twenty-three years. He is said by the historian of the books of Kings to have done "that which was evil in the sight of the Lord"; but he had hardly time to display his qualities as a ruler, when he was deposed and carried to Egypt by Pharaoh Necho, having worn the crown for only three months (608 b.c.). The deep attachment felt for him seems to have given rise to an expectation that he would be restored to his kingdom, a delusion against which the prophet Jeremiah found it necessary to protest (Jer. xxii. 10-12). He was succeeded by his elder brother, Eliakim,[33] the headstrong and selfish tyrant, whose character stands revealed in some passages of the books of Jeremiah and Habakkuk. His reign of nine years gave little occasion to his subjects to cherish a grateful memory of his administration. He died in the crisis of the conflict he had provoked with the king of Babylon, leaving his youthful son Jehoiachin to expiate the folly of his rebellion. Jehoiachin is the second idol of the populace to whom we have referred. He was only eighteen years old when he was called to the throne, and within three months he was doomed to exile in Babylon. In his room Nebuchadnezzar appointed a third son of Josiah--Mattaniah--whose name he changed to Zedekiah. He was apparently a man of weak and vacillating character; but he fell ultimately into the hands of the Egyptian and anti-prophetic party, and so was the means of involving his country in the hopeless struggle in which it perished.

The fact that two of their native princes were languishing, perhaps simultaneously, in foreign confinement, one in Egypt and the other in Babylon, was fitted to evoke in Judah a sympathy with the misfortunes of royalty something like the feeling embalmed in the Jacobite songs of Scotland. It seems to be an echo of this sentiment that we find in the first part of the lament with which Ezekiel closes his references to the fall of the monarchy (ch. xix.). Many critics have indeed found it impossible to suppose that Ezekiel should in any sense have yielded to sympathy with the fate of two princes who are both branded in the historical books as idolaters, and whose calamities on Ezekiel's own view of individual retribution proved them to be sinners against Jehovah. Yet it is certainly unnatural to read the dirge in any other sense than as an expression of genuine pity for the woes that the nation suffered in the fate of her two exiled kings. If Jeremiah, in pronouncing the doom of Shallum or Jehoahaz, could say, "Weep ye sore for him that goeth away; for he shall not return any more, nor see his native country," there is no reason why Ezekiel should not have given lyrical expression to the universal feeling of sadness which the blighted career of these two youths naturally produced. The whole passage is highly poetical, and represents a side of Ezekiel's nature which we have not hitherto been led to study. But it is too much to expect of even the most logical of prophets that he should experience no personal emotion but what fitted into his system, or that his poetic gift should be chained to the wheels of his theological convictions. The dirge expresses no moral judgment on the character or deserts of the two kings to which it refers: it has but one theme--the sorrow and disappointment of the "mother" who nurtured and lost them, that is, the nation of Israel personified according to a usual Hebrew figure of speech. All attempts to go beyond this and to find in the poem an allegorical portrait of Jehoahaz and Jehoiachin are irrelevant. The mother is a lioness, the princes are young lions and behave as stalwart young lions do, but whether their exploits are praiseworthy or the reverse is a question that was not present to the writer's mind.

The chapter is entitled "A Dirge on the Princes of Israel," and embraces not only the fate of Jehoahaz and Jehoiachin, but also of Zedekiah, with whom the old monarchy expired. Strictly speaking, however, the name qînah, or dirge, is applicable only to the first part of the chapter (vv. 2-9), where the rhythm characteristic of the Hebrew elegy is clearly traceable.[34] With a few slight changes of the text[35] the passage may be translated thus:--

The Expositor's Bible: The Book of Ezekiel

i. Jehoahaz.

How was thy mother a lioness!--
Among the lions,
In the midst of young lions she couched--
She reared her cubs;
And she brought up one of her cubs--
A young lion he became,
And he learned to catch the prey--
He ate men.
And nations raised a cry against him--
In their pit he was caught;
And they brought him with hooks--
To the land of Egypt (vv. 2-4).

ii. Jehoiachin.

And when she saw that she was disappointed [36] --
Her hope was lost.
She took another of her cubs--
A young lion she made him;
And he walked in the midst of lions--
A young lion he became;
And he learned to catch prey--
He ate men.
And he lurked in his lair--
The forests he ravaged;
Till the land was laid waste and its fulness--
With the noise of his roar.
The nations arrayed themselves against him--
From the countries around;
And spread over him their net--
In their pit he was caught.
And they brought him with hooks--
To the king of Babylon;
And he put him in a cage, ...
That his voice might no more be heard--
On the mountains of Israel (vv. 5-9).

The poetry here is simple and sincere. The mournful cadence of the elegiac measure, which is maintained throughout, is adapted to the tone of melancholy which pervades the passage and culminates in the last beautiful line. The dirge is a form of composition often employed in songs of triumph over the calamities of enemies; but there is no reason to doubt that here it is true to its original purpose, and expresses genuine sorrow for the accumulated misfortunes of the royal house of Israel.

The closing part of the "dirge" dealing with Zedekiah is of a somewhat different character. The theme is similar, but the figure is abruptly changed, and the elegiac rhythm is abandoned. The nation, the mother of the monarchy, is here compared to a luxuriant vine planted beside great waters; and the royal house is likened to a branch towering above the rest and bearing rods which were kingly sceptres. But she has been plucked up by the roots, withered, scorched by the fire, and finally planted in an arid region where she cannot thrive. The application of the metaphor to the ruin of the nation is very obvious. Israel, once a prosperous nation, richly endowed with all the conditions of a vigorous national life, and glorying in her race of native kings, is now humbled to the dust. Misfortune after misfortune has destroyed her power and blighted her prospects, till at last she has been removed from her own land to a place where national life cannot be maintained. But the point of the passage lies in the closing words: fire went out from one of her twigs and consumed her branches, so that she has no longer a proud rod to be a ruler's sceptre (ver. 14). The monarchy, once the glory and strength of Israel, has in its last degenerate representative involved the nation in ruin.

Such is Ezekiel's final answer to those of his hearers who clung to the old Davidic kingdom as their hope in the crisis of the people's fate.

John J. Skinner

Footnotes:

30. It is noteworthy that in the dirge of ch. xix. Ezekiel ignores the reign of Jehoiakim. Is this because he too owed his elevation to the intervention of a foreign power?

31. Especially if we read ver. 12, as in LXX., "That he may not be seen by any eye, and he shall not see the earth."

32. By this name for Chaldæa Ezekiel seems to express his contempt for the commercial activity which formed so large an element in the greatness of Babylon (ch. xvi. 29 R.V.), perhaps also his sense of the uncongenial environment in which the disinherited king and the nobility of Judah now found themselves.

33. Jehoiakim.

34. The long line is divided into two unequal parts by a cæsura over the end.

35. Mostly adopted from Cornill. The English reader may refer to Dr. Davidson's commentary.

36. This word is uncertain.

Chapter VIII - Prophecy And Its Abuses.
Chapters xii. 21-xiv. 11

There is perhaps nothing more perplexing to the student of Old Testament history than the complicated phenomena which may be classed under the general name of "prophecy." In Israel, as in every ancient state, there was a body of men who sought to influence public opinion by prognostications of the future. As a rule the repute of all kinds of divination declined with the advance of civilisation and general intelligence, so that in the more enlightened communities matters of importance came to be decided on broad grounds of reason and political expediency. The peculiarity in the case of Israel was that the very highest direction in politics, as well as religion and morals, was given in a form capable of being confounded with superstitious practices which flourished alongside of it. The true prophets were not merely profound moral thinkers, who announced a certain issue as the probable result of a certain line of conduct. In many cases their predictions are absolute, and their political programme is an appeal to the nation to accept the situation which they foresee, as the basis of its public action. For this reason prophecy was readily brought into competition with practices with which it had really nothing in common. The ordinary individual who cared little for principles and only wished to know what was likely to happen might readily think that one way of arriving at knowledge of the future was as good as another, and when the spiritual prophet's anticipations displeased him he was apt to try his luck with the sorcerer. It is not improbable that in the last days of the monarchy spurious prophecy of various kinds gained an additional vitality from its rivalry with the great spiritual teachers who in the name of Jehovah foretold the ruin of the state.

This is not the place for an exhaustive account of the varied developments in Israel of what may be broadly termed prophetic manifestations. For the understanding of the section of Ezekiel now before us it will be enough to distinguish three classes of phenomena. At the lowest end of the scale there was a rank growth of pure magic or sorcery, the ruling idea of which is the attempt to control or forecast the future by occult arts which are believed to influence the supernatural powers which govern human destiny. In the second place we have prophecy in a stricter sense--that is, the supposed revelation of the will of the deity in dreams or "visions" or half-articulate words uttered in a state of frenzy. Last of all there is the true prophet, who, though subject to extraordinary mental experiences, yet had always a clear and conscious grasp of moral principles, and possessed an incommunicable certainty that what he spoke was not his own word but the word of Jehovah.

It is obvious that a people subjected to such influences as these was exposed to temptations both intellectual and moral from which modern life is exempt. One thing is certain--the existence of prophecy did not tend to simplify the problems of national life or individual conduct. We are apt to think of the great prophets as men so signally marked out by God as His witnesses that it must have been impossible for any one with a shred of sincerity to question their authority. In reality it was quite otherwise. It was no more an easy thing then than now to distinguish between truth and error, between the voice of God and the speculations of men. Then, as now, divine truth had no available credentials at the moment of its utterance except its self-evidencing power on hearts that were sincere in their desire to know it. The fact that truth came in the guise of prophecy only stimulated the growth of counterfeit prophecy, so that only those who were "of the truth" could discern the spirits, whether they were of God.

The passage which forms the subject of this chapter is one of the most important passages of the Old Testament in its treatment of the errors and abuses incident to a dispensation of prophecy. It consists of three parts: the first deals with difficulties occasioned by the apparent failure of prophecy (ch. xii. 21-28); the second with the character and doom of the false prophets (ch. xiii.); and the third with the state of mind which made a right use of prophecy impossible (ch. xiv. 1-11).

I

It is one of Ezekiel's peculiarities that he pays close attention to the proverbial sayings which indicated the drift of the national mind. Such sayings were like straws, showing how the stream flowed, and had a special significance for Ezekiel, inasmuch as he was not in the stream himself, but only observed its motions from a distance. Here he quotes a current proverb, giving expression to a sense of the futility of all prophetic warnings: "The days are drawn out, and every vision faileth" (ch. xii. 22). It is difficult to say what the feeling is that lies behind it, whether it is one of disappointment or of relief. If, as seems probable, ver. 27 is the application of the general principle to the particular case of Ezekiel, the proverb need not indicate absolute disbelief in the truth of prophecy. "The vision which he sees is for many days, and remote times does he prophesy"--that is to say, The prophet's words are no doubt perfectly true, and come from God; but no man can ever tell when they are to be fulfilled: all experience shows that they relate to a remote future which we are not likely to see. For men whose concern was to find direction in the present emergency, that was no doubt equivalent to a renunciation of the guidance of prophecy.

There are several things which may have tended to give currency to this view and make it plausible. First of all, of course, the fact that many of the "visions" that were published had nothing in them; they were false in their origin, and were bound to fail. Accordingly one thing necessary to rescue prophecy from the discredit into which it had fallen was the removal of those who uttered false predictions in the name of Jehovah: "There shall no more be any false vision or flattering divination in the midst of the house of Israel" (ver. 24). But besides the prevalence of false prophecy there were features of true prophecy which partly explained the common misgiving as to its trustworthiness. Even in true prophecy there is an element of idealism, the future being depicted in forms derived from the prophet's circumstances, and represented as the immediate continuation of the events of his own time. In support of the proverb it might have been equally apt to instance the Messianic oracles of Isaiah, or the confident predictions of Hananiah, the opponent of Jeremiah. Further, there is a contingent element in prophecy: the fulfilment of a threat or promise is conditional on the moral effect of the prophecy itself on the people. These things were perfectly understood by thoughtful men in Israel. The principle of contingency is clearly expounded in the eighteenth chapter of Jeremiah, and it was acted on by the princes who on a memorable occasion saved him from the doom of a false prophet (Jer. xxvi.). Those who used prophecy to determine their practical attitude towards Jehovah's purposes found it to be an unerring guide to right thinking and action. But those who only took a curious interest in questions of external fulfilment found much to disconcert them; and it is hardly surprising that many of them became utterly sceptical of its divine origin. It must have been to this turn of mind that the proverb with which Ezekiel is dealing owed its origin.

It is not on these lines, however, that Ezekiel vindicates the truth of the prophetic word, but on lines adapted to the needs of his own generation. After all, prophecy is not wholly contingent. The bent of the popular character is one of the elements which it takes into account, and it foresees an issue which is not dependent on anything that Israel might do. The prophets rise to a point of view from which the destruction of the sinful people and the establishment of a perfect kingdom of God are seen to be facts unalterably decreed by Jehovah. And the point of Ezekiel's answer to his contemporaries seems to be that a final demonstration of the truth of prophecy was at hand. As the fulfilment drew near, prophecy would increase in distinctness and precision, so that when the catastrophe came it would be impossible for any man to deny the inspiration of those who had announced it: "Thus saith Jehovah, I will suppress this proverb, and it shall no more circulate in Israel; but say unto them, The days are near, and the content [literally word or matter] of every vision" (ver. 23). After the extinction of every form of lying prophecy, Jehovah's words shall still be heard, and the proclamation of them shall be immediately followed by their accomplishment: "For I Jehovah will speak My words; I will speak and perform, it shall not be deferred any more: in your days, O house of rebellion, I will speak a word and perform it, saith Jehovah" (ver. 25). The immediate reference is to the destruction of Jerusalem which the prophet saw to be one of those events which were unconditionally decreed, and an event which must bulk more and more largely in the vision of the true prophet until it was accomplished.

II

The thirteenth chapter deals with what was undoubtedly the greatest obstacle to the influence of prophecy--viz., the existence of a division in the ranks of the prophets themselves. That division had been of long standing. The earliest indication of it is the story of the contest between Micaiah and four hundred prophets of Jehovah, in presence of Ahab and Jehoshaphat (1 Kings xxii. 5-28). All the canonical prophets show in their writings that they had to contend against the mass of the prophetic order--men who claimed an authority equal to theirs, but used it for diametrically opposite interests. It is not, however, till we come to Jeremiah and Ezekiel that we find a formal apologetic of true prophecy against false. The problem was serious: where two sets of prophets systematically and fundamentally contradicted each other, both might be false, but both could not be true. The prophet who was convinced of the truth of his own visions must be prepared to account for the rise of false visions, and to lay down some criterion by which men might discriminate between the one and the other. Jeremiah's treatment of the question is of the two perhaps the more profound and interesting. It is thus summarised by Professor Davidson: "In his encounters with the prophets of his day Jeremiah opposes them in three spheres--that of policy, that of morals, and that of personal experience. In policy the genuine prophets had some fixed principles, all arising out of the idea that the kingdom of the Lord was not a kingdom of this world. Hence they opposed military preparation, riding on horses, and building of fenced cities, and counselled trust in Jehovah.... The false prophets, on the other hand, desired their country to be a military power among the powers around, they advocated alliance with the eastern empires and with Egypt, and relied on their national strength. Again, the true prophets had a stringent personal and state morality. In their view the true cause of the destruction of the state was its immoralities. But the false prophets had no such deep moral convictions, and seeing nothing unwonted or alarming in the condition of things prophesied of peace.' They were not necessarily irreligious men; but their religion had no truer insight into the nature of the God of Israel than that of the common people.... And finally Jeremiah expresses his conviction that the prophets whom he opposed did not stand in the same relation to the Lord as he did: they had not his experiences of the word of the Lord, into whose counsel they had not been admitted; and they were without that fellowship of mind with the mind of Jehovah which was the true source of prophecy. Hence he satirises their pretended supernatural dreams,' and charges them from conscious want of any true prophetic word with stealing words from one another." [37]

The passages in Jeremiah on which this statement is mainly founded may have been known to Ezekiel, who in this matter, as in so many others, follows the lines laid down by the elder prophet.

The first thing, then, that deserves attention in Ezekiel's judgment on false prophecy is his assertion of its purely subjective or human origin. In the opening sentence he pronounces a woe upon the prophets "who prophesy from their own mind without having seen" [38] (ver. 3). The words put in italics sum up Ezekiel's theory of the genesis of false prophecy. The visions these men see and the oracles they utter simply reproduce the thoughts, the emotions, the aspirations, natural to their own minds. That the ideas came to them in a peculiar form, which was mistaken for the direct action of Jehovah, Ezekiel does not deny. He admits that the men were sincere in their professions, for he describes them as "waiting for the fulfilment of the word" (ver. 6). But in this belief they were the victims of a delusion. Whatever there might be in their prophetic experiences that resembled those of a true prophet, there was nothing in their oracles that did not belong to the sphere of worldly interests and human speculation.

If we ask how Ezekiel knew this, the only possible answer is that he knew it because he was sure of the source of his own inspiration. He possessed an inward experience which certified to him the genuineness of the communications which came to him, and he necessarily inferred that those who held different beliefs about God must lack that experience. Thus far his criticism of false prophecy is purely subjective. The true prophet knew that he had that within him which authenticated his inspiration, but the false prophet could not know that he wanted it. The difficulty is not peculiar to prophecy, but arises in connection with religious belief as a whole. It is an interesting question whether the assent to a truth is accompanied by a feeling of certitude differing in quality from the confidence which a man may have in giving his assent to a delusion. But it is not possible to elevate this internal criterion to an objective test of truth. A man who is awake may be quite sure he is not dreaming, but a man in a dream may readily enough fancy himself awake.

But there were other and more obvious tests which could be applied to the professional prophets, and which at least showed them to be men of a different spirit from the few who were "full of power by the spirit of the Lord, and of judgment, and of might, to declare to Israel his sin" (Mic. iii. 8). In two graphic figures Ezekiel sums up the character and policy of these parasites who disgraced the order to which they belonged. In the first place he compares them to jackals burrowing in ruins and undermining the fabric which it was their professed function to uphold (vv. 4, 5). The existence of such a class of men is at once a symptom of advanced social degeneration and a cause of greater ruin to follow. A true prophet fearlessly speaking the words of God is a defence to the state; he is like a man who stands in the breach or builds a wall to ward off the danger which he foresees. Such were all genuine prophets whose names were held in honour in Israel--men of moral courage, never hesitating to incur personal risk for the welfare of the nation they loved. If Israel now was like a heap of ruins, the fault lay with the selfish crowd of hireling prophets who had cared more to find a hole in which they could shelter themselves than to build up a stable and righteous polity.

The prophet's simile calls to mind the type of churchman represented by Bishop Blougram in Browning's powerful satire. He is one who is content if the corporation to which he belongs can provide him with a comfortable and dignified position in which he can spend good days; he is triumphant if, in addition to this, he can defy any one to prove him more of a fool or a hypocrite than an average man of the world. Such utter abnegation of intellectual sincerity may not be common in any Church; but the temptation which leads to it is one to which ecclesiastics are exposed in every age and every communion. The tendency to shirk difficult problems, to shut one's eyes to grave evils, to acquiesce in things as they are, and calculate that the ruin will last one's own time, is what Ezekiel calls playing the jackal; and it hardly needs a prophet to tell us that there could not be a more fatal symptom of the decay of religion than the prevalence of such a spirit in its official representatives.

The second image is equally suggestive. It exhibits the false prophets as following where they pretended to lead, as aiding and abetting the men into whose hands the reins of government had fallen. The people build a wall and the prophets cover it with plaster (ver. 10)--that is to say, when any project or scheme of policy is being promoted they stand by glozing it over with fine words, flattering its promoters, and uttering profuse assurances of its success. The uselessness of the whole activity of these prophets could not be more vividly described. The white-washing of the wall may hide its defects, but will not prevent its destruction; and when the wall of Jerusalem's shaky prosperity tumbles down, those who did so little to build and so much to deceive shall be overwhelmed with confusion. "Behold, when the wall is fallen, shall it not be said to them, Where is the plaster which ye plastered?" (ver. 12).

This will be the beginning of the judgment on false prophets in Israel. The overthrow of their vaticinations, the collapse of the hopes they fostered, and the demolition of the edifice in which they found a refuge shall leave them no more a name or a place in the people of God. "I will stretch out My hand against the prophets that see vanity and divine falsely: in the council of My people they shall not be, and in the register of the house of Israel they shall not be written, and into the land of Israel they shall not come" (ver. 9).

There was, however, a still more degraded type of prophecy, practised chiefly by women, which must have been exceedingly prevalent in Ezekiel's time. The prophets spoken of in the first sixteen verses were public functionaries who exerted their evil influence in the arena of politics. The prophetesses spoken of in the latter part of the chapter are private fortune-tellers who practised on the credulity of individuals who consulted them. Their art was evidently magical in the strict sense, a trafficking with the dark powers which were supposed to enter into alliance with men irrespective of moral considerations. Then, as now, such courses were followed for gain, and doubtless proved a lucrative means of livelihood. The "fillets" and "veils" mentioned in ver. 18 are either a professional garb worn by the women, or else implements of divination whose precise significance cannot now be ascertained. To the imagination of the prophet they appear as the snares and weapons with which these wretched creatures "hunted souls"; and the extent of the evil which he attacks is indicated by his speaking of the whole people as being entangled in their meshes. Ezekiel naturally bestows special attention on a class of practitioners whose whole influence tended to efface moral landmarks and to deal out to men weal or woe without regard to character. "They slew souls that should not die, and saved alive souls that should not live; they made sad the heart of the righteous, and strengthened the hands of the wicked, that he should not return from his wicked way and be saved alive" (ver. 22). That is to say, while Ezekiel and all true prophets were exhorting men to live resolutely in the light of clear ethical conceptions of providence, the votaries of occult superstitions seduced the ignorant into making private compacts with the powers of darkness in order to secure their personal safety. If the prevalence of sorcery and witchcraft was at all times dangerous to the religion and public order of the state, it was doubly so at a time when, as Ezekiel perceived, everything depended on maintaining the strict rectitude of God in His dealings with individual men.

III

Having thus disposed of the external manifestations of false prophecy, Ezekiel proceeds in the fourteenth chapter to deal with the state of mind amongst the people at large which rendered such a condition of things possible. The general import of the passage is clear, although the precise connection of ideas is somewhat difficult to explain. The following observations may suffice to bring out all that is essential to the understanding of the section.

The oracle was occasioned by a particular incident, undoubtedly historical--namely, a visit, such as was perhaps now common, from the elders to inquire of the Lord through Ezekiel. As they sit before him it is revealed to the prophet that the minds of these men are preoccupied with idolatry, and therefore it is not fitting that any answer should be given to them by a prophet of Jehovah. Apparently no answer was given by Ezekiel to the particular question they had asked, whatever it may have been. Generalising from the incident, however, he is led to enunciate a principle regulating the intercourse between Jehovah and Israel through the medium of a prophet: "Whatever man of the house of Israel sets his thoughts upon his idols, and puts his guilty stumbling-block before him, and comes to the prophet, I Jehovah will make Myself intelligible to him; [39] that I may take the house of Israel in their own heart, because they are all estranged from Me by their idols" (vv. 4, 5). It seems clear that one part of the threat here uttered is that the very withholding of the answer will unmask the hypocrisy of men who pretend to be worshippers of Jehovah, but in heart are unfaithful to Him and servants of false gods. The moral principle involved in the prophet's dictum is clear and of lasting value. It is that for a false heart there can be no fellowship with Jehovah, and therefore no true and sure knowledge of His will. The prophet occupies the point of view of Jehovah, and when consulted by an idolater he finds it impossible to enter into the point of view from which the question is put, and therefore cannot answer it. [40] Ezekiel assumes for the most part that the prophet consulted is a true prophet of Jehovah like himself, who will give no answer to such questions as he has before him. He must, however, allow for the possibility that men of this stamp may receive answers in the name of Jehovah from those reputed to be His true prophets. In that case, says Ezekiel, the prophet is "deceived" by God; he is allowed to give a response which is not a true response at all, but only confirms the people in their delusions and unbelief. But this deception does not take place until the prophet has incurred the guilt of deceiving himself in the first instance. It is his fault that he has not perceived the bent of his questioners' minds, that he has accommodated himself to their ways of thought, has consented to occupy their standpoint in order to be able to say something coinciding with the drift of their wishes. Prophet and inquirers are involved in a common guilt and share a common fate, both being sentenced to exclusion from the commonwealth of Israel.

The purification of the institution of prophecy necessarily appeared to Ezekiel as an indispensable feature in the restoration of the theocracy. The ideal of Israel's relation to Jehovah is "that they may be My people, and that I may be their God" (ver. 11). That implies that Jehovah shall be the source of infallible guidance in all things needful for the religious life of the individual and the guidance of the state. But it was impossible for Jehovah to be to Israel all that a God should be, so long as the regular channels of communication between Him and the nation were choked by false conceptions in the minds of the people and false men in the position of prophets. Hence the constitution of a new Israel demands such special judgments on false prophecy and the false use of true prophecy as have been denounced in these chapters. When these judgments have been executed, the ideal will have become possible which is described in the words of another prophet: "Thine eyes shall see thy teachers: and thine ears shall hear a word behind thee, saying, This is the way, walk ye in it" (Isa. xxx. 20, 21).

Footnotes:

37. Ezekiel, p. 85.

38. Translating with LXX.

39. The exact force of the reflexive form used (na' anêthi, niphal) is doubtful. The translation given is that of Cornill, which is certainly forcible.

40. The same rule is applied to direct communion with God in prayer in Psalm lxvi. 18: "If I regard iniquity in my heart, the Lord will not hear."

John J. Skinner

Chapter IX - Jerusalem--An Ideal History.
Chapter xvi.

In order to understand the place which the sixteenth chapter occupies in this section [41] of the book, we must remember that a chief source of the antagonism between Ezekiel and his hearers was the proud national consciousness which sustained the courage of the people through all their humiliations. There were, perhaps, few nations of antiquity in which the flame of patriotic feeling burned more brightly than in Israel. No people with a past such as theirs could be indifferent to the many elements of greatness embalmed in their history. The beauty and fertility of their land, the martial exploits and signal deliverances of the nation, the great kings and heroes she had reared, her prophets and lawgivers--these and many other stirring memories were witnesses to Jehovah's peculiar love for Israel and His power to exalt and bless His people. To cherish a deep sense of the unique privileges which Jehovah had conferred on her in giving her a distinct place among the nations of the earth was thus a religious duty often insisted on in the Old Testament. But in order that this sense might work for good it was necessary that it should take the form of grateful recognition of Jehovah as the source of the nation's greatness, and be accompanied by a true knowledge of His character. When allied with false conceptions of Jehovah's nature, or entirely divorced from religion, patriotism degenerated into racial prejudice and became a serious moral and political danger. That this had actually taken place is a common complaint of the prophets. They feel that national vanity is a great obstacle to the acceptance of their message, and pour forth bitter and scornful words intended to humble the pride of Israel to the dust. No prophet addresses himself to the task so remorselessly as Ezekiel. The utter worthlessness of Israel, both absolutely in the eyes of Jehovah and relatively in comparison with other nations, is asserted by him with a boldness and emphasis which at first startle us. From a different point of view prophecy and its results might have been regarded as fruits of the national life, under the divine education vouchsafed to that people. But that is not Ezekiel's standpoint. He seizes on the fact that prophecy was in opposition to the natural genius of the people, and was not to be regarded as in any sense an expression of it. Accepting the final attitude of Israel toward the word of Jehovah as the genuine outcome of her natural proclivities, he reads her past as an unbroken record of ingratitude and infidelity. All that was good in Israel was Jehovah's gift, freely bestowed and justly withdrawn; all that was Israel's own was her weakness and her sin. It was reserved for a later prophet to reconcile the condemnation of Israel's actual history with the recognition of the divine power working there and moulding a spiritual kernel of the nation into a true "servant of the Lord" (Isa. xl. ff.).

In chs. xv. and xvi., therefore, the prophet exposes the hollowness of Israel's confidence in her national destiny. The first of these appears to be directed against the vain hopes cherished in Jerusalem at the time. It is not necessary to dwell on it at length. The image is simple and its application to Jerusalem obvious. Earlier prophets had compared Israel to a vine, partly to set forth the exceptional privileges she enjoyed, but chiefly to emphasise the degeneration she had undergone, as shown by the bad moral fruits which she had borne (cf. Isa. v. 1 ff.; Jer. ii. 21; Hos. x. 1). The popular imagination had laid hold of the thought that Israel was the vine of God's planting, ignoring the question of the fruit. But Ezekiel reminds his hearers that apart from its fruit the vine is the most worthless of trees. Even at the best its wood can be employed for no useful purpose; it is fit only for fuel. Such was the people of Israel, considered simply as a state among other states, without regard to its religious vocation. Even in its pristine vigour, when the national energies were fresh and unimpaired, it was but a weak nation, incapable of attaining the dignity of a great power. But now the strength of the nation has been worn away by a long succession of disasters, until only a shadow of her former glory remains. Israel is no longer like a green and living vine, but like a branch burned at both ends and charred in the middle, and therefore doubly unfit for any worthy function in the affairs of the world. By the help of this illustration men may read in the present state of the nation the irrevocable sentence of rejection which Jehovah has passed on His people.

We now turn to the striking allegory of ch. xvi., where the same subject is treated with far greater penetration and depth of feeling. There is no passage in the book of Ezekiel at once so powerful and so full of religious significance as the picture of Jerusalem, the foundling child, the unfaithful spouse, and the abandoned prostitute, which is here presented. The general conception is one that might have been presented in a form as beautiful as it is spiritually true. But the features which offend our sense of propriety are perhaps introduced with a stern purpose. It is the deliberate intention of Ezekiel to present Jerusalem's wickedness in the most repulsive light, in order that if possible he might startle men into abhorrence of their national sin. In his own mind the feelings of moral indignation and physical disgust were very close together, and here he seems to work on the minds of his readers, so that the feeling excited by the image may call forth the feeling appropriate to the reality.

The allegory is a highly idealised history of the city of Jerusalem from its origin to its destruction, and then onward to its future restoration. It falls naturally into four divisions:--

i. Vv. 1-14.--The first emergence of Jerusalem into civic life is compared to a new-born female infant, exposed to perish, after a cruel custom which is known to have prevailed among some Semitic tribes. None of the offices customary on the birth of a child were performed in her case, whether those necessary to preserve life or those which had a merely ceremonial significance. Unblessed and unpitied she lay in the open field, weltering in blood, exciting only repugnance in all who passed by, until Jehovah Himself passed by, and pronounced over her the decree that she should live. Thus saved from death, she grew up and reached maturity, but still "naked and bare," destitute of wealth and the refinements of civilisation. These were bestowed on her when a second time Jehovah passed by and spread His skirt over her, and claimed her for His own. Not till then had she been treated as a human being, with the possibilities of honourable life before her. But now she becomes the bride of her protector, and is provided for as a high-born maiden might be, with all the ornaments and luxuries befitting her new rank. Lifted from the lowest depth of degradation, she is now transcendently beautiful, and has "attained to royal estate." The fame of her loveliness went abroad among the nations: "for it was perfect through My glory, which I put upon thee, saith Jehovah" (ver. 14).

It will be seen that the points of contact with actual history are here extremely few as well as vague. It is indeed doubtful whether the subject of the allegory be the city of Jerusalem conceived as one through all its changes of population, or the Hebrew nation of which Jerusalem ultimately became the capital. The latter interpretation is certainly favoured by ch. xxiii., where both Jerusalem and Samaria are represented as having spent their youth in Egypt. That parallel may not be decisive as to the meaning of ch. xvi.; and the statement "thy father was the Amorite and thy mother an Hittite" may be thought to support the other alternative. Amorite and Hittite are general names for the pre-Israelite population of Canaan, and it is a well-known fact that Jerusalem was originally a Canaanitish city. It is not necessary to suppose that the prophet has any information about the early fortunes of Jerusalem when he describes the stages of the process by which she was raised to royal magnificence. The chief question is whether these details can be fairly applied to the history of the nation before it had Jerusalem as its metropolis. It is usually held that the first "passing by" of Jehovah refers to the preservation of the people in the patriarchal period, and the second to the events of the Exodus and the Sinaitic covenant. Against this it may be urged that Ezekiel would hardly have presented the patriarchal period in a hateful light, although he does go further in discrediting antiquity than any other prophet. Besides, the description of Jerusalem's betrothal to Jehovah contains points which are more naturally understood of the glories of the age of David and Solomon than of the events of Sinai, which were not accompanied by an access of material prosperity such as is suggested. It may be necessary to leave the matter in the vagueness with which the prophet has surrounded it, and accept as the teaching of the allegory the simple truth that Jerusalem in herself was nothing, but had been preserved in existence by Jehovah's will, and owed all her splendour to her association with His cause and His kingdom.

ii. Vv. 15-34.--The dainties and rich attire enjoyed by the highly favoured bride become a snare to her. These represent blessings of a material order bestowed by Jehovah on Jerusalem. Throughout the chapter nothing is said of the imparting of spiritual privileges, or of a moral change wrought in the heart of Jerusalem. The gifts of Jehovah are conferred on one incapable of responding to the care and affection that had been lavished on her. The inborn taint of her nature, the hereditary immorality of her heathen ancestors, breaks out in a career of licentiousness in which all the advantages of her proud position are prostituted to the vilest ends. "As is the mother, so is her daughter" (ver. 44); and Jerusalem betrayed her true origin by the readiness with which she took to evil courses as soon as she had the opportunity. The "whoredom" in which the prophet sums up his indictment against his people is chiefly the sin of idolatry. The figure may have been suggested by the fact that actual lewdness of the most flagrant kind was a conspicuous element in the form of idolatry to which Israel first succumbed--the worship of the Canaanite Baals. But in the hands of the prophets it has a deeper and more spiritual import than this. It signified the violation of all the sacred moral obligations which are enshrined in human marriage, or, in other words, the abandonment of an ethical religion for one in which the powers of nature were regarded as the highest revelation of the divine. To the mind of the prophet it made no difference whether the object of worship was called by the name of Jehovah or of Baal: the character of the worship determined the quality of the religion; and in the one case, as in the other, it was idolatry, or "whoredom."

Two stages in the idolatry of Israel appear to be distinguished in this part of the chapter. The first is the naïve, half-conscious heathenism which crept in insensibly through contact with Phoenician and Canaanite neighbours (vv. 15-25). The tokens of Jerusalem's implication in this sin were everywhere. The "high places" with their tents and clothed images (ver. 17), and the offerings set forth before these objects of adoration, were undoubtedly of Canaanitish origin, and their preservation to the fall of the kingdom was a standing witness to the source to which Israel owed her earliest and dearest "abominations." We learn that this phase of idolatry culminated in the atrocious rite of human sacrifice (vv. 20, 21). The immolation of children to Baal or Molech was a common practice amongst the nations surrounding Israel, and when introduced there seems to have been regarded as part of the worship of Jehovah. [42] What Ezekiel here asserts is that the practice came through Israel's illicit commerce with the gods of Canaan, and there is no question that this is historically true. The allegory exhibits the sin in its unnatural heinousness. The idealised city is the mother of her citizens, the children are Jehovah's children and her own, yet she has taken them and offered them up to the false lovers she so madly pursued. Such was her feverish passion for idolatry that the dearest and most sacred ties of nature were ruthlessly severed at the bidding of a perverted religious sense.

The second form of idolatry in Israel was of a more deliberate and politic kind (vv. 23-34). It consisted in the introduction of the deities and religious practices of the great world-powers--Egypt, Assyria, and Chaldæa. The attraction of these foreign rites did not lie in the fascination of a sensuous type of religion, but rather in the impression of power produced by the gods of the conquering peoples. The foreign gods came in mostly in consequence of a political alliance with the nations whose patrons they were; in other cases a god was worshipped simply because he had shown himself able to do great things for his servants. Jerusalem as Ezekiel knew it was full of monuments of this comparatively recent type of idolatry. In every street and at the head of every way there were erections (here called "arches" or "heights") which, from the connection in which they are mentioned, must have been shrines devoted to the strange gods from abroad. It is characteristic of the political idolatry here referred to that its monuments were found in the capital, while the more ancient and rustic worship was typified by the "high places" throughout the provinces. It is probable that the description applies mainly to the later period of the monarchy, when Israel, and especially Judah, began to lean for support on one or other of the great empires on either side of her. At the same time it must be remembered that Ezekiel elsewhere teaches distinctly that the influence of Egyptian religion had been continuous from the days of the Exodus (ch. xxiii.). There may, however, have been a revival of Egyptian influence, due to the political exigencies which arose in the eighth century.

Thus Jerusalem has "played the harlot"; nay, she has done worse--"she has been as a wife that committeth adultery, who though under her husband taketh strangers." [43] And the result has been simply the impoverishment of the land. The heavy exactions levied on the country by Egypt and Assyria were the hire she had paid to her lovers to come to her. If false religion had resulted in an increase of wealth or material prosperity, there might have been some excuse for the eagerness with which she plunged into it. But certainly Israel's history bore the lesson that false religion means waste and ruin. Strangers had devoured her strength from her youth, yet she never would heed the voice of her prophets when they sought to guide her into the ways of peace. Her infatuation was unnatural; it goes almost beyond the bounds of the allegory to exhibit it: "The contrary is in thee from other women, in that thou committest whoredoms, and none goeth awhoring after thee: and in that thou givest hire, and no hire is given to thee, therefore thou art contrary" (ver. 34).

iii. Vv. 35-58.--Having thus made Jerusalem to "know her abominations" (ver. 2), the prophet proceeds to announce the doom which must inevitably follow such a career of wickedness. The figures under which the judgment is set forth appear to be taken from the punishment meted out to profligate women in ancient Israel. The public exposure of the adulteress and her death by stoning in the presence of "many women" supply images terribly appropriate of the fate in store for Jerusalem. [44] Her punishment is to be a warning to all surrounding nations, and an exhibition of the jealous wrath of Jehovah against her infidelity. These nations, some of them hereditary enemies, others old allies, are represented as assembled to witness and to execute the judgment of the city. The remorseless realism of the prophet spares no detail which could enhance the horror of the situation. Abandoned to the ruthless violence of her former lovers, Jerusalem is stripped of her royal attire, the emblems of her idolatry are destroyed, and so, left naked to her enemies, she suffers the ignominious death of a city that has been false to her religion. The root of her sin had been the forgetfulness of what she owed to the goodness of Jehovah, and the essence of her punishment lies

The Expositor's Bible: The Book of Ezekiel

in the withdrawal of the gifts He had lavished upon her and the protection which amid all her apostasies she had never ceased to expect.

At this point (ver. 44 ff.) the allegory takes a new turn through the introduction of the sister cities of Samaria and Sodom. Samaria, although as a city much younger than Jerusalem, is considered the elder sister because she had once been the centre of a greater political power than Jerusalem, and Sodom, which was probably older than either, is treated as the youngest because of her relative insignificance. The order, however, is of no importance. The point of the comparison is that all three had manifested in different degrees the same hereditary tendency to immorality (ver. 45). All three were of heathen origin--their mother a Hittite and their father an Amorite--a description which it is even more difficult to understand in the case of Samaria than in that of Jerusalem. But Ezekiel is not concerned about history. What is prominent in his mind is the family likeness observed in their characters, which gave point to the proverb "Like mother, like daughter" when applied to Jerusalem. The prophet affirms that the wickedness of Jerusalem had so far exceeded that of Samaria and Sodom that she had "justified" her sisters--i.e., she had made their moral condition appear pardonable by comparison with hers. He knows that he is saying a bold thing in ranking the iniquity of Jerusalem as greater than that of Sodom, and so he explains his judgment on Sodom by an analysis of the cause of her notorious corruptness. The name of Sodom lived in tradition as that of the foulest city of the old world, a ne plus ultra of wickedness. Yet Ezekiel dares to raise the question, What was the sin of Sodom? "This was the sin of Sodom thy sister, pride, superabundance of food, and careless ease was the lot of her and her daughters, but they did not succour the poor and needy. But they became proud, and committed abominations before Me: therefore I took them away as thou hast seen" (vv. 49, 50). The meaning seems to be that the corruptions of Sodom were the natural outcome of the evil principle in the Canaanitish nature, favoured by easy circumstances and unchecked by the saving influences of a pure religion. Ezekiel's judgment is like an anticipation of the more solemn sentence uttered by One who knew what was in man when He said, "If the mighty works which have been done in you had been done in Sodom and Gomorrha, they would have remained until this day."

It is remarkable to observe how some of the profoundest ideas in this chapter attach themselves to the strange conception of these two vanished cities as still capable of being restored to their place in the world. In the ideal future of the prophet's vision Sodom and Samaria shall rise from their ruins through the same power which restores Jerusalem to her ancient glory. The promise of a renewed existence to Sodom and Samaria is perhaps connected with the fact that they lay within the sacred territory of which Jerusalem is the centre. Hence Sodom and Samaria are no longer sisters, but daughters of Jerusalem, receiving through her the blessings of the true religion. And it is her relation to these her sisters that opens the eyes of Jerusalem to the true nature of her own relation to Jehovah. Formerly she had been proud and self-sufficient, and counted her exceptional prerogatives the natural reward of some excellence to which she could lay claim. The name of Sodom, the disgraced sister of the family, was not heard in her mouth in the days of her pride, when her wickedness had not been disclosed as it is now (ver. 57). But when she realises that her conduct has justified and comforted her sister, and when she has to take guilty Sodom to her heart as a daughter, she will understand that she owes all her greatness to the same sovereign grace of Jehovah which is manifested in the restoration of the most abandoned community known to history. And out of this new consciousness of grace will spring the chastened and penitent temper of mind which makes possible the continuance of the bond which unites her to Jehovah.

iv. Vv. 59-63.--The way is thus prepared for the final promise of forgiveness with which the chapter closes. The reconciliation between Jehovah and Jerusalem will be effected by an act of recollection on both sides: "I will remember My covenant with thee.... Thou shalt remember thy ways" (vv. 60, 61). The mind of Jehovah and the mind of Jerusalem both go back on the past; but while Jehovah thinks only of the purpose of love which he had entertained towards Jerusalem in the days of her youth and the indissoluble bond between them, Jerusalem retains the memory of her own sinful history, and finds in the remembrance the source of abiding contrition and shame. It does not fall within the scope of the prophet's purpose to set forth in this place the blessed consequences which flow from this renewal of loving intercourse between Israel and her God. He has accomplished his object when he has shown how the electing love of Jehovah reaches its end in spite of human sin and rebellion, and how through the crushing power of divine grace the failures and transgressions of the past are made to issue in a relation of perfect harmony between Jehovah and His people. The permanence of that relation is expressed by an idea borrowed from Jeremiah-- the idea of an everlasting covenant, which cannot be broken because based on the forgiveness of sin and a renewal of heart. The prophet knows that when once the power of evil has been broken by a full disclosure of redeeming love it cannot resume its old ascendency in human life. So he leaves us on the threshold of the new dispensation with the picture of Jerusalem humbled and bearing her shame, yet in the abjectness of her self-accusation realising the end towards which the love of

John J. Skinner

Jehovah had guided her from the beginning: "I will establish My covenant with thee; and thou shalt know that I am Jehovah: that thou mayest remember, and be ashamed, and not open thy mouth any more for very shame, when I expiate for thee all that thou hast done, saith the Lord Jehovah" (vv. 62, 63).

Throughout this chapter we see that the prophet moves in the region of national religious ideas which are distinctive of the Old Testament. Of the influences that formed his conceptions that of Hosea is perhaps most discernible. The fundamental thoughts embodied in the allegory are the same as those by which the older prophet learned to interpret the nature of God and the sin of Israel through the bitter experiences of his family life. These thoughts are developed by Ezekiel with a fertility of imagination and a grasp of theological principles which were adapted to the more complex situation with which he had to deal. But the conception of Israel as the unfaithful wife of Jehovah, of the false gods and the world-powers as her lovers, of her conversion through affliction, and her final restoration by a new betrothal which is eternal, are all expressed in the first three chapters of Hosea. And the freedom with which Ezekiel handles and expands these conceptions shows how thoroughly he was at home in that national view of religion which he did much to break through. In the next lecture we shall have occasion to examine his treatment of the problem of the individual's relation to God, and we cannot fail to be struck by the contrast. The analysis of individual religion may seem meagre by the side of this most profound and suggestive chapter. This arises from the fact that the full meaning of religion could not then be expressed as an experience of the individual soul. The subject of religion being the nation of Israel, the human side of it could only be unfolded in terms of what we should call the national consciousness. The time was not yet come when the great truths which the prophets and psalmists saw embodied in the history of their people could be translated in terms of individual fellowship with God. Yet the God who spake to the fathers by the prophets is the same who has spoken to us in His Son; and when from the standpoint of a higher revelation we turn back to the Old Testament, it is to find in the form of a nation's history the very same truths which we realise as matters of personal experience.

From this point of view the chapter we have considered is one of the most evangelical passages in the writings of Ezekiel. The prophet's conception of sin, for example, is singularly profound and true. He has been charged with a somewhat superficial conception of sin, as if he saw nothing more in it than the transgression of a law arbitrarily imposed by divine authority. There are aspects of Ezekiel's teaching which give some plausibility to that charge, especially those which deal with the duties of the individual. But we see that to Ezekiel the real nature of sin could not possibly be manifested except as a factor in the national life. Now in this allegory it is obvious that he sees something far deeper in it than the mere transgression of positive commandments. Behind all the outward offences of which Israel had been guilty there plainly lies the spiritual fact of national selfishness, unfaithfulness to Jehovah, insensibility to His love, and ingratitude for His benefits. Moreover, the prophet, like Jeremiah before him, has a strong sense of sin as a tendency in human life, a power which is ineradicable save by the mingled severity and goodness of God. Through the whole history of Israel it is one evil disposition which he sees asserting itself, breaking out now in one form and then in another, but continually gaining strength, until at last the spirit of repentance is created by the experience of God's forgiveness. It is not the case, therefore, that Ezekiel failed to comprehend the nature of sin, or that in this respect he falls below the most spiritual of the prophets who had gone before him.

In order that this tendency to sin may be destroyed, Ezekiel sees that the consciousness of guilt must take its place. In the same way the apostle Paul teaches that "every mouth must be stopped, and all the world become guilty before God." Whether the subject be a nation or an individual, the dominion of sin is not broken till the sinner has taken home to himself the full responsibility for his acts and felt himself to be "without excuse." But the most striking thing in Ezekiel's representation of the process of conversion is the thought that this saving sense of sin is produced less by judgment than by free and undeserved forgiveness. Punishment he conceives to be necessary, being demanded alike by the righteousness of God and the good of the sinful people. But the heart of Jerusalem is not changed till she finds herself restored to her former relation to God, with all the sin of her past blotted out and a new life before her. It is through the grace of forgiveness that she is overwhelmed with shame and sorrow for sin, and learns the humility which is the germ of a new hope towards God. Here the prophet strikes one of the deepest notes of evangelical doctrine. All experience confirms the lesson that true repentance is not produced by the terrors of the law, but by the view of God's love in Christ going forth to meet the sinner and bring him back to the Father's heart and home.

Another question of great interest and difficulty is the attitude towards the heathen world assumed by Ezekiel. The prophecy of the restoration of Sodom is certainly one of the most remarkable things in the book. It is true that Ezekiel as a rule concerns himself very little with the religious state of the outlying world under the Messianic dispensation. Where he speaks of foreign

The Expositor's Bible: The Book of Ezekiel

nations it is only to announce the manifestation of Jehovah's glory in the judgments He executes upon them. The effect of these judgments is that "they shall know that I am Jehovah"; but how much is included in the expression as applied to the heathen it is impossible to say. This, however, may be due to the peculiar limitation of view which leads him to concentrate his attention on the Holy Land in his visions of the perfect kingdom of God. We can hardly suppose that he conceived all the rest of the world as a blank or filled with a seething mass of humanity outside the government of the true God. It is rather to be supposed that Canaan itself appeared to his mind as an epitome of the world such as it must be when the latter-day glory was ushered in. And in Canaan he finds room for Sodom, but Sodom turned to the knowledge of the true God and sharing in the blessings bestowed on Jerusalem. It is surely allowable to see in this the symptom of a more hopeful view of the future of the world at large than we should gather from the rest of the prophecy. If Ezekiel could think of Sodom as raised from the dead and sharing the glories of the people of God, the idea of the conversion of heathen nations could not have been altogether foreign to his mind. It is at all events significant that when he meditates most profoundly on the nature of sin and God's method of dealing with it, he is led to the thought of a divine mercy which embraces in its sweep those communities which had reached the lowest depths of moral corruption.

Footnotes:

41. See above, p. [1]97 f.
42. See below, pp. [2]179 f.
43. Ver. 33 may, however, be an interpolation (Cornill).
44. In ver. 41 the Syriac Version reads, with a slight alteration of the text, "they shall burn thee in the midst of the fire." The reading has something to recommend it. Death by burning was an ancient punishment of harlotry (Gen. xxxviii. 24), although it is not likely that it was still inflicted in the time of Ezekiel.

Chapter X - The Religion Of The Individual.
Chapter xviii

In the sixteenth chapter, as we have seen, Ezekiel has asserted in the most unqualified terms the validity of the principle of national retribution. The nation is dealt with as a moral unity, and the catastrophe which closes its history is the punishment for the accumulated guilt incurred by the past generations. In the eighteenth chapter he teaches still more explicitly the freedom and the independent responsibility of each individual before God. No attempt is made to reconcile the two principles as methods of the divine government; from the prophet's standpoint they do not require to be reconciled. They belong to different dispensations. So long as the Jewish state existed the principle of solidarity remained in force. Men suffered for the sins of their ancestors; individuals shared the punishment incurred by the nation as a whole. But as soon as the nation is dead, when the bonds that unite men in the organism of national life are dissolved, then the idea of individual responsibility comes into immediate operation. Each Israelite stands isolated before Jehovah, the burden of hereditary guilt falls away from him, and he is free to determine his own relation to God. He need not fear that the iniquity of his fathers will be reckoned against him; he is held accountable only for his own sins, and these can be forgiven on the condition of his own repentance.

The doctrine of this chapter is generally regarded as Ezekiel's most characteristic contribution to theology. It might be nearer the truth to say that he is dealing with one of the great religious problems of the age in which he lived. The difficulty was perceived by Jeremiah, and treated in a manner which shows that his thoughts were being led in the same direction as those of Ezekiel (Jer. xxxi. 29, 30). If in any respect the teaching of Ezekiel makes an advance on that of Jeremiah, it is in his application of the new truth to the duty of the present: and even here the difference is more apparent than real. Jeremiah postpones the introduction of personal religion to the future, regarding it as an ideal to be realised in the Messianic age. His own life and that of his contemporaries was bound up with the old dispensation which was passing away, and he knew that he was destined to share the fate of his people. Ezekiel, on the other hand, lives already under the powers of the world to come. The one hindrance to the perfect manifestation of Jehovah's righteousness has been removed by the destruction of Jerusalem, and henceforward it will be made apparent in the correspondence between the desert and the fate of each individual. The new Israel must be organised on the basis of personal religion, and the time has already come when the task of preparing the religious community of the future must be earnestly taken up. Hence the doctrine of individual responsibility has a peculiar and practical importance in the mission of Ezekiel. The call to repentance, which is the keynote of his ministry, is addressed to individual men, and in order that it may take effect their minds must be disabused of all fatalistic preconceptions which would induce paralysis of the moral faculties. It was necessary to affirm in all their breadth and fulness the two fundamental truths of personal religion--the absolute righteousness of God's dealings with individual men, and His readiness to welcome and pardon the penitent.

The eighteenth chapter falls accordingly into two divisions. In the first the prophet sets the individual's immediate relation to God against the idea that guilt is transmitted from father to children (vv. 2-20). In the second he tries to dispel the notion that a man's fate is so determined by his own past life as to make a change of moral condition impossible (vv. 21-32).

I

It is noteworthy that both Jeremiah and Ezekiel, in dealing with the question of retribution, start from a popular proverb which had gained currency in the later years of the kingdom of Judah: "The fathers have eaten sour grapes, and the children's teeth are set on edge." In whatever spirit this saying may have been first coined, there is no doubt that it had come to be used as a witticism at the expense of Providence. It indicates that influences were at work besides the word of prophecy which tended to undermine men's faith in the current conception of the divine government. The doctrine of transmitted guilt was accepted as a fact of experience, but it no longer satisfied the deeper moral instincts of men. In early Israel it was otherwise. There the idea that the son should bear the iniquity of the father was received without challenge and applied without misgiving in judicial procedure. The whole family of Achan perished for the sin of their father; the sons of Saul expiated their father's crime long after he was dead. These are indeed but isolated facts, yet they are sufficient to prove the ascendency of the antique conception of the tribe or family as a unity whose individual members are involved in the guilt of the head. With the spread of purer ethical ideas among the people there came a deeper sense of the value of the individual life, and at a later time the principle of vicarious punishment was banished from the administration of human justice (cf. 2 Kings xiv. 6 with Deut. xxiv. 16). Within that sphere the principle was firmly established that each man shall be put to death for his own sin. But the motives which made this change intelligible and necessary in purely human relations could not be brought to bear immediately on the question of divine retribution. The righteousness of God was thought to act on different lines from the righteousness of man. The experience of the last generation of the state seemed to furnish fresh evidence of the operation of a law of providence by which men were made to inherit the iniquity of their fathers. The literature of the period is filled with the conviction that it was the sins of Manasseh that had sealed the doom of the nation. These sins had never been adequately punished, and subsequent events showed that they were not forgiven. The reforming zeal of Josiah had postponed for a time the final visitation of Jehovah's anger; but no reformation and no repentance could avail to roll back the flood of judgment that had been set in motion by the crimes of the reign of Manasseh. "Notwithstanding Jehovah turned not from the fierceness of His great wrath, wherewith His anger was kindled against Judah, because of all the provocations that Manasseh had provoked Him withal" (2 Kings xxiii. 26).

The proverb about the sour grapes shows the effect of this interpretation of providence on a large section of the people. It means no doubt that there is an irrational element in God's method of dealing with men, something not in harmony with natural laws. In the natural sphere if a man eats sour grapes his own teeth are blunted or set on edge; the consequences are immediate, and they are transitory. But in the moral sphere a man may eat sour grapes all his life and suffer no evil consequences whatever; the consequences, however, appear in his children who have committed no such indiscretion. There is nothing there which answers to the ordinary sense of justice. Yet the proverb appears to be less an arraignment of the divine righteousness than a mode of self-exculpation on the part of the people. It expresses the fatalism and despair which settled down on the minds of that generation when they realised the full extent of the calamity that had overtaken them: "If our transgressions and our sins be upon us, and we pine away in them, how then should we live?" (ch. xxxiii. 10). So the exiles reasoned in Babylon, where they were in no mood for quoting facetious proverbs about the ways of Providence; but they accurately expressed the sense of the adage that had been current in Jerusalem before its fall. The sins for which they suffered were not their own, and the judgment that lay on them was no summons to repentance, for it was caused by sins of which they were not guilty and for which they could not in any real sense repent.

Ezekiel attacks this popular theory of retribution at what must have been regarded as its strongest point--the relation between the father and son. "Why should the son not bear the iniquity of his father?" the people asked in astonishment (ver. 19). "It is good traditional theology, and it has been confirmed by our own experience." Now Ezekiel would probably not have admitted that in any circumstances a son suffers because his father has sinned. With that notion he appears to have absolutely broken. He did not deny that the Exile was the punishment for all the sins of the past as well as for those of the present; but that was because the nation was treated as a moral unity, and not because of any law of heredity which bound up the fate of the child with that of the father. It was essential to his purpose to show that the principle of social guilt or collective retribution came to an end with the fall of the state; whereas in the form in which the people held to it, it could never come to an end so long as there are parents to sin and children to suffer. But the important point in the prophet's teaching is that whether in one form or in another the principle of solidarity is now superseded. God will no longer deal with men in the mass, but as individuals; and facts which gave plausibility and a relative justification to cynical views of God's providence shall no more occur. There will be no more occasion to use that objectionable proverb in Israel. On the contrary, it will be manifest in the case of each separate individual that God's righteousness is discriminating, and that each man's destiny corresponds with his own character. And the new principle is embodied in words which may be called the charter of the individual soul--words whose significance is fully revealed only in Christianity: "All souls are Mine.... The soul that sinneth, it shall die."

What is here asserted is of course not a distinction between the soul or spiritual part of man's being and another part of his being which is subject to physical necessity, but one between the individual and his moral environment. The former distinction is real, and it may be necessary for us in our day to insist on it, but it was certainly not thought of by Ezekiel or perhaps by any other Old Testament writer. The word "soul" denotes simply the principle of individual life. "All persons are Mine" expresses the whole meaning which Ezekiel meant to convey. Consequently the death threatened to the sinner is not what we call spiritual death, but death in the literal sense--the death of the individual. The truth taught is the independence and freedom of the individual, or his moral

John J. Skinner

personality. And that truth involves two things. First, each individual belongs to God, stands in immediate personal relation to Him. In the old economy the individual belonged to the nation or the family, and was related to God only as a member of a larger whole. Now he has to deal with God directly--possesses independent personal worth in the eye of God. Secondly, as a result of this, each man is responsible for his own acts, and for these alone. So long as his religious relations are determined by circumstances outside of his own life his personality is incomplete. The ideal relation to God must be one in which the destiny of every man depends on his own free actions. These are the fundamental postulates of personal religion as formulated by Ezekiel.

The first part of the chapter is nothing more than an illustration of the second of these truths in a sufficient number of instances to show both sides of its operation. There is first the case of a man perfectly righteous, who as a matter of course lives by his righteousness, the state of his father not being taken into account. Then this good man is supposed to bear a son who is in all respects the opposite of his father, who answers none of the tests of a righteous man; he must die for his own sins, and his father's righteousness avails him nothing. Lastly, if the son of this wicked man takes warning by his father's fate and leads a good life, he lives just as the first man did because of his own righteousness, and suffers no diminution of his reward because his father was a sinner. In all this argument there is a tacit appeal to the conscience of the hearers, as if the case only required to be put clearly before them to command their assent. This is what shall be, the prophet says; and it is what ought to be. It is contrary to the idea of perfect justice to conceive of Jehovah as acting otherwise than as here represented. To cling to the idea of collective retribution as a permanent truth of religion, as the exiles were disposed to do, destroys belief in the divine righteousness by making it different from the righteousness which expresses itself in the moral judgments of men.

Before we pass from this part of the chapter we may take note of some characteristics of the moral ideal by which Ezekiel tests the conduct of the individual man. It is given in the form of a catalogue of virtues, the presence or absence of which determines a man's fitness or unfitness to enter the future kingdom of God. Most of these virtues are defined negatively; the code specifies sins to be avoided rather than duties to be performed or graces to be cultivated. Nevertheless they are such as to cover a large section of human life, and the arrangement of them embodies distinctions of permanent ethical significance. They may be classed under the three heads of piety, chastity, and beneficence. Under the first head, that of directly religious duties, two offences are mentioned which are closely connected with each other, although to our minds they may seem to involve different degrees of guilt (ver. 6). One is the acknowledgment of other gods than Jehovah, and the other is participation in ceremonies which denoted fellowship with idols.[45] To us who "know that an idol is nothing in the world" the mere act of eating with the blood has no religious significance. But in Ezekiel's time it was impossible to divest it of heathen associations, and the man who performed it stood convicted of a sin against Jehovah. Similarly the idea of sexual purity is illustrated by two outstanding and prevalent offences (ver. 6). The third head, which includes by far the greater number of particulars, deals with the duties which we regard as moral in a stricter sense. They are embodiments of the love which "worketh no ill to his neighbour," and is therefore "the fulfilling of the law." It is manifest that the list is not meant to be an exhaustive enumeration of all the virtues that a good man must practise, or all the vices he must shun. The prophet has before his mind two broad classes of men--those who feared God, and those who did not; and what he does is to lay down outward marks which were practically sufficient to discriminate between the one class and the other.

The supreme moral category is Righteousness, and this includes the two ideas of right character and a right relation to God. The distinction between an active righteousness manifested in the life and a "righteousness which is by faith" is not explicitly drawn in the Old Testament. Hence the passage contains no teaching on the question whether a man's relation to God is determined by his good works, or whether good works are the fruit and outcome of a right relation to God. The essence of morality, according to the Old Testament, is loyalty to God, expressed by obedience to His will; and from that point of view it is self-evident that the man who is loyal to Jehovah stands accepted in His sight. In other connections Ezekiel makes it abundantly clear that the state of grace does not depend on any merit which man can have towards God.

The fact that Ezekiel defines righteousness in terms of outward conduct has led to his being accused of the error of legalism in his moral conceptions. He has been charged with resolving righteousness into "a sum of separate tzedaqôth," or virtues. But this view strains his language unduly, and seems moreover to be negatived by the presuppositions of his argument. As a man must either live or die at the day of judgment, so he must at any moment be either righteous or wicked. The problematic case of a man who should conscientiously observe some of these requirements and deliberately violate others would have been dismissed by Ezekiel as an idle speculation: "Whosoever shall keep the whole law, and yet offend in one point, he is guilty of all" (James ii. 10). The very fact that former good deeds are not remembered to a man in the day when he turns from his righteousness shows that the state of righteousness is something different from an average struck from the statistics of his moral career. The bent of the character towards or away from goodness is no doubt spoken of as subject to sudden fluctuations, but for the time being each man is conceived as dominated by the one tendency or the other; and it is the bent of the whole nature towards the good that constitutes the righteousness by which a man shall live. It is at all events a mistake to suppose that the prophet is concerned only about the external act and indifferent to the state of heart from which it proceeds. It is true that he does not attempt to penetrate beneath the surface of the outward life. He does not analyse motives. But this is because he assumes that if a man keeps God's law he does it from a sincere desire to please God and with a sense of the rightness of the law to which he subjects his life. When we recognise this the charge of externalism amounts to very little. We can never get behind the principle that "he that doeth righteousness is righteous" (1 John iii. 7), and that principle covers all that Ezekiel really teaches. Compared with the more spiritual teaching of the New Testament his moral ideal is no doubt defective in many directions, but his insistence on action as a test of character is hardly one of them. We must remember that the New Testament itself contains as many warnings against a false spirituality as it does against the opposite error of reliance on good works.

II

The second great truth of personal religion is the moral freedom of the individual to determine his own destiny in the day of judgment. This is illustrated in the latter part of the chapter by the two opposite cases of a wicked man turning from his wickedness (vv. 21, 22) and a righteous man turning from his righteousness (ver. 24). And the teaching of the passage is that the effect of such a change of mind, as regards a man's relation to God, is absolute. The good life subsequent to conversion is not weighed against the sins of past years; it is the index of a new state of heart in which the guilt of former transgressions is entirely blotted out: "All his transgressions that he hath committed shall not be remembered in regard to him; in his righteousness that he hath done he shall live." But in like manner the act of apostasy effaces the remembrance of good deeds done in an earlier period of the man's life. The standing of each soul before God, its righteousness or its wickedness, is thus wholly determined by its final choice of good or evil, and is revealed by the conduct which follows that great moral decision. There can be no doubt that Ezekiel regards these two possibilities as equally real, falling away from righteousness being as much a fact of experience as repentance. In the light of the New Testament we should perhaps interpret both cases somewhat differently. In genuine conversion we must recognise the imparting of a new spiritual principle which is ineradicable, containing the pledge of perseverance in the state of grace to the end. In the case of final apostasy we are compelled to judge that the righteousness which is renounced was only apparent, that it was no true indication of the man's character or of his condition in the sight of God. But these are not the questions with which the prophet is directly dealing. The essential truth which he inculcates is the emancipation of the individual, through repentance, from his own past. In virtue of his immediate personal relation to God each man has the power to accept the offer of salvation, to break away from his sinful life and escape the doom which hangs over the impenitent. To this one point the whole argument of the chapter tends. It is a demonstration of the possibility and efficacy of individual repentance, culminating in the declaration which lies at the very foundation of evangelical religion, that God has no pleasure in the death of him that dieth, but will have all men to repent and live (ver. 32).

It is not easy for us to conceive the effect of this revelation on the minds of people so utterly unprepared for it as the generation in which Ezekiel lived. Accustomed as they were to think of their individual fate as bound up in that of their nation, they could not at once adjust themselves to a doctrine which had never previously been enunciated with such incisive clearness. And it is not surprising that one effect of Ezekiel's teaching was to create fresh doubts of the rectitude of the divine government. "The way of the Lord is not equal," it was said (vv. 25, 29). So long as it was admitted that men suffered for the sins of their ancestors or that God dealt with them in the mass, there was at least an appearance of consistency in the methods of Providence. The justice of God might not be visible in the life of the individual, but it could be roughly traced in the history of the nation as a whole. But when that principle was discarded, then the question of the divine righteousness was raised in the case of each separate Israelite, and there immediately appeared all those perplexities about the lot of the individual which so sorely exercised the faith of Old Testament believers. Experience did not show that correspondence between a man's attitude towards God and his earthly fortunes which the doctrine of individual freedom seemed to imply; and even in Ezekiel's time it must have been evident that the calamities which overtook the state fell indiscriminately on the righteous and the wicked. The prophet's purpose, however, is a practical one, and he does not attempt to offer a theoretical solution of the difficulties which thus arose. There were several considerations in his mind which turned aside the edge of the people's complaint against the righteousness of Jehovah. One was the imminence of the final judgment, in which the absolute rectitude of the divine procedure would be clearly manifested. Another seems to be the irresolute and unstable attitude of the people themselves towards the great moral issues which were set before them. While they professed to be more righteous than their fathers, they showed no settled purpose of amendment in their lives. A man might be apparently righteous to-day and a sinner to-morrow; the "inequality" of which they complained was in their own ways, and not in the way of the Lord (vv. 25, 29). But the most important element in the case was the prophet's conception of the character of God as one who, though strictly just, yet desired that men should live. The Lord is longsuffering, not willing that any should perish; and He postpones the day of decision that His goodness may lead men to repentance. "Have I any pleasure in the death of the wicked? saith the Lord: and not that he should turn from his ways, and live?" (ver. 23). And all these considerations lead up to the urgent call to repentance with which the chapter closes.

The importance of the questions dealt with in this eighteenth chapter is shown clearly enough by the hold which they have over the minds of men in the present day. The very same difficulties which Ezekiel had to encounter in his time confront us still in a somewhat altered form, and are often keenly felt as obstacles to faith in God. The scientific doctrine of heredity, for example, seems to be but a more precise modern rendering of the old proverb about the eating of sour grapes. The biological controversy over the possibility of the transmission of acquired characteristics scarcely touches the moral problem. In whatever way that controversy may be ultimately settled, it is certain that in all cases a man's life is affected both for good and evil by influences which descend upon him from his ancestry. Similarly within the sphere of the individual life the law of habit seems to exclude the possibility of complete emancipation from the penalty due to past transgressions. Hardly anything, in short, is better established by experience than that the consequences of past actions persist through all changes of spiritual condition, and, further, that children do suffer from the consequences of their parents' sin.

Do not these facts, it may be asked, amount practically to a vindication of the theory of retribution against which the prophet's argument is directed? How can we reconcile them with the great principles enunciated in this chapter? Dictates of morality, fundamental truths of religion, these may be; but can we say in the face of experience that they are true?

It must be admitted that a complete answer to these questions is not given in the chapter before us, nor perhaps anywhere in the Old Testament. So long as God dealt with men mainly by temporal rewards and punishments, it was impossible to realise fully the separateness of the soul in its spiritual relations to God; the fate of the individual is necessarily merged in that of the community, and Ezekiel's doctrine remains a prophecy of better things to be revealed. This indeed is the light in which he himself teaches us to regard it; although he applies it in all its strictness to the men of his own generation, it is nevertheless essentially a feature of the ideal kingdom of God, and is to be exhibited in the judgment by which that kingdom is introduced. The great value of his teaching therefore lies in his having formulated with unrivalled clearness principles which are eternally true of the spiritual life, although the perfect manifestation of these principles in the experience of believers was reserved for the final revelation of salvation in Christ.

The solution of the contradiction referred to lies in the separation between the natural and the penal consequences of sin. There is a sphere within which natural laws have their course, modified, it may be, but not wholly suspended by the law of the spirit of life in Christ. The physical effects of vicious indulgence are not turned aside by repentance, and a man may carry the scars of sin upon him to the grave. But there is also a sphere into which natural law does not enter. In his immediate personal relation to God a believer is raised above the evil consequences which flow from his past life, so that they have no power to separate him from the love of God. And within that sphere his moral freedom and independence are as much matter of experience as is his subjection to law in another sphere. He knows that all things work together for his good, and that tribulation itself is a means of bringing him nearer to God. Amongst those tribulations which work out his salvation there may be the evil conditions imposed on him by the sin of others, or even the natural consequences of his own former transgressions. But tribulations no longer bear the aspect of penalty, and are no longer a token of the wrath of God. They are transformed into chastisements by which the Father of spirits makes His children perfect in holiness. The hardest cross to bear will always be that which is the result of one's own sin; but He who has borne the guilt of it can strengthen us to bear even this and follow Him. [46]

Footnotes:

45. "To eat upon the mountains" (if that reading can be retained) must mean to take part in the sacrificial feasts which were held on the high places in honour of idols. But if with W. R. Smith and others we substitute the phrase "eat with the blood," assimilating the reading to that of ch. xxxiii. 25, the offence is still of the same nature. In the time of Ezekiel to eat with the blood probably

meant not merely to eat that which had not been sacrificed to Jehovah, but to engage in a rite of distinctly heathenish character. Cf. Lev. xix. 20, and see the note in Smith's Kinship and Marriage in Early Arabia, p. 310.

46. In the striking passage ch. xiv. 12-23 the application of the doctrine of individual retribution to the destruction of Jerusalem is discussed. It is treated as "an exception to the rule" (Smend)--perhaps the exception which proves the rule. The rule is that in a national judgment the most eminent saints save neither son nor daughter by their righteousness, but only their own lives (vv. 13-20). At the fall of Jerusalem, however, a remnant escapes and goes into captivity with sons and daughters, in order that their corrupt lives may prove to the earlier exiles how necessary the destruction of the city was (vv. 21-23). The argument is an admission that the judgment on Israel was not carried out in accordance with the strict principle laid down in ch. xviii. It is difficult, indeed, to reconcile the various utterances of Ezekiel on this subject. In ch. xxi. 3, 4 he expressly announces that in the downfall of the state righteous and wicked shall perish together. In the vision of ch. ix., on the other hand, the righteous are marked for exemption from the fate of the city. The truth appears to be that the prophet is conscious of standing between two dispensations, and does not hold a consistent view regarding the time when the law proper to the perfect dispensation comes into operation. The point on which there is no ambiguity is that in the final judgment which ushers in the Messianic age the principle of individual retribution shall be fully manifested.

Chapter XI - The Sword Unsheathed. Chapter xxi

The date at the beginning of ch. xx. introduces the fourth and last section of the prophecies delivered before the destruction of Jerusalem. It also divides the first period of Ezekiel's ministry into two equal parts. The time is the month of August, 590 b.c., two years after his prophetic inauguration and two years before the investment of Jerusalem. It follows that if the book of Ezekiel presents anything like a faithful picture of his actual work, by far his most productive year was that which had just closed. It embraces the long and varied series of discourses from ch. viii. to ch. xix.; whereas five chapters are all that remain as a record of his activity during the next two years. This result is not so improbable as at first sight it might appear. From the character of Ezekiel's prophecy, which consists largely of homiletic amplifications of one great theme, it is quite intelligible that the main lines of his teaching should have taken shape in his mind at an early period of his ministry. The discourses in the earlier part of the book may have been expanded in the act of committing them to writing; but there is no reason to doubt that the ideas they contain were present to the prophet's mind and were actually delivered by him within the period to which they are assigned. We may therefore suppose that Ezekiel's public exhortations became less frequent during the two years that preceded the siege, just as we know that for two years after that event they were altogether discontinued.

In this last division of the prophecies relating to the destruction of Jerusalem we can easily distinguish two different classes of oracles. On the one hand we have two chapters dealing with contemporary incidents--the march of Nebuchadnezzar's army against Jerusalem (ch. xxi.), and the commencement of the siege of the city (ch. xxiv.). In spite of the confident opinion of some critics that these prophecies could not have been composed till after the fall of Jerusalem, they seem to me to bear the marks of having been written under the immediate influence of the events they describe. It is difficult otherwise to account for the excitement under which the prophet labours, especially in ch. xxi., which stands by the side of ch. vii. as the most agitated utterance in the whole book. On the other hand we have three discourses of the nature of formal indictments--one directed against the exiles (ch. xx.), one against Jerusalem (ch. xxii.), and one against the whole nation of Israel (ch. xxiii.). It is impossible in these chapters to discover any advance in thought upon similar passages that have already been before us. Two of them (chs. xx. and xxiii.) are historical retrospects after the manner of ch. xvi., and there is no obvious reason why they should be placed in a different section of the book. The key to the unity of the section must therefore be sought in the two historical prophecies and in the situation created by the events they describe.[47] It will therefore help to clear the ground if we commence with the oracle which throws most light on the historical background of this group of prophecies--the oracle of Jehovah's sword against Jerusalem in ch. xxi.[48]

The long-projected rebellion has at length broken out. Zedekiah has renounced his allegiance to the king of Babylon, and the army of the Chaldæans is on its way to suppress the insurrection. The precise date of these events is not known. For some reason the conspiracy of the Palestinian states had hung fire; many years had been allowed to slip away since the time when their envoys had met in Jerusalem to concert measures of united resistance (Jer. xxvii.). This procrastination was, as usual, a sure presage of disaster. In the interval the league had dissolved. Some of its members had made terms with Nebuchadnezzar; and it would appear that only Tyre, Judah, and Ammon ventured on open defiance of his power. The hope was cherished in Jerusalem, and probably also among the Jews in Babylon, that the first assault of the Chaldæans would be directed against the Ammonites, and that time would thus be gained to complete the defences of Jerusalem. To dispel this illusion is one obvious purpose of the prophecy before us. The movements of Nebuchadnezzar's army are directed by a wisdom higher than his own; he is the unconscious instrument by which Jehovah is executing His own purpose. The real object of his expedition is not to punish a few refractory tribes for an act of disloyalty, but to vindicate the righteousness of Jehovah in the destruction of the city which had profaned His holiness. No human calculations will be allowed even for a moment to turn aside the blow which is aimed directly at Jerusalem's sins, or to obscure the lesson taught by its sure and unerring aim.

We can imagine the restless suspense and anxiety with which the final struggle for the national cause was watched by the exiles in Babylon. In imagination they would follow the long march of the Chaldæan hosts by the Euphrates and their descent by the valleys of the Orontes and Leontes upon the city. Eagerly would they wait for some tidings of a reverse which would revive their drooping hope of a speedy collapse of the great world-empire and a restoration of Israel to its ancient freedom. And when at length they heard that Jerusalem was enclosed in the iron grip of these victorious legions, from which no human deliverance was possible, their mood would harden into one in which fanatical hope and sullen despair contended for the mastery. Into an atmosphere charged with such excitement Ezekiel hurls the series of predictions comprised in chs. xxi. and xxiv. With far other feelings than his fellows, but with as keen an interest as theirs, he follows the development of what he knows to be the last act in the long controversy between Jehovah and Israel. It is his duty to repeat once more the irrevocable decree--the divine delenda est against the guilty Jerusalem. But he does so in this instance in language whose vehemence betrays the agitation of his mind, and perhaps also the restlessness of the society in which he lived. The twenty-first chapter is a series of rhapsodies, the product of a state bordering on ecstasy, where different aspects of the impending judgment are set forth by the help of vivid images which pass in quick succession through the prophet's mind.

I

The first vision which the prophet sees of the approaching catastrophe (vv. 1-4) is that of a forest conflagration, an occurrence which must have been as frequent in Palestine as a prairie fire in America. He sees a fire break out in the "forest of the south," and rage with such fierceness that "every green tree and every dry tree" is burned up; the faces of all who are near it are scorched, and all men are convinced that so terrible a calamity must be the work of Jehovah Himself. This we may suppose to have been the form in which the truth first laid hold of Ezekiel's imagination; but he appears to have hesitated to proclaim his message in this form. His figurative manner of speech had become notorious among the exiles (ver. 5), and he was conscious that a "parable" so vague and general as this would be dismissed as an ingenious riddle which might mean anything or nothing. What follows (vv. 7-10) gives the key to the original vision. Although it is in form an independent oracle, it is closely parallel to the preceding and elucidates each feature in detail. The "forest of the south" is explained to mean the land of Israel; and the mention of the sword of Jehovah instead of the fire intimates less obscurely that the instrument of the threatened calamity is the Babylonian army. It is interesting to observe that Ezekiel expressly admits that there were righteous men even in the doomed Israel. Contrary to his conception of the normal methods of the divine righteousness, he conceives of this judgment as one which involves righteous and wicked in a common ruin. Not that God is less than righteous in this crowning act of vengeance, but His justice is not brought to bear on the fate of individuals. He is dealing with the nation as a whole, and in the exterminating judgment of the nation good men will no more be spared than the green tree of the forest escapes the fate of the dry. It was the fact that righteous men perished in the fall of Jerusalem; and Ezekiel does not shut his eyes to it, firmly as he believed that the time was come when God would reward every man according to his own character. The indiscriminateness of the judgment in its bearing on different classes of persons is obviously a feature which Ezekiel here seeks to emphasise.

But the idea of the sword of Jehovah drawn from its scabbard, to return no more till it has accomplished its mission, is the one that has fixed itself most deeply in the prophet's imagination, and forms the connecting link between this vision and the other amplifications of the same theme which follow.

II

Passing over the symbolic action of vv. 11-13, representing the horror and astonishment with which the dire tidings of Jerusalem's fall will be received, we come to the point where the prophet breaks into the wild strain of dithyrambic poetry, which has been called the "Song of the Sword" (vv. 14-22). The following translation, although necessarily imperfect and in some places uncertain, may convey some idea both of the structure and the rugged vigour of the original. It will be seen that there is a clear division into four stanzas: [49] --

(i) Vv. 14-16.
A sword, a sword! It is sharpened and burnished withal.
For a work of slaughter is it sharpened!
To gleam like lightning burnished!

And 'twas given to be smoothed for the grip of the hand,
--Sharpened is it, and furbished--
To put in the hand of the slayer.

(ii) Vv. 17, 18.
Cry and howl, son of man!
For it has come among my people;
Come among all the princes of Israel!
Victims of the sword are they, they and my people;
Therefore smite upon thy thigh!

It shall not be, saith Jehovah the Lord.

(iii) Vv. 19, 20.
But, thou son of man, prophesy, and smite hand on hand;
Let the sword be doubled and tripled (?).
A sword of the slain is it, the great sword of the slain whirling around them,--
That hearts may fail, and many be the fallen in all their gates.

It is made like lightning, furbished for slaughter!

(iv) Vv. 21, 22.
Gather thee together! Smite to the right, to the left,
Whithersoever thine edge is appointed!
And I also will smite hand on hand,
And appease My wrath:
I Jehovah have spoken it.

In spite of its obscurity, its abrupt transitions, and its strange blending of the divine with the human personality, the ode exhibits a definite poetic form and a real progress of thought from the beginning to the close. Throughout the passage we observe that the prophet's gaze is fascinated by the glittering sword which symbolised the instrument of Jehovah's vengeance. In the opening stanza (i) he describes the preparation of the sword; he notes the keenness of its edge and its glittering sheen with an awful presentiment that an implement so elaborately fashioned is destined for some terrible day of slaughter. Then (ii) he announces the purpose for which the sword is prepared, and breaks into loud lamentation as he realises that its doomed victims are his own people and the princes of Israel. In the next stanza (iii) he sees the sword in action; wielded by an invisible hand, it flashes hither and thither, circling round its hapless victims as if two or three swords were at work instead of one. All hearts are paralysed with fear, but the sword does not cease its ravages until it has filled the ground with slain. Then at length the sword is at rest (iv), having accomplished its work. The divine Speaker calls on it in a closing apostrophe "to gather itself together" as if for a final sweep to right and left, indicating the thoroughness with which the judgment has been executed. In the last verse the vision of the sword fades away, and the poem closes with an announcement, in the usual prophetic manner, of Jehovah's fixed purpose to "assuage" His wrath against Israel by the crowning act of retribution.

III

If any doubt still remained as to what the sword of Jehovah meant, it is removed in the next section (vv. 23-32), where the prophet indicates the way by which the sword is to come on the kingdom of Judah. The Chaldæan monarch is represented as pausing on his march, perhaps at Riblah or some place to the north of Palestine, and deliberating whether he shall advance first against Judah or the Ammonites. He stands at the parting of the ways--on the left hand is the road to Rabbath-ammon, on the right that to Jerusalem. In his perplexity he invokes supernatural guidance, resorting to various expedients then in use for ascertaining the will of the gods and the path of good fortune. He "rattles the arrows" (two of them in some kind of vessel, one for Jerusalem and the other for Riblah); he consults the teraphim and inspects the entrails of a sacrificial victim. This consulting of the omens was no doubt an invariable preliminary to every campaign, and was resorted to whenever an important military decision had to be made. It might seem a matter of indifference to a powerful monarch like Nebuchadnezzar which of two petty opponents he determined to crush first. But the kings of Babylon were religious men in their way, and never doubted that success depended on their following the indications that were given by the higher powers. In this case Nebuchadnezzar gets a true answer, but not from the deities whose aid he had invoked. In his right hand he finds the arrow marked "Jerusalem." The die is cast, his resolution is taken, but it is Jehovah's sentence sealing the fate of Jerusalem that has been uttered.

Such is the situation which Ezekiel in Babylon is directed to represent through a piece of obvious symbolism. A road diverging into two is drawn on the ground, and at the meeting-point a sign-post is erected indicating that the one leads to Ammon and the other to Judah. It is of course not necessary to suppose that the incident so graphically described actually occurred. The divination scene may only be imaginary, although it is certainly a true reflection of Babylonian ideas and customs. The truth conveyed is that the Babylonian army is moving under the immediate guidance of Jehovah, and that not only the political projects of the king, but his secret thoughts and even his superstitious reliance on signs and omens, are all overruled for the furtherance of the one purpose for which Jehovah has raised him up.

Meanwhile Ezekiel is well aware that in Jerusalem a very different interpretation is put on the course of events. When the news of the great king's decision reaches the men at the head of affairs they are not dismayed. They view the decision as the result of "false divination"; they laugh to scorn the superstitious rites which have determined the course of the campaign,--not that they suppose the king will not act on his omens, but they do not believe they are an augury of success. They had hoped for a short breathing space while Nebuchadnezzar was engaged on the east of the Jordan, but they will not shrink from the conflict whether it be to-day or to-morrow. Addressing himself to this state of mind, Ezekiel once more [50] reminds those who hear him that these men are fighting against the moral laws of the universe. The existing kingdom of Judah occupies a false position before God and in the eyes of just men. It has no religious foundation; for the hope of the Messiah does not lie with that wearer of a dishonoured crown, the king Zedekiah, but with the legitimate heir of David now in exile. The state has no right to be except as part of the Chaldæan empire, and this right it has forfeited by renouncing its allegiance to its earthly superior. These men forget that in this quarrel the just cause is that of Nebuchadnezzar, whose enterprise only seems to "call to mind their iniquity" (ver. 28)--i.e., their political crime. In provoking this conflict, therefore, they have put themselves in the wrong; they shall be caught in the toils of their own villainy.

The heaviest censure is reserved for Zedekiah, the "wicked one, the prince of Israel, whose day is coming in the time of final retribution." This part of the prophecy has a close resemblance to the latter part of ch. xvii. The prophet's sympathies are still with the exiled king, or at least with that branch of the royal family which he represents. And the sentence of rejection on Zedekiah is again accompanied by a promise of the restoration of the kingdom in the person of the Messiah. The crown which has been dishonoured by the last king of Judah shall be taken from his head; that which is low shall be exalted (the exiled branch of the Davidic house), and that which is high shall be abased (the reigning king); the whole existing order of things shall be overturned "until He comes who has the right." [51]

IV

The last oracle is directed against the children of Ammon. By Nebuchadnezzar's decision to subdue Jerusalem first the Ammonites had gained a short respite. They even exulted in the humiliation of their former ally, and had apparently drawn the sword in order to seize part of the land of Judah. Misled by false diviners, they had dared to seek their own advantage in the calamities which Jehovah had brought on His own people. The prophet threatens the complete annihilation of Ammon, even in its own land, and the blotting out of its remembrance among the nations. That is the substance of the prophecy; but its form presents several points of difficulty. It begins with what appears to be an echo of the "Song of the Sword" in the earlier part of the chapter:--

> *A sword! a sword!*
> *It is drawn for slaughter; it is furbished to shine like lightning* (ver. 33).

But as we proceed we find that it is the sword of the Ammonites that is meant, and they are ordered to return it to its sheath. If this be so, the tone of the passage must be ironical. It is in mockery that the prophet uses such magnificent language of the puny pretensions of Ammon to take a share in the work for which Jehovah has fashioned the mighty weapon of the Chaldæan army. There are other reminiscences of the earlier part of the chapter, such as the "lying divination" of ver. 34, and the "time of final retribution" in the same verse. The allusion to the "reproach" of Ammon and its aggressive attitude seems to point to the time after the destruction of Jerusalem and the withdrawal of the army of Nebuchadnezzar. Whether the Ammonites had previously made their submission or not we cannot tell; but the fortieth and forty-first chapters of Jeremiah show that Ammon was still a hotbed of conspiracy against the Babylonian interest in the days after the fall of Jerusalem. These appearances make it probable that this part of the chapter is an appendix, added at a later time, and dealing with a situation which was developed after the destruction of the city. Its insertion in its present place is easily accounted for by the circumstance that the fate of Ammon had been linked with that of Jerusalem in the previous part of the chapter. The vindictive little nationality had used its respite to gratify its hereditary hatred of Israel, and now the judgment, suspended for a time, shall return with redoubled fury and sweep it from the earth.

Looking back over this series of prophecies, there seems reason to believe that, with the exception of the last, they are really contemporaneous with the events they deal with. It is true that they do not illuminate the historical situation to the same degree as those in which Isaiah depicts the advance of another invader and the development of another crisis in the people's history. This is due partly to the bent of Ezekiel's genius, but partly also to the very peculiar circumstances in which he was placed. The events which form the theme of his prophecy were transacted on a distant stage; neither he nor his immediate hearers were actors in the drama. He addresses himself to an audience wrought to the highest pitch of excitement, but swayed by hopes and rumours and vague surmises as to the probable issue of events. It was inevitable in these circumstances that his prophecy, even in those passages which deal with contemporary facts, should present but a pale reflection of the actual situation. In the case before us the one historical event which stands out clearly is the departure of Nebuchadnezzar with his army to Jerusalem. But what we read is genuine prophecy; not the artifice of a man using prophetic speech as a literary form, but the utterance of one who discerns the finger of God in the present, and interprets His purpose beforehand to the men of his day.

Footnotes:

47. This is true whether (as some expositors think) the date in ch. xx. is merely an external mark introducing a new division of the book, or whether (as seems more natural) it is due to the fact that here Ezekiel recognised a turning-point of his ministry. Such visits of the elders as that here recorded must have been of frequent occurrence. Two others are mentioned, and of these one is undated (ch. xiv. 1); the other at least admits the supposition that it was connected with a very definite change of opinion among the exiles (ch. viii. 1: see above, p. ^{3}80). We may therefore reasonably suppose that the precise note of time here introduced marks this particular incident as having possessed a peculiar significance in the relations between the prophet and his fellow-exiles. What its significance may have been we shall consider in the next lecture, see p. ^{4}174.

48. The verses xx. 45-49 of the English Version really belong to ch. xxi., and are so placed in the Hebrew. In what follows the verses will be numbered according to the Hebrew text.

49. At three places the meaning is entirely lost, through corruption of the text.

50. Cf. ch. xvii.

51. The reference is to the Messiah, and seems to be based on the ancient prophecy of Gen. xlix. 10, reading there slh instead of slh.

Chapter XII - Jehovah's Controversy With Israel. Chapter xx

By far the hardest trial of Ezekiel's faith must have been the conduct of his fellow-exiles. It was amongst them that he looked for the great spiritual change which must precede the establishment of the kingdom of God; and he had already addressed to them words of consolation based on the knowledge that the hope of the future was theirs (ch. xi. 18). Yet the time passed on without bringing any indications that the promise was about to be fulfilled. There were no symptoms of national repentance; there was nothing even to show that the lessons of the Exile as interpreted by the prophet were beginning to be laid to heart. For these men, among whom he lived, were still inveterately addicted to idolatry. Strange as it must seem to us, the very men who cherished a fanatical faith in Jehovah's power to save His people were assiduously practising the worship of other gods. It is too readily assumed by some writers that the idolatry of the exiles was of the ambiguous kind which had prevailed so long in the land of Israel, that it was the worship of Jehovah under the form of images--a breach of the second commandment, but not of the first. The people who carried Jeremiah down to Egypt were as eager as Ezekiel's companions to hear a word from Jehovah; yet they were devoted to the worship of the "Queen of Heaven," and dated all their misfortunes from the time when their women had ceased to pay court to her. There is no reason to believe that the Jews in Babylon were less catholic in their superstitions than those of Judæa; and indeed the whole drift of Ezekiel's expostulations goes to show that he has the worship of false gods in view. The ancient belief that the worship of Jehovah was specially associated with the land of Canaan is not likely to have been without influence on the minds of those who felt the fascination of idolatry, and must have strengthened the tendency to seek the aid of foreign gods in a foreign land.

The twentieth chapter deals with this matter of idolatry; and the fact that this important discourse was called forth by a visit from the elders of Israel shows how heavily the subject weighed on the prophet's mind. Whatever the purpose of the deputation may have been (and of that we have no information), it was certainly not to consult Ezekiel about the propriety of worshipping false gods. It is only because this great question dominates all his thoughts concerning them and their destiny that he connects the warning against idolatry with a casual inquiry addressed to him by the elders. The circumstances are so similar to those of ch. xiv. that Ewald was led to conjecture that both oracles originated in one and the same incident, and were separated from each other in writing because of the difference of their subjects. Ch. xiv. on that view justifies the refusal of an answer from a consideration of the true function of prophecy, while ch. xx. expands the admonition of the sixth verse of ch. xiv. into an elaborate review of the religious history of Israel. But there is really no good reason for identifying the two incidents. In neither passage does the prophet think it worth while to record the object of the inquiry addressed to him, and therefore conjecture is useless.

But the very fact that a definite date is given for this visit leads us to consider whether it had not some peculiar significance to lodge it so firmly in Ezekiel's mind. Now the most suggestive hint which the chapter affords is the idea put into the lips of the exiles in ver. 32: "And as for the thought which arises in your mind, it shall not be, in that ye are thinking, We will become like the heathen, like the families of the lands, in worshipping wood and stone." These words contain the key to the whole discourse. It is difficult, no doubt, to decide how much exactly is implied in them. They may mean no more than the determination to keep up the external conformity to heathen customs which already existed in matters of worship--as, for example, in the use of images. But the form of expression used, "that which is coming up in your mind," almost suggests that the prophet was face to face with an incipient tendency among the exiles, a deliberate resolve to apostatise and assimilate themselves for all religious purposes to the surrounding heathen. It is by no means improbable that, amidst the many conflicting tendencies that distracted the exiled community, this idea of a complete abandonment of the national religion should have crystallised into a settled purpose in the event of their last hope being disappointed. If this was the situation with which Ezekiel had to deal, we should be able to understand how his denunciation takes the precise form which it assumes in this chapter.

For what is, in the main, the purport of the chapter? Briefly stated the argument is as follows.

John J. Skinner

The religion of Jehovah had never been the true expression of the national genius of Israel. Not now for the first time has the purpose of Israel come into conflict with the immutable purpose of Jehovah; but from the very beginning the history had been one long struggle between the natural inclinations of the people and the destiny which was forced on it by the will of God. The love of idols had been the distinguishing feature of the national character from the beginning; and if it had been suffered to prevail, Israel would never have been known as Jehovah's people. Why had it not been suffered to prevail? Because of Jehovah's regard for the honour of His name; because in the eyes of the heathen His glory was identified with the fortunes of this particular people, to whom He had once revealed Himself. And as it has been in the past, so it will be in the future. The time has come for the age-long controversy to be brought to an issue, and it cannot be doubtful what the issue will be. "That which comes up in their mind"--this new resolve to live like the heathen--cannot turn aside the purpose of Jehovah to make of Israel a people for His own glory. Whatever further judgments may be necessary for that end, the land of Israel shall yet be the seat of a pure and acceptable worship of the true God, and the people shall recognise with shame and contrition that the goal of all its history has been accomplished in spite of its perversity by the "irresistible grace" of its divine King.

I

The Lesson of History (vv. 5-29).--It is a magnificent conception of national election which the prophet here unfolds. It takes the form of a parallel between two desert scenes, one at the beginning and the other at the close of Israel's history. The first part of the chapter deals with the religious significance of the transactions in the wilderness of Sinai and the events in Egypt which were introductory to them. It starts from Jehovah's free choice of the people while they were still living as idolaters in Egypt. Jehovah there revealed Himself to them as their God, and entered into a covenant [52] with them; and the covenant included on the one hand the promise of the land of Canaan, and on the other hand a requirement that the people should separate themselves from all forms of idolatry whether native or Egyptian. "In the day that I chose Israel, ... and made Myself known to them in the land of Egypt, ... saying, I am Jehovah your God; in that day I lifted up My hand to them, to bring them out of the land of Egypt, into a land which I had sought out for them. And I said to them, Cast away each man the abomination of his eyes, and defile not yourselves with the block-gods of Egypt. I am Jehovah your God" (vv. 5-7). The point which Ezekiel specially emphasises is that this vocation to be the people of the true God was thrust on Israel without its consent, and that the revelation of Jehovah's purpose evoked no response in the heart of the people. By persistence in idolatry they had virtually renounced the kingship of Jehovah and forfeited their right to the fulfilment of the promise He had given them. And only from regard to His name, that it might not be profaned in the sight of the nations, before whose eyes He had made Himself known to them, did He turn from the purpose He had formed to destroy them in the land of Egypt.

In several respects this account of the occurrences in Egypt goes beyond what we learn from any other source. The historical books contain no reference to the prevalence of specifically Egyptian forms of idolatry among the Hebrews, nor do they mention any threat to exterminate the people for their rebellion. It is not to be supposed, however, that Ezekiel possessed other records of the period before the Exodus than those preserved in the Pentateuch. The fundamental conceptions are those attested by the history, that God first revealed Himself to Israel by the name Jehovah through Moses, and that the revelation was accompanied by a promise of deliverance from Egypt. That the people in spite of this revelation continued to worship idols is an inference from the whole of their subsequent history. And the conflict in the mind of Jehovah between anger against the people's sin and jealousy for His own name is not a matter of history at all, but is an inspired interpretation of the history in the light of the divine holiness, which embraces both these elements.

In the wilderness Israel entered on the second and decisive stage of its probation which falls into two acts, and whose determining factor was the legislation. To the generation of the Exodus Jehovah made known the way of life in a code of law which on its own intrinsic merits ought to have commended itself to their moral sense. The statutes and judgments that were then given were such that "if a man do them he shall live by them" (ver. 11). This thought of the essential goodness of the law as originally given reveals Ezekiel's view of God's relation to men. It derives its significance no doubt from the contrast with legislation of an opposite character afterwards mentioned. Yet even that contrast expresses a conviction in the prophet's mind that morality is not constituted by arbitrary enactments on the part of God, but that there are eternal conditions of ethical fellowship between God and man, and that the law first offered for Israel's acceptance was the embodiment of those ethical relations which flow from the nature of Jehovah. It is probable that Ezekiel has in view the moral precepts of the Decalogue. If so, it is instructive to notice that the Sabbath law is separately mentioned, not as one of the laws by which a man lives, but as a sign of the covenant between Jehovah and Israel. The divine purpose was again defeated by the idolatrous proclivities of the people: "They despised My judgments, and they did not walk in My statutes, and they profaned My Sabbaths, because their heart went after their idols" (ver. 16).

To the second generation in the wilderness the offer of the covenant was renewed, with the same result (vv. 18-24). It should be observed that in both cases the disobedience of the people is answered by two distinct utterances of Jehovah's wrath. The first is a threat of immediate extermination, which is expressed as a momentary purpose of Jehovah, no sooner formed than withdrawn for the sake of His honour (vv. 14, 21). The other is a judgment of a more limited character, uttered in the form of an oath, and in the first case at least actually carried out. For the threat of exclusion from the Promised Land (ver. 15) was enforced so far as the first generation was concerned. Now the parallelism between the two sections leads us to expect that the similar threat of dispersion in ver. 23 is meant to be understood of a judgment actually inflicted. We may conclude, therefore, that ver. 23 refers to the Babylonian exile and the dispersion among the nations, which hung like a doom over the nation during its whole history in Canaan, and is represented as a direct consequence of their transgressions in the wilderness. There seems reason to believe that the particular allusion is to the twenty-eighth chapter of Deuteronomy, where the threat of a dispersion among the nations concludes the long list of curses which will follow disobedience to the law (Deut. xxviii. 64-68). It is true that in that chapter the threat is only conditional; but in the time of Ezekiel it had already been fulfilled, and it is in accordance with his whole conception of the history to read the final issue back into the early period when the national character was determined.

But in addition to this, as if effectually to "conclude them under sin," Jehovah met the hardness of their hearts by imposing on them laws of an opposite character to those first given, and laws which accorded only too well with their baser inclinations: "And I also gave them statutes that were not good, and judgments by which they should not live; and I rendered them unclean in their offerings, by making over all that opened the womb, that I might horrify them" (vv. 25, 26).

This division of the wilderness legislation into two kinds, one good and life-giving and the other not good, presents difficulties both moral and critical which cannot perhaps be altogether removed. The general direction in which the solution must be sought is indeed tolerably clear. The reference is to the law which required the consecration of the firstborn of all animals to Jehovah. This was interpreted in the most rigorous sense as dedication in sacrifice; and then the principle was extended to the case of human beings. The divine purpose in appearing to sanction this atrocious practice was to "horrify" the people--that is to say, the punishment of their idolatry consisted in the shock to their natural instincts and affections caused by the worst development of the idolatrous spirit to which they were delivered. We are not to infer from this that human sacrifice was an element of the original Hebrew religion, and that it was actually based on legislative enactment. The truth appears to be that the sacrifice of children was originally a feature of Canaanitish worship, particularly of the god Melek or Molech, and was only introduced into the religion of Israel in the evil days which preceded the fall of the state.[53] The idea took hold of men's minds that this terrible rite alone revealed the full potency of the sacrificial act; and when the ordinary means of propitiation seemed to fail, it was resorted to as the last desperate expedient for appeasing an offended deity. All that Ezekiel's words warrant us in assuming is that when once the practice was established it was defended by an appeal to the ancient law of the firstborn, the principle of which was held to cover the case of human sacrifices. These laws, relating to the consecration of firstborn animals, are therefore the statutes referred to by Ezekiel; and their defect lies in their being open to such an immoral misinterpretation. This view is in accordance with the probabilities of the case. When we consider the tendency of the Old Testament writers to refer all actual events immediately to the will of God, we can partly understand the form in which Ezekiel expresses the facts; and this is perhaps all that can be said on the moral aspect of the difficulty. It is but an application of the principle that sin is punished by moral obliquity, and precepts which are accommodated to the hardness of men's hearts are by that same hardness perverted to fatal issues. It cannot even be said that there is a radical divergence of view between Ezekiel and Jeremiah on this subject. For when the older prophet, speaking of child-sacrifice, says that Jehovah "commanded it not, neither came it into His mind" (ch. vii. 31 and ch. xix. 5), he must have in view men who justified the custom by an appeal to ancient legislation. And although Jeremiah indignantly repudiates the suggestion that such horrors were contemplated by the law of Jehovah, he hardly in this goes beyond Ezekiel, who declares that the ordinance in question does not represent the true mind of Jehovah, but belongs to a part of the law which was intended to punish sin by delusion.[54]

In consequence of these transactions in the desert Israel entered the land of Canaan under the threat of eventual exile and under the curse of a polluted worship. The subsequent history has little significance from the point of view occupied throughout this discourse; and accordingly Ezekiel disposes of it in three verses (27-29). The entrance on the Promised Land, he says, furnished the opportunity for a new manifestation of disloyalty to Jehovah. He refers to the multiplication of heathen or semi-heathen sanctuaries throughout the land. Wherever they saw a high hill or a leafy tree, they made it a place of sacrifice, and there they practised the impure rites which were the outcome of their false conception of the Deity. To the mind of Ezekiel the unity of Jehovah and the unity of the sanctuary were inseparable ideas: the offence here alluded to is therefore of the same kind as the abominations practised in Egypt and the desert; it is a violation of the holiness of Jehovah. The prophet condenses his scorn for the whole system of religion which led to a multiplication of sanctuaries into a play on the etymology of the word bamah (high places), the point of which, however, is obscure. [55]

II

The Application (vv. 30-44).--Having thus described the origin of idolatry in Israel, and having shown that the destiny of the nation had been determined neither by its deserts nor by its inclinations, but by Jehovah's consistent regard for the honour of His name, the prophet proceeds to bring the lesson of the history to bear on his contemporaries. The Captivity has as yet produced no change in their spiritual condition; in Babylon they still defile themselves with the same abominations as their ancestors, even to the crowning atrocity of child-sacrifice. Their idolatry is if anything more conscious than before, for it takes the shape of a deliberate intention to be as other nations, worshipping wood and stone. It is necessary therefore that once for all Jehovah should assert His sovereignty over Israel, and bend their stubborn will to the accomplishment of His purpose. "As I live, saith the Lord Jehovah, surely with a strong hand, and with an outstretched arm, and wrath poured out, will I be king over you" (ver. 33). But how was this to be done? A heavier chastisement than that which had been inflicted on the exiles could hardly be conceived, yet it had effected nothing for the regeneration of Israel. Surely the time is come when the divine method must be changed, when those who have hardened themselves against the severity of God must be won by His goodness? Such, however, is not the thought expressed in Ezekiel's delineation of the future. It is possible that the description which follows (vv. 34-38) may only be meant as an ideal picture of spiritual processes to be effected by ordinary providential agencies. But certain it is that what Ezekiel is chiefly convinced of is the necessity for further acts of judgment--judgment which shall be decisive, because discriminating, and issuing in the annihilation of all who cling to the evil traditions of the past. This idea, indeed, of further chastisement in store for the exiles is a fixed element of Ezekiel's prophecy. It appears in his earliest public utterance (ch. v.), although it is perhaps only in this chapter that we perceive its full significance.

The scene of God's final dealings with Israel's sin is to be the "desert of the nations." That great barren plateau which stretches between the Jordan and the Euphrates valley, round which lay the nations chiefly concerned in Israel's history, occupies a place in the restoration analogous to that of the wilderness of Sinai (here called the "wilderness of Egypt") at the time of the Exodus. Into that vast solitude Jehovah will gather His people from the lands of their exile, and there He will once more judge them face to face. This judgment will be conducted on the principle laid down in ch. xviii. Each individual shall be dealt with according to his own character as a righteous man or a wicked. They shall be made to "pass under the rod," like sheep when they are counted by the shepherd. [56] The rebels and transgressors shall perish in the wilderness; for "out of the land of their sojournings will I bring them, and into the land of Israel they shall not come" (ver. 38). Those that emerge from the trial are the righteous remnant, who are to be brought into the land by number:[57] these constitute the new Israel, for whom is reserved the glory of the latter days.

The idea that the spiritual transformation of Israel was to be effected during a second sojourn in the wilderness, although a very striking one, occurs only here in the book of Ezekiel, and it can hardly be considered as one of the cardinal ideas of his eschatology. It is in all probability derived from the prophecies of Hosea, although it is modified in accordance with the very different estimate of the nation's history represented by Ezekiel. It is instructive to compare the teaching of these two prophets on this point. To Hosea the idea of a return to the desert presents itself naturally as an element of the process by which Israel is to be brought back to its allegiance to Jehovah. The return to the desert restores the conditions under which the nation had first known and followed Jehovah. He looks back to the sojourn in the wilderness of Sinai as the time of uninterrupted communion between Jehovah and Israel--a time of youthful innocence, when the sinful tendencies which may have been latent in the nation had not developed into actual infidelity. The decay of religion and morality dates from the possession of the land of Canaan, and is traced to the corrupting influence of Canaanitish idolatry and civilisation. It was at Baal-peor that they first succumbed to the attractions of a false religion and became contaminated with the spirit of heathenism. Then the rich produce of the land came to be regarded as the gift of the deities who were worshipped at the local sanctuaries, and this worship with its sensuous accompaniments was the means of estranging the people more and more from the knowledge of Jehovah. Hence the first step towards a renewal of the relation between God and Israel is the withdrawal of the gifts of nature, the suppression of religious ordinances and political institutions; and this is represented as effected by a return to the primitive life of the desert. Then in her desolation and affliction the heart of Israel shall respond once more to the love of Jehovah, who has never ceased to yearn after His unfaithful people. "I will allure her, and bring her into the wilderness, and speak to her heart: ... and she shall make answer there, as in the days of her youth, and as in the day when she came up out of the land of Egypt" (Hos. ii. 14, 15). Here there may be a doubt whether the wilderness is to be taken literally or as a figure for exile, but in either case the image naturally arises out of Hosea's profoundly simple conception of religion.

To Ezekiel, on the other hand, the "wilderness" is a synonym for contention and judgment. It is the scene where the meanness and perversity of man stand out in unrelieved contrast with the majesty and purity of God. He recognises no glad springtime of promise and hope in the history of Israel, no "kindness of her youth" or "love of her espousals" when she went after Jehovah in the land that was not sown (Jer. ii. 2). The difference between Hosea's conception and Ezekiel's is that in the view of the exilic prophet there never has been any true response on the part of Israel to the call of God. Hence a return to the desert can only mean a repetition of the judgments that had marked the first sojourn of the people in the wilderness of Sinai, and the carrying of them to the point of a final decision between the claims of Jehovah and the stubbornness of His people.

If it be asked which of these representations of the past is the true one, the only answer possible is that from the standpoint from which the prophets viewed history both are true. Israel did follow Jehovah through the wilderness, and took possession of the land of Canaan animated by an ardent faith in His power. It is equally true that the religious condition of the people had its dark side, and that they were far from understanding the nature of the God whose name they bore. And a prophet might emphasise the one truth or the other according to the idea of God which it was given him to teach. Hosea, reading the religious symptoms of his own time, sees in it a contrast to the happier period when life was simple and religion comparatively pure, and finds in the desert sojourn an image of the purifying process by which the national life must be renewed. Ezekiel had to do with a more difficult problem. He saw that there was a power of evil which could not be eradicated merely by banishment from the land of Israel--a hard bed-rock of unbelief and superstition in the national character which had never yielded to the influence of revelation; and he dwells on all the manifestations of this which he read in the past. His hope for the future of the cause of God rests no longer on the moral influence of the divine love on the heart of man, but on the power of Jehovah to accomplish His purpose in spite of the resistance of human sin. That was not the whole truth about God's relation to Israel, but it was the truth that needed to be impressed on the generation of the Exile.

Of the final issue at all events Ezekiel is not doubtful. He is a man who is "very sure of God" and sure of nothing else. In man he finds nothing to inspire him with confidence in the ultimate victory of the true religion over polytheism and superstition. His own generation has shown itself fit only to perpetuate the evils of the past--the love of sensuous worship, the insensibility to the claims and nature of Jehovah, which had marked the whole history of Israel. He is compelled for the present to abandon them to their corrupt inclinations, [58] expecting no signs of amendment until his appeal is enforced by signal acts of judgment.

But all this does not shake his sublime faith in the fulfilment of Israel's destiny. Despairing of men, he falls back on what St. Paul calls the "purpose of God according to election" (Rom. ix. 11). And with an insight akin to that of the apostle of the Gentiles, he discerns through all Jehovah's dealings with Israel a principle and an ideal which must in the end prevail over the sin of men. The goal to which the history points stands out clear before the mind of the prophet; and already he sees in vision the restored Israel--a holy people in a renovated land--rendering acceptable worship to the one God of heaven and earth. "For in My holy mountain, in the mountain heights of Israel, saith the Lord Jehovah, there shall serve Me the whole house of Israel: there will I be gracious to them, and there will I require your oblations, and the firstfruits of your offerings, in all your holy things" (ver. 40).

There we have the thought which is expanded in the vision of the purified theocracy which occupies the closing chapters of the book. And it is important to notice this indication that the idea of that vision was present to Ezekiel during the earlier part of his ministry.

Footnotes:

52. The word "covenant" is not here used.

53. Apart from the case of Jephthah, which is entirely exceptional, the first historical instance is that of Ahaz (2 Kings xvi. 3).

54. There still remain the critical difficulties. What are the ambiguous laws to which the prophet refers? It is of course not to be assumed as certain that they are to be found in the Pentateuch, at least in the exact form which Ezekiel has in view. There may have been at that time a

considerable amount of uncodified legislative material which passed vaguely as the law of Jehovah. The "lying pen of the scribes" seems to have been busy in the multiplication of such enactments (Jer. viii. 8). Still, it is a legitimate inquiry whether any of the extant laws of the Pentateuch are open to the interpretation which Ezekiel seems to have in view. The parts of the Pentateuch in which the regulation about the dedication of the firstborn occurs are the so-called Book of the Covenant (Exod. xxii. 29, 30), the short code of Exod. xxxiv. 17-26 (vv. 19 f.), the enactment connected with the institution of the Passover (Exod. xiii. 12 f.), and the priestly ordinance (Numb. xviii. 15). Now, in three of these four passages, the inference to which Ezekiel refers is expressly excluded by the provision that the firstborn of men shall be redeemed. The only one which bears the appearance of ambiguity is that in the Book of the Covenant, where we read: "The firstborn of thy sons shalt thou give unto Me; likewise shalt thou do with thine oxen and thy sheep: seven days it shall be with its dam, on the eighth day thou shalt give it to Me." Here the firstborn children and the firstlings of animals are put on a level; and if any passage in our present Pentateuch would lend itself to the false construction which the later Israelites favoured, it would be this. On the other hand this passage does not contain the particular technical word (he'ebîr) used by Ezekiel. The word probably means simply "dedicate," although this was understood in the sense of dedication by sacrifice. The only passage of the four where the verb occurs is Exod. xiii. 12; and this accordingly is the one generally fixed on by critics as having sanctioned the abuse in question. But apart from its express exemption of firstborn children from the rule, the passage fails in another respect to meet the requirements of the case. The prophet appears to speak here of legislation addressed to the second generation in the wilderness, and this could not refer to the Passover ordinance in its present setting. On the whole we seem to be driven to the conclusion that Ezekiel is not thinking of any part of our present Pentateuch, but to some other law similar in its terms to that of Exod. xiii. 12 f., although equivocal in the same way as Exod. xxii. 29 f. In the text above I have given what appears to me the most natural interpretation of the passage, without referring to the numerous other views which have been put forward. Van Hoonacker, in Le Museon (1893), subjects the various theories to a searching criticism, and arrives himself at the nebulous conclusion that the "statutes which were not good" are not statutes at all, but providential chastisements. That cuts the knot, it does not untie it.

  55. None of the interpretations of ver. 29 gives a satisfactory sense. Cornill rejects it as "absonderlich und aus dem Tenor des ganzen Cap. herausfallend."

  56. See Dillmann's note on Lev. xxvii. 32, quoted by Davidson.

  57. Reading vmsphr for vmsrt with the LXX.

  58. The transition ver. 39 is, however, very difficult. As it stands in the Hebrew text it contains an ironical concession (a good-natured one, Smend thinks) to the persistent advocates of idolatry, the only tolerable translation being, "So serve ye every man his idols, but hereafter ye shall surely hearken to Me, and My holy name ye shall no longer profane with your gifts and your idols." But this sense is not in itself very natural, and the Hebrew construction by which it is expressed would be somewhat strained. The most satisfactory rendering is perhaps that given in the Syriac Version, where two clauses of our Hebrew text are transposed: "But as for you, O house of Israel, if ye will not hearken to Me, go serve every man his idols! Yet hereafter ye shall no more profane My holy name in you," etc.

Chapter XIII - Ohola And Oholibah. Chapter xxiii

The allegory of ch. xxiii. adds hardly any new thought to those which have already been expounded in connection with ch. xvi. and ch. xx. The ideas which enter into it are all such as we are now familiar with. They are: the idolatry of Israel, learned in Egypt and persisted in to the end of her history; her fondness for alliances with the great Oriental empires, which was the occasion of new developments of idolatry; the corruption of religion by the introduction of human sacrifice into the service of Jehovah; and, finally, the destruction of Israel by the hands of the nations whose friendship she had so eagerly courted. The figure under which these facts are presented is the same as in ch. xvi., and many of the details of the earlier prophecy are reproduced here with little variation. But along with these resemblances we find certain characteristic features in this chapter which require attention, and perhaps some explanation.

In its treatment of the history this passage is distinguished from the other two by the recognition of the separate existence of the northern and southern kingdoms. In the previous retrospects Israel has either been treated as a unity (as in ch. xx.), or attention has been wholly concentrated on the fortunes of Judah, Samaria being regarded as on a level with a purely heathen city like Sodom (ch. xvi.). Ezekiel may have felt that he has not yet done justice to the truth that the history of Israel ran in two parallel lines, and that the full significance of God's dealings with the nation can only be understood when the fate of Samaria is placed alongside of that of Jerusalem. He did not forget that he was sent as a prophet to the "whole house of Israel," and indeed all the great pre-exilic prophets realised that their message concerned "the whole family which Jehovah had brought up out of Egypt" (Amos iii. 1). Besides this the chapter affords in many ways an interesting illustration of the workings of the prophet's mind in the effort to realise vividly the nature of his people's sin and the meaning of its fate. In this respect it is perhaps the most finished and comprehensive product of his imagination, although it may not reveal the depth of religious insight exhibited in the sixteenth chapter.

The main idea of the allegory is no doubt borrowed from a prophecy of Jeremiah belonging to the earlier part of his ministry (Jer. iii. 6-13). The fall of Samaria was even then a somewhat distant memory, but the use which Jeremiah makes of it seems to show that the lesson of it had not altogether ceased to impress the mind of the southern kingdom. In the third chapter he reproaches Judah the "treacherous" for not having taken warning from the fate of her sister the "apostate" Israel, who has long since received the reward of her infidelities. The same lesson is implied in the representation of Ezekiel (ver. 11); but as is usual with our prophet, the simple image suggested by Jeremiah is drawn out in an elaborate allegory, into which as many details are crowded as it will bear. In place of the epithets by which Jeremiah characterises the moral condition of Israel and Judah, Ezekiel coins two new and somewhat obscure names--Ohola for Samaria, and Oholibah for Jerusalem. [59]

These women are children of one mother, and afterwards become wives of one husband--Jehovah. This need occasion no surprise in an allegorical representation, although it is contrary to a law which Ezekiel doubtless knew (Lev. xviii. 18). Nor is it strange, considering the freedom with which he handles the facts of history, that the division between Israel and Judah is carried back to the time of the oppression in Egypt. We have indeed no certainty that this view is not historical. The cleavage between the north and the south did not originate with the revolt of Jeroboam. That great schism only brought out elements of antagonism which were latent in the relations of the tribe of Judah to the northern tribes. Of this there are many indications in the earlier history, and for what we know the separation might have existed among the Hebrews in Goshen. Still, it is not probable that Ezekiel was thinking of any such thing. He is bound by the limits of his allegory; and there was no other way by which he could combine the presentation of the two essential elements of his conception--that Samaria and Jerusalem were branches of the one people of Jehovah, and that the idolatry which marked their history had been learned in the youth of the nation in the land of Egypt.

That neither Israel nor Judah ever shook off the spell of their adulterous connection with Egypt, but returned to it again and again down to the close of their history, is certainly one point which the prophet means to impress on the minds of his readers (vv. 8, 19, 27). With this exception the earlier part of the chapter (to ver. 35) deals exclusively with the later developments of idolatry from the eighth century and onwards. And one of the most remarkable things in it is the description of the manner in which first Israel and then Judah was entangled in political relations with the Oriental empires. There seems to be a vein of sarcasm in the sketch of the gallant Assyrian officers who turned the heads of the giddy and frivolous sisters and seduced them from their allegiance to Jehovah: "Ohola doted on her lovers, on the Assyrian warriors [60] clad in purple, governors and satraps, charming youths all of them, horsemen riding on horses; and she lavished on them her fornications, the élite of the sons of Asshur all of them, and with all the idols of all on whom she doted she defiled herself" (vv. 6, 7). The first intimate contact of North Israel with Assyria was in the reign of Menahem (2 Kings xv. 19), and the explanation of it given in these words of Ezekiel must be historically true. It was the magnificent equipment of the Assyrian armies, the imposing display of military power which their appearance suggested, that impressed the politicians of Samaria with a sense of the value of their alliance. The passage therefore throws light on what Ezekiel and the prophets generally mean by the figure of "whoredom." What he chiefly deplores is the introduction of Assyrian idolatry, which was the inevitable sequel to a political union. But that was a secondary consideration in the intention of those who were responsible for the alliance. The real motive of their policy was undoubtedly the desire of one party in the state to secure the powerful aid of the king of Assyria against the rival party. None the less it was an act of infidelity and rebellion against Jehovah.

Still more striking is the account of the first approaches of the southern kingdom to Babylon. After Samaria had been destroyed by the lovers whom she had gathered to her side, Jerusalem still kept up the illicit connection with the Assyrian empire. After Assyria had vanished from the stage of history, she eagerly sought an opportunity to enter into friendly relations with the new Babylonian empire. She did not even wait till she had made their acquaintance, but "when she saw men portrayed on the wall, pictures of Chaldæans portrayed in vermilion, girt with waist-cloths on their loins, with flowing turbans on their heads, all of them champions to look upon, the likeness of the sons of Babel whose native land is Chaldæa--then she doted upon them when she saw them with her eyes, and sent messengers to them to Chaldæa" (vv. 14-16). The brilliant pictures referred to are those with which Ezekiel must have been familiar on the walls of the temples and palaces of Babylon. The representation, however, cannot be understood literally, since the Jews could have had no opportunity of even seeing the Babylonian pictures "on the wall" until they had sent ambassadors there. [61]

The meaning of the prophet is clear. The mere report of the greatness of Babylon was sufficient to excite the passions of Oholibah, and she began with blind infatuation to court the advances of the distant strangers who were to be her ruin. The exact historic reference, however, is uncertain. It cannot be to the compact between Merodach-baladan and Hezekiah, since at that time the initiative seems to have been taken by the rebel prince, whose sovereignty over Babylon proved to be of short duration. It may rather be some transaction about the time of the battle of Carchemish (604) that Ezekiel is thinking of; but we have not as yet sufficient knowledge of the circumstances to clear up the allusion.

Before the end came the soul of Jerusalem was alienated from her latest lovers--another touch of fidelity to the historical situation. But it was now too late. The soul of Jehovah is alienated from Oholibah (vv. 17, 18), and she is already handed over to the fate which had overtaken her less guilty sister Ohola. The principal agents of her punishment are the Babylonians and all the Chaldæans; but under their banner marches a host of other nations--Pekod and Shoa and Koa, [62] and, somewhat strangely, the sons of Asshur. In the pomp and circumstance of war which had formerly fascinated her imagination, they shall come against her, and after their cruel manner execute upon her the judgment meted out to adulterous women: "Thou hast walked in the way of thy sister, and I will put her cup into thy hand. Thus saith the Lord Jehovah, The cup of thy sister shalt thou drink,--deep and wide, and of large content,--filled with drunkenness and anguish--the cup of horror and desolation, the cup of thy sister Samaria. And thou shalt drink it and drain it out,[63] ... for I have spoken it, saith the Lord Jehovah" (vv. 31-34).

Up to this point the allegory has closely followed the actual history of the two kingdoms. The remainder of the chapter (vv. 36-49) forms a pendant to the principal picture, and works out the central theme from a different point of view. Here Samaria and Jerusalem are regarded as still existent, and judgment is pronounced on both as if it were still future. This is thoroughly in keeping with Ezekiel's ideal delineations. The limitations of space and time are alike transcended. The image, once clearly conceived, fixes itself in the writer's mind, and must be allowed to exhaust its meaning before it is finally dismissed. The distinctions of far and near, of past and present and future, are apt to disappear in the intensity of his reverie. It is so here. The figures of Ohola and Oholibah are so real to the prophet that they are summoned once more to the tribunal to hear the recital of their "abominations" and receive the sentence which has in fact been already partly executed. Whether he is thinking at all of the ten tribes then in exile and awaiting further punishment it would be difficult to say. We see, however, that the picture is enriched with many features for which there was no room in the more historic form of the allegory, and perhaps the desire for completeness was the chief motive for thus amplifying the figure. The description of the conduct of the two harlots (vv. 40-44) is exceedingly graphic, [64] and is no doubt a piece of realism drawn from life. Otherwise the section contains nothing that calls for elucidation. The ideas are those which we have already met with in other connections, and even the setting in which they are placed presents no element of novelty.

Thus with words of judgment, and without a ray of hope to lighten the darkness of the picture, the prophet closes this last survey of his people's history.

Footnotes:

59. It is not certain what is the exact meaning wrapped up in these designations. A very slight change in the pointing of the Hebrew would give the sense "her tent" for Ohola and "my tent in her" for Oholibah. This is the interpretation adopted by most commentators, the idea being that while the tent or temple of Jehovah was in Judah, Samaria's "tent" (religious system) was of her own making. It is not likely, however, that Ezekiel has any such sharp contrast in his mind, since the whole of the argument proceeds on the similarity of the course pursued by the two kingdoms. It is simpler to take the word Ohola as meaning "tent," and Oholibah as "tent in her," the signification of the names being practically identical. The allusion is supposed to be to the tents of the high places which formed a marked feature of the idolatrous worship practised in both divisions of the country (cf. ch. xvi. 16). This is better, though not entirely convincing, since it does not explain how Ezekiel came to fix on this particular emblem as a mark of the religious condition of Israel. It may be worth noting that the word 'hlh contains the same number of consonants as smrn (= Samaria, although the word is always written smrvn in the Old Testament), and 'hlyvh the same number as yrvslm. The Eastern custom of giving similar names to children of the same family (like Hasan and Husein) is aptly instanced by Smend and Davidson.

60. This word is of doubtful meaning.

61. Smend thinks that the illustration is explained by the secluded life of females in the East, which makes it quite intelligible that a woman might be captivated by the picture of a man she had never seen, and try to induce him to visit her.

62. On these names of nations see Davidson's Commentary, p. 168, and the reference there to Delitzsch.

63. The words rendered in E.V., "thou shalt be laughed to scorn and had in derision" (ver. 32), "and pluck off thy own breasts" (ver. 34), are wanting in the LXX. The passage gains in force by the omission. The words translated "break the sherds thereof" (ver. 34) are unintelligible.

64. Although the text in parts of vv. 42, 43 is very imperfect.

John J. Skinner

Chapter XIV - Final Oracles Against Jerusalem. Chapters xxii., xxiv

The close of the first period of Ezekiel's work was marked by two dramatic incidents, which made the day memorable both in the private life of the prophet and in the history of the nation. In the first place it coincided exactly with the commencement of the siege of Jerusalem. The prophet's mysterious knowledge of what was happening at a distance was duly recorded, in order that its subsequent confirmation through the ordinary channels of intelligence might prove the divine origin of his message (ch. xxiv. 1, 2). That Ezekiel actually did this we have no reason to doubt. Then the sudden death of his wife on the evening of the same day, and his unusual behaviour under the bereavement, caused a sensation among the exiles which the prophet was instructed to utilise as a means of driving home the appeal just made to them. These transactions must have had a profound effect on Ezekiel's fellow-captives. They made his personality the centre of absorbing interest to the Jews in Babylon; and the two years of silence on his part which ensued were to them years of anxious foreboding about the result of the siege.

At this juncture the prophet's thoughts naturally are occupied with the subject which hitherto formed the principal burden of his prophecy. The first part of his career accordingly closes, as it had begun, with a symbol of the fall of Jerusalem. Before this, however, he had drawn out the solemn indictment against Jerusalem which is given in ch. xxii., although the finishing touches were probably added after the destruction of the city. The substance of that chapter is so closely related to the symbolic representation in the first part of ch. xxiv. that it will be convenient to consider it here as an introduction to the concluding oracles addressed more directly to the exiles of Tel-abib.

I

The purpose of this arraignment--the most stately of Ezekiel's orations--is to exhibit Jerusalem in her true character as a city whose social condition is incurably corrupt. It begins with an enumeration of the prevalent sins of the capital (vv. 2-16); it ends with a denunciation of the various classes into which society was divided (vv. 23-31); while the short intervening passage is a figurative description of the judgment which is now inevitable (vv. 17-22).

1. The first part of the chapter, then, is a catalogue of the "abominations" which called down the vengeance of Heaven upon the city of Jerusalem. The offences enumerated are nearly the same as those mentioned in the definitions of personal righteousness and wickedness given in ch. xviii. It is not necessary to repeat what was there said about the characteristics of the moral ideal which had been formed in the mind of Ezekiel. Although he is dealing now with a society, his point of view is quite different from that represented by purely allegorical passages like chs. xvi. and xxiii. The city is not idealised and treated as a moral individual, whose relations to Jehovah have to be set forth in symbolic and figurative language. It is conceived as an aggregate of individuals bound together in social relations; and the sins charged against it are the actual transgressions of the men who are members of the community. Hence the standard of public morality is precisely the same as that which is elsewhere applied to the individual in his personal relation to God; and the sins enumerated are attributed to the city merely because they are tolerated and encouraged in individuals by laxity of public opinion and the force of evil example. Jerusalem is a community in which these different crimes are perpetrated: "Father and mother are despised in thee; the stranger is oppressed in the midst of thee; orphan and widow are wronged in thee; slanderous men seeking blood have been in thee; flesh with the blood is eaten in thee; lewdness is committed in the midst of thee; the father's shame is uncovered in thee; she that was unclean in her separation hath been humbled in thee." So the grave and measured indictment runs on. It is because of these things that Jerusalem as a whole is "guilty" and "unclean" and has brought near her day of retribution (ver. 4). Such a conception of corporate guilt undoubtedly appeals more directly to our ordinary conscience of public morality than the more poetic representations where Jerusalem is compared to a faithless and treacherous woman. We have no difficulty in judging of any modern city in the very same way as Ezekiel here judges Jerusalem; and in this respect it is interesting to notice the social evils which he regards as marking out that city as ripe for destruction.

There are three features of the state of things in Jerusalem in which the prophet recognises the symptoms of an incurable social condition. The first is the loss of a true conception of God. In ancient Israel this defect necessarily assumed the form of idolatry. Hence the multiplication of idols appropriately finds a place among the marks of the "uncleanness" which made Jerusalem hateful in the eyes of Jehovah (ver. 3). But the root of idolatry in Israel was the incapacity or the unwillingness of the people to live up to the lofty conception of the divine nature which was taught by the prophets. Throughout the ancient world religion was felt to be the indispensable bond of society, and the gods that were worshipped reflected more or less fully the ideals that swayed the life of the community. To Israel the religion of Jehovah represented the highest social ideal that was then known on earth. It meant righteousness, and purity, and brotherhood, and compassion for the poor and distressed. When these virtues decayed she forgot Jehovah (ver. 12)--forgot His character even if she remembered His name--and the service of false gods was the natural and obvious expression of the fact. There is therefore a profound truth in Ezekiel's mind when he numbers the idols of Jerusalem amongst the indications of a degenerate society. They were the evidence that she had lost the sense of God as a holy and righteous spiritual presence in her midst, and that loss was at once the source and the symptom of widespread moral declension. It is one of the chief lessons of the Old Testament that a religion which was neither the product of national genius nor the embodiment of national aspiration, but was based on supernatural revelation, proved itself in the history of Israel to be the only possible safeguard against the tendencies which made for social disintegration.

A second mark of depravity which Ezekiel discovers in the capital is the perversion of certain moral instincts which are just as essential to the preservation of society as a true conception of God. For if society rests at one end on religion, it rests at the other on instinct. The closest and most fundamental of human relations depend on innate perceptions which may be easily destroyed, but which when destroyed can scarcely be recovered. The sanctities of marriage and the family will hardly bear the coarse scrutiny of utilitarian ethics; yet they are the foundation on which the whole social fabric is built. And there is no part of Ezekiel's indictment of Jerusalem which conveys to our minds a more vivid sense of utter corruption than where he speaks of the loss of filial piety and revolting forms of sexual impurity as prevalent sins in the city. Here at least he carries the conviction of every moralist with him. He instances no offence of this kind which would not be branded as unnatural by any system of ethics as heartily as it is by the Old Testament. It is possible, on the other hand, that he ranks on the same level with these sins ceremonial impurities appealing to feelings of a different order, to which no permanent moral value can be attached. When, for example, he instances eating with the blood [65] as an "abomination," he appeals to a law which is no longer binding on us. But even that regulation was not so worthless, from a moral point of view, at that time as we are apt to suppose. The abhorrence of eating blood was connected with certain sacrificial ideas which attributed a mystic significance to the blood as the seat of animal life. So long as these ideas existed no man could commit this offence without injuring his moral nature and loosening the divine sanctions of morality as a whole. It is a false illuminism which seeks to disparage the moral insight of the prophet on the ground that he did not teach an abstract system of ethics in which ceremonial precepts were sharply distinguished from duties which we consider moral. [66]

The third feature of Jerusalem's guilty condition is lawless violation of human rights. Neither life nor property was secure. Judicial murders were frequent in the city, and minor forms of oppression, such as usury, spoliation of the unprotected, and robbery, were of daily occurrence. The administration of justice was corrupted by systematic bribery and perjury, and the lives of innocent men were ruthlessly sacrificed under the forms of law. This after all is the aspect of things which bulks most largely in the prophet's indictment. Jerusalem is addressed as a "city shedding blood in her midst," and throughout the accusation the charge of bloodshed is that which constantly recurs. Misgovernment and party strife, and perhaps religious persecution, had converted the city into a vast human shambles, and the blood of the innocent slain cried aloud to heaven for vengeance. "Of what avail," asks the prophet, "are the stores of wealth piled up in the hands of a few against this damning witness of blood? Jehovah smites His hand [in derision] against her gains that she has made, and against her blood which is in her midst. How can her heart stand or her hands be strong in the days when He deals with her?" (vv. 13, 14). Drained of her best blood, given over to internecine strife, and stricken with the cowardice of conscious guilt, Jerusalem, already disgraced among the nations, must fall an easy victim to the Chaldæan invaders, who are the agents of Jehovah's judgments.

2. But the most serious aspect of the situation is that which is dealt with in the peroration of the chapter (vv. 23-31). Outbursts of vice and lawlessness such as has been described may occur in any society, but they are not necessarily fatal to a community so long as it possesses a conscience which can be roused to effective protest against them. Now the worst thing about Jerusalem was

that she lacked this indispensable condition of recovery. No voice was raised on the side of righteousness, no man dared to stem the tide of wickedness that swept through her streets. Not merely that she harboured within her walls men guilty of incest and robbery and murder, but that her leading classes were demoralised, that public spirit had decayed among her citizens, marked her as incapable of reformation. She was "a land not watered," [67] "and not rained upon in a day of indignation" (ver. 24); the springs of her civic virtue were dried up, and a blight spread through all sections of her population. [68] Ezekiel's impeachment of different classes of society brings out this fact with great force. First of all the ancient institutions of social order, government, priesthood, and prophecy were in the hands of men who had lost the spirit of their office and abused their position for the advancement of private interests. Her princes [69] have been, instead of humane rulers and examples of noble living, cruel and rapacious tyrants, enriching themselves at the cost of their subjects (ver. 25). The priests, whose function was to maintain the outward ordinances of religion and foster the spirit of reverence, have done their utmost, by falsification of the Torah, to bring religion into contempt and obliterate the distinction between the holy and the profane (ver. 26). The nobles had been a pack of ravening wolves, imitating the rapacity of the court, and hunting down prey which the royal lion would have disdained to touch (ver. 27). As for the professional prophets--those degenerate representatives of the old champions of truth and mercy--we have already seen what they were worth (ch. xiii.). They who should have been foremost to denounce civil wrong are fit for nothing but to stand by and bolster up with lying oracles in the name of Jehovah a constitution which sheltered crimes like these (ver. 28).

From the ruling classes the prophet's glance turns for a moment to the "people of the land," the dim common population, where virtue might have been expected to find its last retreat. It is characteristic of the age of Ezekiel that the prophets begin to deal more particularly with the sins of the masses as distinct from the classes. This was due partly perhaps to a real increase of ungodliness in the body of the people, but partly also to a deeper sense of the importance of the individual apart from his position in the state. These prophets seem to feel that if there had been anywhere among rich or poor an honest response to the will of Jehovah it would have been a token that God had not altogether rejected Israel. Jeremiah puts this view very strongly when in the fifth chapter he says that if one man could be found in Jerusalem who did justice and sought truth the Lord would pardon her; and his vain search for that man begins among the poor. It is this same motive that leads Ezekiel to include the humble citizen in his survey of the moral condition of Jerusalem. It is little wonder that under such leaders they had cast off the restraints of humanity, and oppressed those who were still more defenceless than themselves. But it showed nevertheless that real religion had no longer a foothold in the city. It proved that the greed of gain had eaten into the very heart of the people and destroyed the ties of kindred and mutual sympathy, through which alone the will of Jehovah could be realised. No matter although they were obscure householders, without political power or responsibility; if they had been good men in their private relations, Jerusalem would have been a better place to live in. Ezekiel indeed does not go so far as to say that a single good life would have saved the city. He expects of a good man that he be a man in the full sense--a man who speaks boldly on behalf of righteousness and resists the prevalent evils with all his strength: "I sought among them a man to build up a fence, and to stand in the breach before Me on behalf of the land, that it might not be destroyed; and I found none. So I poured out My indignation upon them; with the fire of My wrath I consumed them: I have returned their way upon their head, saith the Lord Jehovah" (vv. 30, 31).

3. But we should misunderstand Ezekiel's position if we supposed that his prediction of the speedy destruction of Jerusalem was merely an inference from his clear insight into the necessary conditions of social welfare which were being violated by her rulers and her citizens. That is one part of his message, but it could not stand alone. The purpose of the indictment we have considered is simply to explain the moral reasonableness of Jehovah's action in the great act of judgment which the prophet knows to be approaching. It is no doubt a general law of history that moribund communities are not allowed to die a natural death. Their usual fate is to perish in the struggle for existence before some other and sounder nation. But no human sagacity can foresee how that law will be verified in any particular case. It may seem clear to us now that Israel must have fallen sooner or later before the advance of the great Eastern empires, but an ordinary observer could not have foretold with the confidence and precision which mark the predictions of Ezekiel in what manner and within what time the end would come. Of that aspect of the prophet's mind no explanation can be given save that God revealed His secret to His servants the prophets.

Now this element of the prophecy seems to be brought out by the image of Jerusalem's fate which occupies the middle verses of the chapter (vv. 17-22). The city is compared to the crucible in which all the refuse of Israel's national life is to undergo its final trial by fire. The prophet sees in imagination the terror-stricken provincial population swept into the capital before the approach of the Chaldæans; and he says, "Thus does Jehovah cast His ore into the furnace--the silver, the brass, the iron, the lead, and the tin; and He will kindle the fire with His anger, and blow upon it till He have consumed the impurities of the land." The image of the smelting-pot had been used by Isaiah as an emblem of purifying judgment, the object of which was the removal of injustice and the restoration of the state to its former splendour: "I will again bring My hand upon thee, smelting out thy dross with lye and taking away all thine alloy; and I will make thy judges to be again as aforetime, and thy counsellors as at the beginning: thereafter thou shalt be called the city of righteousness, the faithful city" (Isa. i. 25, 26). Ezekiel, however, can hardly have contemplated such a happy result of the operation. The whole house of Israel has become dross, from which no precious metal can be extracted; and the object of the smelting is only the demonstration of the utter worthlessness of the people for the ends of God's kingdom. The more refractory the material to be dealt with the fiercer must be the fire that tests it; and the severity of the exterminating judgment is the only thing symbolised by the metaphor as used by Ezekiel. In this he follows Jeremiah, who applies the figure in precisely the same sense: "The bellows snort, the lead is consumed of the fire; in vain he smelts and smelts: but the wicked are not taken away. Refuse silver shall men call them, for the Lord hath rejected them" (Jer. vi. 29, 30). In this way the section supplements the teaching of the rest of the chapter. Jerusalem is full of dross--that has been proved by the enumeration of her crimes and the estimate of her social condition. But the fire which consumes the dross represents a special providential intervention bringing the history of the state to a summary and decisive conclusion. And the Refiner who superintends the process is Jehovah, the Holy One of Israel, whose righteous will is executed by the march of conquering hosts, and revealed to men in His dealings with the people whom He had known of all the families of the earth.

II

The chapter we have just studied was evidently not composed with a view to immediate publication. It records the view of Jerusalem's guilt and punishment which was borne in upon the mind of the prophet in the solitude of his chamber, but it was not destined to see the light until the whole of his teaching could be submitted in its final form to a wider and more receptive audience. It is equally obvious that the scenes described in ch. xxiv. were really enacted in the full view of the exiled community. We have reached the crisis of Ezekiel's ministry. For the last time until his warnings of doom shall be fulfilled he emerges from his partial seclusion, and in symbolism whose vivid force could not have failed to impress the most listless hearer he announces once more the destruction of the Hebrew nation. The burden of his message is that that day--the tenth day of the tenth month of the ninth year--marked the beginning of the end. "On that very day"--a day to be commemorated for seventy long years by a national fast (Zech. viii. 19; cf. vii. 5)--Nebuchadnezzar was drawing his lines round Jerusalem. The bare announcement to men who knew what a Chaldæan siege meant must have sent a thrill of consternation through their minds. If this vision of what was happening in a distant land should prove true, they must have felt that all hope of deliverance was now cut off. Sceptical as they may have been of the moral principles that lay behind Ezekiel's prediction, they could not deny that the issue he foresaw was only the natural sequel to the fact he so confidently announced.

The image here used of the fate of Jerusalem would recall to the minds of the exiles the ill-omened saying which expressed the reckless spirit prevalent in the city: "This city is the pot, and we are the flesh" (ch. xi. 3). It was well understood in Babylon that these men were playing a desperate game, and did not shrink from the horrors of a siege. "Set on the pot," then, cries the prophet to his listeners, "set it on, and pour in water also, and gather the pieces into it, every good joint, leg and shoulder; fill it with the choicest bones. Take them from the best of the flock, and then pile up the wood [70] under it; let its pieces be boiled and its bones cooked within it" (vv. 3-5). This part of the parable required no explanation; it simply represents the terrible miseries endured by the population of Jerusalem during the siege now commencing. But then by a sudden transition the speaker turns the thoughts of his hearers to another aspect of the judgment (vv. 6-8). The city itself is like a rusty caldron, unfit for any useful purpose until by some means it has been cleansed from its impurity. It is as if the crimes that had been perpetrated in Jerusalem had stained her very stones with blood. She had not even taken steps to conceal the traces of her wickedness; they lie like blood on the bare rock, an open witness to her guilt. Often Jehovah had sought to purify her by more measured chastisements, but it has now been proved that "her much rust will not go from her except by fire" [71] (ver. 12). Hence the end of the siege will be twofold. First of all the contents of the caldron will be indiscriminately thrown out--a figure for the dispersion and captivity of the inhabitants; and then the pot must be set empty on the glowing coals till its rust is thoroughly burned out--a symbol of the burning of the city and its subsequent desolation (ver. 11). The idea that the material world may contract defilement through the sins of those who live in it is one that is hard for us to realise, but it is in keeping with the view of sin presented by Ezekiel, and indeed by the Old Testament generally. There are certain natural emblems of sin, such as uncleanness or

John J. Skinner

disease or uncovered blood, etc., which had to be largely used in order to educate men's moral perceptions. Partly these rest on the analogy between physical defect and moral evil; but partly, as here, they result from a strong sense of association between human deeds and their effects or circumstances. Jerusalem is unclean as a place where wicked deeds have been done, and even the destruction of the sinners cannot in the mind of Ezekiel clear her from the unhallowed associations of her history. She must lie empty and dreary for a generation, swept by the winds of heaven before devout Israelites can again twine their affections round the hope of her glorious future. [72]

Even while delivering this message of doom to the people the prophet's heart was burdened by the presentiment of a great personal sorrow. He had received an intimation that his wife was to be taken from him by a sudden stroke, and along with the intimation a command to refrain from all the usual signs of mourning. "So I spake to the people" (as recorded in vv. 1-14) "in the morning, and my wife died in the evening" (ver. 18). Just one touch of tenderness escapes him in relating this mysterious occurrence. She was the "delight of his eyes": that phrase alone reveals that there was a fountain of tears sealed up within the breast of this stern preacher. How the course of his life may have been influenced by a bereavement so strangely coincident with a change in his whole attitude to his people we cannot even surmise. Nor is it possible to say how far he merely used the incident to convey a lesson to the exiles, or how far his private grief was really swallowed up in concern for the calamity of his country. All we are told is that "in the morning he did as he was commanded." He neither uttered loud lamentations, nor disarranged his raiment, nor covered his head, nor ate the "bread of men," [73] nor adopted any of the customary signs of mourning for the dead. When the astonished neighbours inquire the meaning of his strange demeanour, he assures them that his conduct now is a sign of what theirs will be when his words have come true. When the tidings reach them that Jerusalem has actually fallen, when they realise how many interests dear to them have perished--the desolation of the sanctuary, the loss of their own sons and daughters--they will experience a sense of calamity which will instinctively discard all the conventional and even the natural expressions of grief. They shall neither mourn nor weep, but sit in dumb bewilderment, haunted by a dull consciousness of guilt which yet is far removed from genuine contrition of heart. They shall pine away in their iniquities. For while their sorrow will be too deep for words, it will not yet be the godly sorrow that worketh repentance. It will be the sullen despair and apathy of men disenchanted of the illusions on which their national life was based, of men left without hope and without God in the world.

Here the curtain falls on the first act of Ezekiel's ministry. He appears to have retired for the space of two years into complete privacy, ceasing entirely his public appeals to the people, and waiting for the time of his vindication as a prophet. The sense of restraint under which he has hitherto exercised the function of a public teacher cannot be removed until the tidings have reached Babylon that the city has fallen. Meanwhile, with the delivery of this message, his contest with the unbelief of his fellow-captives comes to an end. But when that day arrives "his mouth shall be open, and he shall be no more dumb." A new career will open out before him, in which he can devote all his powers of mind and heart to the inspiring work of reviving faith in the promises of God, and so building up a new Israel out of the ruins of the old.

Footnotes:

65. On the reading here see above, p. [5]150.

66. The eighth verse, referring to the Sabbath and the sanctuary, is rejected by Cornill on internal grounds, but for that there is no justification. If the verse is retained, it will be seen that the enumeration of sins corresponds pretty closely in substance, though not in arrangement, with the precepts of the Decalogue.

67. Read with the LXX. mtrh, instead of mthrh, "purified."

68. This appears to be the meaning of the simile in ver. 24; the judgment is conceived as a parching drought, and the point of the comparison is that its severity is not tempered by the fertilising streams which should have descended on the people in the shape of sound political and religious guidance.

69. Following the LXX. we should read "whose princes" ('sr nsy'yh) for "the conspiracy of her prophets" (qsr nvy'yh) in ver. 25.

70. Read tsym, "wood," instead of tsmym, "bones" (Boettcher and others).

71. The words "except by fire" represent an emendation proposed by Cornill, which may be somewhat bold, but certainly expresses an idea in the passage.

72. Cf. Jer. xiii. 27: "Thou shalt not be pronounced clean, for how long a time yet!"

73. I.e., as generally explained, bread brought by sympathising friends, to be shared with the mourning household: cf. Jer. xvi. 7; 2 Sam. iii. 35. Wellhausen, however, proposes to read "bread of mourners" ('nsym for 'nsym).

Part III - Prophecies Against Foreign Nations

Chapter XV - Ammon, Moab, Edom, And Philistia. Chapter xxv

The next eight chapters (xxv.-xxxii.) form an intermezzo in the book of Ezekiel. They are inserted in this place with the obvious intention of separating the two sharply contrasted situations in which our prophet found himself before and after the siege of Jerusalem. The subject with which they deal is indeed an essential part of the prophet's message to his time, but it is separate from the central interest of the narrative, which lies in the conflict between the word of Jehovah in the hands of Ezekiel and the unbelief of the exiles among whom he lived. The perusal of this group of chapters is intended to prepare the reader for the completely altered conditions under which Ezekiel was to resume his public ministrations. The cycle of prophecies on foreign peoples is thus a sort of literary analogue of the period of suspense which interrupted the continuity of Ezekiel's work in the way we have seen. It marks the shifting of the scenes behind the curtain before the principal actors again step on the stage.

It is natural enough to suppose that the prophet's mind was really occupied during this time with the fate of Israel's heathen neighbours; but that alone does not account for the grouping of the oracles before us in this particular section of the book. Not only do some of the chronological notices carry us far past the limit of the time of silence referred to, but it will be found that nearly all these prophecies assume that the fall of Jerusalem is already known to the nations addressed. It is therefore a mistaken view which holds that in these chapters we have simply the result of Ezekiel's meditations during his period of enforced seclusion from public duty. Whatever the nature of his activity at this time may have been, the principle of arrangement here is not chronological, but literary; and no better motive for it can be suggested than the writer's sense of dramatic propriety in unfolding the significance of his prophetic life.

In uttering a series of oracles against heathen nations, Ezekiel follows the example set by some of his greatest predecessors. The book of Amos, for example, opens with an impressive chapter of judgments on the peoples lying immediately round the borders of Palestine. The thundercloud of Jehovah's anger is represented as moving over the petty states of Syria before it finally breaks in all its fury over the two kingdoms of Judah and Israel. Similarly the books of Isaiah and Jeremiah contain continuous sections dealing with various heathen powers, while the book of Nahum is wholly occupied with a prediction of the ruin of the Assyrian empire. And these are but a few of the more striking instances of a phenomenon which is apt to cause perplexity to close and earnest students of the Old Testament. We have here to do, therefore, with a standing theme of Hebrew prophecy; and it may help us better to understand the attitude of Ezekiel if we consider for a moment some of the principles involved in this constant preoccupation of the prophets with the affairs of the outer world.

At the outset it must be understood that prophecies of this kind form part of Jehovah's message to Israel. Although they are usually cast in the form of direct address to foreign peoples, this must not lead us to imagine that they were intended for actual publication in the countries to which they refer. A prophet's real audience always consisted of his own countrymen, whether his discourse was about themselves or about their neighbours. And it is easy to see that it was impossible to declare the purpose of God concerning Israel in words that came home to men's business and bosoms, without taking account of the state and the destiny of other nations. Just as it would not be possible nowadays to forecast the future of Egypt without alluding to the fate of the Ottoman empire, so it was not possible then to describe the future of Israel in the concrete manner characteristic of the prophets without indicating the place reserved for those peoples with whom it had close intercourse. Besides this, a large part of the national consciousness of Israel was made up of interests, friendly or the reverse, in neighbouring states. The Hebrews had a keen eye for national idiosyncrasies, and the simple international relations of those days were almost as vivid and personal as of neighbours living in the same village. To be an Israelite was to be something characteristically different from a Moabite, and that again from an Edomite or a Philistine, and every patriotic Israelite had a shrewd sense of what the difference was. We cannot read the utterances of the prophets with regard to any of these nationalities without seeing that they often appeal to perceptions deeply lodged in the popular mind, which could be utilised to convey the spiritual lessons which the prophets desired to teach.

It must not be supposed, however, that such prophecies are in any degree the expression of national vanity or jealousy. What the prophets aim at is to elevate the thoughts of Israel to the sphere of eternal truths of the kingdom of God; and it is only in so far as these can be made to touch the conscience of the nation at this point that they appeal to what we may call its international sentiments. Now the question we have to ask is, What spiritual purpose for Israel is served by the announcements of the destiny of the outlying heathen populations? There are of course special interests attaching to each particular prophecy which it would be difficult to classify. But, speaking generally, prophecies of this class had a moral value for two reasons. In the first place they re-echo and confirm the sentence of judgment passed on Israel herself. They do this in two ways: they illustrate the principle on which Jehovah deals with His own people, and His character as the righteous judge of men. Israel was to be destroyed for her national sins, her contempt of Jehovah, and her breaches of the moral law. But other nations, though more excusable, were not less guilty than Israel. The same spirit of ungodliness, in different forms, was manifested by Tyre, by Egypt, by Assyria, and by the petty states of Syria. Hence, if Jehovah was really the righteous ruler of the world, He must visit upon these nations their iniquities. Wherever a "sinful kingdom" was found, whether in Israel or elsewhere, that kingdom must be removed from its place among the nations. This appears most clearly in the book of Amos, who, though he enunciates the paradoxical truth that Israel's sin must be punished just because it was the only people that Jehovah had known, nevertheless, as we have seen, thundered forth similar judgments on other nations for their flagrant violation of the universal law written in the human heart. In this way therefore the prophets enforced on their contemporaries the fundamental lesson of their teaching that the disasters which were coming on them were not the result of the caprice or impotence of their Deity, but the execution of His moral purpose, to which all men everywhere are subject. But again, not only was the principle of the judgment emphasised, but the manner in which it was to be carried out was more clearly exhibited. In all cases the pre-exilic prophets announce that the overthrow of the Hebrew states was to be effected either by the Assyrians or the Babylonians. These great world-powers were in succession the instruments fashioned and used by Jehovah for the performance of His great work in the earth. Now it was manifest that if this anticipation was well founded it involved the overthrow of all the nations in immediate contact with Israel. The policy of the Mesopotamian monarchs was well understood; and if their wonderful successes were the revelation of the divine purpose, then Israel would not be judged alone. Accordingly we find in most instances that the chastisement of the heathen is either ascribed directly to the invaders or else to other agencies set in motion by their approach. The people of Israel or Judah were thus taught to look on their fate as involved in a great scheme of divine providence, overturning all the existing relations which gave them a place among the nations of the world and preparing for a new development of the purpose of Jehovah in the future.

When we turn to that ideal future we find a second and more suggestive aspect of these prophecies against the heathen. All the prophets teach that the destiny of Israel is inseparably bound up with the future of God's kingdom on earth. The Old Testament never wholly shakes off the idea that the preservation and ultimate victory of the true religion demands the continued existence of the one people to whom the revelation of the true God had been committed. The indestructibility of Israel's national life depends on its unique position in relation to the purposes of Jehovah, and it is for this reason that the prophets look forward with unwavering confidence to a time when the knowledge of Jehovah shall go forth from Israel to all the nations of mankind. And this point of view we must try to enter into if we are to understand the meaning of their declarations concerning the fate of the surrounding nations. If we ask whether an independent future is reserved in the new dispensation for the peoples with whom Israel had dealings in the past, we find that different and sometimes conflicting answers are given. Thus Isaiah predicts a restoration of Tyre after the lapse of seventy years, while Ezekiel announces its complete and final destruction. It is only when we consider these utterances in the light of the prophets' general conception of the kingdom of God that we discern the spiritual truth that gives them an abiding significance for the instruction of all ages. It was not a matter of supreme religious importance to know whether Phoenicia or Egypt or Assyria would retain their old place in the world, and share indirectly in the blessings of the Messianic age. What men needed to be taught then, and what we need to remember still, is that each nation holds its position in subordination to the ends of God's government, that no power or wisdom or refinement will save a state from destruction when it ceases to serve the interests of His kingdom. The foreign peoples that come under the survey of the prophets are as yet strangers to the true God, and are therefore destitute of that which could secure them a place in the reconstruction of political relationships of which Israel is to be the religious centre. Sometimes they are represented as having by their hostility to Israel or their pride of heart so encroached on the sovereignty of Jehovah that their doom is already sealed. At other times they are conceived as converted to the knowledge of the true God, and as gladly accepting the place assigned to them in the humanity of the future by consecrating their wealth and power to the service of His people Israel. In all cases it is their attitude to Israel and the God of Israel that determines their destiny: that is the great truth which the prophets design to impress on their countrymen. So long as the cause of religion was identified with the fortunes of the people of Israel no higher conception of the redemption of mankind could be formed than that of a willing subjection of the nations of the earth to the word of Jehovah which went forth from Jerusalem (cf. Isa. ii. 2-4). And whether any particular nation should survive to participate in the glories of that latter day depends on the view taken of its present condition and its fitness for incorporation in the universal empire of Jehovah soon to be established.

We now know that this was not the form in which Jehovah's purpose of salvation was destined to be realised in the history of the world. Since the coming of Christ the people of Israel has lost its distinctive and central position as the bearer of the hopes and promises of the true religion. In its place we have a spiritual kingdom of men united by faith in Jesus Christ, and in the worship of one Father in spirit and in truth--a kingdom which from its very nature can have no local centre or political organisation. Hence the conversion of the heathen can no longer be conceived as national homage paid to the seat of Jehovah's sovereignty on Zion; nor is the unfolding of the divine plan of universal salvation bound up with the extinction of the nationalities which once symbolised the hostility of the world to the kingdom of God. This fact has an important bearing on the question of the fulfilment of the foreign prophecies of the Old Testament. Literal fulfilment is not to be looked for in this case any more than in the delineations of Israel's future, which are after all the predominant element of Messianic prediction. It is true that the nations passed under review have now vanished from history, and in so far as their fall was brought about by causes operating in the world in which the prophets moved, it must be recognised as a partial but real vindication of the truth of their words. But the details of the prophecies have not been historically verified. All attempts to trace their accomplishment in events that took place long afterwards and in circumstances which the prophets themselves never contemplated only lead us astray from the real interest which belongs to them. As concrete embodiments of the eternal principles exhibited in the rise and fall of nations they have an abiding significance for the Church in all ages; but the actual working out of these principles in history could not in the nature of things be complete within the limits of the world known to the inhabitants of Judæa. If we are to look for their ideal fulfilment, we shall only find it in the progressive victory of Christianity over all forms of error and superstition, and in the dedication of all the resources of human civilisation--its wealth, its commercial enterprise, its political power--to the advancement of the kingdom of our God and His Christ.

***

It was natural from the special circumstances in which he wrote, as well as from the general character of his teaching, that Ezekiel, in his oracles against the heathen powers, should present only the dark side of God's providence. Except in the case of Egypt, the nations addressed are threatened with annihilation, and even Egypt is to be reduced to a condition of utter impotence and humiliation. Very characteristic also is his representation of the purpose which comes to light in this series of judgments. It is to be a great demonstration to all the earth of the absolute sovereignty of Jehovah. "Ye shall know that I am Jehovah" is the formula that sums up the lesson of each nation's fall. We observe that the prophet starts from the situation created by the fall of Jerusalem. That great calamity bore in the first instance the appearance of a triumph of heathenism over Jehovah the God of Israel. It was, as the prophet elsewhere expresses it, a profanation of His holy name in the eyes of the nations. And in this light it was undoubtedly regarded by the petty principalities around Palestine, and perhaps also by the more distant and powerful spectators, such as Tyre and Egypt. From the standpoint of heathenism the downfall of Israel meant the defeat of its tutelary Deity; and the neighbouring nations, in exulting over the tidings of Jerusalem's fate, had in their minds the idea of the prostrate Jehovah unable to save His people in their hour of need. It is not necessary to suppose that Ezekiel attributes to them any consciousness of Jehovah's claim to be the only living and true God. It is the paradox of revelation that He who is the Eternal and Infinite first revealed Himself to the world as the God of Israel; and all the misconceptions that sprang out of that fact had to be cleared away by His self-manifestation in historical acts that appealed to the world at large. Amongst these acts the judgment of the heathen nations holds the first place in the mind of Ezekiel. A crisis has been reached at which it becomes necessary for Jehovah to vindicate His divinity by the destruction of those who have exalted themselves against Him. The world must learn once for all that Jehovah is no mere tribal god, but the omnipotent ruler of the universe. And this is the preparation for the final disclosure of His power and Godhead in the restoration of Israel to its own land, which will speedily follow the overthrow of its ancient foes. This series of prophecies forms thus an appropriate introduction to the third division of the book, which deals with the formation of the new people of Jehovah.

It is somewhat remarkable that Ezekiel's survey of the heathen nations is restricted to those in the immediate vicinity of the land of Canaan. Although he had unrivalled opportunities of becoming acquainted with the remote countries of the East, he confines his attention to the Mediterranean states which had long played a part in Hebrew history. The peoples dealt with are seven in number--Ammon, Moab, Edom, the Philistines, Tyre, Sidon, and Egypt. The order of the enumeration is geographical: first the inner circle of Israel's immediate neighbours, from Ammon on the east round to Sidon in the extreme north; then outside the circle the preponderating world-power of Egypt. It is not altogether an accidental circumstance that five of these nations are named in the twenty-seventh chapter of Jeremiah as concerned in the project of rebellion against Nebuchadnezzar in the early part of Zedekiah's reign. Egypt and Philistia are not mentioned there, but we may surmise at least that Egyptian diplomacy was secretly at work pulling the wires which set the puppets in motion. This fact, together with the omission of Babylon from the list of threatened nations, shows that Ezekiel regards the judgment as falling within the period of Chaldæan supremacy, which he appears to have estimated at forty years. What is to be the fate of Babylon itself he nowhere intimates, a conflict between that great world-power and Jehovah's purpose being no part of his system. That Nebuchadnezzar is to be the agent of the overthrow of Tyre and the humiliation of Egypt is expressly stated; and although the crushing of the smaller states is ascribed to other agencies, we can hardly doubt that these were conceived as indirect consequences of the upheaval caused by the Babylonian invasion.

***

Ch. xxv., then, consists of four brief prophecies addressed respectively to Ammon, Moab, Edom, and the Philistines. A few words on the fate prefigured for each of these countries will suffice for the explanation of the chapter.

1. Ammon (vv. 2-7) lay on the edge of the desert, between the upper waters of the Jabbok and the Arnon, separated from the Jordan by a strip of Israelitish territory from twenty to thirty miles wide. Its capital, Rabbah, mentioned here (ver. 5), was situated on a southern tributary of the Jabbok, and its ruins still bear amongst the Arabs the ancient national name Ammân. Although their country was pastoral (milk is referred to in ver. 4 as one of its chief products), the Ammonites seem to have made some progress in civilisation. Jeremiah (ch. xlix. 4) speaks of them as trusting in their treasures; and in this chapter Ezekiel announces that they shall be for a spoil to the nations (ver. 7). After the deportation of the transjordanic tribes by Tiglath-pileser, Ammon seized the country that had belonged to the tribe of Gad, its nearest neighbour on the west. This encroachment is denounced by the prophet Jeremiah in the opening words of his oracle against Ammon: "Hath Israel no children? or has he no heir? why doth Milcom [the national deity of the Ammonites] inherit Gad, why hath his [Milcom's] folk settled in his [Gad's] cities" (Jer. xlix. 1). We have already seen (ch. xxi.) that the Ammonites took part in the rebellion against Nebuchadnezzar, and stood out after the other members of the league had gone back from their purpose. But this temporary union with Jerusalem did nothing to abate the old national animosity, and the disaster of Judah was the signal for an exhibition of malignant satisfaction on the part of Ammon. "Because thou hast said, Aha, against My sanctuary when it was profaned, and the land of Israel when it was laid waste, and the house of Judah when it went into captivity," etc. (ver. 3)--for this crowning offence against the majesty of Jehovah, Ezekiel denounces an exterminating judgment on Ammon. The land shall be given up to the "children of the East"--i.e., the Bedouin Arabs--who shall pitch their tent encampments in it, eating its fruits and drinking its milk, and turning the "great city" Rabbah itself into a resting-place for camels (vv. 4, 5). It is not quite clear (though it is commonly assumed) that the children of the East are regarded as the actual conquerors of Ammon. Their possession of the country may be the consequence rather than the cause of the destruction of civilisation, the encroachment of the nomads being as inevitable under these circumstances as the extension of the desert itself where water fails.

2. Moab [74] (vv. 8-11) comes next in order. Its proper territory, since the settlement of Israel in Canaan, was the elevated tableland south of the Arnon, along the lower part of the Dead Sea. But the tribe of Reuben, which bordered it on the north, was never able to hold its ground against the

superior strength of Moab, and hence the latter nation is found in possession of the lower and more fertile district stretching northwards from the Arnon, now called the Belka. All the cities, indeed, which are mentioned in this chapter as belonging to Moab--Beth-jeshimoth, Baal-meon, and Kirjathaim--were situated in this northern and properly Israelite region. These were the "glory of the land," which were now to be taken away from Moab (ver. 9). In Israel Moab appears to have been regarded as the incarnation of a peculiarly offensive form of national pride, [75] of which we happen to have a monument in the famous Moabite Stone, which was erected by Mesha in the ninth century b.c. to commemorate the victories of Chemosh over Jehovah and Israel. The inscription shows, moreover, that in the arts of civilised life Moab was at that early time no unworthy rival of Israel itself. It is for a special manifestation of this haughty and arrogant spirit in the day of Jerusalem's calamity that Ezekiel pronounces Jehovah's judgment on Moab: "Because Moab hath said, Behold, the house of Judah is like all the nations" (ver. 8). These words no doubt reflect accurately the sentiment of Moab towards Israel, and they presuppose a consciousness on the part of Moab of some unique distinction pertaining to Israel in spite of all the humiliations it had undergone since the time of David. And the thought of Moab may have been more widely disseminated among the nations than we are apt to suppose: "The kings of the earth believed not, neither all the inhabitants of the world, that the adversary and the enemy should enter into the gates of Jerusalem" (Lam. iv. 12). The Moabites at all events breathed a sigh of relief when Israel's pretensions to religious ascendency seemed to be confuted, and thereby they sealed their own doom. They share the fate of the Ammonites, their land being handed over for a possession to the sons of the East (ver. 10).

Both these nations, Ammon and Moab, were absorbed by the Arabs, as Ezekiel had foretold; but Ammon at least preserved its separate name and nationality through many changes of fortune down to the second century after Christ.

3. Edom (vv. 12-14), famous in the Old Testament for its wisdom (Jer. xlix. 7; Obad. 8), occupied the country to the south of Moab from the Dead Sea to the head of the Gulf of Akaba. In Old Testament times the centre of its power was in the region to the east of the Arabah Valley, a position of great commercial importance, as commanding the caravan route from the Red Sea port of Elath to Northern Syria. From this district the Edomites were afterwards driven (about 300 b.c.) by the Arabian tribe of the Nabatæans, when they took up their abode in the south of Judah. None of the surrounding nations were so closely akin to Israel as Edom, and with none were its relations more embittered and hostile. The Edomites had been subjugated and nearly exterminated by David, had been again subdued by Amaziah and Uzziah, but finally recovered their independence during the attack of the Syrians and Ephraimites on Judah in the reign of Ahaz. The memory of this long struggle produced in Edom a "perpetual enmity," an undying hereditary hatred towards the kingdom of Judah. But that which made the name of Edom to be execrated by the later Jews was its conduct after the fall of Jerusalem. The prophet Obadiah represents it as sharing in the spoil of Jerusalem (ver. 10), and as "standing in the crossway to cut off those that escaped" (ver. 14). Ezekiel also alludes to this in the thirty-fifth chapter (ver. 5), and tells us further that in the time of the captivity the Edomites seized part of the territory of Israel (vv. 10-12), from which indeed the Jews were never able altogether to dislodge them. For the guilt they thus incurred by taking advantage of the humiliation of Jehovah's people, Ezekiel here threatens them with extinction; and the execution of the divine vengeance is in their case entrusted to the children of Israel themselves (vv. 13, 14). They were, in fact, finally subdued by John Hyrcanus in 126 b.c., and compelled to adopt the Jewish religion. But long before then they had lost their prestige and influence, their ancient seats having passed under the dominion of the Arabs in common with all the neighbouring countries.

4. The Philistines (vv. 15-17)--the "immigrants" who had settled along the Mediterranean coast, and who were destined to leave their name to the whole country--had evidently played a part very similar to the Edomites at the time of the destruction of Jerusalem; but of this nothing is known beyond what is here said by Ezekiel. They were at this time a mere "remnant" (ver. 16), having been exhausted by the Assyrian and Egyptian wars. Their fate is not precisely indicated in the prophecy. They were in point of fact gradually extinguished by the revival of Jewish domination under the Asmonean dynasty.

One other remark may here be made, as showing the discrimination which Ezekiel brought to bear in estimating the characteristics of each separate nation. He does not ascribe to the greater powers, Tyre and Sidon and Egypt, the same petty and vindictive jealousy of Israel which actuated the diminutive nationalities dealt with in this chapter. These great heathen states, which played so imposing a part in ancient civilisation, had a wide outlook over the affairs of the world; and the injuries they inflicted on Israel were due less to the blind instinct of national hatred than to the pursuit of far-reaching schemes of selfish interest and aggrandisement. If Tyre rejoices over the fall of Jerusalem, it is because of the removal of an obstacle to the expansion of her commercial enterprise. When Egypt is described as having been an occasion of sin to the people of God, what is meant is that she had drawn Israel into the net of her ambitious foreign policy, and led her away from the path of safety pointed out by Jehovah's will through the prophets. Ezekiel pays a tribute to the grandeur of their position by the care he bestows on the description of their fate. The smaller nations embodying nothing of permanent value for the advancement of humanity, he dismisses each with a short and pregnant oracle announcing its doom. But when he comes to the fall of Tyre and of Egypt his imagination is evidently impressed; he lingers over all the details of the picture, he returns to it again and again, as if he would penetrate the secret of their greatness and understand the potent fascination which their names exercised throughout the world. It would be entirely erroneous to suppose that he sympathises with them in their calamity, but certainly he is conscious of the blank which will be caused by their disappearance from history; he feels that something will have vanished from the earth whose loss will be mourned by the nations far and near. This is most apparent in the prophecy on Tyre, to which we now proceed.

Footnotes:

74. The words "and Seir" in ver. 8 are wanting in the true text of the LXX., and should probably be omitted.

75. Isa. xvi. 6, xxv. 11; Jer. xlviii. 29, 42.

Chapter XVI - Tyre. Chapters xxvi., xxix. 17-21

In the time of Ezekiel Tyre was still at the height of her commercial prosperity. Although not the oldest of the Phoenician cities, she held a supremacy among them which dated from the thirteenth century b.c., [76] and she had long been regarded as the typical embodiment of the genius of the remarkable race to which she belonged. The Phoenicians were renowned in antiquity for a combination of all the qualities on which commercial greatness depends. Their absorbing devotion to the material interests of civilisation, their amazing industry and perseverance, their resourcefulness in assimilating and improving the inventions of other peoples, the technical skill of their artists and craftsmen, but above all their adventurous and daring seamanship, conspired to give them a position in the old world such as has never been quite rivalled by any other nation of ancient or modern times. In the grey dawn of European history we find them acting as pioneers of art and culture along the shores of the Mediterranean, although even then they had been displaced from their earliest settlements in the Ægean and the coast of Asia Minor by the rising commerce of Greece. Matthew Arnold has drawn a brilliant imaginative picture of this collision between the two races, and the effect it had on the dauntless and enterprising spirit of Phoenicia:--

> As some grave Tyrian trader, from the sea,
> Descried at sunrise an emerging prow
> Lifting the cool-hair'd creepers stealthily,
> The fringes of a southward-facing brow
> Among the Ægæan isles;
> And saw the merry Grecian coaster come,
> Freighted with amber grapes, and Chian wine,
> Green, bursting figs, and tunnies steep'd in brine--
> And knew the intruders on his ancient home,
> The young light-hearted masters of the waves--
> And snatch'd his rudder and shook out more sail;
> And day and night held on indignantly
> O'er the blue Midland waters with the gale,
> Betwixt the Syrtes and soft Sicily,
> To where the Atlantic raves
> Outside the western straits; and unbent sails
> There, where down cloudy cliffs, through sheets of foam,
> Shy traffickers, the dark Iberians, come;
> And on the beach undid his corded bales. [77]

It is that spirit of masterful and untiring ambition kept up for so many centuries that throws a halo of romance round the story of Tyre.

In the oldest Greek literature, however, Tyre is not mentioned, the place which she afterwards held being then occupied by Sidon. But after the decay of Sidon the rich harvest of her labours fell into the lap of Tyre, which thenceforth stands out as the foremost city of Phoenicia. She owed her pre-eminence partly to the wisdom and energy with which her affairs were administered, but partly also to the strength of her natural situation. The city was built both on the mainland and on a row of islets about half a mile from the shore. This latter portion contained the principal buildings (temples and palaces), the open place where business was transacted, and the two harbours. It was no doubt from it that the city derived its name (tsvr = Rock); and it always was looked on as the central part of Tyre. There was something in the appearance of the island city--the Venice of antiquity, rising from mid-ocean with her "tiara of proud towers"--which seemed to mark her out as destined to be mistress of the sea. It also made a siege of Tyre an arduous and a tedious undertaking, as many a conqueror found to his cost. Favoured then by these advantages, Tyre speedily gathered the traffic of Phoenicia into her own hands, and her wealth and luxury were the wonder of the nations. She was known as "the crowning city, whose merchants were princes, and her traffickers the honourable of the earth" (Isa. xxiii. 8). She became the great commercial emporium of the world. Her colonies were planted all over the islands and coasts of the Mediterranean, and the one most frequently mentioned in the Bible, Tarshish, was in Spain, beyond Gibraltar. Her seamen had ventured beyond the Pillars of Hercules, and undertook distant Atlantic voyages to the Canary Islands on the south and the coasts of Britain on the north. The most barbarous and inhospitable regions were ransacked for the metals and other products needed to supply the requirements of civilisation, and everywhere she found a market for her own wares and manufactures. The carrying trade of the Mediterranean was almost entirely conducted in her ships, while her richly laden caravans traversed all the great routes that led into the heart of Asia and Africa.

It so happens that the twenty-seventh chapter of Ezekiel is one of the best sources of information we possess as to the varied and extensive commercial relations of Tyre in the sixth century b.c. [78] It will therefore be better to glance shortly at its contents here rather than in its proper connection in the development of the prophet's thought. It will easily be seen that the description is somewhat idealised; no details are given of the commodities which Tyre sold to the nations--only as an afterthought (ver. 33) is it intimated that by sending forth her wares she has enriched and satisfied many nations. So the goods which she bought of them are not represented as given in exchange for anything else; Tyre is poetically conceived as an empress ruling the peoples by the potent spell of her influence, compelling them to drudge for her and bring to her feet the gains they have acquired by their heavy labour. Nor can the list of nations [79] or their gifts be meant as exhaustive; it only includes such things as served to exhibit the immense variety of useful and costly articles which ministered to the wealth and luxury of Tyre. But making allowance for this, and for the numerous difficulties which the text presents, the passage has evidently been compiled with great care; it shows a minuteness of detail and fulness of knowledge which could not have been got from books, but displays a lively personal interest in the affairs of the world which is surprising in a man like Ezekiel.

The order followed in the enumeration of nations is not quite clear, but is on the whole geographical. Starting from Tarshish in the extreme west (ver. 12), the prophet mentions in succession Javan (Ionia), Tubal, and Meshech (two tribes to the south-east of the Black Sea), and Togarmah (usually identified with Armenia) (vv. 13, 14). These represent the northern limit of the Phoenician markets. The reference in the next verse (v. 15) is doubtful, on account of a difference between the Septuagint and the Hebrew text. If with the former we read "Rhodes" instead of "Dedan," it embraces the nearer coasts and islands of the Mediterranean, and this is perhaps on the whole the more natural sense. In this case it is possible that up to this point the description has been confined to the sea trade of Phoenicia, if we may suppose that the products of Armenia reached Tyre by way of the Black Sea. At all events the overland traffic occupies a space in the list out of proportion to its actual importance, a fact which is easily explained from the prophet's standpoint. First, in a line from south to north, we have the nearer neighbours of Phoenicia--Edom, Judah, Israel, and Damascus (vv. 16-18). Then the remoter tribes and districts of Arabia--Uzal [80] (the chief city of Yemen), Dedan (on the eastern side of the Gulf of Akaba), Arabia and Kedar (nomads of the eastern desert), Havilah, [81] Sheba, and Raamah (in the extreme south of the Arabian peninsula) (vv. 19-22). Finally the countries tapped by the eastern caravan route--Haran (the great trade centre in Mesopotamia), Canneh (? Calneh, unknown), Eden (differently spelt from the garden of Eden, also unknown), Assyria, and Chilmad (unknown) (ver. 23). These were the "merchants" and "traders" of Tyre, who are represented as thronging her market-place with the produce of their respective countries.

The imports, so far as we can follow the prophet's enumeration, are in nearly all cases characteristic products of the regions to which they are assigned. Spain is known to have furnished all the metals here mentioned--silver, iron, lead, and tin. Greece and Asia Minor were centres of the slave traffic (one of the darkest blots on the commerce of Phoenicia), and also supplied hardware. Armenia was famous as a horse-breeding country, and thence Tyre procured her supply of horses and mules. The ebony and tusks of ivory must have come from Africa; and if the Septuagint is right in reading "Rhodes" in ver. 15, these articles can only have been collected there for shipment to Tyre. [82] Through Edom come pearls and precious stones. [83] Judah and Israel furnish Tyre with agricultural and natural produce, as they had done from the days of David and Solomon--wheat and oil, wax and honey, balm and spices. Damascus yields the famous "wine of Helbon"--said to be the only vintage that the Persian kings would drink--perhaps also other choice wines. [84] A rich variety of miscellaneous articles, both natural and manufactured, is contributed by Arabia,--wrought iron (perhaps sword-blades) from Yemen; saddle-cloths from Dedan; sheep and goats from the Bedouin tribes; gold, precious stones, and aromatic spices from the caravans of Sheba. Lastly, the Mesopotamian countries provide the costly textile fabrics from the looms of Babylon so highly prized in antiquity--"costly garments, mantles of blue, purple, and broidered work," "many-coloured carpets," and "cords twisted and durable." [85]

This survey of the ramifications of Tyrian commerce will have served its purpose if it enables us to realise in some measure the conception which Ezekiel had formed of the power and prestige of the maritime city, whose destruction he so confidently announced. He knew, as did Isaiah before him, how deeply Tyre had struck her roots in the life of the old world, how indispensable her existence seemed to be to the whole fabric of civilisation as then constituted. Both prophets represent the nations as lamenting the downfall of the city which had so long ministered to their material welfare. The overthrow of Tyre would be felt as a world-wide calamity; it could hardly be contemplated except as part of a radical subversion of the established order of things. This is what Ezekiel has in view, and his attitude towards Tyre is governed by his expectation of a great shaking of the nations which is to usher in the perfect kingdom of God. In the new world to which he looks forward no place will be found for Tyre, not even the subordinate position of a handmaid to the people of God which Isaiah's vision of the future had assigned to her. Beneath all her opulence and refinement the prophet's eye detected that which was opposed to the mind of Jehovah--the irreligious spirit which is the temptation of a mercantile community, manifesting itself in overweening pride and self-exaltation, and in sordid devotion to gain as the highest end of a nation's existence.

The twenty-sixth chapter is in the main a literal prediction of the siege and destruction of Tyre by Nebuchadnezzar. It is dated from the year in which Jerusalem was captured, and was certainly written after that event. The number of the month has accidentally dropped out of the text, so that we cannot tell whether at the time of writing the prophet had received actual intelligence of the fall of the city. At all events it is assumed that the fate of Jerusalem is already known in Tyre, and the manner in which the tidings were sure to have been received there is the immediate occasion of the prophecy. Like many other peoples, Tyre had rejoiced over the disaster which had befallen the Jewish state; but her exultation had a peculiar note of selfish calculation, which did not escape the notice of the prophet. Ever mindful of her own interest, she sees that a barrier to the free development of her commerce has been removed, and she congratulates herself on the fortunate turn which events have taken: "Aha! the door of the peoples is broken, it is turned towards me; she that was full hath been laid waste!" [86] (ver. 2). Although the relations of the two countries had often been friendly and sometimes highly advantageous to Tyre, she had evidently felt herself hampered by the existence of an independent state on the mountain ridge of Palestine. The kingdom of Judah, especially in days when it was strong enough to hold Edom in subjection, commanded the caravan routes to the Red Sea, and doubtless prevented the Phoenician merchants from reaping the full profit of their ventures in that direction. It is probable that at all times a certain proportion of the revenue of the kings of Judah was derived from toll levied on the Tyrian merchandise that passed through their territory; and what they thus gained represented so much loss to Tyre. It was, to be sure, a small item in the mass of business transacted on the exchange of Tyre. But nothing is too trivial to enter into the calculations of a community given over to the pursuit of gain; and the satisfaction with which the fall of Jerusalem was regarded in Tyre showed how completely she was debased by her selfish commercial policy, how oblivious she was to the spiritual interests bound up with the future of Israel.

Having thus exposed the sinful cupidity and insensibility of Tyre, the prophet proceeds to describe in general terms the punishment that is to overtake her. Many nations shall be brought up against her, irresistible as the sea when it comes up with its waves; her walls and fortifications shall be rased; the very dust shall be scraped from her site, so that she is left "a naked rock" rising out of the sea, a place where fishermen spread their nets to dry, as in the days before the city was built.

Then follows (vv. 7-14) a specific announcement of the manner in which judgment shall be executed on Tyre. The recent political attitude of the city left no doubt as to the quarter from which immediate danger was to be apprehended. The Phoenician states had been the most powerful members of the confederacy that was formed about 596 to throw off the yoke of the Chaldæans, and they were in open revolt at the time when Ezekiel wrote. They had apparently thrown in their lot with Egypt, and a conflict with Nebuchadnezzar was therefore to be expected. Tyre had every reason to avoid a war with a first-rate power, which could not fail to be disastrous to her commercial interests. But her inhabitants were not destitute of martial spirit; they trusted in the strength of their position and their command of the sea, and they were in the mood to risk everything rather than again renounce their independence and their freedom. But all this avails nothing against the purpose which Jehovah has purposed concerning Tyre. It is He who brings Nebuchadnezzar, the king of kings, from the north with his army and his siege-train, and Tyre shall fall before his assault, as Jerusalem has already fallen. First of all, the Phoenician cities on the mainland shall be ravaged and laid waste, and then operations commence against the mother-city herself. The description of the siege and capture of the island fortress is given with an abundance of graphic details, although, strangely enough, without calling attention to the peculiar method of attack that was necessary for the reduction of Tyre. The great feature of the siege would be the construction of a huge mole between the shore and the island; once the wall was reached the attack would proceed precisely as in the case of an inland town, in the manner depicted on Assyrian monuments. When the breach is made in the fortifications the whole army pours into the city, and for the first time in her history the walls of Tyre shake with the rumbling of chariots in her streets. The conquered city is then given up to slaughter and pillage, her songs and her music are stilled for ever, her stones and timber and dust are cast into the sea, and not a trace remains of the proud mistress of the waves.

In the third strophe (vv. 15-21) the prophet describes the dismay which will be caused when the crash of the destruction of Tyre resounds along the coasts of the sea. All the "princes of the sea" (perhaps the rulers of the Phoenician colonies in the Mediterranean) are represented as rising from their thrones, and putting off their stately raiment, and sitting in the dust bewailing the fate of the city. The dirge in which they lift up their voices (vv. 17, 18) is given by the Septuagint in a form which preserves more nearly than the Hebrew the structure as well as the beauty which we should expect in the original:--

> *How is perished from the sea--*
> *The city renowned!*
> *She that laid her terror--*
> *On all its inhabitants!*
> *[Now] are the isles affrighted--*
> *In the day of thy falling!*

But this beautiful image is not strong enough to express the prophet's sense of the irretrievable ruin that hangs over Tyre. By a bold flight of imagination he turns from the mourners on earth to follow in thought the descent of the city into the under-world (vv. 19-21). The idea that Tyre might rise from her ruins after a temporary eclipse and recover her old place in the world was one that would readily suggest itself to any one who understood the real secret of her greatness. To the mind of Ezekiel the impossibility of her restoration lies in the fixed purpose of Jehovah, which includes, not only her destruction, but her perpetual desolation. "When I make thee a desolate city, like the cities that are not inhabited; when I bring up against thee the deep, and the great waters cover thee; then I will bring thee down with them that go down to the pit, with the people of old time, and I will make thee dwell in the lowest parts of the earth, like the immemorial waste places, with them that go down to the pit, that thou be not inhabited nor establish thyself in the land of the living." The whole passage is steeped in weird poetic imagery. The "deep" [87] suggests something more than the blue waters of the Mediterranean: it is the name of the great primeval Ocean, out of which the habitable world was fashioned, and which is used as an emblem of the irresistible judgments of God. [88] The "pit" is the realm of the dead, Sheôl, conceived as situated under the earth, where the shades of the departed drag out a feeble existence from which there is no deliverance. The idea of Sheôl is a frequent subject of poetical embellishment in the later books of the Old Testament; and of this we have an example here when the prophet represents the once populous and thriving city as now a denizen of that dreary place. But the essential meaning he wishes to convey is that Tyre is numbered among the things that were. She "shall be sought, and shall not be found any more for ever," because she has entered the dismal abode of the dead, whence there is no return to the joys and activities of the upper world.

Such then is the anticipation which Ezekiel in the year 586 had formed of the fate of Tyre. No candid reader will suppose that the prophecy is anything but what it professes to be--a bonâ-fide prediction of the total destruction of the city in the immediate future and by the hands of Nebuchadnezzar. When Ezekiel wrote, the siege of Tyre had not begun; and however clear it may have been to observant men that the next stage in the campaign would be the reduction of the Phoenician cities, the prophet is at least free from the suspicion of having prophesied after the event. The remarkable absence of characteristic and special details from the account of the siege is the best proof that he is dealing with the future from the true prophetic standpoint and clothing a divinely imparted conviction in images supplied by a definite historical situation. Nor is there any reason to doubt that in some form the prophecy was actually published among his fellow-exiles at the date to which it is assigned. On these points critical opinion is fairly unanimous. But when we come to the question of the fulfilment of the prediction we find ourselves in the region of controversy, and, it must be admitted, of uncertainty. Some expositors, determined at all hazards to vindicate Ezekiel's prophetic authority, maintain that Tyre was actually devastated by Nebuchadnezzar in the manner described by the prophet, and seek for confirmations of their view in the few historical notices we possess of this period of Nebuchadnezzar's reign. Others, reading the history differently, arrive at the conclusion that Ezekiel's calculations were entirely at fault, that Tyre was not captured by the Babylonians at all, and that his oracle against Tyre must be reckoned amongst the unfulfilled prophecies of the Old Testament. Others again seek to reconcile an impartial historical judgment with a high conception of the function of prophecy, and find in the

The Expositor's Bible: The Book of Ezekiel

undoubted course of events a real though not an exact verification of the words uttered by Ezekiel. It is indeed almost by accident that we have any independent corroboration of Ezekiel's anticipation with regard to the immediate future of Tyre. Oriental discoveries have as yet brought to light no important historical monuments of the reign of Nebuchadnezzar; and outside of the book of Ezekiel itself we have nothing to guide us except the statement of Josephus, based on Phoenician and Greek authorities, [89] that Tyre underwent a thirteen years' siege by the Babylonian conqueror. There is no reason whatever to call in question the reliability of this important information, although the accompanying statement that the siege began in the seventh year of Nebuchadnezzar is certainly erroneous. But unfortunately we are not told how the siege ended. Whether it was successful or unsuccessful, whether Tyre was reduced or capitulated, or was evacuated or beat off her assailants, is nowhere indicated. To argue from the silence of the historians is impossible; for if one man argues that a catastrophe that took place "before the eyes of all Asia" would not have passed unrecorded in historical books, another might urge with equal force that a repulse of Nebuchadnezzar was too uncommon an event to be ignored in the Phoenician annals. [90] On the whole the most reasonable hypothesis is perhaps that after the thirteen years the city surrendered on not unfavourable terms; but this conclusion is based on other considerations than the data or the silence of Josephus.

The chief reason for believing that Nebuchadnezzar was not altogether successful in his attack on Tyre is found in a supplementary prophecy of Ezekiel's, given in the end of the twenty-ninth chapter (vv. 17-21). It was evidently written after the siege of Tyre was concluded, and so far as it goes it confirms the accuracy of Josephus' sources. It is dated from the year 570, sixteen years after the fall of Jerusalem; and it is, in fact, the latest oracle in the whole book. The siege of Tyre therefore, which had not commenced in 586, when ch. xxvi. was written, was finished before 570; and between these terminal dates there is just room for the thirteen years of Josephus. The invasion of Phoenicia must have been the next great enterprise of the Babylonian army in Western Asia after the destruction of Judah, and it was only the extraordinary strength of Tyre that enabled it to protract the struggle so long. Now what light does Ezekiel throw on the issue of the siege? His words are: "Nebuchadnezzar, king of Babylon, has made his army to serve a great service against Tyre; every head made bald and every shoulder peeled, yet he and his army got no wages out of Tyre for the service which he served against her." The prophet then goes on to announce that the spoils of Egypt should be the recompense to the army for their unrequited labour against Tyre, inasmuch as it was work done for Jehovah. Here then, we have evidence first of all that the long siege of Tyre had taxed the resources of the besiegers to the utmost. The "peeled shoulders" and the "heads made bald" is a graphic detail which alludes not obscurely to the monotonous navvy work of carrying loads of stones and earth to fill up the narrow channel between the mainland and the island, [91] so as to allow the engines to be brought up to the walls. Ezekiel was well aware of the arduous nature of the undertaking, the expenditure of human effort and life which was involved, in the struggle with natural obstacles; and his striking conception of these obscure and toiling soldiers as unconscious servants of the Almighty shows how steadfast was his faith in the word he proclaimed against Tyre. But the important point is that they obtained from Tyre no reward--at least no adequate reward--for their herculean labours. The expression used is no doubt capable of various interpretations. It might mean that the siege had to be abandoned, or that the city was able to make extremely easy terms of capitulation, or, as Jerome suggests, that the Tyrians had carried off their treasures by sea and escaped to one of their colonies. In any case it shows that the historical event was not in accordance with the details of the earlier prophecy. That the wealth of Tyre would fall to the conquerors is there assumed as a natural consequence of the capture of the city. But whether the city was actually captured or not, the victors were somehow disappointed in their expectation of plunder. The rich spoil of Tyre, which was the legitimate reward of their exhausting toil, had slipped from their eager grasp; to this extent at least the reality fell short of the prediction, and Nebuchadnezzar had to be compensated for his losses at Tyre by the promise of an easy conquest of Egypt.

But if this had been all it is not probable that Ezekiel would have deemed it necessary to supplement his earlier prediction in the way we have seen after an interval of sixteen years. The mere circumstance that the sack of Tyre had failed to yield the booty that the besiegers counted on was not of a nature to attract attention amongst the prophet's auditors, or to throw doubt on the genuineness of his inspiration. And we know that there was a much more serious difference between the prophecy and the event than this. It is from what has just been said extremely doubtful whether Nebuchadnezzar actually destroyed Tyre, but even if he did she very quickly recovered much of her former prosperity and glory. That her commerce was seriously crippled during the struggle with Babylonia we may well believe, and it is possible that she never again was what she had been before this humiliation came upon her. But for all that the enterprise and prosperity of Tyre continued for many ages to excite the admiration of the most enlightened nations of antiquity.

The destruction of the city, therefore, if it took place, had not the finality which Ezekiel had anticipated. Not till after the lapse of eighteen centuries could it be said with approximate truth that she was like "a bare rock in the midst of the sea."

The most instructive fact for us, however, is that Ezekiel reissued his original prophecy, knowing that it had not been literally fulfilled. In the minds of his hearers the apparent falsification of his predictions had revived old prejudices against him which interfered with the prosecution of his work. They reasoned that a prophecy so much out of joint with the reality was sufficient to discredit his claim to be an authoritative exponent of the mind of Jehovah; and so the prophet found himself embarrassed by a recurrence of the old unbelieving attitude which had hindered his public activity before the destruction of Jerusalem. He has not for the present "an open mouth" amongst them, and he feels that his words will not be fully received until they are verified by the restoration of Israel to its own land. But it is evident that he himself did not share the view of his audience, otherwise he would certainly have suppressed a prophecy which lacked the mark of authenticity. On the contrary he published it for the perusal of a wider circle of readers, in the conviction that what he had spoken was a true word of God, and that its essential truth did not depend on its exact correspondence with the facts of history. In other words, he believed in it as a true reading of the principles revealed in God's moral government of the world--a reading which had received a partial verification in the blow which had been dealt at the pride of Tyre, and which would receive a still more signal fulfilment in the final convulsions which were to introduce the day of Israel's restoration and glory. Only we must remember that the prophet's horizon was necessarily limited; and as he did not contemplate the slow development and extension of the kingdom of God through long ages, so he could not have taken into account the secular operation of historic causes which eventually brought about the ruin of Tyre.

Footnotes:

76. Rawlinson, History of Phoenicia.
77. Closing stanzas of The Scholar Gipsy.
78. Both Movers and Rawlinson make it the basis of their survey of Tyrian commerce.
79. Babylon and Egypt are probably omitted because of the peculiar point of view assumed by the prophet. They were too powerful to be represented as slaves of Tyre, even in poetry.
80. E.V., "going to and fro."
81. So Cornill, chvylh for rkly (= merchants).
82. See ch. xxvii. 6, where ivory is said to come from Chittim or Cyprus.
83. The Hebrew text adds "purple, embroidered work, and byssus"; but most of these things are omitted in the LXX.
84. The text of vv. 18, 19 is in confusion, and Cornill, from a comparison with a contemporary wine-list of Nebuchadnezzar, and also an Assyrian one from the library of Asshurbanipal, makes it read thus: "Wine of Helbon and Zimin and Arnaban they furnished in thy markets. From Uzal," etc. Both lists are quoted in Schrader's Cuneiform Inscriptions and the Old Testament, under this verse.
85. The latter half of this verse, however, is of very uncertain interpretation. For full explanation of the archæological details in this chapter it will be necessary to consult the commentaries and the lexicon. See also Rawlinson's History of Phoenicia, pp. 285 ff.
86. With a change of one letter in the Hebrew text, hml'h for 'ml'h, as in the LXX. and Targum.
87. Hebrew, TEhôm; Babylonian, Tiamat.
88. Psalm xxxvi. 6: cf. Gen. vii, 11.
89. Contra Ap., I. 21; Ant., X. xi. 1.
90. Cf. Hävernick against Hitzig and Winer, Ezekiel, pp. 436 f.
91. The same engineering feat was accomplished by Alexander the Great in seven months, but the Greek general probably adopted more scientific methods (such as pile-driving) than the Babylonians; and, besides, it is possible that the remains of Nebuchadnezzar's embankment may have facilitated the operation.

Chapter XVII - Tyre (Continued): Sidon. Chapters xxvii., xxviii

The remaining oracles on Tyre (chs. xxvii., xxviii. 1-19) are somewhat different both in subject and mode of treatment from the chapter we have just finished. Ch. xxvi. is in the main a direct announcement of the fall of Tyre, delivered in the oratorical style which is the usual vehicle of prophetic address. She is regarded as a state occupying a definite place among the other states of the world, and sharing the fate of other peoples who by their conduct towards Israel or their ungodliness and arrogance have incurred the anger of Jehovah. The two great odes which follow are purely ideal delineations of what Tyre is in herself; her destruction is assumed as certain rather than directly predicted, and the prophet gives free play to his imagination in the effort to set forth the conception of the city which was impressed on his mind. In ch. xxvii. he dwells on the external greatness and magnificence of Tyre, her architectural splendour, her political and military power, and above all her amazing commercial enterprise. Ch. xxviii., on the other hand, is a meditation on the peculiar genius of Tyre, her inner spirit of pride and self-sufficiency, as embodied in the person of her king. From a literary point of view the two chapters are amongst the most beautiful in the whole book. In the twenty-seventh chapter the fiery indignation of the prophet almost disappears, giving place to the play of poetic fancy, and a flow of lyric emotion more perfectly rendered than in any other part of Ezekiel's writings. The distinctive feature of each passage is the elegy pronounced over the fall of Tyre; and although the elegy seems just on the point of passing into the taunt-song, yet the accent of triumph is never suffered to overwhelm the note of sadness to which these poems owe their special charm.

I

Ch. xxvii. is described as a dirge over Tyre. In the previous chapter the nations were represented as bewailing her fall, but here the prophet himself takes up a lamentation for her; and, as may have been usual in real funeral dirges, he commences by celebrating the might and riches of the doomed city. The fine image which is maintained throughout the chapter was probably suggested to Ezekiel by the picturesque situation of Tyre on her sea-girt rock at "the entries of the sea." He compares her to a stately vessel riding at anchor [92] near the shore, taking on board her cargo of precious merchandise, and ready to start on the perilous voyage from which she is destined never to return. Meanwhile the gallant ship sits proudly in the water, tight and seaworthy and sumptuously furnished; and the prophet's eye runs rapidly over the chief points of her elaborate construction and equipment (vv. 3-11). Her timbers are fashioned of cypress from Hermon, [93] her mast is a cedar of Lebanon, her oars are made of the oak of Bashan, her deck of sherbîn-wood [94] (a variety of cedar) inlaid with ivory imported from Cyprus. Her canvas fittings are still more exquisite and costly. The sail is of Egyptian byssus with embroidered work, and the awning over the deck was of cloth resplendent in the two purple dyes procured from the coasts of Elishah. [95] The ship is fitted up for pleasure and luxury as well as for traffic, the fact symbolised being obviously the architectural and other splendours which justified the city's boast that she was "the perfection of beauty."

But Tyre was wise and powerful as well as beautiful; and so the prophet, still keeping up the metaphor, proceeds to describe how the great ship is manned. Her steersmen are the experienced statesmen whom she herself has bred and raised to power; her rowers are the men of Sidon and Aradus, who spend their strength in her service. The elders and wise men of Gebal are her shipwrights (literally "stoppers of leaks"); and so great is her influence that all the naval resources of the world are subject to her control. Besides this Tyre employs an army of mercenaries drawn from the remotest quarters of the earth--from Persia and North Africa, as well as the subordinate towns of Phoenicia; and these, represented as hanging their shields and helmets on her sides, make her beauty complete. [96] In these verses the prophet pays a tribute of admiration to the astuteness with which the rulers of Tyre used their resources to strengthen her position as the head of the Phoenician confederacy. Three of the cities mentioned--Sidon, Aradus, and Gebal or Byblus--were the most important in Phoenicia; two of them at least had a longer history than herself, yet they are here truly represented as performing the rough menial labour which brought wealth and renown to

Tyre. It required no ordinary statecraft to preserve the balance of so many complex and conflicting interests, and make them all co-operate for the advancement of the glory of Tyre; but hitherto her "wise men" had proved equal to the task.

The second strophe (vv. 12-25) contains the survey of Tyrian commerce, which has already been analysed in another connection. [97] At first sight it appears as if the allegory were here abandoned, and the impression is partly correct. In reality the city, although personified, is regarded as the emporium of the world's commerce, to which all the nations stream with their produce. But at the end it appears that the various commodities enumerated represent the cargo with which the ship is laden. Ships of Tarshish--i.e., the largest class of merchant vessels then afloat, used for the long Atlantic voyage--wait upon her, and fill her with all sorts of precious things (ver. 25). Then in the last strophe (vv. 26-36), which speaks of the destruction of Tyre, the figure of the ship is boldly resumed. The heavily freighted vessel is rowed into the open sea; there she is struck by an east wind and founders in deep water. The image suggests two ideas, which must not be pressed, although they may have an element of historic truth in them: one is that Tyre perished under the weight of her own commercial greatness, and the other that her ruin was hastened through the folly of her rulers. But the main idea is that the destruction of the city was wrought by the power of God, which suddenly overwhelmed her at the height of her prosperity and activity. As the waves close over the doomed vessel the cry of anguish that goes up from the drowning mariners and passengers strikes terror into the hearts of all seafaring men. They forsake their ships, and having reached the safety of the shore abandon themselves to frantic demonstrations of grief, joining their voices in a lamentation over the fate of the goodly ship which symbolised the mistress of the sea (vv. 32-36)[98] :--

> *Who was like Tyre [so glorious]--*
> *In the midst of the sea?*
> *When thy wares went forth from the seas--*
> *Thou filledst the peoples;*
> *With thy wealth and thy merchandise--*
> *Thou enrichedst the earth.*
> *Now art thou broken from the seas--*
> *In depths of the waters;*
> *Thy merchandise and all thy multitude--*
> *Are fallen therein.*
> *All the inhabitants of the islands--*
> *Are shocked at thee,*
> *And their kings shudder greatly--*
> *With tearful countenances.*
> *They that trade among the peoples ...--*
> *Hiss over thee;*
> *Thou art become a terror--*
> *And art no more for ever.*

Such is the end of Tyre. She has vanished utterly from the earth; the imposing fabric of her greatness is like an unsubstantial pageant faded; and nothing remains to tell of her former glory but the mourning of the nations who were once enriched by her commerce.

II

Ch. xxviii. 1-19.--Here the prophet turns to the prince of Tyre, who is addressed throughout as the impersonation of the consciousness of a great commercial community. We happen to know from Josephus that the name of the reigning king at this time was Ithobaal or Ethbaal II. But it is manifest that the terms of Ezekiel's message have no reference to the individuality of this or any other prince of Tyre. It is not likely that the king could have exercised any great political influence in a city "whose merchants were all princes"; indeed, we learn from Josephus that the monarchy was abolished in favour of some sort of elective constitution not long after the death of Ithobaal. Nor is there any reason to suppose that Ezekiel has in view any special manifestation of arrogance on the part of the royal house, such as a pretension to be descended from the gods. The king here is simply the representative of the genius of the community, the sins of heart charged against him are the expression of the sinful principle which the prophet detected beneath the refinement and luxury of Tyre, and his shameful death only symbolises the downfall of the city. The prophecy consists of two parts: first, an accusation against the prince of Tyre, ending with a threat of destruction (vv. 2-10); and second, a lament over his fall (vv. 11-19). The point of view is very different in these two sections. In the first the prince is still conceived as a man; and the language put into his mouth, although extravagant, does not exceed the limits of purely human arrogance. In the second, however, the king appears as an angelic being, an inhabitant of Eden and a companion of the cherub, sinless at first, and falling from his high estate through his own transgression. It almost seems as if the prophet had in his mind the idea of a tutelary spirit or genius of Tyre, like the angelic princes in the book of Daniel who preside over the destinies of different nations. [99] But in spite of its enhanced idealism, the passage only clothes in forms drawn from Babylonian mythology the boundless self-glorification of Tyre; and the expulsion of the prince from paradise is merely the ideal counterpart of the overthrow of the city which is his earthly abode.

The sin of Tyre is an overweening pride, which culminated in an attitude of self-deification on the part of its king. Surrounded on every hand by the evidences of man's mastery over the world, by the achievements of human art and industry and enterprise, the king feels as if his throne on the sea-girt island were a veritable seat of the gods, and as if he himself were a being truly divine. His heart is lifted up; and, forgetful of the limits of his mortality, he "sets his mind like the mind of a god." The godlike quality on which he specially prides himself is the superhuman wisdom evinced by the extraordinary prosperity of the city with which he identifies himself. Wiser than Daniel! the prophet ironically exclaims; "no secret thing is too dark for thee!" "By thy wisdom and thine insight thou hast gotten thee wealth, and hast gathered gold and silver into thy treasuries: by thy great wisdom in thy commerce thou hast multiplied thy wealth, and thy heart is lifted up because of thy riches." The prince sees in the vast accumulation of material resources in Tyre nothing but the reflection of the genius of her inhabitants; and being himself the incarnation of the spirit of the city, he takes the glory of it to himself and esteems himself a god. Such impious self-exaltation must inevitably call down the vengeance of Him who is the only living God; and Ezekiel proceeds to announce the humiliation of the prince by the "most ruthless of the nations"--i.e., the Chaldæans. He shall then know how much of divinity doth hedge a king. In face of them that seek his life he shall learn that he is man and not God, and that there are forces in the world against which the vaunted wisdom of Tyre is of no avail. An ignominious death [100] at the hand of strangers is the fate reserved for the mortal who so proudly exalted himself against all that is called God.

The thought thus expressed, when disengaged from its peculiar setting, is one of permanent importance. To Ezekiel, as to the prophets generally, Tyre is the representative of commercial greatness, and the truth which he here seeks to illustrate is that the abnormal development of the mercantile spirit had in her case destroyed the capacity of faith in that which is truly divine. Tyre no doubt, like every other ancient state, still maintained a public religion of the type common to Semitic paganism. She was the sacred seat of a special cult, and the temple of Melkarth was considered the chief glory of the city. But the public and perfunctory worship which was there celebrated had long ceased to express the highest consciousness of the community. The real god of Tyre was not Baal nor Melkarth, but the king, or any other object that might serve as a symbol of her civic greatness. Her religion was one that embodied itself in no outward ritual; it was the enthusiasm which was kindled in the heart of every citizen of Tyre by the magnificence of the imperial city to which he belonged. The state of mind which Ezekiel regards as characteristic of Tyre was perhaps the inevitable outcome of a high civilisation informed by no loftier religious conceptions than those common to heathenism. It is the idea which afterwards found expression in the deification of the Roman emperors--the idea that the state is the only power higher than the individual to which he can look for the furtherance of his material and spiritual interests, the only power, therefore, which rightly claims his homage and his reverence. None the less it is a state of mind which is destructive of all that is essential to living religion; and Tyre in her proud self-sufficiency was perhaps further from a true knowledge of God than the barbarous tribes who in all sincerity worshipped the rude idols which represented the invisible power that ruled their destinies. And in exposing the irreligious spirit which lay at the heart of the Tyrian civilisation the prophet lays his finger on the spiritual danger which attends the successful pursuit of the finite interests of human life. The thought of God, the sense of an immediate relation of the spirit of man to the Eternal and the Infinite, are easily displaced from men's minds by undue admiration for the achievements of a culture based on material progress, and supplying every need of human nature except the very deepest, the need of God. "For that is truly a man's religion, the object of which fills and holds captive his soul and heart and mind, in which he trusts above all things, which above all things he longs for and hopes for." [101] The commercial spirit is indeed but one of the forms in which men devote themselves to the service of this present world; but in any community where it reigns supreme we may confidently look for the same signs of religious decay which Ezekiel detected in Tyre in his own day. At all events his message is not superfluous in an age and country where energies are well-nigh exhausted in the accumulation of the means of living, and whose social problems all run up into the great question of the distribution of wealth. It is essentially the same truth which Ruskin, with something of the power and insight of a Hebrew prophet, has so eloquently enforced on the men who make modern England--that the true religion of a community does not live in the venerable institutions to which it yields a formal and conventional deference, but in the objects which inspire its most eager ambitions, the ideals which govern its standard of worth, in those things wherein it finds the ultimate ground of its confidence and the reward of its work. [102]

The lamentation over the fall of the prince of Tyre (vv. 11-19) reiterates the same lesson with a boldness and freedom of imagination not usual with this prophet. The passage is full of obscurities and difficulties which cannot be adequately discussed here, but the main lines of the conception are easily grasped. It describes the original state of the prince as a semi-divine being, and his fall from that state on account of sin that was found in him. The picture is no doubt ironical; Ezekiel actually means nothing more than that the soaring pride of Tyre enthroned its king or its presiding genius in the seat of the gods, and endowed him with attributes more than mortal. The prophet accepts the idea, and shows that there was sin in Tyre enough to hurl the most radiant of celestial creatures from heaven to hell. The passage presents certain obvious affinities with the account of the Fall in the second and third chapters of Genesis; but it also contains reminiscences of a mythology the key to which is now lost. It can hardly be supposed that the vivid details of the imagery, such as the "mountain of God," the "stones of fire," "the precious gems," are altogether due to the prophet's imagination. The mountain of the gods is now known to have been a prominent idea of the Babylonian religion; and there appears to have been a widespread notion that in the abode of the gods were treasures of gold and precious stones, jealously guarded by griffins, of which small quantities found their way into the possession of men. It is possible that fragments of these mythical notions may have reached the knowledge of Ezekiel during his sojourn in Babylon and been used by him to fill up his picture of the glories which surrounded the first estate of the king of Tyre. It should be observed, however, that the prince is not to be identified with the cherub or one of the cherubim. The words "Thou art the anointed cherub that covereth, and I have set thee so" (ver. 14) may be translated "With the ... cherub I set thee"; and similarly the words of ver. 16, "I will destroy thee, O covering cherub," should probably be rendered "And the cherub hath destroyed thee." The whole conception is greatly simplified by these changes, and the principal features of it, so far as they can be made out with clearness, are as follows: The cherub is the warden of the "holy mountain of God," and no doubt also (as in ch. i.) the symbol and bearer of the divine glory. When it is said that the prince of Tyre was placed with the cherub, the meaning is that he had his place in the abode of God, or was admitted to the presence of God, so long as he preserved the perfection in which he was created (ver. 15). The other allusions to his original glory, such as the "covering" of precious stones and the "walking amidst fiery stones," cannot be explained with any degree of certainty. [103] When iniquity is found in him so that he must be banished from the presence of God, the cherub is said to destroy him from the midst of the stones of fire--i.e., is the agent of the divine judgment which descends on the prince. It is thus doubtful whether the prince is conceived as a perfect human being, like Adam before his fall, or as an angelic, superhuman creature; but the point is of little importance in an ideal delineation such as we have here. It will be seen that even on the first supposition there is no very close correspondence with the story of Eden in the book of Genesis, for there the cherubim are placed to guard the way of the tree of life only after man has been expelled from the garden.

But what is the sin that tarnished the sanctity of this exalted personage and cost him his place among the immortals? Ideally, it was an access of pride that caused his ruin, a spiritual sin, such as might originate in the heart of an angelic being.

By that sin fell the angels: how can man, then,
The image of his Maker, hope to win by it?

His heart was lifted up because of his beauty, and he forfeited his godlike wisdom over his brilliance (ver. 17). But really, this change passing over the spirit of the prince in the seat of God is only the reflection of what is done on earth in Tyre. As her commerce increased, the proofs of her unjust and unscrupulous use of wealth were accumulated against her, and her midst was filled with violence (ver. 16). This is the only allusion in the three chapters to the wrong and oppression and the outrages on humanity which were the inevitable accompaniments of that greed of gain which had taken possession of the Tyrian community. And these sins are regarded as a demoralisation taking place in the nature of the prince who is the representative of the city; by the "iniquity of his traffic he has profaned his holiness," and is cast down from his lofty seat to the earth, a spectacle of abject humiliation for kings to gloat over. By a sudden change of metaphor the destruction of the city is also represented as a fire breaking out in the vitals of the prince and reducing his body to ashes--a conception which has not unnaturally suggested to some commentators the fable of the phoenix which was supposed periodically to immolate herself in a fire of her own kindling.

III

A short oracle on Sidon completes the series of prophecies dealing with the future of Israel's immediate neighbours (vv. 20-23). Sidon lay about twenty miles farther north than Tyre, and was, as we have seen, at this time subject to the authority of the younger and more vigorous city. From the book of Jeremiah, [104] however, we see that Sidon was an autonomous state, and preserved a measure of independence even in matters of foreign policy. There is therefore nothing arbitrary in assigning a separate oracle to this most northerly of the states in immediate contact with the people of Israel, although it must be admitted that Ezekiel has nothing distinctive to say of Sidon. Phoenicia was in truth so overshadowed by Tyre that all the characteristics of the people have been amply illustrated in the chapters that have dealt with the latter city. The prophecy is accordingly delivered in the most general terms, and indicates rather the purpose and effect of the judgment than the manner in which it is to come or the character of the people against whom it is directed. It passes insensibly into a prediction of the glorious future of Israel, which is important as revealing the underlying motive of all the preceding utterances against the heathen nations. The restoration of Israel and the destruction of her old neighbours are both parts of one comprehensive scheme of divine providence, the ultimate object of which is a demonstration before the eyes of the world of the holiness of Jehovah. That men might know that He is Jehovah, God alone, is the end alike of His dealings with the heathen and with His own people. And the two parts of God's plan are in the mind of Ezekiel intimately related to each other; the one is merely a condition of the realisation of the other. The crowning proof of Jehovah's holiness will be seen in His faithfulness to the promise made to the patriarchs of the possession of the land of Canaan, and in the security and prosperity enjoyed by Israel when brought back to their land a purified nation. Now in the past Israel had been constantly interfered with, crippled, humiliated, and seduced by the petty heathen powers around her borders. These had been a pricking brier and a stinging thorn (ver. 24), constantly annoying and harassing her and impeding the free development of her national life. Hence the judgments here denounced against them are no doubt in the first instance a punishment for what they had been and done in the past; but they are also a clearing of the stage that Israel might be isolated from the rest of the world, and be free to mould her national life and her religious institutions in accordance with the will of her God. That is the substance of the last three verses of the chapter; and while they exhibit the peculiar limitations of the prophet's thinking, they enable us at the same time to do justice to the singular unity and consistency of aim which guided him in his great forecast of the future of the kingdom of God. There remains now the case of Egypt to be dealt with; but Egypt's relations to Israel and her position in the world were so unique that Ezekiel reserves consideration of her future for a separate group of oracles longer than those on all the other nations put together.

Footnotes:

92. For the word gvvlyk, rendered "thy borders," Cornill proposes to read zvvlk, which he thinks might mean "thine anchorage." The translation is doubtful, but the sense is certainly appropriate.

93. Senir was the Amorite name of Mount Hermon, the Phoenician name being Sirion (Deut. iii. 9). Senir, however, occurs on the Assyrian monuments, and was probably widely known.

94. Teasshur (read bch'srym instead of bt-'svrym), a kind of tree mentioned several times in the Old Testament, is generally identified with the sherbîn tree.

95. Elishah is one of the sons of Javan (Ionia) (Gen. x. 4), and must have been some part of the Mediterranean coast, subject to the influence of Greece. Italy, Sicily, and the Peloponnesus have been suggested.

96. The details of the description are nearly all illustrated in pictures of Phoenician war-galleys found on Assyrian monuments. They show the single mast with its square sail, the double row of oars, the fighting men on the deck, and the row of shields along the bulwarks. In an Egyptian picture we have a representation of the embroidered sail (ancient ships are said not to have carried a flag). The canvas is richly ornamented with various devices over its whole surface, and beneath the sail we see the cabin or awning of coloured stuff mentioned in the text.

97. See above, pp. [6]232 ff.

98. It is not clear whether the dirge is continued to the end of the chapter, or whether vv. 33 ff. are spoken by the prophet in explanation of the distress of the nations. The proper elegiac measure cannot be made out without some alteration of the text.

99. Dan. x. 20, 21, xii. 1.

100. "The death of the uncircumcised"--i.e., a death which involves exclusion from the rites of honourable burial; like burial in unconsecrated ground among Christian nations.

101. Dean Church, Cathedral and University Sermons, p. 150.

102. "We have, indeed, a nominal religion, to which we pay tithes of property and sevenths of time; but we have also a practical and earnest religion, to which we devote nine-tenths of our

property, and six-sevenths of our time. And we dispute a great deal about the nominal religion: but we are all unanimous about this practical one; of which I think you will admit that the ruling goddess may be best generally described as the Goddess of Getting-on,' or Britannia of the Market.' The Athenians had an Athena Agoraia,' or Athena of the Market; but she was a subordinate type of their goddess, while our Britannia Agoraia is the principal type of ours. And all your great architectural works are, of course, built to her. It is long since you built a great cathedral; and how you would laugh at me if I proposed building a cathedral on the top of one of these hills of yours, to make it an Acropolis! But your railroad mounds, vaster than the walls of Babylon; your railroad stations, vaster than the temple of Ephesus, and innumerable; your chimneys, how much more mighty and costly than cathedral spires! your harbour-piers; your warehouses; your exchanges!--all these are built to your great Goddess of Getting-on;' and she has formed, and will continue to form, your architecture, as long as you worship her; and it is quite vain to ask me to tell you how to build to her; you know far better than I."--The Crown of Wild Olive.

103. The "fiery stones" may represent the thunderbolts, which were harmless to the prince in virtue of his innocence. It may be noted that the "precious stones" that were his covering (ver. 13) correspond with nine out of the twelve jewels that covered the high-priestly breastplate (Exod. xxviii. 17-19), the stones of the third row being those not here represented. This suggests that the allusion is rather to bejewelled garments than to the plumage of the wings of the cherub with whom the prince has been wrongly identified.

104. Jer. xxv. 22, xxvii. 3.

Chapter XVIII - Egypt. Chapters xxix.-xxxii

Egypt figures in the prophecies of Ezekiel as a great world-power cherishing projects of universal dominion. Once more, as in the age of Isaiah, the ruling factor in Asiatic politics was the duel for the mastery of the world between the rival empires of the Nile and the Euphrates. The influence of Egypt was perhaps even greater in the beginning of the sixth century than it had been in the end of the eighth, although in the interval it had suffered a signal eclipse. Isaiah (ch. xix.) had predicted a subjugation of Egypt by the Assyrians, and this prophecy had been fulfilled in the year 672, when Esarhaddon invaded the country and incorporated it in the Assyrian empire. He divided its territory into twenty petty principalities governed by Assyrian or native rulers, and this state of things had lasted with little change for a generation. During the reign of Asshurbanipal Egypt was frequently overrun by Assyrian armies, and the repeated attempts of the Ethiopian monarchs, aided by revolts among the native princes, to reassert their sovereignty over the Nile Valley were all foiled by the energy of the Assyrian king or the vigilance of his generals. At last, however, a new era of prosperity dawned for Egypt about the year 645. Psammetichus, the ruler of Saïs, with the help of foreign mercenaries, succeeded in uniting the whole land under his sway; he expelled the Assyrian garrison, and became the founder of the brilliant twenty-sixth (Saïte) dynasty. From this time Egypt possessed in a strong central administration the one indispensable condition of her material prosperity. Her power was consolidated by a succession of vigorous rulers, and she immediately began to play a leading part in the affairs of Asia. The most distinguished king of the dynasty was Necho II., the son and successor of Psammetichus. Two striking facts mentioned by Herodotus are worthy of mention, as showing the originality and vigour with which the Egyptian administration was at this time conducted. One is the project of cutting a canal between the Nile and the Red Sea, an undertaking which was abandoned by Necho in consequence of an oracle warning him that he was only working for the advantage of foreigners--meaning no doubt the Phoenicians. Necho, however, knew how to turn the Phoenician seamanship to good account, as is proved by the other great stroke of genius with which he is credited--the circumnavigation of Africa. It was a Phoenician fleet, despatched from Suez by his orders, which first rounded the Cape of Good Hope, returning to Egypt by the Straits of Gibraltar after a three years' voyage. And if Necho was less successful in war than in the arts of peace, it was not from want of activity. He was the Pharaoh who defeated Josiah in the plain of Megiddo, and afterwards contested the lordship of Syria with Nebuchadnezzar. His defeat at Carchemish in 604 compelled him to retire to his own land; but the power of Egypt was still unbroken, and the Chaldæan king knew that he would yet have to reckon with her in his schemes for the conquest of Palestine.

At the time to which these prophecies belong the king of Egypt was Pharaoh Hophra (in Greek, Apries), the grandson of Necho II. Ascending the throne in 588 b.c., he found it necessary for the protection of his own interests to take an active part in the politics of Syria. He is said to have attacked Phoenicia by sea and land, capturing Sidon and defeating a Tyrian fleet in a naval engagement. His object must have been to secure the ascendency of the Egyptian party in the Phoenician cities; and the stubborn resistance which Nebuchadnezzar encountered from Tyre was no doubt the result of the political arrangements made by Hophra after his victory. No armed intervention was needed to ensure a spirited defence of Jerusalem; and it was only after the Babylonians were encamped around the city that Hophra sent an Egyptian army to its relief. He was unable, however, to effect more than a temporary suspension of the siege, and returned to Egypt, leaving Judah to its fate, apparently without venturing on a battle (Jer. xxxvii. 5-7). No further hostilities between Egypt and Babylon are recorded during the lifetime of Hophra. He continued to reign with vigour and success till 571, when he was dethroned by Amasis, one of his own generals.

These circumstances show a remarkable parallel to the political situation with which Isaiah had to deal at the time of Sennacherib's invasion. Judah was again in the position of the "earthen pipkin between two iron pots." It is certain that neither Jehoiakim nor Zedekiah, any more than the advisers of Hezekiah in the earlier period, would have embarked on a conflict with the Mesopotamian empire but for delusive promises of Egyptian support. There was the same vacillation and division of counsels in Jerusalem, the same dilatoriness on the part of Egypt, and the same futile effort to retrieve a desperate situation after the favourable moment had been allowed to slip. In both cases the conflict was precipitated by the triumph of an Egyptian party in the Judæan court; and it is probable that in both cases the king was coerced into a policy of which his judgment did not approve. And the prophets of the later period, Jeremiah and Ezekiel, adhere closely to the lines laid down by Isaiah in the time of Sennacherib, warning the people against putting their trust in the vain help of Egypt, and counselling passive submission to the course of events which expressed the unalterable judgment of the Almighty. Ezekiel indeed borrows an image that had been current in the days of Isaiah in order to set forth the utter untrustworthiness and dishonesty of Egypt towards the nations who were induced to rely on her power. He compares her to a staff of reed, which breaks when one grasps it, piercing the hand and making the loins to totter when it is leant upon. [105] Such had Egypt been to Israel through all her history, and such she will again prove herself to be in her last attempt to use Israel as the tool of her selfish designs. The great difference between Ezekiel and Isaiah is that, whereas Isaiah had access to the councils of Hezekiah and could bring his influence to bear on the inception of schemes of state, not without hope of averting what he saw to be a disastrous decision, Ezekiel could only watch the development of events from afar, and throw his warnings into the form of predictions of the fate in store for Egypt.

The oracles against Egypt are seven in number: (i) ch. xxix. 1-16; (ii) 17-21; (iii) xxx. 1-19; (iv) 20-26; (v) xxxi.; (vi) xxxii. 1-16; (vii) 17-32. They are all variations of one theme, the annihilation of the power of Egypt by Nebuchadnezzar, and little progress of thought can be traced from the first to the last. Excluding the supplementary prophecy of ch. xxix. 17-21, which is a later addition, the order appears to be strictly chronological. [106] The series begins seven months before the capture of Jerusalem (ch. xxix. 1), and ends about eight months after that event. [107] How far the dates refer to actual occurrences coming to the knowledge of the prophet it is impossible for us to say. It is clear that his interest is centred on the fate of Jerusalem then hanging in the balance; and it is possible that the first oracles (chs. xxix. 1-16, xxx. 1-19) may be called forth by the appearance of Hophra's army on the scene, while the next (ch. xxx. 20-26) plainly alludes to the repulse of the Egyptians by the Chaldæans. But no attempt can be made to connect the prophecies with incidents of the campaign; the prophet's thoughts are wholly occupied with the moral and religious issues involved in the contest, the vindication of Jehovah's holiness in the overthrow of the great world-power which sought to thwart His purposes.

***

Ch. xxix. 1-16 is an introduction to all that follows, presenting a general outline of the prophet's conceptions of the fate of Egypt. It describes the sin of which she has been guilty, and indicates the nature of the judgment that is to overtake her and her future place among the nations of the world. The Pharaoh is compared to a "great dragon," wallowing in his native waters, and deeming himself secure from molestation in his reedy haunts. The crocodile was a natural symbol of Egypt, and the image conveys accurately the impression of sluggish and unwieldy strength which Egypt in the days of Ezekiel had long produced on shrewd observers of her policy. Pharaoh is the incarnate genius of the country; and as the Nile was the strength and glory of Egypt, he is here represented as arrogating to himself the ownership and even the creation of the wonderful river. "My river is mine, and I have made it" is the proud and blasphemous thought which expresses his consciousness of a power that owns no superior in earth or heaven. That the Nile was worshipped by the Egyptians with divine honours did not alter the fact that beneath all their ostentatious religious observances there was an immoral sense of irresponsible power in the use of the natural resources to which the land owed its prosperity. For this spirit of ungodly self-exaltation the king and people of Egypt are to be visited with a signal judgment, from which they shall learn who it is that is God over all. The monster of the Nile shall be drawn from his waters with hooks, with all his fishes sticking to his scales, and left to perish ignominiously on the desert sands. The rest of the prophecy (vv. 8-16) gives the explanation of the allegory in literal, though still general, terms. The meaning is that Egypt shall be laid waste by the sword, its teeming population led into captivity, and the land shall lie desolate, untrodden by the foot of man or beast for the space of forty years. "From Migdol to Syene" [108] --the extreme limits of the country--the rich valley of the Nile shall be uncultivated and uninhabited for that period of time.

The most interesting feature of the prophecy is the view which is given of the final condition of the Egyptian empire (vv. 13-16). In all cases the prophetic delineations of the future of different nations are coloured by the present circumstances of those nations as known to the writers. Ezekiel knew that the fertile soil of Egypt would always be capable of supporting an industrious peasantry, and that her existence did not depend on her continuing to play the rôle of a great power. Tyre depended on her commerce, and apart from that which was the root of her sin could never be anything but the resort of poor fishermen, who would not even make their dwelling on the barren rock in the midst of the sea. But Egypt could still be a country, though shorn of the glory and power which had made her a snare to the people of God. On the other hand the geographical isolation of the land made it impossible that she should lose her individuality amongst the nations of the world. Unlike the small states, such as Edom and Ammon, which were obviously doomed to be swallowed up by the surrounding population as soon as their power was broken, Egypt would retain her distinct and characteristic life as long as the physical condition of the world remained what it was. Accordingly the prophet does not contemplate an utter annihilation of Egypt, but only a temporary chastisement succeeded by her permanent degradation to the lowest rank among the kingdoms. The forty years of her desolation represent in round numbers the period of Chaldæan supremacy during which Jerusalem lies in ruins. Ezekiel at this time expected the invasion of Egypt to follow soon after the capture of Jerusalem, so that the restoration of the two peoples would be simultaneous. At the end of forty years the whole world will be reorganised on a new basis, Israel occupying the central position as the people of God, and in that new world Egypt shall have a separate but subordinate place. Jehovah will bring back the Egyptians from their captivity, and cause them to return to "Pathros, [109] the land of their origin," and there make them a "lowly state," no longer an imperial power, but humbler than the surrounding kingdoms. The righteousness of Jehovah and the interest of Israel alike demand that Egypt should be thus reduced from her former greatness. In the old days her vast and imposing power had been a constant temptation to the Israelites, "a confidence, a reminder of iniquity," leading them to put their trust in human power and luring them into paths of danger by deceitful promises (vv. 6-7). In the final dispensation of history this shall no longer be the case: Israel shall then know Jehovah, and no form of human power shall be suffered to lead their hearts astray from Him who is the rock of their salvation.

***

Ch. xxx. 1-19.--The judgment on Egypt spreads terror and dismay among all the neighbouring nations. It signalises the advent of the great day of Jehovah, the day of His final reckoning with the powers of evil everywhere. It is the "time of the heathen" that has come (ver. 3). Egypt being the chief embodiment of secular power on the basis of pagan religion, the sudden collapse of her might is equivalent to a judgment on heathenism in general, and the moral effect of it conveys to the world a demonstration of the omnipotence of the one true God whom she had ignored and defied. The nations immediately involved in the fall of Egypt are the allies and mercenaries whom she has called to her aid in the time of her calamity. Ethiopians, and Lydians, and Libyans, and Arabs, and Cretans, [110] the "helpers of Egypt," who have furnished contingents to her motley army, fall by the sword along with her, and their countries share the desolation that overtakes the land of Egypt. Swift messengers are then seen speeding up the Nile in ships to convey to the careless Ethiopians the alarming tidings of the overthrow of Egypt (ver. 9). From this point the prophet confines his attention to the fate of Egypt, which he describes with a fulness of detail that implies a certain acquaintance both with the topography and the social circumstances of the country. In ver. 10 Nebuchadnezzar and the Chaldæans are for the first time mentioned by name as the human instruments employed by Jehovah to execute His judgment on Egypt. After the slaughter of the inhabitants, the next consequence of the invasion is the destruction of the canals and reservoirs and the decay of the system of irrigation on which the productiveness of the country depended. "The rivers [canals] are dried up, and the land is made waste, and the fulness thereof, by the hand of strangers" (ver. 12). And with the material fabric of her prosperity the complicated system of religious and civil institutions which was entwined with the hoary civilisation of Egypt vanishes for ever. "The idols are destroyed; the potentates [111] are made to cease from Memphis, and princes from the land of Egypt, so that they shall be no more" (ver. 13). Faith in the native gods shall be extinguished, and a trembling fear of Jehovah shall fill the whole land. The passage ends with an enumeration of various centres of the national life, which formed as it were the sensitive ganglia where the universal calamity was most acutely felt. On these cities, [112] each of which was identified with the worship of a particular deity, Jehovah executes the judgments in which He makes known to the Egyptians His sole divinity and destroys their confidence in false gods. They also possessed some special military or political importance, so that with their destruction the sceptres of Egypt were broken and the pride of her strength was laid low (ver. 18).

***

Ch. xxx. 20-26.--A new oracle, dated three months later than the preceding. Pharaoh is represented as a combatant, already disabled in one arm and sore pressed by his powerful antagonist the king of Babylon. Jehovah announces that the wounded arm cannot be healed, although he has retired from the contest for that purpose. On the contrary, both his arms shall be broken and the sword struck from his grasp, while the arms of Nebuchadnezzar are strengthened by Jehovah, who puts His own sword into his hand. The land of Egypt, thus rendered defenceless, falls an easy prey to the Chaldæans, and its people are dispersed among the nations. The occasion of the prophecy is the repulse of Hophra's expedition for the relief of Jerusalem, which is referred to as a past event. The date may either mark the actual time of the occurrence (as in ch. xxiv. 1), or the time when it came to the knowledge of Ezekiel. The prophet at all events accepts this reverse to the Egyptian arms as an earnest of the speedy realisation of his predictions in the total submission of the proud empire of the Nile.

***

Ch. xxxi. occupies the same position in the prophecies against Egypt as the allegory of the richly laden ship in those against Tyre (ch. xxvii.). The incomparable majesty and overshadowing power of Egypt are set forth under the image of a lordly cedar in Lebanon, whose top reaches to the clouds and whose branches afford shelter to all the beasts of the earth. The exact force of the allegory is somewhat obscured by a slight error of the text, which must have crept in at a very early period. As it stands in the Hebrew and in all the ancient versions the whole chapter is a description of the greatness not of Egypt but of Assyria. "To whom art thou like in thy greatness?" asks the prophet (ver. 2); and the answer is, "Assyria was great as thou art, yet Assyria fell and is no more." There is thus a double comparison: Assyria is compared to a cedar, and then Egypt is tacitly compared to Assyria. This interpretation may not be altogether indefensible. That the fate of Assyria contained a warning against the pride of Pharaoh is a thought in itself intelligible, and such as Ezekiel might very well have expressed. But if he had wished to express it, he would not have done it so awkwardly as this interpretation supposes. When we follow the connection of ideas we cannot fail to see that Assyria is not in the prophet's thoughts at all. The image is consistently pursued without a break to the end of the chapter, and then we learn that the subject of the description is "Pharaoh and all his multitude" (ver. 18). But if the writer is thinking of Egypt at the end, he must have been thinking of it from the beginning, and the mention of Assyria is out of place and misleading. The confusion has been caused by the substitution of the word Asshur (in ver. 3) for T'asshur, the name of the sherbîn tree, itself a species of cedar. We should therefore read, "Behold a T'asshur, a cedar in Lebanon," etc.; [113] and the answer to the question of ver. 2 is that the position of Egypt is as unrivalled among the kingdoms of the world as this stately tree among the trees of the forest.

With this alteration the course of thought is perfectly clear, although incongruous elements are combined in the representation. The towering height of the cedar with its top in the clouds symbolises the imposing might of Egypt and its ungodly pride (cf. vv. 10, 14). The waters of the flood which nourish its roots are those of the Nile, the source of Egypt's wealth and greatness. The birds that build their nests in its branches and the beasts that bring forth their young under its shadow are the smaller nations that looked to Egypt for protection and support. Finally, the trees in the garden of God who envy the luxuriant pride of this monarch of the forest represent the other great empires of the earth who vainly aspired to emulate the prosperity and magnificence of Egypt (vv. 3-9).

In the next strophe (vv. 10-14) we see the great trunk lying prone across mountain and valley, while its branches lie broken in all the water-courses. A "mighty one of the nations" (Nebuchadnezzar) has gone up against it, and felled it to the earth. The nations have been scared from under its shadow; and the tree which "but yesterday might have stood against the world" now lies prostrate and dishonoured--"none so poor as do it reverence." And the fall of the cedar reveals a moral principle and conveys a moral lesson to all other proud and stately trees. Its purpose is to remind the other great empires that they too are mortal, and to warn them against the soaring ambition and lifting up of the heart which had brought about the humiliation of Egypt: "that none of the trees by the water should exalt themselves in stature or shoot their tops between the clouds, and that their mighty ones should not stand proudly in their loftiness (all who are fed by water); for they are all delivered to death, to the under-world with the children of men, to those that go down to the pit." In reality there is no more impressive intimation of the vanity of earthly glory than the decay of those mighty empires and civilisations which once stood in the van of human progress; nor is there a fitter emblem of their fate than the sudden crash of some great forest tree before the woodman's axe.

The development of the prophet's thought, however, here reaches a point where it breaks through the allegory, which has been hitherto consistently maintained. All nature shudders in sympathy with the fallen cedar: the deep mourns and withholds her streams from the earth; Lebanon is clothed with blackness, and all the trees languish. Egypt was so much a part of the established order that the world does not know itself when she has vanished. While this takes place on earth, the cedar itself has gone down to Sheôl, where the other shades of vanished dynasties are comforted because this mightiest of them all has become like to the rest. This is the answer to the question that introduced the allegory. To whom art thou like? None is fit to be compared to thee; yet "thou shalt be brought down with the trees of Eden to the lower parts of the earth, thou shalt lie in the midst of the uncircumcised, with them that are slain of the sword." It is needless to enlarge on this idea, which is out of keeping here, and is more adequately treated in the next chapter.

***

Ch. xxxii. consists of two lamentations to be chanted over the fall of Egypt by the prophet and the daughters of the nations (vv. 16, 18). The first (vv. 1-16) describes the destruction of Pharaoh, and the effect which is produced on earth; while the second (vv. 17-32) follows his shade into the abode of the dead, and expatiates on the welcome that awaits him there. Both express the spirit of exultation over a fallen foe, which was one of the uses to which elegiac poetry was turned amongst the Hebrews. The first passage, however, can hardly be considered a dirge in any proper sense of the word. It is essential to a true elegy that the subject of it should be conceived as dead, and that whether serious or ironical it should celebrate a glory that has passed away. In this case the elegiac note (of the elegiac measure there is hardly a trace) is just struck in the opening line: "O young lion of the nations! [How] art thou undone!" But this is not sustained: the passage immediately falls into the style of direct prediction and threatening, and is indeed closely parallel to the opening prophecy of the series (ch. xxix.). The fundamental image is the same: that of a great Nile monster spouting from his nostrils and fouling the waters with his feet (ver. 2). His capture by many nations and his lingering death on the open field are described with the realistic and ghastly details naturally suggested by the figure (vv. 3-6). The image is then abruptly changed in order to set forth the effect of so great a calamity on the world of nature and of mankind. Pharaoh is compared to a brilliant luminary, whose sudden extinction is followed by a darkening of all the lights of heaven and by consternation amongst the nations and kings of earth (vv. 7-10). It is thought by some that the violence of the transition is to be explained by the idea of the heavenly constellation of the dragon, answering to the dragon of the Nile, to which Egypt had just been likened. [114] Finally all metaphors are abandoned, and the desolation of Egypt is announced in literal terms as accomplished by the sword of the king of Babylon and the "most terrible of the nations" (vv. 11-16).

But all the foregoing oracles are surpassed in grandeur of conception by the remarkable Vision of Hades which concludes the series--"one of the most weird passages in literature" (Davidson). In form it is a dirge supposed to be sung at the burial of Pharaoh and his host by the prophet along with the daughters of famous nations (ver. 18). But the theme, as has been already observed, is the entrance of the deceased warriors into the under-world, and their reception by the shades that have gone down thither before them. In order to understand it we must bear in mind some features of the conception of the under-world, which it is difficult for the modern mind to realise distinctly. First of all, Sheôl or the "pit," the realm of the dead, is pictured to the imagination as an adumbration of the grave or sepulchre, in which the body finds its last resting-place; or rather it is the aggregate of all the burying-grounds scattered over the earth's surface. There the shades are grouped according to their clans and nationalities, just as on earth the members of the same family would usually be interred in one burying-place. The grave of the chief or king, the representative of the nation, is surrounded by those of his vassals and subjects, earthly distinctions being thus far preserved. The condition of the dead appears to be one of rest or sleep; yet they retain some consciousness of their state, and are visited at least by transient gleams of human emotion, as when in this chapter the heroes rouse themselves to address the Pharaoh when he comes among them. The most material point is that the state of the soul in Hades reflects the fate of the body after death. Those who have received the honour of decent burial on earth enjoy a corresponding honour among the shades below. They have as it were a definite status and individuality in their eternal abode, whilst the spirits of the unburied slain are laid in the lowest recesses of the pit, in the limbo of the uncircumcised. On this distinction the whole significance of the passage before us seems to depend. The dead are divided into two great classes: on the one hand the "mighty ones," who lie in state with their weapons of war around them; and on the other hand the multitude of "the uncircumcised,[115] slain by the sword"--i.e., those who have perished on the field of battle and been buried promiscuously without due funereal rites. [116] There is, however, no moral distinction between the two classes. The heroes are not in a state of blessedness; nor is the condition of the uncircumcised one of acute suffering. The whole of existence in Sheôl is essentially of one character; it is on the whole a pitiable existence, destitute of joy and of all that makes up the fulness of life on earth. Only there is "within that deep a lower deep," and it is reserved for those who in the manner of their death have experienced the penalty of great wickedness. The moral truth of Ezekiel's representation lies here. The real judgment of Egypt was enacted in the historical scene of its final overthrow; and it is the consciousness of this tremendous visitation of divine justice, perpetuated amongst the shades to all eternity, that gives ethical significance to the lot assigned to the nation in the other world. At the same time it should not be overlooked that the passage is in the highest degree poetical, and cannot be taken as an exact statement of what was known or believed about the state after death in Old Testament times. It deals only with the fate of armies and nationalities and great warriors who filled the earth with their renown. These, having vanished from history, preserve through all time in the under-world the memory of Jehovah's mighty acts of judgment; but it is impossible to determine whether this sublime vision implies a real belief in the persistence of national identities in the region of the dead.

These, then, are the principal ideas on which the ode is based, and the course of thought is as follows. Ver. 18 briefly announces the occasion for which the dirge is composed; it is to celebrate the passage of Pharaoh and his host to the lower world, and consign him to his appointed place there. Then follows a scene which has a certain resemblance to a well-known representation in the fourteenth chapter of Isaiah (vv. 9-11). The heroes who occupy the place of honour among the dead are supposed to rouse themselves at the approach of this great multitude, and hailing them from the midst of Sheôl, direct them to their proper place amongst the dishonoured slain. "The mighty ones speak to him: Be thou in the recesses of the pit: whom dost thou excel in beauty? Go down and be laid to rest with the uncircumcised, in the midst of them that are slain with the sword.'?" [117] Thither Pharaoh has been preceded by other great conquerors who once set their terror in the earth, but now bear their shame amongst those that go down to the pit. For there is Asshur and all his company: there too are Elam and Meshech and Tubal, each occupying its own allotment amongst nations that have perished by the sword (vv. 22-26). Not theirs is the enviable lot of the heroes of old time [118] who went down to Sheôl in their panoply of war, and rest with their swords under their heads and their shields [119] covering their bones. And so Egypt, which has perished like these other nations, must be banished with them into the bottom of the pit (vv. 27, 28). The enumeration of the nations of the uncircumcised is then resumed; Israel's immediate neighbours are amongst them--Edom and the dynasties of the north (the Syrians), and the Phoenicians, inferior states which played no great part as conquerors, but nevertheless perished in battle and bear their humiliation along with the others (vv. 29, 30). These are to be Pharaoh's companions in his last resting-place, and at the sight of them he will lay aside his presumptuous thoughts and comfort himself over the loss of his mighty army (vv. 31 f.).

***

It is necessary to say a few words in conclusion about the historical evidence for the fulfilment of these prophecies on Egypt. The supplementary oracle of ch. xxix. 17-21 shows us that the threatened invasion by Nebuchadnezzar had not taken place sixteen years after the fall of Jerusalem. Did it ever take place at all? Ezekiel was at that time confident that his words were on the point of being fulfilled, and indeed he seems to stake his credit with his hearers on their verification. Can we suppose that he was entirely mistaken? Is it likely that the remarkably definite predictions uttered both by him and Jeremiah [120] failed of even the partial fulfilment which that on Tyre received? A number of critics have strongly maintained that we are shut up by the historical evidence to this conclusion. They rely chiefly on the silence of Herodotus, and on the unsatisfactory character of the statement of Josephus. The latter writer is indeed sufficiently explicit in his affirmations. He tells us [121] that five years after the capture of Jerusalem Nebuchadnezzar invaded Egypt, put to death the reigning king, appointed another in his stead, and carried the Jewish refugees in Egypt captive to Babylon. But it is pointed out that the date is impossible, being inconsistent with Ezekiel's own testimony, that the account of the death of Hophra is contradicted by what we know of the matter from other sources (Herodotus and Diodorus), and that the whole passage bears the appearance of a translation into history of the prophecies of Jeremiah which it professes to substantiate. That is vigorous criticism, but the vigour is perhaps not altogether unwarrantable, especially as Josephus does not mention any authority. Other allusions by secular writers hardly count for much, and the state of the question is such that historians would probably have been content to confess their ignorance if the credit of a prophet had not been mixed up with it.

Within the last seventeen years, however, a new turn has been given to the discussion through the discovery of monumental evidence which was thought to have an important bearing on the point in dispute. In the same volume of an Egyptological magazine [122] Wiedemann directed the attention of scholars to two inscriptions, one in the Louvre and the other in the British Museum, both of which he considered to furnish proof of an occupation of Egypt by Nebuchadnezzar. The first was an Egyptian inscription of the reign of Hophra. It was written by an official of the highest rank, named Nes-hor, to whom was entrusted the responsible task of defending Egypt on its southern or Ethiopian frontier. According to Wiedemann's translation, it relates among other things an irruption of Asiatic bands (Syrians, people of the north, Asiatics), which penetrated as far as the first cataract, and did some damage to the temple of Chnum in Elephantine. There they were checked by Nes-hor, and afterwards they were crushed or expelled by Hophra himself. Now the most natural explanation of this incident, in connection with the circumstances of the time, would seem to be that Nebuchadnezzar, finding himself fully occupied for the present with the siege of Tyre, incited roving bands of Arabs and Syrians to plunder Egypt, and that they succeeded so far as to penetrate to the extreme south of the country. But a more recent examination of the text, by Maspero and Brugsch, [123] reduces the incident to much smaller dimensions. They find that it refers to a mutiny of Egyptian mercenaries (Syrians, Ionians, and Bedouins) stationed on the southern frontier. The governor, Nes-hor, congratulates himself on a successful stratagem by which he got the rebels into a position where they were cut down by the king's troops. In any case it is evident that it falls very far short of a confirmation of Ezekiel's prophecy. Not only is there no mention of Nebuchadnezzar or a regular Babylonian army, but the invaders or mutineers are actually said to have been annihilated by Hophra. It may be said, no doubt, that an Egyptian governor was likely to be silent about an event which cast discredit on his country's arms, and would be tempted to magnify some temporary success into a decisive victory. But still the inscription must be taken for what it is worth, and the story it tells is certainly not the story of a Chaldæan supremacy in the valley of the Nile. The only thing that suggests a connection between the two is the general probability that a campaign against Egypt must have been contemplated by Nebuchadnezzar about that time.

The second and more important document is a cuneiform fragment of the annals of Nebuchadnezzar. It is unfortunately in a very mutilated condition, and all that the Assyriologists have made out is that in the thirty-seventh year of his reign Nebuchadnezzar fought a battle with the king of Egypt. As the words of the inscription are those of Nebuchadnezzar himself, we may presume that the battle ended in a victory for him, and a few disconnected words in the later part are thought to refer to the tribute or booty which he acquired. [124] The thirty-seventh year of Nebuchadnezzar is the year 568 b.c., about two years after the date of Ezekiel's last utterance against Egypt. The Egyptian king at this time was Amasis, whose name (only the last syllable of which is legible) is supposed to be that mentioned in the inscription. [125] What the ulterior consequences of this victory were on Egyptian history, or how long the Babylonian domination lasted, we cannot at present say. These are questions on which we may reasonably look for further light from the researches of Assyriology. In the meantime it appears to be established beyond reasonable doubt that Nebuchadnezzar did attack Egypt, and the probable issue of his expedition was in accordance with Ezekiel's latest prediction: "Behold, I give to Nebuchadnezzar, king of Babylon, the land of Egypt; and he shall spoil her spoil, and plunder her plunder, and it shall be the wages for his army" (ch. xxix. 19). There can of course be no question of a fulfilment of the earlier prophecies in their literal terms. History knows nothing of a total captivity of the population of Egypt or a blank of forty years in her annals when her land was untrodden by the foot of man or of beast. These are details belonging to the dramatic form in which the prophet clothed the spiritual lesson which it was necessary to impress on his countrymen--the inherent weakness of the Egyptian empire as a power based on material resources and rearing itself in opposition to the great ends of God's kingdom. And it may well have been that for the illustration of that truth the humiliation that Egypt endured at the hands of Nebuchadnezzar was as effective as her total destruction would have been.

Footnotes:

105. Ezek. xxix. 6, 7: cf. Isa. xxxvi. 6 (the words of Rabshakeh). In ver. 7 read kph, "hand," for ktph, "shoulder," and hmdt, "madest to totter," for hmdt, "madest to stand."

106. This is probable according to the Hebrew text, which, however, omits the number of the month in ch. xxxii. 17. The Septuagint reads "in the first month"; if this is accepted, it would be better to read the eleventh year instead of the twelfth in ch. xxxii. 1, as is done by some ancient versions and Hebrew codices. The change involves a difference of only one letter in Hebrew.

107. Ch. xxxii. 17, following the LXX. reading.

108. Migdol was on the north-east border of Egypt, twelve miles south of Pelusium (Sin), at the mouth of the eastern arm of the Nile. Syene is the modern Assouan, at the first cataract of the Nile, and has always been the boundary between Egypt proper and Ethiopia.

109. Pathros is the name of Upper Egypt, the narrow valley of the Nile above the Delta. In the Egyptian tradition it was regarded as the original home of the nation and the seat of the oldest dynasties. Whether Ezekiel means that the Egyptians shall recover only Pathros, while the Delta is allowed to remain uncultivated, is a question that must be left undecided.

110. Hebrew, "Cush, and Put, and Lud, and all the mixed multitude, and Chub, and the sons of the land of the covenant." Cornill reads, "Cush, and Put, and Lud, and Lub, and all Arabia, and the sons of Crete." The emendations are partly based on somewhat intricate reasoning from the text

of the Greek and Ethiopic versions; but they have the advantage of yielding a series of proper names, as the context seems to demand. Put and Lud are tribes lying to the west of Egypt, and so also is Lub, which may be safely substituted for the otherwise unknown Chub of the Hebrew text.

111. Reading 'lym, "strong ones," instead of 'lylym, "not-gods," as in the LXX. The latter term is common in Isaiah, but does not occur elsewhere in Ezekiel, although he had constant occasion to use it.

112. The cities are not mentioned in any geographical order. Memphis (Noph) and Thebes (No) are the ancient and populous capitals of Lower and Upper Egypt respectively; Tanis (Zoan) was the city of the Hyksos, and subsequently a royal seat; Pelusium (Sin), "the bulwark of Egypt," and Daphne (Tahpanhes) guarded the approach to the Delta from the East; Heliopolis (On, wrongly pointed Aven) was the famous centre of Egyptian wisdom, and the chief seat of the worship of the sun-god Ra; and Bubastis (Pi-beseth), besides being a celebrated religious centre, was one of the possessions of the Egyptian military caste.

113. It is only fair to say that the construction "a T'asshur, a cedar," or, still more, "a T'asshur of a cedar," is somewhat harsh. It is not unlikely that the word "cedar" may have been added after the reading "Assyrian" had been established, in order to complete the sense.

114. See Smend on the passage. Dr. Davidson, however, doubts the possibility of this: see his commentary.

115. This use of the word "uncircumcised" is peculiar. The idea seems to be that circumcision, among nations which like the Israelites practised the rite, was an indispensable mark of membership in the community; and those who lacked this mark were treated as social outcasts, not entitled to honourable sepulture. Hence the word could be used, as here, in the sense of unhallowed.

116. Cf. Isa. xiv. 18-20: "All of the kings of the nations, all of them, sleep in glory, every one in his own house. But thou art cast forth away from thy sepulchre, like an abominable branch, clothed with the slain, that are thrust through with the sword, that go down to the stones of the pit; as a carcase trodden underfoot. Thou shalt not be joined with them in burial," etc.

117. The text of these verses (19-21) is in some confusion. The above is a translation of the reading proposed by Cornill, who in the main follows the LXX.

118. LXX. mvlm for mrlm = "of the uncircumcised."

119. "Shields," a conjecture of Cornill, seems to be demanded by the parallelism.

120. Jer. xliii. 8-13; xliv. 12-14, 27-30; xlvi. 13-26.

121. Ant., X. ix. 7.

122. Zeitschrift für Aegyptische Sprache, 1878, pp. 2 ff. and pp. 87 ff.

123. Ibid., 1884, pp. 87 ff., 93 ff.

124. See Schrader, Keilinschriftliche Bibliothek, III. ii., pp. 140 f.

125. The hypothesis of a joint reign of Hophra and Amasis from 570 to 564 (Wiedemann) may or may not be necessary to establish a connection between the Babylonian inscription and that of Nes-hor; it is certain that Amasis began to reign in 570, and that Hophra is not the Pharaoh mentioned by Nebuchadnezzar.

Part IV − The Formation Of The New Israel

Chapter XIX - The Prophet A Watchman.
Chapter xxxiii

One day in January of the year 586 the tidings circulated through the Jewish colony at Tel-abib that "the city was smitten." The rapidity with which in the East intelligence is transmitted through secret channels has often excited the surprise of European observers. In this case there is no extraordinary rapidity to note, for the fate of Jerusalem had been decided nearly six months before it was known in Babylon. [126] But it is remarkable that the first intimation of the issue of the siege was brought to the exiles by one of their own countrymen, who had escaped at the capture of the city. It is probable that the messenger did not set out at once, but waited until he could bring some information as to how matters were settling down after the war. Or he may have been a captive who had trudged the weary road to Babylon in chains under the escort of Nebuzaradan, captain of the guard, [127] and afterwards succeeded in making his escape to the older settlement where Ezekiel lived. All we know is that his message was not delivered with the despatch which would have been possible if his journey had been unimpeded, and that in the meantime the official intelligence which must have already reached Babylon had not transpired among the exiles who were waiting so anxiously for tidings of the fate of Jerusalem. [128]

The immediate effect of the announcement on the mind of the exiles is not recorded. It was doubtless received with all the signs of public mourning which Ezekiel had anticipated and foretold. [129] They would require some time to adjust themselves to a situation for which, in spite of all the warnings that had been sent them, they were utterly unprepared; and it must have been uncertain at first what direction their thoughts would take. Would they carry out their half-formed intention of abandoning their national faith and assimilating themselves to the surrounding heathenism? Would they sink into the lethargy of despair, and pine away under a confused consciousness of guilt? Or would they repent of their unbelief, and turn to embrace the hope which God's mercy held out to them in the teaching of the prophet whom they had despised? All this was for the moment uncertain; but one thing was certain--they could no more return to the attitude of complacent indifference and incredulity in which they had hitherto resisted the word of Jehovah. The day on which the tidings of the city's destruction fell like a thunderbolt in the community of Tel-abib was the turning-point of Ezekiel's ministry. In the arrival of the "fugitive" he recognises the sign which was to break the spell of silence which had lain so long upon him, and set him free for the ministry of consolation and upbuilding which was henceforth to be his chief vocation. A presentiment of what was coming had visited him the evening before his interview with the messenger, and from that time "his mouth was opened, and he was no more dumb" (ver. 22). Hitherto he had preached to deaf ears, and the echo of his ineffectual appeals had come back in a deadening sense of failure which had paralysed his activity. But now in one moment the veil of prejudice and vain self-confidence is torn from the heart of his hearers, and gradually but surely the whole burden of his message must disclose itself to their intelligence. The time has come to work for the formation of a new Israel, and a new spirit of hopefulness stimulates the prophet to throw himself eagerly into the career which is thus opened up before him.

It may be well at this point to try to realise the state of mind which emerged amongst Ezekiel's hearers after the first shock of consternation had passed away. The seven chapters (xxxiii.-xxxix.) with which we are to be occupied in this section all belong to the second period of the prophet's work, and in all probability to the earlier part of that period. It is obvious, however, that they were not written under the first impulse of the tidings of the fall of Jerusalem. They contain allusions to certain changes which must have occupied some time; and simultaneously a change took place in the temper of the people resulting ultimately in a definite spiritual situation to which the prophet had to address himself. It is this situation which we have to try to understand. It supplies the external conditions of Ezekiel's ministry, and unless we can in some measure interpret it we shall lose the full meaning of his teaching in this important period of his ministry.

At the outset we may glance at the state of those who were left in the land of Israel, who in a sense formed part of Ezekiel's audience. The very first oracle uttered by him after he had received his emancipation was a threat of judgment against these survivors of the nation's calamity (vv. 23-29). The fact that this is recorded in connection with the interview with the "fugitive" may mean that the information on which it is based was obtained from that somewhat shadowy personage. Whether in this way or through some later channel, Ezekiel had apparently some knowledge of the disastrous feuds which had followed the destruction of Jerusalem. These events are minutely described in the end of the book of Jeremiah (chs. xl.-xliv.). With a clemency which in the circumstances is surprising the king of Babylon had allowed a small remnant of the people to settle in the land, and had appointed over them a native governor, Gedaliah, the son of Ahikam, who fixed his residence at Mizpah. The prophet Jeremiah elected to throw in his lot with this remnant, and for a time it seemed as if through peaceful submission to the Chaldæan supremacy all might go well with the survivors. The chiefs who had conducted the guerilla warfare in the open against the Babylonian army came in and placed themselves under the protection of Gedaliah, and there was every prospect that by refraining from projects of rebellion they might be left to enjoy the fruits of the land without disturbance. But this was not to be. Certain turbulent spirits under Ishmael, a member of the royal family, entered into a conspiracy with the king of Ammon to destroy this last refuge of peace-loving Israelites. Gedaliah was treacherously murdered; and although the murder was partially avenged, Ishmael succeeded in making his escape to the Ammonites, while the remains of the party of order, dreading the vengeance of Nebuchadnezzar, took their departure for Egypt and carried Jeremiah forcibly with them. What happened after this we do not know; but it is not improbable that Ishmael and his followers may have held possession of the land by force for some years. We read of a fresh deportation of Judæan captives to Babylon five years after the capture of Jerusalem (Jer. lii. 30); and this may have been the result of an expedition to suppress the depredations of the robber band that Ishmael had gathered round him. How much of this story had reached the ears of Ezekiel we do not know; but there is one allusion in his oracle which makes it probable that he had at least heard of the assassination of Gedaliah. Those he addresses are men who "stand upon their sword"--that is to say, they hold that might is right, and glory in deeds of blood and violence that gratify their passionate desire for revenge. Such language could hardly be used of any section of the remaining population of Judæa except the lawless banditti that enrolled themselves under the banner of Ishmael, the son of Nethaniah.

What Ezekiel is mainly concerned with, however, is the moral and religious condition of those to whom he speaks. Strange to say, they were animated by a species of religious fanaticism, which led them to regard themselves as the legitimate heirs to whom the reversion of the land of Israel belonged. "Abraham was one," so reasoned these desperadoes, "and yet he inherited the land: but we are many; to us the land is given for a possession" (ver. 24). Their meaning is that the smallness of their number is no argument against the validity of their claim to the heritage of the land. They are still many in comparison with the solitary patriarch to whom it was first promised; and if he was multiplied so as to take possession of it, why should they hesitate to claim the mastery of it? This thought of the wonderful multiplication of Abraham's seed after he had received the promise seems to have laid fast hold of the men of that generation. It is applied by the great teacher who stands next to Ezekiel in the prophetic succession to comfort the little flock who followed after righteousness and could hardly believe that it was God's good pleasure to give them the kingdom. "Look unto Abraham your father, and unto Sarah that bare you: for I called him alone, and blessed him, and increased him" (Isa. li. 2). The words of the infatuated men who exulted in the havoc they were making on the mountains of Judæa may sound to us like a blasphemous travesty of this argument; but they were no doubt seriously meant. They afford one more instance of the boundless capacity of the Jewish race for religious self-delusion, and their no less remarkable insensibility to that in which the essence of religion lay. The men who uttered this proud boast were the precursors of those who in the days of the Baptist thought to say within themselves, "We have Abraham to our father," not understanding that God was able "of these stones to raise up children to Abraham" (Matt. iii. 9). All the while they were perpetuating the evils for which the judgment of God had descended on the city and the Hebrew state. Idolatry, ceremonial impurity, bloodshed, and adultery were rife amongst them (vv. 25, 26); and no misgiving seems to have entered their minds that because of these things the wrath of God comes on the children of disobedience. And therefore the prophet repudiates their pretensions with indignation. "Shall ye possess the land?" Their conduct simply showed that judgment had not had its perfect work, and that Jehovah's purpose would not be accomplished until "the land was laid waste and desolate, and the pomp of her strength should cease, and the mountains of Israel be desolate, so that none passed through" (ver. 28). We have seen that in all likelihood this prediction was fulfilled by a punitive expedition from Babylonia in the

The Expositor's Bible: The Book of Ezekiel
twenty-third year of Nebuchadnezzar.

But we knew before that Ezekiel expected no good thing to come of the survivors of the judgment in Judæa. His hope was in those who had passed through the fires of banishment, the men amongst whom his own work lay, and amongst whom he looked for the first signs of the outpouring of the divine Spirit. We must now return to the inner circle of Ezekiel's immediate hearers, and consider the change which the calamity had produced on them. The chapter now before us yields two glimpses into the inner life of the people which help us to realise the kind of men with whom the prophet had to do.

In the first place it is interesting to learn that in his more frequent public appearances the prophet rapidly acquired a considerable reputation as a popular preacher (vv. 30-33). It is true that the interest which he excited was not of the most wholesome kind. It became a favourite amusement of the people hanging about the walls and doors to come and listen to the fervid oratory of their one remaining prophet as he declared to them "the word that came forth from Jehovah." It is to be feared that the substance of his message counted for little in their appreciative and critical listening. He was to them "as a very lovely song of one that hath a pleasant voice, and can play well on an instrument": "they heard his words, but did them not." It was pleasant to subject oneself now and then to the influence of this powerful and heart-searching preacher; but somehow the heart was never searched, the conscience was never stirred, and the hearing never ripened into serious conviction and settled purpose of amendment. The people were thoroughly respectful in their demeanour and apparently devout, coming in crowds and sitting before him as God's people should. But they were preoccupied: "their heart went after their gain" (ver. 31) or their advantage. Self-interest prevented them from receiving the word of God in honest and good hearts, and no change was visible in their conduct. Hence the prophet is not disposed to regard the evidences of his newly acquired popularity with much satisfaction. It presents itself to his mind as a danger against which he has to be on his guard. He has been tried by opposition and apparent failure; now he is exposed to the more insidious temptation of a flattering reception and superficial success. It is a tribute to his power, and an opportunity such as he had never before enjoyed. Whatever may have been the case heretofore, he is now sure of an audience, and his position has suddenly become one of great influence in the community. But the same resolute confidence in the truth of his message which sustained Ezekiel amidst the discouragements of his earlier career saves him now from the fatal attractions of popularity to which many men in similar circumstances have yielded. He is not deceived by the favourable disposition of the people towards himself, nor is he tempted to cultivate his oratorical gifts with a view to sustaining their admiration. His one concern is to utter the word that shall come to pass, and so to declare the counsel of God that men shall be compelled in the end to acknowledge that he has been "a prophet among them" (ver. 33). We may be thankful to the prophet for this little glimpse from a vanished past--one of those touches of nature that make the whole world kin. But we ought not to miss its obvious moral. Ezekiel is the prototype of all popular preachers, and he knew their peculiar trials. He was perhaps the first man who ministered regularly to an attached congregation, who came to hear him because they liked it and because they had nothing better to do. If he passed unscathed through the dangers of the position, it was through his overpowering sense of the reality of divine things and the importance of men's spiritual destiny; and also we may add through his fidelity in a department of ministerial duty which popular preachers are sometimes apt to neglect--the duty of close personal dealing with individual men about their sins and their state before God. To this subject we shall revert by-and-by.

This passage reveals to us the people in their lighter moods, when they were able to cast off the awful burden of life and destiny and take advantage of such sources of enjoyment as their circumstances afforded. Mental dejection in a community, from whatever cause it originates, is rarely continuous. The natural elasticity of the mind asserts itself in the most depressing circumstances; and the tension of almost unendurable sorrow is relieved by outbursts of unnatural gaiety. Hence we need not be surprised to find that beneath the surface levity of these exiles there lurked the feeling of despair expressed in the words of ver. 10 and more fully in those of ch. xxxvii. 11: "Our transgressions and our sins are upon us, and we waste away in them: how should we then live?" "Our bones are dried, and our hope is lost: we are cut off." These accents of despondency reflect the new mood into which the more serious-minded portion of the community had been plunged by the calamities that had befallen them. The bitterness of unavailing remorse, the consciousness of national death, had laid fast hold of their spirits and deprived them of the power of hope. In sober truth the nation was dead beyond apparent hope of revival; and to an Israelite, whose spiritual interests were all identified with those of his nation, religion had no power of consolation apart from a national future. The people therefore abandoned themselves to despair, and hardened themselves against the appeals which the prophet addressed to them in the name of Jehovah. They looked on themselves as the victims of an inexorable fate, and were disposed perhaps to resent the call to repentance as a trifling with the misery of the unfortunate.

John J. Skinner

And yet, although this state of mind was as far removed as possible from the godly sorrow that worketh repentance, it was a step towards the accomplishment of the promise of redemption. For the present, indeed, it rendered the people more impenetrable than ever to the word of God. But it meant that they had accepted in principle the prophetic interpretation of their history. It was no longer possible to deny that Jehovah the God of Israel had revealed His secret to His servants the prophets. He was not such a Being as the popular imagination had figured. Israel had not known Him; only the prophets had spoken of Him the thing that was right. Thus for the first time a general conviction of sin, a sense of being in the wrong, was produced in Israel. That this conviction should at first lead to the verge of despair was perhaps inevitable. The people were not familiar with the idea of the divine righteousness, and could not at once perceive that anger against sin was consistent in God with pity for the sinner and mercy towards the contrite. The chief task that now lay before the prophet was to transform their attitude of sullen impenitence into one of submission and hope by teaching them the efficacy of repentance. They have learned the meaning of judgment; they have now to learn the possibility and the conditions of forgiveness. And this can only be taught to them through a revelation of the free and infinite grace of God, who has "no pleasure in the death of the wicked, but that the wicked should turn from his way and live" (ver. 11). Only thus can the hard and stony heart be taken away from their flesh and a heart of flesh given to them.

We can now understand the significance of the striking passage which stands as the introduction to this whole section of the book (ch. xxxiii. 1-20). At this juncture of his ministry Ezekiel's thoughts went back on an aspect of his prophetic vocation which had hitherto been in abeyance. From the first he had been conscious of a certain responsibility for the fate of each individual within reach of his words (ch. iii. 16-21). This truth had been one of the keynotes of his ministry; but the practical developments which it suggested had been hindered by the solidarity of the opposition which he had encountered. As long as Jerusalem stood the exiles had been swayed by one common current of feeling--their thoughts were wholly occupied by the expectation of an issue that would annul the gloomy predictions of Ezekiel; and no man dared to break away from the general sentiment and range himself on the side of God's prophet. In these circumstances anything of the nature of pastoral activity was obviously out of the question. But now that this great obstacle to faith was removed there was a prospect that the solidity of popular opinion would be broken up, so that the word of God might find an entrance here and there into susceptible hearts. The time was come to call for personal decisions, to appeal to each man to embrace for himself the offer of pardon and salvation. Its watchword might have been found in words uttered in another great crisis of religious destiny: "The kingdom of heaven suffereth violence, and the violent take it by force." Out of such "violent men" who act for themselves and have the courage of their convictions the new people of God must be formed; and the mission of the prophet is to gather round him all those who are warned by his words to "flee from the wrath to come."

Let us look a little more closely at the teaching of these verses. We find that Ezekiel restates in the most emphatic manner the theological principles which underlie this new development of his prophetic duties (vv. 10-20). These principles have been considered already in the exposition of ch. xviii.; and it is not necessary to do more than refer to them here. They are such as these: the exact and absolute righteousness of God in His dealings with individuals; His unwillingness that any should perish, and His desire that all should be saved and live; the necessity of personal repentance; the freedom and independence of the individual soul through its immediate relation to God. On this closely connected body of evangelical doctrine Ezekiel bases the appeal which he now makes to his hearers. What we are specially concerned with here, however, is the direction which they imparted to his activity. We may study in the light of Ezekiel's example the manner in which these fundamental truths of personal religion are to be made effective in the ministry of the gospel for the building up of the Church of Christ.

The general conception is clearly set forth in the figure of the watchman, with which the chapter opens (vv. 1-9). The duties of the watchman are simple, but responsible. He is set apart in a time of public danger to warn the city of the approach of an enemy. The citizens trust him and go about their ordinary occupations in security so long as the trumpet is not sounded. Should he sleep at his post or neglect to give the signal, men are caught unprepared and lives are lost through his fault. Their blood is required at the watchman's hand. If, on the other hand, he gives the alarm as soon as he sees the sword coming, and any man disregards the warning and is cut down in his iniquity, his blood is upon his own head. Nothing could be clearer than this. Office always involves responsibility, and no responsibility could be greater than that of a watchman in time of invasion. Those who suffer are in either case the citizens whom the sword cuts off; but it makes all the difference in the world whether the blame of their death rests on themselves for their foolhardiness or on the watchman for his unfaithfulness. Such then, as Ezekiel goes on to explain, is his own position as a prophet. The prophet is one who sees further into the spiritual issues of things than other men, and discovers the coming calamity which is to them invisible. We must notice that a background of danger is presupposed. In what form it was to come is not indicated; but Ezekiel knows that judgment follows hard at the heels of sin, and seeing sin in his fellow-men he knows that their state is one of spiritual peril. The prophet's course therefore is clear. His business is to announce as in trumpet tones the doom that hangs over every man who persists in his wickedness, to re-echo the divine sentence which he alone may have heard, "O wicked man, thou shalt surely die." And again the main question is one of responsibility. The watchman cannot ensure the safety of every citizen, because any man may refuse to take the warning he gives. No more can the prophet ensure the salvation of all his hearers, for each one is free to accept or despise the message. But whether men hear or whether they forbear, it is of the utmost moment for himself that that warning should be faithfully proclaimed and that he should thus "deliver his soul." Ezekiel seems to feel that it is only by frankly accepting the responsibility which thus devolves on himself that he can hope to impress on his hearers the responsibility that rests on them for the use they make of his message.

These thoughts appear to have occupied the mind of Ezekiel on the eve of his emancipation, and must have influenced his subsequent action to an extent which we can but vaguely estimate. It is generally considered that this description of the prophet's functions covers a whole department of work of which no express account is given. Ezekiel writes no "Pastor's Sketches," and records no instances of individual conversion through his ministry. The unwritten history of the Babylonian captivity must have been rich in such incidents of spiritual experience, and nothing could have been more instructive to us than the study of a few typical cases had it been possible. One of the most interesting features of the early history of Mohammedanism is found in the narratives of personal adhesion to the new religion; and the formation of the new Israel in the age of the Exile is a process of infinitely greater importance for humanity at large than the genesis of Islam. But neither in this book nor elsewhere are we permitted to follow that process in its details. Ezekiel may have witnessed the beginnings of it, but he was not called upon to be its historian. Still, the inference is probably correct that a conception of the prophet's office which holds him accountable to God for the fate of individuals led to something more than mere general exhortations to repentance. The preacher must have taken a personal interest in his hearers; he must have watched for the first signs of a response to his message, and been ready to advise and encourage those who turned to him for guidance in their perplexities. And since the sphere of his influence and responsibility included the whole Hebrew community in which he lived, he must have been eager to seize every opportunity to warn individual sinners of the error of their ways, lest their blood should be required at his hand. To this extent we may say that Ezekiel held a position amongst the exiles somewhat analogous to that of a spiritual director in the Catholic Church or the pastor of a Protestant congregation. But the analogy must not be pressed too far. The nurture of the spiritual life of individuals could not have presented itself to him as the chief end of his ministrations. His business was first to lay down the conditions of entrance into the new kingdom of God, and then out of the ruins of the old Israel to make ready a people prepared for the Lord. Perhaps the nearest parallel to this department of his work which history affords is the mission of the Baptist. The keynote of Ezekiel's preaching was the same as that of John: "Repent, for the kingdom of heaven is at hand." Both prophets were alike animated by a sense of crisis and urgency, based on the conviction that the impending Messianic age would be ushered in by a searching judgment in which the chaff would be separated from the wheat. Both laboured for the same end--the formation of a new circle of religious fellowship, in anticipation of the advent of the Messianic kingdom. And as John, by an inevitable spiritual selection, gathered round him a band of disciples, amongst whom our Lord found some of His most devoted followers, so we may believe that Ezekiel, by a similar process, became the acknowledged leader of those whom he taught to wait for the hope of Israel's restoration.

There is nothing in Ezekiel's ministry that appeals more directly to the Christian conscience than the serious and profound sense of pastoral responsibility to which this passage bears witness. It is a feeling which would seem to be inseparable from the right discharge of the ministerial office. In this, as in many other respects, Ezekiel's experience is repeated, on a higher level, in that of the apostle of the Gentiles, who could take his hearers to record that he was "pure from the blood of all men," inasmuch as he had "taught them publicly and from house to house," and "ceased not to warn every one night and day with tears" (Acts xx. 17-35). That does not mean, of course, that a preacher is to occupy himself with nothing else than the personal salvation of his hearers. St. Paul would have been the last to agree to such a limitation of the range of his teaching. But it does mean that the salvation of men and women is the supreme end which the minister of Christ is to set before him, and that to which all other instruction is subordinated. And unless a man realises that the truth he utters is of tremendous importance on the destiny of those to whom he speaks, he can hardly hope to approve himself as an ambassador for Christ. There are doubtless temptations, not in themselves ignoble, to use the pulpit for other purposes than this. The desire for public influence may be one of them, or the desire to utter one's mind on burning questions of the day. To say that these are temptations is not to say that matters of public interest are to be rigorously excluded from treatment in the pulpit. There are many questions of this kind on which the will of God is as clear and imperative as it can possibly be on any point of private conduct; and even in matters as to which there is legitimate difference of opinion amongst Christian men there are underlying principles of righteousness which may need to be fearlessly enunciated at the risk of obloquy and misunderstanding. Nevertheless it remains true that the great end of the gospel ministry is to reconcile men to God and to cultivate in individual lives the fruits of the Spirit, so as at the last to present every man perfect in Christ. And the preacher who may be most safely entrusted with the handling of all other questions is he who is most intent on the formation of Christian character and most deeply conscious of his responsibility for the effect of his teaching on the eternal destiny of those to whom he ministers. What is called preaching to the age may certainly become a very poor and empty thing if it is forgotten that the age is made up of individuals each of whom has a soul to save or lose. What shall it profit a man if the preacher teaches him how to win the whole world and lose his own life? It is fashionable to hold up the prophets of Israel as models of all that a Christian minister ought to be. If that is true, prophecy must at least be allowed to speak its whole lesson; and amongst other elements Ezekiel's consciousness of responsibility for the individual life must receive due recognition.

Footnotes:

126. Jerusalem was taken in the fourth month of the eleventh year of Zedekiah or of Ezekiel's captivity. The announcement reached Ezekiel, according to the reading of the Hebrew text, in the tenth month of the twelfth year (ch. xxxiii. 21)--that is, about eighteen months after the event. It is hardly credible that the transmission of the news should have been delayed so long as this; and therefore the reading "eleventh year," found in some manuscripts and in the Syriac Version, is now generally regarded as correct.

127. Jer. xxxix. 9.

128. It is possible, however, that the word happalît, "the fugitive," may be used in a collective sense, of the whole body of captives carried away after the destruction of the city.

129. Ch. xxiv. 21-24.

Chapter XX - The Messianic Kingdom. Chapter xxxiv

The term "Messianic" as commonly applied to Old Testament prophecy bears two different senses, a wider and a narrower. In its wider use it is almost equivalent to the modern word "eschatological." It denotes that unquenchable hope of a glorious future for Israel and the world which is an all but omnipresent feature of the prophetic writings, and includes all predictions of the kingdom of God in its final and perfect manifestation. In its stricter sense it is applied only to the promise of the ideal king of the house of David, which, although a very conspicuous element of prophecy, is by no means universal, and perhaps does not bulk quite so largely in the Old Testament as is generally supposed. The later Jews were guided by a true instinct when they seized on this figure of the ideal ruler as the centre of the nation's hope; and to them we owe this special application of the name "Messiah," the "Anointed," which is never used of the Son of David in the Old Testament itself. To a certain extent we follow in their steps when we enlarge the meaning of the word "Messianic" so as to embrace the whole prophetic delineation of the future glories of the kingdom of God.

This distinction may be illustrated from the prophecies of Ezekiel. If we take the word in its more general sense, we may say that all the chapters from the thirty-fourth to the end of the book are Messianic in character. That is to say, they describe under various aspects the final condition of things which is introduced by the restoration of Israel to its own land. Let us glance for a moment at the elements which enter into this general conception of the last things as they are set forth in the section of the book with which we are now dealing. We exclude from view for the present the last nine chapters, because there the prophet's point of view is somewhat different, and it is better to reserve them for separate treatment.

The chapters from the thirty-fourth to the thirty-seventh are the necessary complement of the call to repentance in the first part of ch. xxxiii. Ezekiel has enunciated the conditions of entrance to the new kingdom of God, and has urged his hearers to prepare for its appearing. He now proceeds to unfold the nature of that kingdom, and the process by which Jehovah is to bring it to pass. As has been said, the central fact is the restoration of Israel to the land of Canaan. Here the prophet found a point of contact with the natural aspirations of his fellow-exiles. There was no prospect to which they had clung with more eager longing than that of a return to national independence in their own land; and the feeling that this was no longer possible was the source of the abject despair from which the prophet sought to rouse them. How was this to be done? Not simply by asserting in the face of all human probability that the restoration would take place, but by presenting it to their minds in its religious aspects as an object worthy of the exercise of almighty power, and an object in which Jehovah was interested for the glory of His great name. Only by being brought round to Ezekiel's faith in God could the exiles recover their lost hope in the future of the nation. Thus the return to which Ezekiel looks forward has a Messianic significance; it is the establishment of the kingdom of God, a symbol of the final and perfect union between Jehovah and Israel.

Now in the chapters before us this general conception is exhibited in three separate pictures of the Restoration, the leading ideas being the Monarchy (ch. xxxiv.), the Land (chs. xxxv., xxxvi.), and the Nation (ch. xxxvii.). The order in which they are arranged is not that which might seem most natural. We should have expected the prophet to deal first with the revival of the nation, then with its settlement on the soil of Palestine, and last of all with its political organisation under a Davidic king. Ezekiel follows the reverse order. He begins with the kingdom, as the most complete embodiment of the Messianic salvation, and then falls back on its two presuppositions--the recovery and purification of the land on the one hand, and the restitution of the nation on the other. It is doubtful, indeed, whether any logical connection between the three pictures is intended. It is perhaps better to regard them as expressing three distinct and collateral aspects of the idea of redemption, to each of which a certain permanent religious significance is attached. They are at all events the outstanding elements of Ezekiel's eschatology so far as it is expounded in this section of his prophecies.

We thus see that the promise of the perfect king--the Messianic idea in its more restricted signification--holds a distinct but not a supreme place in Ezekiel's vision of the future. It appears for the first time in ch. xvii. at the end of an oracle denouncing the perfidy of Zedekiah and foretelling the overthrow of his kingdom; and again, in a similar connection, in an obscure verse of ch. xxi.[130] Both these prophecies belong to the time before the fall of the state, when the prophet's thoughts were not continuously occupied with the hope of the future. The former is remarkable, nevertheless, for the glowing terms in which the greatness of the future kingdom is depicted. From the top of the lofty cedar which the great eagle had carried away to Babylon Jehovah will take a tender shoot and plant it in the mountain height of Israel. There it will strike root and grow up into a lordly cedar, under whose branches all the birds of the air find refuge. The terms of the allegory have been explained in the proper place. [131] The great cedar is the house of David; the topmost bough which was taken to Babylon is the family of Jehoiachin, the direct heirs to the throne. The planting of the tender shoot in the land of Israel represents the founding of the Messiah's kingdom, which is thus proclaimed to be of transcendent earthly magnificence, overshadowing all the other kingdoms of the world, and convincing the nations that its foundation is the work of Jehovah Himself. In this short passage we have the Messianic idea in its simplest and most characteristic expression. The hope of the future is bound up with the destiny of the house of David; and the re-establishment of the kingdom in more than its ancient splendour is the great divine act to which all the blessings of the final dispensation are attached.

But it is in the thirty-fourth chapter that we find the most comprehensive exposition of Ezekiel's teaching on the subject of the monarchy and the Messianic kingdom. It is perhaps the most political of all his prophecies. It is pervaded by a spirit of genuine sympathy with the sufferings of the common people, and indignation against the tyranny practised and tolerated by the ruling classes. The disasters that have befallen the nation down to its final dispersion among the heathen are all traced to the misgovernment and anarchy for which the monarchy was primarily responsible. In like manner the blessings of the coming age are summed up in the promise of a perfect king, ruling in the name of Jehovah and maintaining order and righteousness throughout his realm. Nowhere else does Ezekiel approach so nearly to the political ideal foreshadowed by the statesman-prophet Isaiah of a "king reigning in righteousness and princes ruling in judgment" (Isa. xxxii. 1), securing the enjoyment of universal prosperity and peace to the redeemed people of God. It must be remembered of course that this is only a partial expression of Ezekiel's conception both of the past condition of the nation and of its future salvation. We have had abundant evidence [132] to show that he considered all classes of the community to be corrupt, and the people as a whole implicated in the guilt of rebellion against Jehovah. The statement that the kings have brought about the dispersion of the nation must not therefore be pressed to the conclusion that civic injustice was the sole cause of Israel's calamities. Similarly we shall find that the redemption of the people depends on other and more fundamental conditions than the establishment of good government under a righteous king. But that is no reason for minimising the significance of the passage before us as an utterance of Ezekiel's profound interest in social order and the welfare of the poor. It shows moreover that the prophet at this time attached real importance to the promise of the Messiah as the organ of Jehovah's rule over His people. If civil wrongs and legalised tyranny were not the only sins which had brought about the destruction of the state, they were at least serious evils, which could not be tolerated in the new Israel; and the chief safeguard against their recurrence is found in the character of the ideal ruler whom Jehovah will raise up from the seed of David. How far this high conception of the functions of the monarchy was modified in Ezekiel's subsequent teaching we shall see when we come to consider the position assigned to the prince in the great vision at the end of the book. [133]

In the meantime let us examine somewhat more closely the contents of ch. xxxiv. Its leading ideas seem to have been suggested by a Messianic prophecy of Jeremiah's with which Ezekiel was no doubt acquainted: "Woe to the shepherds that destroy and scatter the flock of My pasture! saith Jehovah. Therefore thus saith Jehovah, the God of Israel, against the shepherds that tend My people, Ye have scattered My flock, and dispersed them, and have not visited them: behold, I will visit upon you the evil of your doings, saith Jehovah. And I will gather the remnant of My flock from all the lands whither I have dispersed them, and will restore them to their folds; and they shall be fruitful and multiply. And I will set shepherds over them who shall feed them: and they shall not fear any more, nor be frightened, nor be lacking, saith Jehovah" (Jer. xxiii. 1-4). Here we have the simple image of the flock and its shepherds, which Ezekiel, as his manner is, expands into an allegory of the past history and future prospects of the nation. How closely he follows the guidance of his predecessor will be seen from the analysis of the chapter. It may be divided into four parts.

i. The first ten verses are a strongly worded denunciation of the misgovernment to which the people of Jehovah had been subjected in the past. The prophet goes straight to the root of the evil when he indignantly asks, "Should not the shepherds feed the flock?" (ver. 2). The first principle of all true government is that it must be in the interest of the governed. But the universal vice of Oriental despotism, as we see in the case of the Turkish empire at the present day, or Egypt before

The Expositor's Bible: The Book of Ezekiel

the English occupation, is that the rulers rule for their own advantage, and treat the people as their lawful spoil. So it had been in Israel: the shepherds had fed themselves, and not the flock. Instead of carefully tending the sick and the maimed, and searching out the strayed and the lost, they had been concerned only to eat the milk [134] and clothe themselves with the wool and slaughter the fat; they had ruled with "violence and rigour." That is to say, instead of healing the sores of the body politic, they had sought to enrich themselves at the expense of the people. Such misconduct in the name of government always brings its own penalty; it kills the goose that lays the golden eggs. The flock which is spoiled by its own shepherds is scattered on the mountains and becomes the prey of wild beasts; and so the nation that is weakened by internal misrule loses its powers of defence and succumbs to the attacks of some foreign invader. But the shepherds of Israel have to reckon with Him who is the owner of the flock, whose affection still watches over them, and whose compassion is stirred by the hapless condition of His people. "Therefore, O ye shepherds, hear the word of Jehovah; ... Behold, I am against the shepherds; and I will require My flock at their hand; and I will make them to cease from feeding [My] flock, that they who feed themselves may no longer shepherd them; and I will deliver My flock from their mouth, that they be not food for them" (vv. 9, 10).

ii. But Jehovah not only removes the unworthy shepherds; He Himself takes on Him the office of shepherd to the flock that has been so mishandled (vv. 11-16). As the shepherd goes out after the thunderstorm to call in his frightened sheep, so will Jehovah after the storm of judgment is over go forth to "gather together the outcasts of Israel" (Psalm cxlvii. 2). He will seek them out and deliver them from all places whither they were scattered in the day of clouds and darkness; then He will lead them back to the mountain height of Israel, where they shall enjoy abundant prosperity and security under His just and beneficent rule. By what agencies this deliverance is to be accomplished is nowhere indicated. It is the unanimous teaching of the prophets that the final salvation of Israel will be effected in a "day of Jehovah"--i.e., a day in which Jehovah's own power will be specially manifested. Hence there is no need to describe the process by which the Almighty works out His purpose of salvation; it is indescribable: the results are certain, but the intermediate agencies are supernatural, and the precise method of Jehovah's intervention is as a rule left indefinite. It is particularly to be noted that the Messiah plays no part in the actual work of deliverance. He is not the hero of a national struggle for independence, but comes on the scene and assumes the reins of government after Jehovah has gotten the victory and restored peace to Israel.[135]

iii. The next six verses (17-22) add a feature to the allegory which is not found in the corresponding passage in Jeremiah. Jehovah will judge between one sheep and another, especially between the rams and he-goats on the one hand and the weaker animals on the other. The strong cattle had monopolised the fat meadows and clear settled waters, and as if this were not enough, they had trampled down the residue of the pastures and fouled the waters with their feet. Those addressed are the wealthy and powerful upper class, whose luxury and wanton extravagance had consumed the resources of the country, and left no sustenance for the poorer members of the community. Allusions to this kind of selfish tyranny are frequent in the older prophets. Amos speaks of the nobles as panting after the dust on the head of the poor, and of the luxurious dames of Samaria as oppressing the poor and crushing the needy, and saying to their lords, "Bring us to drink" (Amos ii. 7, iv. 1). Micah says of the same class in the southern kingdom that they cast out the women of Jehovah's people from their pleasant houses, and robbed their children of His glory for ever (Micah ii. 9). And Isaiah, to take one other example, denounces those who "take away the right from the poor of My people, that widows may be their prey, and that they may rob the orphans" (Isa. x. 2). Under the corrupt administration of justice which the kings had tolerated for their own convenience litigation had been a farce; the rich man had always the ear of the judge, and the poor found no redress. But in Israel the true fountain of justice could not be polluted; it was only its channels that were obstructed. For Jehovah Himself was the supreme judge of His people; and in the restored commonwealth to which Ezekiel looks forward all civil relations will be regulated by a regard to His righteous will. He will "save His flock that they be no more a prey, and will judge between cattle and cattle."

iv. Then follows in the last section (vv. 23-31) the promise of the Messianic king, and a description of the blessings that accompany his reign: "I will set up one shepherd over them, and he shall feed them--My servant David: he shall feed them, and he shall be their shepherd. And I Jehovah will be their God, and My servant David shall be a prince in their midst: I Jehovah have spoken it." There are one or two difficulties connected with the interpretation of this passage, the consideration of which may be postponed till we have finished our analysis of the chapter. It is sufficient in the meantime to notice that a Davidic kingdom in some sense is to be the foundation of social order in the new Israel. A prince will arise, endowed with the spirit of his exalted office, to discharge perfectly the royal functions in which the former kings had so lamentably failed. Through him the divine government of Israel will become a reality in the national life. The Godhead of

Jehovah and the kingship of the Messiah will be inseparably associated in the faith of the people: "Jehovah their God, and David their king" (Hosea iii. 5) is the expression of the ground of Israel's confidence in the latter days. And this kingdom is the pledge of the fulness of divine blessing descending on the land and the people. The people shall dwell in safety, none making them afraid, because of the covenant of peace which Jehovah will make for them, securing them against the assaults of other nations. [136] The heavens shall pour forth fertilising "showers of blessing"; and the land shall be clothed with a luxuriant vegetation which shall be the admiration of the whole earth. [137] Thus happily situated Israel shall shake off the reproach of the heathen, which they had formerly to endure because of the poverty of their land and their unfortunate history. In the plenitude of material prosperity they shall recognise that Jehovah their God is with them, and they shall know what it is to be His people and the flock of His pasture. [138]

We have now before us the salient features of the Messianic hope, as it is presented in the pages of Ezekiel. We see that the idea is developed in contrast with the abuses that had characterised the historic monarchy in Israel. It represents the ideal of the kingdom as it exists in the mind of Jehovah, an ideal which no actual king had fully realised, and which most of them had shamefully violated. The Messiah is the vicegerent of Jehovah on earth, and the representative of His kingly authority and righteous government over Israel. We see further that the promise is based on the "sure mercies of David," the covenant which secured the throne to David's descendants for ever. Messianic prophecy is legitimist, the ideal king being regarded as standing in the direct line of succession to the crown. And to these features we may add another, which is explicitly developed in ch. xxxvii. 22-26, although it is implied in the expression "one shepherd" in the passage with which we have been dealing. The Messianic kingdom represents the unity of all Israel, and particularly the reunion of the two kingdoms under one sceptre. The prophets attach great importance to this idea. [139] The existence of two rival monarchies, divided in interest and often at war with each other, although it had never effaced the consciousness of the original unity of the nation, was felt by the prophets to be an anomalous state of things, and seriously detrimental to the national religion. The ideal relation of Jehovah to Israel was as incompatible with two kingdoms as the ideal of marriage is incompatible with two wives to one husband. Hence in the glorious future of the Messianic age the schism must be healed, and the Davidic dynasty restored to its original position at the head of an undivided empire. The prominence given to this thought in the teaching of Hosea shows that even in the northern kingdom devout Israelites cherished the hope of reunion with their brethren under the house of David as the only form in which the redemption of the nation could be achieved. And although, long before Ezekiel's day, the kingdom of Samaria had disappeared from history, he too looks forward to a restoration of the ten tribes as an essential element of the Messianic salvation.

In these respects the teaching of Ezekiel reflects the general tenor of the Messianic prophecy of the Old Testament. There are just two questions on which some obscurity and uncertainty must be felt to rest. In the first place, what is the precise meaning of the expression "My servant David"? It will not be supposed that the prophet expected David, the founder of the Hebrew monarchy, to reappear in person and inaugurate the new dispensation. Such an interpretation would be utterly false to Eastern modes of thought and expression, besides being opposed to every indication we have of the prophetic conception of the Messiah. Even in popular language the name of David was current, after he had been long dead, as the name of the dynasty which he had founded. When the ten tribes revolted from Rehoboam they said, exactly as they had said in David's lifetime, "What portion have we in David? neither have we inheritance in the son of Jesse: to your tents, O Israel: now see to thine own house, David." [140] If the name of David could thus be invoked in popular speech at a time of great political excitement, we need not be surprised to find it used in a similar sense in the figurative style of the prophets. All that the word means is that the Messiah will be one who comes in the spirit and power of David, a representative of the ancient family who carries to completion the work so nobly begun by his great ancestor.

The real difficulty is whether the title "David" denotes a unique individual or a line of Davidic kings. To that question it is hardly possible to return a decided answer. That the idea of a succession of sovereigns is a possible form of the Messianic hope is shown by a passage in the thirty-third chapter of Jeremiah. There the promise of the righteous sprout of the house of David is supplemented by the assurance that David shall never want a man to sit on the throne of Israel;[141] the allusion therefore appears to be to the dynasty, and not to a single person. And this view finds some support in the case of Ezekiel from the fact that in the later vision of chs. xl.-xlviii. the prophet undoubtedly anticipates a perpetuation of the dynasty through successive generations.[142] On the other hand it is difficult to reconcile this view with the expressions used in this and the thirty-seventh chapters. When we read that "My servant David shall be their prince for ever," [143] we can scarcely escape the impression that the prophet is thinking of a personal Messiah reigning eternally. If it were necessary to decide between these two alternatives, it might be safest to adhere to the idea

The Expositor's Bible: The Book of Ezekiel

of a personal Messiah, as conveying the fullest rendering of the prophet's thought. There is reason to think that in the interval between this prophecy and his final vision Ezekiel's conception of the Messiah underwent a certain modification, and therefore the teaching of the later passage cannot be used to control the explanation of this. But the obscurity is of such a nature that we cannot hope to remove it. In the prophets' delineations of the future there are many points on which the light of revelation had not been fully cast; for they, like the Christian apostle, "knew in part and prophesied in part." And the question of the way in which the Messiah's office is to be prolonged is precisely one of those which did not greatly occupy the mind of the prophets. There is no perspective in Messianic prophecy: the future kingdom of God is seen, as it were, in one plane, and how it is to be transmitted from one age to another is never thought of. Thus it may become difficult to say whether a particular prophet, in speaking of the Messiah, has a single individual in view or whether he is thinking of a dynasty or a succession. To Ezekiel the Messiah was a divinely revealed ideal, which was to be fulfilled in a person; whether the prophet himself distinctly understood this is a matter of inferior importance.

The second question is one that perhaps would not readily occur to a plain man. It relates to the meaning of the word "prince" as applied to the Messiah. It has been thought by some critics that Ezekiel had a special reason for avoiding the title "king"; and from this supposed reason a somewhat sweeping conclusion has been deduced. We are asked to believe that Ezekiel had in principle abandoned the Messianic hope of his earlier prophecies--i.e., the hope of a restoration of the Davidic kingdom in its ancient splendour. What he really contemplates is the abolition of the Hebrew monarchy, and the institution of a new political system entirely different from anything that had existed in the past. Although the Davidic prince will hold the first place in the restored community, his dignity will be less than royal; he will only be a titular monarch, his power being overshadowed by the presence of Jehovah, the true king of Israel. Now so far as this view is suggested by the use of the word "prince" (literally "leader" or "president") in preference to "king,"[144] it is sufficiently answered by pointing to the Messianic passage in ch. xxxvii., where the name "king" is used three times and in a peculiarly emphatic manner of the Messianic prince.[145] There is no reason to suppose that Ezekiel drew a distinction between "princely" and "kingly" rank, and deliberately withheld the higher dignity from the Messiah. Whatever may be the exact relation of the Messiah to Jehovah, there is no doubt that he is conceived as a king in the full sense of the term, possessed of all regal qualities, and shepherding his people with the authority which belonged to a true son of David.

But there is another consideration which weighs more seriously with the writers referred to. There is reason to believe that Ezekiel's conception of the final kingdom of God underwent a change which might not unfairly be described as an abandonment of the Messianic expectation in its more restricted sense. In his latest vision the functions of the prince are defined in such a way that his position is shorn of the ideal significance which properly invests the office of the Messiah. The change does not indeed affect his merely political status. He is still son of David and king of Israel, and all that is here said about his duty towards his subjects is there presupposed. But his character seems to be no longer regarded as thoroughly reliable, or equal to all the temptations that arise wherever absolute power is lodged in human hands. The possibility that the king may abuse his authority for his private advantage is distinctly contemplated, and provision is made against it in the statutory constitution to which the king himself is subject. Such precautions are obviously inconsistent with the ideal of the Messianic kingdom which we find, for example, in the prophecy of Isaiah. The important question therefore comes to be, whether this lower view of the monarchy is anticipated in the thirty-fourth and thirty-seventh chapters. This does not appear to be the case. The prophet still occupies the same standpoint as in ch. xvii., regarding the Davidic monarchy as the central religious institution of the restored state. The Messiah of these chapters is a perfect king, endowed with the Spirit of God for the discharge of his great office, one whose personal character affords an absolute security for the maintenance of public righteousness, and who is the medium of communication between God and the nation. In other words, what we have to do with is a Messianic prediction in the fullest sense of the term.

In concluding our study of Ezekiel's Messianic teaching, we may make one remark bearing on its typological interpretation. The attempt is sometimes made to trace a gradual development and enrichment of the Messianic idea in the hands of successive prophets. From that point of view Ezekiel's contribution to the doctrine of the Messiah must be felt to be disappointing. No one can imagine that his portrait of the coming king possesses anything like the suggestiveness and religious meaning conveyed by the ideal which stands out so clearly from the pages of Isaiah. And, indeed, no subsequent prophet excels or even equals Isaiah in the clearness and profundity of his directly Messianic conceptions. This fact shows us that the endeavour to find in the Old Testament a regular progress along one particular line proceeds on too narrow a view of the scope of prophecy. The truth is that the figure of the king is only one of many types of the Christian dispensation which the religious institutions of Israel supplied to the prophets. It is the most perfect of all types, partly because it is personal, and partly because the idea of kingship is the most comprehensive of the offices which Christ executes as our Redeemer. But, after all, it expresses only one aspect of the glorious future of the kingdom of God towards which prophecy steadily points. We must remember also that the order in which these types emerge is determined not altogether by their intrinsic importance, but partly by their adaptation to the needs of the age in which the prophet lived. The main function of prophecy was to furnish present and practical direction to the people of God; and the form under which the ideal was presented to any particular generation was always that best fitted to help it onwards, one stage nearer to the great consummation. Thus while Isaiah idealises the figure of the king, Jeremiah grasps the conception of a new religion under the form of a covenant, the second Isaiah unfolds the idea of the prophetic servant of Jehovah, Zechariah and the writer of the 110th Psalm idealise the priesthood. All these are Messianic prophecies, if we take the word in its widest acceptation; but they are not all cast in one mould, and the attempt to arrange them in a single series is obviously misleading. So with regard to Ezekiel we may say that his chief Messianic ideal (still using the expression in a general sense) is the sanctuary, the symbol of Jehovah's presence in the midst of His people. At the end of ch. xxxvii. the kingdom and the sanctuary are mentioned together as pledges of the glory of the latter days. But while the idea of the Messianic monarchy was a legacy inherited from his prophetic precursors, the Temple was an institution whose typical significance Ezekiel was the first to unfold. It was moreover the one that met the religious requirements of the age in which Ezekiel lived. Ultimately the hope of the personal Messiah loses the importance which it still has in the present section of the book; and the prophet's vision of the future concentrates itself on the sanctuary as the centre of the restored theocracy, and the source from which the regenerating influences of the divine grace flow forth to Israel and the world.

Footnotes:

130. Chs. xvii. 22-24, xxi. 26, 27.
131. See pp. [7]102 ff.
132. Cf. especially ch. xxii.
133. See below, pp. [8]318 f., and ch. xxviii.
134. Pointing the Hebrew text in accordance with the rendering of the LXX.
135. This seems to me to be the clear meaning of Isaiah's prophecy of the Messiah in the beginning of the ninth chapter, although the contrary is often asserted. Micah v. 1-6 may, however, be an exception to the rule stated above.
136. Ver. 25. The idea is based on Hosea ii. 18, where God promises to make a covenant for Israel "with the beasts of the field, and the birds of heaven, and the creeping things of the ground." This is to be understood quite literally: it means immunity from the ravages of wild beasts and other noxious creatures. Ezekiel's promise, however, is probably to be explained in accordance with the terms of the allegory: the "evil beasts" are the foreign nations from whom Israel had suffered so severely in the past.
137. This is the sense of the expression mt lsm in ver. 29 (literally "a plantation for a name"). The LXX., however, read mt slm, which may be translated "a perfect vegetation." At all events the phrase is not a title of the Messiah.
138. The word "men" in ver. 31 should be omitted, as in the LXX.
139. Cf. Amos ix. 11 f.; Hosea ii. 2, iii. 5; Isa. xi. 13; Micah ii. 12 f., v. 3.
140. 1 Kings xii. 16 (cf. 2 Sam. xx. 1). It should be mentioned, however, that the last clause in the LXX. is replaced by a more prosaic sentence: "for this man is not fit to be a ruler nor a prince."
141. Jer. xxxiii. 15-17.
142. Cf. ch. xliii. 7, xlv. 8, xlvi. 16 ff.
143. Ch. xxxvii. 25.
144. "Das Königthum wird diese [the Davidic] Familie nicht wieder erhalten, denn Ezechiel fährt fort: Ich Iahwe werde ihnen Gott sein und mein Knecht David wird nâsî d. h. Fürst in ihrer Mitte sein.' Also nur ein Fürstenthum wird der Familie Davids in der besseren Zukunft Israel's zu Theil."--Stade, Geschichte des Volkes Israel, vol. ii., p. 39.
145. Ch. xxxvii. 22-24.

Chapter XXI - Jehovah's Land. Chapters xxxv., xxxvi

The teaching of this important passage turns on certain ideas regarding the land of Canaan which enter very deeply into the religion of Israel. These ideas are no doubt familiar in a general way to all thoughtful readers of the Old Testament; but their full import is scarcely realised until we understand that they are not peculiar to the Bible, but form part of the stock of religious conceptions common to Israel and its heathen neighbours. [146] In the more advanced Semitic religions of antiquity each nation had its own god as well as its own land, and the bond between the god and the land was supposed to be quite as strong as that between the god and the nation. The god, the land, and the people formed a triad of religious relationship, and so closely were these three elements associated that the expulsion of a people from its land was held to dissolve the bond between it and the god. Thus while in practice the land of a god was coextensive with the territory inhabited by his worshippers, yet in theory the relation of the god to his land is independent of his relation to the inhabitants; it was his land whether the people in it were his worshippers or not. The peculiar confusion of ideas that arose when the people of one god came to reside permanently in the territory of another is well illustrated by the case of the heathen colony which the king of Assyria planted in Samaria after the exile of the ten tribes. These settlers brought their own gods with them; but when some of them were slain by lions, they perceived that they were making a mistake in ignoring the rights of the god of the land. They sent accordingly for a priest to instruct them in the religion of the god of the land; and the result was that they "feared Jehovah and served their own gods" (2 Kings xvii. 24-41). It was expected no doubt that in course of time the foreign deities would be acclimatised.

In the Old Testament we find many traces of the influence of this conception on the Hebrew religion. Canaan was the land of Jehovah (Hosea ix. 3) apart altogether from its possession by Israel, the people of Jehovah. It was Jehovah's land before Israel entered it, the inheritance which He had selected for His people out of all the countries of the world, the Land of Promise, given to the patriarchs while as yet they were but strangers and sojourners in it. Although the Israelites took possession of it as a nation of conquerors, they did so in the consciousness that they were expelling from Jehovah's dwelling-place a population which had polluted it by their abominations. From that time onwards the tenure of the soil of Palestine was regarded as an essential factor of the national religion. The idea that Jehovah could not be rightly worshipped outside of Hebrew territory was firmly rooted in the mind of the people, and was accepted by the prophets as a principle involved in the special relations that Jehovah maintained with the people of Israel. [147] Hence no threat could be more terrible in the ears of the Israelites than that of expatriation from their native soil; for it meant nothing less than the dissolution of the tie that subsisted between them and their God. When that threat was actually fulfilled there was no reproach harder to bear than the taunt which Ezekiel here puts into the mouth of the heathen: "These are Jehovah's people--and yet they are gone forth out of His land" (ch. xxxvi. 20). They felt all that was implied in that utterance of malicious satisfaction over the collapse of a religion and the downfall of a deity.

There is another way in which the thought of Canaan as Jehovah's land enters into the religious conceptions of the Old Testament, and very markedly into those of Ezekiel. As the God of the land Jehovah is the source of its productiveness and the author of all the natural blessings enjoyed by its inhabitants. It is He who gives the rain in its season or else withholds it in token of His displeasure; it is He who multiplies or diminishes the flocks and herds which feed on its pastures, as well as the human population sustained by its produce. This view of things was a primary factor in the religious education of an agricultural people, as the ancient Hebrews mainly were. They felt their dependence on God most directly in the influences of their uncertain climate on the fertility of their land, with its great possibilities of abundant provision for man and beast, and on the other hand its extreme risk of famine and all the hardships that follow in its train. In the changeful aspects of nature they thus read instinctively the disposition of Jehovah towards themselves. Fruitful seasons and golden harvests, diffusing comfort and affluence through the community, were regarded as proofs that all was well between them and their God; while times of barrenness and scarcity brought home to them the conviction that Jehovah was alienated. From the allusions in the prophets to droughts and famines, to blastings and mildew, to the scourge of locusts, we seem to gather that on the whole the later history of Israel had been marked by agricultural distress. The impression is confirmed by a hint of Ezekiel's in the passage now before us. The land of Canaan had apparently acquired an unenviable reputation for barrenness. The reproach of the heathen lay upon it as a land that "devoured men and bereaved its population."[148] The reference may be partly (as Smend thinks) to the ravages of war, to which Palestine was peculiarly exposed on account of its important strategic situation. But the "reproach of famine"[149] was certainly one point in its ill fame among the surrounding nations, and it is quite sufficient to explain the strong language in which they expressed their contempt. Now this state of things was plainly inconsistent with amicable relations between the nation and its God. It was evidence that the land lay under the blight of Jehovah's displeasure, and the ground of that displeasure lay in the sin of the people. Where the land counted for so much as an index to the mind of God, it was a postulate of faith that in the ideal future when God and Israel were perfectly reconciled the physical condition of Canaan should be worthy of Him whose land it was. And we have already seen that amongst the glories of the Messianic age the preternatural fertility of the Holy Land holds a prominent place.

This conception of Canaan as the land of Jehovah undoubtedly has its natural affinities with religious notions of a somewhat primitive kind. It belongs to the stage of thought at which the power of a god is habitually regarded as subject to local limitations, and in which accordingly a particular territory is assigned to every deity as the sphere of his influence. It is probable that the great mass of the Hebrew people had never risen above this idea, but continued to think of their country as Jehovah's land in precisely the same way as Assyria was Asshur's land and Moab the land of Chemosh. The monotheism of the Old Testament revelation breaks through this system of ideas, and interprets Jehovah's relation to the land in an entirely different sense. It is not as the exclusive sphere of His influence that Canaan is peculiarly associated with Jehovah's presence, but mainly because it is the scene of His historical manifestation of Himself, and the stage on which events were transacted which revealed His Godhead to all the world. No prophet has a clearer perception of the universal sweep of the divine government than Ezekiel, and yet no prophet insists more strongly than he on the possession of the land of Canaan as an indispensable symbol of communion between God and His people. He has met with God in the "unclean land" of his exile, and he knows that the moral government of the universe is not suspended by the departure of Jehovah from His earthly sanctuary. Nevertheless he cannot think of this separation as other than temporary. The final reconciliation must take place on the soil of Palestine. The kingdom of God can only be established by the return both of Israel and Jehovah to their own land; and their joint possession of that land is the seal of the everlasting covenant of peace that subsists between them.

We must now proceed to study the way in which these conceptions influenced the Messianic expectations of Ezekiel at this period of his life. The passage we are to consider consists of three sections. The thirty-fifth chapter is a prophecy of judgment on Edom. The first fifteen verses of ch. xxxvi. contain a promise of the restoration of the land of Israel to its rightful owner. And the remainder of that chapter presents a comprehensive view of the divine necessity for the restoration and the power by which the redemption of the people is to be accomplished.

I

At the time when these prophecies were written the land of Israel was in the possession of the Edomites. By what means they had succeeded in effecting a lodgment in the country we do not know. It is not unlikely that Nebuchadnezzar may have granted them this extension of their territory as a reward for their services to his army during the last siege of Jerusalem. At all events their presence there was an accomplished fact, and it appeals to the mind of the prophet in two aspects. In the first place it was an outrage on the majesty of Jehovah which filled the cup of Edom's iniquity to the brim. In the second place it was an obstacle to the restoration of Israel which had to be removed by the direct intervention of the Almighty. These are the two themes which occupy the thoughts of Ezekiel, the one in ch. xxxv. and the other in ch. xxxvi. Hitherto he has spoken of the return to the land of Canaan as a matter of course, as a thing necessary and self-evident and not needing to be discussed in detail. But as the time draws near he is led to think more clearly of the historical circumstances of the return, and especially of the hindrances arising from the actual situation of affairs.

But besides this one cannot fail to be struck by the effective contrast which the two pictures-- one of the mountain land of Israel, and the other of the mountain land of Seir--present to the imagination. It is like a prophetic amplification of the blessing and curse which Isaac pronounced on the progenitors of these two nations. Of the one it is said:--

The Expositor's Bible: The Book of Ezekiel
> *God give thee of the dew of heaven, and of the fatness of the earth,*
> *And abundance of corn and wine.*

And of the other:--

> *Surely far from the fatness of the earth shall thy dwelling be,*
> *And far from the dew of heaven from above.* [150]

In that forecast of the destiny of the two brothers the actual characteristics of their respective countries are tersely and accurately expressed. But now, when the history of both nations is about to be brought to an issue, the contrast is emphasised and perpetuated. The blessing of Jacob is confirmed and expanded into a promise of unimagined felicity, and the equivocal blessing on Esau is changed into an unqualified and permanent curse. Thus, when the mountains of Israel break forth into singing, and are clothed with all the luxuriance of vegetation in which the Oriental imagination revels, and cultivated by a happy and contented people, those of Seir are doomed to perpetual sterility and become a horror and desolation to all that pass by.

Confining ourselves, however, to the thirty-fifth chapter, what we have first to notice is the sins by which the Edomites had incurred this judgment. These may be summed up under three heads: first, their unrelenting hatred of Israel, which in the day of Judah's calamity had broken out in savage acts of revenge (ver. 5); second, their rejoicing over the misfortunes of Israel and the desolation of its land (ver. 15); and third, their eagerness to seize the land as soon as it was vacant (ver. 10). The first and second of these have been already spoken of under the prophecies on foreign nations; it is only the last that is of special interest in the present connection. Of course the motive that prompted Edom was natural, and it may be difficult to say how far real moral guilt was involved in it. The annexation of vacant territory, as the land of Israel practically was at this time, would be regarded according to modern ideas as not only justifiable but praiseworthy. Edom had the excuse of seeking to better its condition by the possession of a more fertile country than its own, and perhaps also the still stronger plea of pressure by the Arabs from behind. But in the consciousness of an ancient people there was always another thought present; and it is here if anywhere that the sin of Edom lies. The invasion of Israel did not cease to be an act of aggression because there were no human defenders to bar the way. It was still Jehovah's land, although it was unoccupied; and to intrude upon it was a conscious defiance of His power. The arguments by which the Edomites justified their seizure of it were none of those which a modern state might use in similar circumstances, but were based on the religious ideas which were common to all the world in those days. They were aware that by the unwritten law which then prevailed the step they meditated was sacrilege; and the spirit that animated them was arrogant exultation over what was esteemed the humiliation of Israel's national deity: "The two nations and the two countries shall be mine, and I will possess them, although Jehovah was there" (ver. 12, 13). That is to say, the defeat and captivity of Israel have proved the impotence of Jehovah to guard His land; His power is broken, and the two countries called by His name lie open to the invasion of any people that dares to trample religious scruples underfoot. This was the way in which the action of Edom would be interpreted by universal consent; and the prophet is only reflecting the general sense of the age when he charges them with this impiety. Now it is true that the Edomites could not be expected to understand all that was involved in a defiance of the God of Israel. To them He was only one among many national gods, and their religion did not teach them to reverence the gods of a foreign state. But though they were not fully conscious of the degree of guilt they incurred, they nevertheless sinned against the light they had; and the consequences of transgression are never measured by the sinner's own estimate of his culpability. There was enough in the history of Israel to have impressed the neighbouring peoples with a sense of the superiority of its religion and the difference in character between Jehovah and all other gods. If the Edomites had utterly failed to learn that lesson, they were themselves partly to blame; and the spiritual insensibility and dulness of conscience which everywhere suppressed the knowledge of Jehovah's name is the very thing which in the view of Ezekiel needs to be removed by signal and exemplary acts of judgment.

It is not necessary to enter minutely into the details of the judgment threatened against Edom. We may simply note that it corresponds point for point with the demeanour exhibited by the Edomites in the time of Israel's final retribution. The "perpetual hatred" is rewarded by perpetual desolation (ver. 9); their seizure of Jehovah's land is punished by their annihilation in the land that was their own (vv. 6-8); and their malicious satisfaction over the depopulation of Palestine recoils on their own heads when their mountain land is made desolate "to the rejoicing of the whole earth" (vv. 14, 15). And the lesson that will be taught to the world by the contrast between the renewed Israel and the barren mountain of Seir will be the power and holiness of the one true God: "they shall know that I am Jehovah."

II

The prophet's mind is still occupied with the sin of Edom as he turns in the thirty-sixth chapter to depict the future of the land of Israel. The opening verses of the chapter (vv. 1-7) betray an intensity of patriotic feeling not often expressed by Ezekiel. The utterance of the single idea which he wishes to express seems to be impeded by the multitude of reflections that throng upon him as he apostrophises "the mountains and the hills, the watercourses and the valleys, the desolate ruins and deserted cities" of his native country (ver. 4). The land is conceived as conscious of the shame and reproach that rest upon it; and all the elements that might be supposed to make up the consciousness of the land--its naked desolation, the tread of alien feet, the ravages of war, and the derisive talk of the surrounding heathen (Edom being specially in view)--present themselves to the mind of the prophet before he can utter the message with which he is charged: "Thus saith the Lord Jehovah; Behold, I speak in My jealousy and My anger, because ye have borne the shame of the heathen: therefore ... I lift up My hand, Surely the nations that are round about you--even they shall bear their shame" (vv. 6, 7).

The jealousy of Jehovah is here His holy resentment against indignities done to Himself, and this attribute of the divine nature is now enlisted on the side of Israel because of the despite which the heathen had heaped on His land. But it is noteworthy that it is through the land and not the people that this feeling is first called into operation. Israel is still sinful and alienated from God; but the honour of Jehovah is bound up with the land not less than with the nation, and it is in reference to it that the necessity of vindicating His holy name first becomes apparent. There is what we might almost venture to call a divine patriotism, which is stirred into activity by the desolate condition of the land where the worship of the true God should be celebrated. On this feature of Jehovah's character Ezekiel builds the assurance of his people's redemption. The idea expressed by the verses is simply the certainty that Canaan shall be recovered from the heathen dominion for the purposes of the kingdom of God.

The following verses (8-15) speak of the positive aspects of the approaching deliverance. Continuing his apostrophe to the mountains of Israel, the prophet describes the transformation which is to pass over them in view of the return of the exiled nation, which is now on the eve of accomplishment (ver. 8). It might almost seem as if the return of the inhabitants were here treated as a mere incident of the rehabilitation of the land. That of course is only an appearance, caused by the peculiar standpoint assumed throughout these chapters. Ezekiel was not one who could look on complacently

Where wealth accumulates and men decay;

nor was he indifferent to the social welfare of his people. On the contrary we have seen from ch. xxxiv. that he regards that as a supreme interest in the future kingdom of God. And even in this passage he does not make the interests of humanity subservient to those of nature. His leading idea is a reunion of land and people under happier auspices than had obtained of old. Formerly the land, in mysterious sympathy with the mind of Jehovah, had seemed to be animated by a hostile disposition towards its inhabitants. The reluctant and niggardly subsistence that had been wrung from the soil justified the evil report which the spies had brought up of it at the first as a "land that eateth up the inhabitants thereof."[151] Its inhospitable character was known among the heathen, so that it bore the reproach of being a land that "devoured men and bereaved its nation." But in the glorious future all this will be changed in harmony with Jehovah's altered relations with His people. In the language of a later prophet,[152] the land shall be "married" to Jehovah, and endowed with exuberant fertility. Yielding its fruits freely and generously, it will wipe off the reproach of the heathen; its cities shall be inhabited, its ruins rebuilt, and man and beast multiplied on its surface, so that its last state shall be better than its first (ver. 11). And those who till it and enjoy the benefits of its wonderful transformation shall be none other than the house of Israel, for whose sins it had borne the reproach of barrenness in the past (vv. 12-15).

III

The next passage (vv. 16-38) deals more with the renewal of the nation than with that of the land; and thus forms a link of connection between the main theme of this chapter and that of ch. xxxvii. It contains the clearest and most comprehensive statement of the process of redemption to be found in the whole book, exhibiting as it does in logical order all the elements which enter into the divine scheme of salvation. The fact that it is inserted just at this point affords a fresh illustration of the importance attached by the prophet to the religious associations which gathered round the Holy Land. The land indeed is still the pivot on which his thoughts turn; he starts from it in his short review of God's past judgments on His people, and finally returns to it in summing up the world-wide effects of His gracious dealings with them in the immediate future. Although the connection of ideas is singularly clear, the passage throws so much light on the deepest theological conceptions of Ezekiel that it will be well to recapitulate the principal steps of the argument.

We need not linger on the cause of the rejection of Israel, for here the prophet only repeats the main lesson which we have found so often enforced in the first part of his book. Israel went into exile because its manner of life as a nation had been abhorrent to Jehovah, and it had defiled the land which was Jehovah's house. As in ch. xxii. and elsewhere bloodshed and idols are the chief emblems of the people's sinful condition; these constitute a real physical defilement of the land, which must be punished by the eviction of its inhabitants: "So I poured out My wrath upon them [on account of the blood which they had shed upon the land, and the idols wherewith they had polluted it]: and I scattered them among the nations, and they were dispersed through the countries." [153]

Thus the Exile was necessary for the vindication of Jehovah's holiness as reflected in the sanctity of His land. But the effect of the dispersion on other nations was such as to compromise the honour of Israel's God in another direction. Knowing Jehovah only as a tribal god, the heathen naturally concluded that He had been too feeble to protect His land from invasion and His people from captivity. They could not penetrate to the moral reasons which rendered the chastisement inevitable; they only saw that these were Jehovah's people, and yet they were gone forth out of His land (ver. 20), and drew the natural inference. The impression thus produced by the presence of Israelites amongst the heathen was derogatory to the majesty of Jehovah, and obscured the knowledge of the true principles of His government which was destined to extend to all the earth. This is all that seems to be meant by the expression "profaned My holy name." [154] It is not implied that the exiles scandalised the heathen by their vicious lives, and so brought disgrace on "that glorious name by which they were called," [155] although that idea is implied in ch. xii. 16. The profanation spoken of here was caused directly not by the sin but by the calamities of Israel. Yet it was their sins which brought down judgment upon them, and so indirectly gave occasion to the enemies of the Lord to blaspheme. There were probably already some of Ezekiel's compatriots who realised the bitterness of the thought that their fate was the means of bringing discredit on their God. Their experience would be similar to that of the lonely exile who composed the forty-second psalm:--

> As with a sword in my bones, mine enemies reproach me;
> While they say daily unto me, Where is thy God? [156]

Now in this fact the prophet recognises an absolute ground of confidence in Israel's restoration. Jehovah cannot endure that His name should thus be held up to derision before the eyes of mankind. To allow this would be to frustrate the end of His government of the world, which is to manifest His Godhead in such a way that all men shall be brought to acknowledge it. Although He is known as yet only as the national God of a particular people, He must be disclosed to the world as all that the inspired teachers of Israel know Him to be--the one Being worthy of the homage of the human heart. There must be some way by which His name can be sanctified before the heathen, some means of reconciling the partial revelation of His holiness in Israel's dispersion with the complete manifestation of His power to the world at large. And this reconciliation can only be effected through the redemption of Israel. God cannot disown His ancient people, for that would be to stultify the whole past revelation of His character and leave the name by which He had made Himself known to contempt. That is divinely impossible; and therefore Jehovah must carry through His purpose by sanctifying Himself in the salvation of Israel. The outward token of salvation will be their restoration to their own land (ver. 24); but the inward reality of it will be a change in the national character which will make their dwelling in the land consistent with the revelation of Jehovah's holiness already given by their banishment from it.

At this point accordingly (ver. 25) Ezekiel passes to speak of the spiritual process of regeneration by which Israel is to be transformed into a true people of God. This is a necessary part of the sanctification of the divine name before the world. The new life of the people will reveal the character of the God whom they serve, and the change will explain the calamities that had befallen them in the past. The world will thus see "that the house of Israel went into captivity for their iniquity," [157] and will understand the holiness which the true God requires in His worshippers. But for the present the prophet's thoughts are concentrated on the operations of the divine grace by which the renewal is effected. His analysis of the process of conversion is profoundly instructive, and anticipates to a remarkable degree the teaching of the New Testament. We shall content ourselves at present with merely enumerating the different parts of the process. The first step is the removal of the impurities contracted by past transgressions. This is represented under the figure of sprinkling with clean water, suggested by the ablutions or lustrations which are so common a feature of the Levitical ritual (ver. 25). The truth symbolised is the forgiveness of sins, the act of grace which takes away the effect of moral uncleanness as a barrier to fellowship with God. The second point is what is properly called regeneration, the giving of a new heart and spirit (ver. 26). The stony heart of the old nation, whose obduracy had dismayed so many prophets, making them feel that they had spent their labour for nought and in vain, shall be taken away, and instead of it they shall receive a heart of flesh, sensitive to spiritual influences and responsive to the divine will. And to this is added in the third place the promise of the Spirit of God to be in them as the ruling principle of a new life of obedience to the law of God (ver. 27). The law, both moral and ceremonial, is the expression of Jehovah's holy nature, and both the will and the power to keep it perfectly must proceed from the indwelling of His holy Spirit in the people. [158] It is thus Jehovah Himself who "saves" the people "out of all their uncleannesses" (ver. 29), caused by the depravity and infirmity of their natural hearts. When these conditions are realised the harmony between Jehovah and Israel will be completely restored: He will be their God, and they shall be His people. They shall dwell for ever in the land promised to their fathers; and the blessing of God resting on land and people will multiply the fruit of the tree and the produce of the field, so that they receive no more the reproach of famine among the nations (vv. 28-30).

Having thus described the process of salvation as from first to last the work of Jehovah, the prophet proceeds to consider the impression which it will produce first on Israel and then on the surrounding nations (vv. 31-36). On Israel the effect of the goodness of God will be to lead them to repentance. Remembering what their past history has been, and contrasting it with the blessedness they now enjoy, they shall be filled with shame and self-contempt, loathing themselves for their iniquities and their abominations. It is not meant that all feelings of joy and gratitude will be swallowed up in the consciousness of unworthiness; but this is the feeling that will be called forth by the memory of their past transgressions. Their horror of sin will be such that they cannot think of what they have been without the deepest compunction and self-abasement. And this sense of the exceeding sinfulness of sin, reacting on their consciousness of themselves, will be the best moral guarantee against their relapse into the uncleanness from which they have been delivered.

To the heathen, on the other hand, the state of Israel will be a convincing demonstration of the power and godhead of Jehovah. Men will say, "Yonder land, which was desolate, has become like the garden of Eden; and the cities that were ruined and waste and destroyed are fenced and inhabited" (ver. 35). They will know that it is Jehovah's doing, and it will be marvellous in their eyes.

The last two verses seem to be an appendix. They deal with a special feature of the restoration, about which the minds of the exiles may have been exercised in thinking of the possibility of their deliverance. Where was the population of the new Israel to come from? The population of Judah must have been terribly reduced by the disastrous wars that had desolated the country since the time of Hezekiah. How was it possible, with a few thousands in exile, and a miserable remnant left in the land, to build up a strong and prosperous nation? This thought of theirs is met by the announcement of a great increase of the inhabitants of the land. Jehovah is ready to meet the questionings of human anxiety on this point: He will "let Himself be inquired of" for this. [159] The remembrance of the sacrificial flocks that used to throng the streets leading to the Temple at the time of the great festivals supplies Ezekiel with an image of the teeming population that shall be in all the cities of Canaan when this prophecy is fulfilled.

Such is in outline the scheme of redemption which Ezekiel presents to the minds of his readers. We shall reserve a fuller consideration of its more important doctrines for a separate chapter. [160] One general application of its teaching, however, may be pointed out before leaving the subject. We see that for Ezekiel the mysteries and perplexities of the divine government find their solution in the idea of redemption. He is aware of the false impression necessarily produced on the heathen mind by God's dealings with His people, as long as the process is incomplete. On account of Israel's sin the revelation of God in providence is gradual and fragmentary, and seems even for a time to defeat its own end. The omnipotence of God was obscured by the very act of vindicating His holiness; and what was in itself a great step towards the complete revelation of His character came on the world in the first instance as an evidence of His impotence. But the prophet, looking beyond this to the final effect of God's work upon the world, sees that Jehovah can be truly known only in the manifestation of His redeeming grace. All the enigmas and contradictions that arise from imperfect comprehension of His purpose find their answer in this truth, that God will yet redeem Israel from its iniquities. God is His own interpreter, and when His work of salvation is finished the result will be a conclusive demonstration of that lofty conception of God to which the prophet had attained.

Now this argument of Ezekiel's illustrates a principle of wide application. Many objections that are advanced against the theistic view of the universe seem to proceed on the assumption that the actual state of the world adequately represents the mind of its Creator. The heathen of Ezekiel's day have their modern representatives amongst dispassionate critics of Providence like J. S. Mill, who prove to their own satisfaction that the world cannot be the work of a being answering to the Christian idea of God. Do what you will, they say, to minimise the evils of existence, there is still an amount of undeniable pain and misery in the world which is fatal to your doctrine of an all-powerful and perfectly good Creator. Omnipotence could, and benevolence would, find a remedy; the Author of the universe, therefore, cannot possess both. God, in short, if there be a God, may be benevolent, or He may be omnipotent; but if benevolent He is not omnipotent, and if omnipotent He cannot be benevolent. How very convincing this is--from the standpoint of the neutral, non-Christian observer! And how poor a defence is sometimes made by the optimism which tries to make out that most evils are blessings in disguise, and the rest not worth minding! The Christian religion rises superior to such criticism, mainly in virtue of its living faith in redemption. It does not explain away evil, nor does it profess to account for its origin. It speaks of the whole creation groaning and travailing in pain together even until now. But it also describes the creation as waiting for the manifestation of the sons of God. It teaches us to discover in history the unfolding of a purpose of redemption, the end of which will be the deliverance of mankind from the dominion of sin and their eternal blessedness in the kingdom of our God and His Christ. What Ezekiel foresaw in the form of a national restoration will be accomplished in a world-wide salvation, in a new heavens and a new earth, where there shall be no more curse. But meanwhile to judge of God from what is, apart from what is yet to be revealed, is to repeat the mistake of those who judged Jehovah to be an effete tribal deity because He had suffered His people to go forth out of their land. Those who have been brought into sympathy with the divine purpose, and have experienced the power of the Spirit of God in subduing the evil of their own hearts, can hold with unwavering confidence the hope of a universal victory of good over evil; and in the light of that hope the mysteries that surround the moral government of God cease to disturb their faith in the eternal Love which labours patiently and unceasingly for the redemption of man.

Footnotes:

146. On the whole subject of the relation of the gods to the land see Robertson Smith, Religion of the Semites, pp. 91 ff.

147. Josh. xxii. 19; 1 Sam. xxvi. 19; Hosea ix. 3-5.

148. Ch. xxxvi. 13.

149. Ch. xxxvi. 30: cf. xxxiv. 29.

150. Gen. xxvii. 28, 39.

151. Numb. xiii. 32.

152. Isa. lxii. 4.

153. Vv. 18, 19. The words in brackets are wanting in the LXX.

154. Vv. 20, 22, 23.

155. James ii. 7.

156. Psalm xlii. 10.

157. Ch. xxxix. 23.

158. The phrase "cause you to walk" (ver. 27) is very strong in the Hebrew, almost "I will bring it about that ye walk."

159. The thirty-seventh verse hardly bears the sense which is sometimes put upon it: "I am ready to do this for the house of Israel, yet I will not do it until they have learned to pray for it." That is true of spiritual blessings generally; but Ezekiel's idea is simpler. The particle "yet" is not adversative but temporal, and the "this" refers to what follows, and not to what precedes. The meaning is, "The time shall come when I will answer the prayer of the house of Israel," etc.

160. Chapter XXIII. below.

John J. Skinner

Chapter XXII - Life From The Dead. Chapter xxxvii

The most formidable obstacle to faith on the part of the exiles in the possibility of a national redemption was the complete disintegration of the ancient people of Israel. Hard as it was to realise that Jehovah still lived and reigned in spite of the cessation of His worship, and hard to hope for a recovery of the land of Canaan from the dominion of the heathen, these things were still conceivable. What almost surpassed conception was the restoration of national life to the feeble and demoralised remnant who had survived the fall of the state. It was no mere figure of speech that these exiles employed when they thought of their nation as dead. Cast off by its God, driven from its land, dismembered and deprived of its political organisation, Israel as a people had ceased to exist. Not only were the outward symbols of national unity destroyed, but the national spirit was extinct. Just as the destruction of the bodily organism implies the death of each separate member and organ and cell, so the individual Israelites felt themselves to be as dead men, dragging out an aimless existence without hope in the world. While Israel was alive they had lived in her and for her; all the best part of their life, religion, duty, liberty, and loyalty had been bound up with the consciousness of belonging to a nation with a proud history behind them and a brilliant future for their posterity. Now that Israel had perished all spiritual and ideal significance had gone out of their lives; there remained but a selfish and sordid struggle for existence, and this they felt was not life, but death in life. And thus a promise of deliverance which appealed to them as members of a nation seemed to them a mockery, because they felt in themselves that the bond of national life was irrevocably broken.

The hardest part of Ezekiel's task at this time was therefore to revive the national sentiment, so as to meet the obvious objection that even if Jehovah were able to drive the heathen from His land there was still no people of Israel to whom He could give it. If only the exiles could be brought to believe that Israel had a future, that although now dead it could be raised from the dead, the spiritual meaning of their life would be given back to them in the form of hope, and faith in God would be possible. Accordingly the prophet's thoughts are now directed to the idea of the nation as the third factor of the Messianic hope. He has spoken of the kingdom and the land, and each of these ideals has led him on to the contemplation of the final condition of the world, in which Jehovah's purpose is fully manifested. So in this chapter he finds in the idea of the nation a new point of departure, from which he proceeds to delineate once more the Messianic salvation in its completeness.

I

The vision of the valley of dry bones described in the first part of the chapter contains the answer to the desponding thoughts of the exiles, and seems indeed to be directly suggested by the figure in which the popular feeling was currently expressed: "Our bones are dried; our hope is lost: we feel ourselves cut off" (ver. 11). The fact that the answer came to the prophet in a state of trance may perhaps indicate that his mind had brooded over these words of the people for some time before the moment of inspiration. Recognising how faithfully they represented the actual situation, he was yet unable to suggest an adequate solution of the difficulty by means of the prophetic conceptions hitherto revealed to him. Such a vision as this seems to presuppose a period of intense mental activity on the part of Ezekiel, during which the despairing utterance of his compatriots sounded in his ears; and the image of the dried bones of the house of Israel so fixed itself in his mind that he could not escape its gloomy associations except by a direct communication from above. When at last the hand of the Lord came upon him, the revelation clothed itself in a form corresponding to his previous meditations; the emblem of death and despair is transformed into a symbol of assured hope through the astounding vision which unfolds itself before his inner eye.

In the ecstasy he feels himself led out in spirit to the plain which had been the scene of former appearances of God to His prophet. But on this occasion he sees it covered with bones--"very many on the surface of the valley, and very dry." He is made to pass round about them, in order that the full impression of this spectacle of desolation might sink into his mind. His attention is engrossed by two facts--their exceeding great number, and their parched appearance, as if they had lain there long. In other circumstances the question might have suggested itself, How came these bones there? What countless host has perished here, leaving its unburied bones to bleach and wither on the open plain? But the prophet has no need to think of this. They are the bones which had been familiar to his waking thoughts, the dry bones of the house of Israel. The question he hears addressed to him is not, Whence are these bones? but, Can these bones live? It is the problem which had exercised his faith in thinking of a national restoration which thus comes back to him in vision, to receive its final solution from Him who alone can give it.

The prophet's hesitating answer probably reveals the struggle between faith and sight, between hope and fear, which was latent in his mind. He dare not say No, for that would be to limit the power of Him whom he knows to be omnipotent, and also to shut out the last gleam of hope from his own mind. Yet in presence of that appalling scene of hopeless decay and death he cannot of his own initiative assert the possibility of resurrection. In the abstract all things are possible with God; but whether this particular thing, so inconceivable to men, is within the active purpose of God, is a question which none can answer save God Himself. Ezekiel does what man must always do in such a case--he throws himself back on God, and reverently awaits the disclosure of His will, saying, "O Jehovah God, Thou knowest."

It is instructive to notice that the divine answer comes through the consciousness of a duty. Ezekiel is commanded first of all to prophesy over these dry bones; and in the words given him to utter the solution of his own inward perplexity is wrapped up. "Say unto them, O ye dry bones, hear the word of Jehovah.... Behold, I will cause breath to enter into you, and ye shall live" (vv. 4, 5). In this way he is not only taught that the agency by which Jehovah will effect His purpose is the prophetic word, but he is also reminded that the truth now revealed to him is to be the guide of his practical ministry, and that only in the steadfast discharge of his prophetic duty can he hold fast the hope of Israel's resurrection. The problem that has exercised him is not one that can be settled in retirement and inaction. What he receives is not a mere answer, but a message, and the delivery of the message is the only way in which he can realise the truth of it, his activity as a prophet being indeed a necessary element in the fulfilment of his words. Let him preach the word of God to these dry bones, and he will know that they can live; but if he fails to do this, he will sink back into the unbelief to which all things are impossible. Faith comes in the act of prophesying.

Ezekiel did as he was commanded; he prophesied over the dry bones, and immediately he was sensible of the effect of his words. He heard a rustling, and looking he saw that the bones were coming together, bone to his bone. He does not need to tell us how his heart rejoiced at this first sign of life returning to these dead bones, and as he watched the whole process by which they were built up into the semblance of men. It is described in minute detail, so that no feature of the impression produced by the stupendous miracle may be lost. It is divided into two stages, the restoration of the bodily frame and the imparting of the principle of life.

This division cannot have any special significance when applied to the actual nation, such as that the outward order of the state must be first established, and then the national consciousness renewed. It belongs to the imagery of the vision, and follows the order observed in the original creation of man as described in the second chapter of Genesis. God first formed man of the dust of the ground, and afterwards breathed into his nostrils the breath of life, so that he became a living soul. So here we have first a description of the process by which the bodies were built up, the skeletons being formed from the scattered bones, and then clothed successively with sinews and flesh and skin. The reanimation of these still lifeless bodies is a separate act of creative energy, in which, however, the agency is still the word of God in the mouth of the prophet. He is bidden call for the breath to "come from the four winds of heaven, and breathe upon these slain that they may live." In Hebrew the words for wind, breath, and spirit are identical; and thus the wind becomes a symbol of the universal divine Spirit which is the source of all life, while the breath is a symbol of that Spirit as so to speak specialised in the individual man, or in other words of his personal life. In the case of the first man Jehovah breathed into his nostrils the breath of life, and the idea here is precisely the same. The wind from the four quarters of heaven which becomes the breath of this vast assemblage of men is conceived as the breath of God, and symbolises the life-giving Spirit which makes each of them a living person. The resurrection is complete. The men live, and stand up upon their feet an exceeding great army.

This is the simplest, as well as the most suggestive, of Ezekiel's visions, and carries its interpretation on the face of it. The single idea which it expresses is the restoration of the Hebrew nationality through the quickening influence of the Spirit of Jehovah on the surviving members of the old house of Israel. It is not a prophecy of the resurrection of individual Israelites who have perished. The bones are "the whole house of Israel" now in exile; they are alive as individuals, but as members of a nation they are dead and hopeless of revival. This is made clear by the explanation of the vision given in vv. 11-14. It is addressed to those who think of themselves as cut off from the higher interests and activities of the national life. By a slight change of figure they are conceived as dead and buried; and the resurrection is represented as an opening of their graves. But the grave is no more to be understood literally than the dry bones of the vision itself; both are symbols of the gloomy and despairing view which the exiles take of their own condition. The substance of the prophet's message is that the God who raises the dead and calls the things that are not as though they were is able to bring together the scattered members of the house of Israel and form them into a new people through the operation of His life-giving Spirit.

It has often been supposed that, although the passage may not directly teach the resurrection of the body, it nevertheless implies a certain familiarity with that doctrine on the part of Ezekiel, if not of his hearers likewise. If the raising of dead men to life could be used as an analogy of a national restoration, the former conception must have been at least more obvious than the latter, otherwise the prophet would be explaining obscurum per obscurius. This argument, however, has only a superficial plausibility. It confounds two things which are distinct--the mere conception of resurrection, which is all that was necessary to make the vision intelligible, and settled faith in it as an element of the Messianic expectation. That God by a miracle could restore the dead to life no devout Israelite ever doubted. [161] But it is to be noted that the recorded instances of such miracles are all of those recently dead; and there is no evidence of a general belief in the possibility of resurrection for those whose bones were scattered and dry. It is this very impossibility, indeed, that gives point to the metaphor under which the people here express their sense of hopelessness. Moreover, if the prophet had presupposed the doctrine of individual resurrection, he could hardly have used it as an illustration in the way he does. The mere prospect of a resuscitation of the multitudes of Israelites who had perished would of itself have been a sufficient answer to the despondency of the exiles; and it would have been an anti-climax to use it as an argument for something much less wonderful. We must also bear in mind that while the resurrection of a nation may be to us little more than a figure of speech, to the Hebrew mind it was an object of thought more real and tangible than the idea of personal immortality.

It would appear therefore that in the order of revelation the hope of the resurrection is first presented in the promise of a resurrection of the dead nation of Israel, and only in the second instance as the resurrection of individual Israelites who should have passed away without sharing in the glory of the latter days. Like the early converts to Christianity, the Old Testament believers sorrowed for those who fell asleep when the Messiah's kingdom was supposed to be just at hand, until they found consolation in the blessed hope of a resurrection with which Paul comforted the Church at Thessalonica. [162] In Ezekiel we find that doctrine as yet only in its more general form of a national resurrection; but it can hardly be doubted that the form in which he expressed it prepared the way for the fuller revelation of a resurrection of the individual. In two later passages of the prophetic Scriptures we seem to find clear indications of progress in this direction. One is a difficult verse in the twenty-sixth chapter of Isaiah--part of a prophecy usually assigned to a period later than Ezekiel--where the writer, after a lamentation over the disappointments and wasted efforts of the present, suddenly breaks into a rapture of hope as he thinks of a time when departed Israelites shall be restored to life to join the ranks of the ransomed people of God: "Let thy dead live again! Let my dead bodies arise! Awake and rejoice, ye that dwell in the dust, for thy dew is a dew of light, and the earth shall yield up [her] shades." [163] There does not seem to be any doubt that what is here predicted is the actual resurrection of individual members of the people of Israel to share in the blessings of the kingdom of God. The other passage referred to is in the book of Daniel, where we have the first explicit prediction of a resurrection both of the just and the unjust. In the time of trouble when the people is delivered "many of them that sleep in the dust of the earth shall awake, some to everlasting life, and some to shame and everlasting contempt." [164]

These remarks are made merely to show in what sense Ezekiel's vision may be regarded as a contribution to the Old Testament doctrine of personal immortality. It is so not by its direct teaching, nor yet by its presuppositions, but by the suggestiveness of its imagery, opening out a line of thought which under the guidance of the Spirit of truth led to a fuller disclosure of the care of God for the individual life, and His purpose to redeem from the power of the grave those who had departed this life in His faith and hope.

But this line of inquiry lies somewhat apart from the main teaching of the passage before us as a message for the Church in all ages. The passage teaches with striking clearness the continuity of God's redeeming work in the world, in spite of hindrances which to human eyes seem insurmountable. The gravest hindrance, both in appearance and in reality, is the decay of faith and vital religion in the Church itself. There are times when earnest men are tempted to say that the Church's hope is lost and her bones are dried--when laxity of life and lukewarmness in devotion pervade all her members, and she ceases to influence the world for good. And yet when we consider that the whole history of God's cause is one long process of raising dead souls to spiritual life and building up a kingdom of God out of fallen humanity, we see that the true hope of the Church can never be lost. It lies in the life-giving, regenerating power of the divine Spirit, and the promise that the word of God does not return to Him void but prospers in the thing whereto He sends it. That is the great lesson of Ezekiel's vision, and although its immediate application may be limited to the occasion that called it forth, yet the analogy on which it is founded is taken up by our Lord Himself and extended to the proclamation of His truth to the world at large: "The hour is coming, and now is, when the dead shall hear the voice of the Son of God; and they that hear shall live."[165] We perhaps too readily empty these strong terms of their meaning. The Spirit of God is apt to become a mere expression for the religious and moral influences lodged in a Christian society, and we come to rely on these agencies for the dissemination of Christian principles and the formation of Christian character. We forget that behind all this there is something which is compared to the imparting of life where there was none, something which is the work of the Spirit of which we cannot tell whence it cometh and whither it goeth. But in times of low spirituality, when the love of many waxes cold, and there are few signs of zeal and activity in the service of Christ, men learn to fall back in faith on the invisible power of God to make His word effectual for the revival of His cause among men. And this happens constantly in narrow spheres which may never attract the notice of the world. There are positions in the Church still where Christ's servants are called to labour in the faith of Ezekiel, with appearances all against them, and nothing to inspire them but the conviction that the word they preach is the power of God and able even to bring life to the dead.

II

The second half of the chapter speaks of a special feature of the national restoration, the reunion of the kingdoms of Judah and Israel under one sceptre. This is represented first of all by a symbolic action. The prophet is directed to take two pieces of wood, apparently in the form of sceptres, and to write upon them inscriptions dedicating them respectively to Judah and Joseph, the heads of the two confederacies out of which the rival monarchies were formed. The "companions" (ver. 16)--i.e., allies--of Judah are the two tribes of Benjamin and Simeon; those of Joseph are all the other tribes, who stood under the hegemony of Ephraim. If the second inscription is rather more complicated than the first, it is because of the fact that there was no actual tribe of Joseph. It therefore runs thus: "For Joseph, the staff of Ephraim, and all the house of Israel his confederates." These two staves then he is to put together so that they become one sceptre in his hand. It is a little difficult to decide whether this was a sign that was actually performed before the people, or one that is only imagined. It depends partly on what we take to be meant by the joining of the two pieces. If Ezekiel merely took two sticks, put them end to end, and made them look like one, then no doubt he did this in public, for otherwise there would be no use in mentioning the circumstance at all. But if the meaning is, as seems more probable, that when the rods are put together they miraculously grow into one, then we see that such a sign has a value for the prophet's own mind as a symbol of the truth revealed to him, and it is no longer necessary to assume that the action was really performed. The purpose of the sign is not merely to suggest the idea of political unity, which is too simple to require any such illustration, but rather to indicate the completeness of the union and the divine force needed to bring it about. The difficulty of conceiving a perfect fusion of the two parts of the nation was really very great, the cleavage between Judah and the North being much older than the monarchy, and having been accentuated by centuries of political separation and rivalry.

To us the most noteworthy fact is the steadfastness with which the prophets of this period cling to the hope of a restoration of the northern tribes, although nearly a century and a half had now elapsed since "Ephraim was broken from being a people."[166] Ezekiel, like Jeremiah, is unable to think of an Israel which does not include the representatives of the ten northern tribes. Whether any communication was kept up with the colonies of Israelites that had been transported from Samaria to Assyria we do not know, but they are regarded as still existing, and still remembered by Jehovah. The resurrection of the nation which Ezekiel has just predicted is expressly said to apply to the whole house of Israel, and now he goes on to announce that this "exceeding great army" shall march to its land not under two banners, but under one.

We have touched already, in speaking of the Messianic idea, on the reasons which lead the prophets to put so much emphasis on this union. They felt as strongly on the point as a High Churchman does about the sin of schism, and it would not be difficult for the latter to show that his point of view and his ideals closely resemble those of the prophets. The rending of the body of Christ which is supposed to be involved in a breach of external unity is paralleled by the disruption of the Hebrew state, which violates the unity of the one people of Jehovah. The idea of the Church as the bride of Christ, is the same idea under which Hosea expresses the relations between Jehovah and Israel, and it necessarily carries with it the unity of the people of Israel in the one case and of the Church in the other. It must be admitted also that the evils resulting from the division between Judah and Israel have been reproduced, with consequences a thousand times more disastrous to religion, in the strife and uncharitableness, the party spirit and jealousies and animosities, which different denominations of Christians have invariably exhibited towards each other when they were close enough for mutual interest. But granting all this, and granting that what is called schism is essentially the same thing that the prophets desired to see removed, it does not at once follow that dissent is in itself sinful, and still less that the sin is necessarily on the side of the Dissenter. The question is whether the national standpoint of the prophets is altogether applicable to the communion of saints in Christ, whether the body of Christ is really torn asunder by differences in organisation and opinion, whether, in short, anything is necessary to avoid the guilt of schism beyond keeping the unity of the Spirit in the bond of peace. The Old Testament dealt with men in the mass, as members of a nation, and its standards can hardly be adequate to the polity of a religion which has to provide for the freedom of the individual conscience before God. At the worst the Dissenter may point out that the Old Testament schism was necessary as a protest against tyranny and despotism, that in this aspect it was sanctioned by the inspired prophets of the age, that its undoubted evils were partly compensated by a freer expansion of religious life, and finally that even the prophets did not expect it to be healed before the millennium.

From the idea of the reunited nation Ezekiel returns easily to the promise of the Davidic king and the blessings of the Messianic dispensation. The one people implies one shepherd, and also one land, and one spirit to walk in Jehovah's judgments and to observe His statutes to do them. The various elements which enter into the conception of national salvation are thus gathered up and combined in one picture of the people's everlasting felicity. And the whole is crowned by the promise of Jehovah's presence with the people, sanctifying and protecting them from His sanctuary. This final condition of things is permanent and eternal. The sources of internal dispeace are removed by the washing away of Israel's iniquities, and the impossibility of any disturbance from without is illustrated by the onslaught of the heathen nations described in the following chapters.

Footnotes:

161. Cf. 1 Kings xvii.; 2 Kings iv. 13 ff., xiii. 21.
162. 1 Thess. iv. 13 ff.
163. Isa. xxvi. 19.
164. Dan. xii. 2.
165. John v. 25: cf. vv. 28, 29.
166. Isa. vii. 8.

Chapter XXIII - The Conversion Of Israel

In an early chapter of this volume [167] we had occasion to notice some theological principles which appear to have guided the prophet's thinking from the first. It was evident even then that these principles pointed towards a definite theory of the conversion of Israel and the process by which it was to be effected. In subsequent prophecies we have seen how constantly Ezekiel's thoughts revert to this theme, as now one aspect of it and then another is disclosed to him. We have also glanced at one passage [168] which seemed to be a connected statement of the divine procedure as bearing on the restoration of Israel. But we have now reached a stage in the exposition where all this lies behind us. In the chapters that remain to be considered the regeneration of the people is assumed to have taken place; their religion and their morality are regarded as established on a stable and permanent basis, and all that has to be done is to describe the institutions by which the benefits of salvation may be conserved and handed down from age to age of the Messianic dispensation. The present is therefore a fitting opportunity for an attempt to describe Ezekiel's doctrine of conversion as a whole. It is all the more desirable that the attempt should be made because the national salvation is the central interest of the whole book; and if we can understand the prophet's teaching on this subject, we shall have the key to his whole system of theology.

1. The first point to be noticed, and the one most characteristic of Ezekiel, is the divine motive for the redemption of Israel--Jehovah's regard for His own name. This thought finds expression in many parts of the book, but nowhere more clearly than in the twenty-second verse of the thirty-sixth chapter: "Not for your sakes do I act, O house of Israel, but for My holy name, which ye have profaned among the heathen, whither ye went." Similarly in the thirty-second verse: "Not for your sakes do I act, saith the Lord Jehovah, be it known unto you: be ashamed and confounded for your own ways, O house of Israel." There is an apparent harshness in these declarations which makes it easy to present them in a repellent light. They have been taken to mean that Jehovah is absolutely indifferent to the weal or woe of the people except in so far as it reflects on His own credit with the world; that He accepts the relationship between Him and Israel, but does so in the spirit of a selfish parent who exerts himself to save his child from disgrace merely in order to prevent his own name from being dragged in the mire. It would be difficult to explain how such a Being should be at all concerned about what men think of Him. If Jehovah has no interest in Israel, it is hard to see why He should be sensitive to the opinion of the rest of mankind. That is an idea of God which no man can seriously hold, and we may be certain that it is a perversion of Ezekiel's meaning. Everything depends on how much is included in the "name" of Jehovah. If it denotes mere arbitrary power, delighting in its own exercise and the awe which it excites, then we might conceive of the divine action as ruled by a boundless egoism, to which all human interests are alike indifferent. But that is not the conception of God which Ezekiel has. He is a moral Being, one who has compassion on other things besides His own name, [169] one who has no pleasure in the death of the wicked, but that he should turn from his way and live. [170] But when this aspect of His character is included in the name of God, we see that regard for His name cannot mean mere regard for His own interests, as if these were opposed to the interests of His creatures; but means the desire to be known as He is, as a God of mercy and righteousness as well as of infinite power.

The name of God is that by which He is known amongst men. It is more than His honour or reputation, although that is included in it according to Hebrew idiom; it is the expression of His character or His personality. To act for His name's sake, therefore, is to act so that His true character may be more fully revealed, and so that men's thoughts of Him may more truly correspond to that which in Himself He is. There is plainly nothing in this inconsistent with the deepest interest in men's spiritual well-being. Jehovah is the God of salvation, and desires to reveal Himself as such; and whether we say that He saves men in order that He may be known as a Saviour, or that He makes Himself known in order to save them, does not make any real difference. Revelation and redemption are one thing. And when Ezekiel says that regard for His own name is the supreme motive of Jehovah's action, he does not teach that Jehovah is uninfluenced by care for man; if the question had been put to him, he would have said that care for man is one of the attributes included in the Name which Jehovah is concerned to reveal.

The real meaning of Ezekiel's doctrine will perhaps be best understood from its negative statement. What is meant to be excluded by the expression "not for your sakes"? It might no doubt mean, "not because I care at all for you"; but that we have seen to be inconsistent with other aspects of Ezekiel's teaching about the divine character. All that it necessarily implies is "not for any good that I find in you." It is a protest against the idea of Pharisaic self-righteousness that a man may have a legal claim upon God through his own merits. It is true that that was not a prevalent notion amongst the people in the time of Ezekiel. But their state of mind was one in which such a thought might easily arise. They were convinced of having been entirely in the wrong in their conceptions of the relation between them and Jehovah. The pagan notion that the people is indispensable to the god on account of a physical bond between them had broken down in the recent experience of Israel, and with it had vanished every natural ground for the hope of salvation. In such circumstances the promise of deliverance would naturally raise the thought that there must after all be something in Israel that was pleasing to Jehovah, and that the prophet's denunciations of their past sins were overdone. In order to guard against that error Ezekiel explicitly asserts, what was involved in the whole of his teaching, that the mercy of God was not called forth by any good in Israel, but that nevertheless there are immutable reasons in the divine nature on which the certainty of Israel's redemption may be built.

The truth here taught is therefore, in theological language, the sovereignty of the divine grace. Ezekiel's statement of it is liable to all the distortions and misrepresentations to which that doctrine has been subjected at the hands both of its friends and its enemies; but when fairly treated it is no more objectionable than any other expression of the same truth to be found in Scripture. In Ezekiel's case it was the result of a penetrating analysis of the moral condition of his people which led him to see that there was nothing in them to suggest the possibility of their being restored. It is only when he falls back on the thought of what God is, on the divine necessity of vindicating His holiness in the salvation of His people, that his faith in Israel's future finds a sure point of support. And so in general a profound sense of human sinfulness will always throw the mind back on the idea of God as the one immovable ground of confidence in the ultimate redemption of the individual and the world. When the doctrine is pressed to the conclusion that God saves men in spite of themselves, and merely to display His power over them, it becomes false and pernicious, and indeed self-contradictory. But so long as we hold fast to the truth that God is love, and that the glory of God is the manifestation of His love, the doctrine of the divine sovereignty only expresses the unchangeableness of that love and its final victory over the sin of the world.

2. The intellectual side of the conversion of Israel is the acceptance of that idea of God which to the prophet is summed up in the name of Jehovah. This is expressed in the standing formula which denotes the effect of all God's dealings with men, "They shall know that I am Jehovah." We need not, however, repeat what has been already said as to the meaning of these words. [171] Nor shall we dwell on the effect of the national judgment as a means towards producing a right impression of Jehovah's nature. It is possible that as time went on Ezekiel came to see that chastisement alone would not effect the moral change in the exiles which was necessary to bring them into sympathy with the divine purposes. In the early prophecy of ch. vi. the knowledge of Jehovah and the self-condemnation which accompanies it are spoken of as the direct result of His judgment on sin, [172] and this undoubtedly was one element in the conversion of the people to right thoughts about God. But in all other passages this feeling of self-loathing is not the beginning but the end of conversion; it is caused by the experience of pardon and redemption following upon punishment. [173] There is also another aspect of judgment which may be mentioned in passing for the sake of completeness. It is that which is expounded in the end of the twentieth chapter. There the judgment which still stands between the exiles and the return to their own land is represented as a sifting process, in which those who have undergone a spiritual change are finally separated from those who perish in their impenitence. This idea does not occur in the prophecies subsequent to the fall of Jerusalem, and it may be doubtful how it fits into the scheme of redemption there unfolded. The prophet here regards conversion as a process wholly carried through by the operation of Jehovah on the mind of the people; and what we have next to consider is the steps by which this great end is accomplished. They are these two--forgiveness and regeneration.

3. The forgiveness of sins is denoted in the thirty-sixth chapter, as we have already seen, by the symbol of sprinkling with clean water. But it must not be supposed that this isolated figure is the only form in which the doctrine appears in Ezekiel's exposition of the process of salvation. On the contrary forgiveness is the fundamental assumption of the whole argument, and is present in every promise of future blessedness to the people. For the Old Testament idea of forgiveness is extremely simple, resting as it does on the analogy of forgiveness in human life. The spiritual fact which constitutes the essence of forgiveness is the change in Jehovah's disposition towards His people which is manifested by the renewal of those indispensable conditions of national well-being which in His anger He had taken away. The restoration of Israel to its own land is thus not simply a token of forgiveness, but the act of forgiveness itself, and the only form in which the fact could be realised in the experience of the nation. In this sense the whole of Ezekiel's predictions of the

Messianic deliverance and the glories that follow it are one continuous promise of forgiveness, setting forth the truth that Jehovah's love to His people persists in spite of their sin, and works victoriously for their redemption and restoration to the full enjoyment of His favour. There is perhaps one point in which we discover a difference between Ezekiel's conception and that of his predecessors. According to the common prophetic doctrine penitence, including amendment, is the moral effect of Jehovah's chastisement, and is the necessary condition of pardon. We have seen that there is some doubt whether Ezekiel regarded repentance as the result of judgment, and the same doubt exists as to whether in the order of salvation repentance is a preliminary or a consequence of forgiveness. The truth is that the prophet appears to combine both conceptions. In urging individuals to prepare for the coming of the kingdom of God he makes repentance a necessary condition of entering it; but in describing the whole process of salvation as the work of God he makes contrition for sin the result of reflection on the goodness of Jehovah already experienced in the peaceful occupation of the land of Canaan.

4. The idea of regeneration is very prominent in Ezekiel's teaching. The need for a radical change in the national character was impressed on him by the spectacle which he witnessed daily of evil tendencies and practices persisted in, in spite of the clearest demonstration that they were hateful to Jehovah and had been the cause of the nation's calamities. And he does not ascribe this state of things merely to the influence of tradition and public opinion and evil example, but traces it to its source in the hardness and corruption of the individual nature. It was evident that no mere change of intellectual conviction would avail to alter the currents of life among the exiles; the heart must be renewed, out of which are the issues both of personal and national life. Hence the promise of regeneration is expressed as a taking away of the stony, unimpressible heart that was in them, and putting within them a heart of flesh, a new heart and a new spirit. In exhorting individuals to repentance Ezekiel calls on them to make themselves a new heart and a new spirit, [174] meaning that their repentance must be genuine, extending to the inner motives and springs of action, and not be confined to outward signs of mourning. [175] But in other connections the new heart and spirit is represented as a gift, the result of the operation of the divine grace. [176]

Closely connected with this, perhaps only the same truth in another form, is the promise of the outpouring of the Spirit of God. [177] The general expectation of a new supernatural power infused into the national life in the latter days is common in the prophets. It appears in Hosea under the beautiful image of the dew, [178] and in Isaiah it is expressed in the consciousness that the desolation of the land must continue "until spirit be poured upon us from on high." [179] But no earlier prophet presents the idea of the Spirit as a principle of regeneration with the precision and clearness which the doctrine assumes in the hands of Ezekiel. What in Hosea and Isaiah may be only a divine influence, quickening and developing the flagging spiritual energies of the people, is here revealed as a creative power, the source of a new life, and the beginning of all that possesses moral or spiritual worth in the people of God.

5. It only remains for us now to note the twofold effect of these operations of Jehovah's grace in the religious and moral condition of the nation. There will be produced, in the first place, a new readiness and power of obedience to the divine commandments. [180] Like the apostle, they will not only "consent unto the law that it is good"; [181] but in virtue of the new "Spirit of life" given to them, they will be in a real sense "free from the law," [182] because the inward impulse of their own regenerate nature will lead them to fulfil it perfectly. The inefficiency of law as a mere external authority acting on men by hope of reward and fear of punishment was perceived both by Jeremiah and Ezekiel almost as clearly as by Paul, although this conviction on the part of the prophets was based on observation of national depravity rather than on their personal experience. It led Jeremiah to the conception of a new covenant under which Jehovah will write His law on men's hearts; [183] and Ezekiel expresses the same truth in the promise of a new Spirit inclining the people to walk in Jehovah's statutes and to keep His judgments.

The second inward result of salvation is shame and self-loathing on account of past transgressions. [184] It seems strange that the prophet should dwell so much on this as a mark of Israel's saved condition. His strong protest against the doctrine of inherited guilt in the eighteenth chapter would have led us to expect that the members of the new Israel would not be conscious of any responsibility for the sins of the old. But here, as in other instances, the conception of the personified nation proves itself a better vehicle of religious truth from the Old Testament standpoint than the religious relations of the individual. The continuity of the national consciousness sustains that profound sense of unworthiness which is an essential element of true reconciliation to God, although each individual Israelite in the kingdom of God knows that he is not accountable for the iniquity of his fathers.

***

John J. Skinner

This outline of the prophet's conception of salvation illustrates the truth of the remark that Ezekiel is the first dogmatic theologian. In so far as it is the business of a theologian to exhibit the logical connection of the ideas which express man's relation to God, Ezekiel more than any other prophet may claim the title. Truths which are the presuppositions of all prophecy are to him objects of conscious reflection, and emerge from his hands in the shape of clearly formulated doctrines. There is probably no single element of his teaching which may not be traced in the writings of his predecessors, but there is none which has not gained from him a more distinct intellectual expression. And what is specially remarkable is the manner in which the doctrines are bound together in the unity of a system. In grounding the necessity of redemption in the divine nature, Ezekiel may be said to foreshadow the theology which is often called Calvinistic or Augustinian, but which might more truly be called Pauline. Although the final remedy for the sin of the world had not yet been revealed, the scheme of redemption disclosed to Ezekiel agrees with much of the teaching of the New Testament regarding the effects of the work of Christ on the individual. Speaking of the passage ch. xxxvi. 16-38 Dr. Davidson writes as follows:--

"Probably no passage in the Old Testament of the same extent offers so complete a parallel to New Testament doctrine, particularly to that of St. Paul. It is doubtful if the apostle quotes Ezekiel anywhere, but his line of thought entirely coincides with his. The same conceptions and in the same order belong to both,--forgiveness (ver. 25); regeneration, a new heart and spirit (ver. 26); the Spirit of God as the ruling power in the new life (ver. 27); the issue of this, the keeping of the requirements of God's law (ver. 27; Rom. viii. 4); the effect of being under grace' in softening the human heart and leading to obedience (ver. 31; Rom. vi., vii.); and the organic connection of Israel's history with Jehovah's revelation of Himself to the nations (vv. 33-36; Rom. xi.)."

Footnotes:

167. Chapter V., above.
168. Ch. xxxvi. 16-38.
169. Ch. xxxvi. 21.
170. Chs. xviii. 23, xxxiii. 11.
171. See pp. 975 f. above.
172. Ch. vi. 8-10.
173. Chs. xvi. 61-63, xx. 43, 44, xxxvi. 31, 32.
174. Ch. xviii. 31.
175. Cf. Joel's "Rend your heart, and not your garments" (Joel ii. 13).
176. Chs. xi. 19, xxxvi. 26, 27.
177. Chs. xxxvi. 27, xxxvii. 14.
178. Hosea xiv. 5.
179. Isa. xxxii. 15.
180. Chs. xi. 20, xxxvi. 27.
181. Rom. vii. 16.
182. Rom. viii. 2.
183. Jer. xxxi. 33.
184. Chs. vi. 9, xvi. 63, xx. 43, xxxvi. 31, 32.

Chapter XXIV - Jehovah's Final Victory. Chapters xxxviii., xxxix

These chapters give the impression of having been intended to stand at the close of the book of Ezekiel. Their present position is best explained on the supposition that the original collection of Ezekiel's prophecies actually ended here, and that the remaining chapters (xl.-xlviii.) form an appendix, added at a later period without disturbing the plan on which the book had been arranged. In chronological order, at all events, the oracle on Gog comes after the vision of the last nine chapters. It marks the utmost limit of Ezekiel's vision of the future of the kingdom of God. It represents the dénouement of the great drama of Jehovah's self-manifestation to the nations of the world. It describes an event which is to take place in the far-distant future, long after the Messianic age has begun and after Israel has long been settled peacefully in its own land. Certain considerations, which we shall notice at the end of this lecture, brought home to the prophet's mind the conviction that the lessons of Israel's restoration did not afford a sufficient illustration of Jehovah's glory or of the meaning of His past dealings with His people. The conclusive demonstration of this is therefore to be furnished by the destruction of Gog and his myrmidons when in the latter days they make an onslaught on the Holy Land.

The idea of a great world-catastrophe, following after a long interval the establishment of the kingdom of God, is peculiar to Ezekiel amongst the prophets of the Old Testament. According to other prophets the judgment of the nations takes place in a "day of Jehovah" which is the crisis of history; and the Messianic era which follows is a period of undisturbed tranquillity in which the knowledge of the true God penetrates to the remotest regions of the earth. In Ezekiel, on the other hand, the judgment of the world is divided into two acts. The nearer nations which have played a part in the history of Israel in the past form a group by themselves; their punishment is a preliminary to the restoration of Israel, and the impression produced by that restoration is for them a signal, though not perhaps a complete, [185] vindication of the Godhead of Jehovah. But the outlying barbarians, who hover on the outskirts of civilisation, are not touched by this revelation of the divine power and goodness; they seem to be represented as utterly ignorant of the marvellous course of events by which Israel has been brought to dwell securely in the midst of the nations.[186] These, accordingly, are reserved for a final reckoning, in which the power of Jehovah will be displayed with the terrible physical convulsions which mark the great day of the Lord. [187] Only then will the full meaning of Israel's history be disclosed to the world; in particular it will be seen that it was for their sin that they had fallen under the power of the heathen, and not because of Jehovah's inability to protect them. [188]

These are some general features of the prophecy which at once attract attention. We shall now examine the details of the picture, and then proceed to consider its significance in relation to other elements of Ezekiel's teaching.

I

The thirty-eighth chapter may be divided into three sections of seven verses each.

i. Vv. 3-9.--The prophet having been commanded to direct his face towards Gog in the land of Magog, is commissioned to announce the fate that is in store for him and his hosts in the latter days. The name of this mysterious and formidable personage was evidently familiar to the Jewish world of Ezekiel's time, although to us its origin is altogether obscure. The most plausible suggestion, on the whole, is perhaps that which identifies it with the name of the Lydian monarch Gyges, which appears on the Assyrian monuments in the form Gugu, corresponding as closely as is possible to the Hebrew Gog. [189] But in the mind of Ezekiel Gog is hardly an historical figure. He is but the impersonation of the dreaded power of the northern barbarians, already recognised as a serious danger to the peace of the world. His designation as prince of Rosh, Meshech, and Tubal points to the region east of the Black Sea as the seat of his power. [190] He is the captain of a vast multitude of horsemen, gorgeously arrayed, and armed with shield, helmet, and sword. But although Gog himself belongs to the "uttermost north," he gathers under his banner all the most distant nations both of the north and the south. Not only northern peoples like the Cimmerians and Armenians,[191] but Persians and Africans, [192] all of them with shield and helmet, swell the ranks of his motley army. The name of Gog is thus on the way to become a symbol of the implacable enmity of this world to the kingdom of God; as in the book of the Revelation it appears as the designation of the ungodly world-power which perishes in conflict with the saints of God (Rev. xx. 7 ff.).

Gog therefore is summoned to hold himself in readiness, as Jehovah's reserve, [193] against the last days, when the purpose for which he has been raised up will be made manifest. After many days he shall receive his marching orders; Jehovah Himself will lead forth his squadrons and the innumerable hosts of nations that follow in his train, [194] and bring them up against the mountains of Israel, now reclaimed from desolation, and against a nation gathered from among many peoples, dwelling in peace and security. The advance of these destructive hordes is likened to a tempest, and their innumerable multitude is pictured as a cloud covering all the land (ver. 9).

ii. Vv. 10-16.--But like the Assyrian in the time of Isaiah, Gog "meaneth not so"; he is not aware that he is Jehovah's instrument, his purpose being to "destroy and cut off nations not a few."[195] Hence the prophet proceeds to a new description of the enterprise of Gog, laying stress on the "evil thought" that will arise in his heart and lure him to his doom. What urges him on is the lust of plunder. The report of the people of Israel as a people that has amassed wealth and substance, and is at the same time defenceless, dwelling in a land without walls or bolts or gates, will have reached him. These two verses (11, 12) are interesting as giving a picture of Ezekiel's conception of the final state of the people of God. They dwell in the "navel of the world"; they are rich and prosperous, so that the fame of them has gone forth through all lands; they are destitute of military resources, yet are unmolested in the enjoyment of their favoured lot because of the moral effect of Jehovah's name on all nations that know their history. To Gog, however, who knows nothing of Jehovah, they will seem an easy conquest, and he will come up confident of victory to seize spoil and take booty and lay his hand on waste places reinhabited and a people gathered out of the heathen. The news of the great expedition and the certainty of its success will rouse the cupidity of the trading communities from all the ends of the earth, and they will attach themselves as camp-followers to the army of Gog. In historic times this rôle would naturally have fallen to the Phoenicians, who had a keen eye for business of this description. [196] But Ezekiel is thinking of a time when Tyre shall be no more; and its place is taken by the mercantile tribes of Arabia and the ancient Phoenician colony of Tarshish. The whole world will then resound with the fame of Gog's expedition, and the most distant nations will await its issue with eager expectation. This then is the meaning of Gog's destiny. In the time when Israel dwells peacefully he will be restless and eager for spoil; [197] his multitudes will be set in motion, and throw themselves on the land, covering it like a cloud. But this is Jehovah's doing, and the purpose of it is that the nations may know Him and that He may be sanctified in Gog before their eyes.

iii. Vv. 17-23.--These verses are in the main a description of the annihilation of Gog's host by the fierce wrath of Jehovah; but this is introduced by a reference to unfulfilled prophecies which are to receive their accomplishment in this great catastrophe. It is difficult to say what particular prophecies are meant. Those which most readily suggest themselves are perhaps the fourth chapter of Joel and the twelfth and fourteenth of Zechariah; but these probably belong to a later date than Ezekiel. The prophecies of Zephaniah and Jeremiah, called forth by the Scythian invasion, [198] have also been thought of, although the point of view there is different from that of Ezekiel. In Jeremiah and Zephaniah the Scythians are the scourge of God, appointed for the chastisement of the sinful nation; whereas Gog is brought up against a holy people, and for the express purpose of having judgment executed on himself. On the supposition that Ezekiel's vision was coloured by his recollection of the Scythians, this view has no doubt the greatest likelihood. It is possible, however, that the allusion is not to any particular group of prophecies, but to a general idea which pervades prophecy--the expectation of a great conflict in which the power of the world shall be arrayed against Jehovah and Israel, and the issue of which shall exhibit the sole sovereignty of the true God to all mankind. [199] It is of course unnecessary to suppose that any prophet had mentioned Gog by name in a prediction of the future. All that is meant is that Gog is the person in whom the substance of previous oracles is to be accomplished.

The question of ver. 17 leads thus to the announcement of the outpouring of Jehovah's indignation on the violators of His territory. As soon as Gog sets foot on the soil of Israel, Jehovah's wrath is kindled against him. A mighty earthquake shall shatter the mountains and level every wall to the ground and strike terror into the hearts of all creatures. The host of Gog shall be panic-stricken, [200] each man turning his sword against his fellow; while Jehovah completes the slaughter by pestilence and blood, rain and hailstones, fire and brimstone. The deliverance of Israel is effected without the help of any human arm; it is the doing of Jehovah, who thus magnifies and sanctifies Himself and makes Himself known before the eyes of many peoples, so that they may know Him to be Jehovah.

iv. Ch. xxxix. 1-8.--Commencing afresh with a new apostrophe to Gog, Ezekiel here recapitulates the substance of the previous chapter--the bringing up of Gog from the farthest north, his destruction on the mountains of Israel, and the effect of this on the surrounding nations. Mention is expressly made of the bow and arrows which were the distinctive weapons of the Scythian horsemen. [201] These are struck from the grasp of Gog, and the mighty host falls on the open field to be devoured by wild beasts and by ravenous birds of every feather. But the judgment is universal in its extent; it reaches to Magog, the distant abode of Gog, and all the remote lands whence his auxiliaries were drawn. This is the day whereof Jehovah has spoken by His servants the prophets of Israel, the day which finally manifests His glory to all the ends of the earth.

v. Vv. 9-16.--Here the prophet falls into a more prosaic strain, as he proceeds to describe with characteristic fulness of detail the sequel of the great invasion. As the English story of the Invincible Armada would be incomplete without a reference to the treasures cast ashore from the wrecked galleons on the Orkneys and the Hebrides, so the fate of Gog's ill-starred enterprise is vividly set forth by the minute description of the traces it left behind in the peaceful life of Israel. The irony of the situation is unmistakable, and perhaps a touch of conscious exaggeration is permissible in such a picture. In the first place the weapons of the slain warriors furnish wood enough to serve for fuel to the Israelites for the space of seven years. Then follows a picture of the process of cleansing the land from the corpses of the fallen enemy. A burying-place is assigned to them in the valley of Abarim [202] on the eastern side of the Dead Sea, outside of the sacred territory. The whole people of Israel will be engaged for seven months in the operation of burying them; after this the mouth of the valley will be sealed, [203] and it will be known ever afterwards as the Valley of the Host of Gog. But even after the seven months have expired the scrupulous care of the people for the purity of their land will be shown by the precautions they take against its continued defilement by any fragment of a skeleton that may have been overlooked. They will appoint permanent officials, whose business will be to search for and remove relics of the dead bodies, that the land may be restored to its purity. Whenever any passer-by lights on a bone he will set up a mark beside it to attract the attention of the buriers. "Thus [in course of time] they shall cleanse the land."

vi. Vv. 17-24.--The overwhelming magnitude of the catastrophe is once more set forth under the image of a sacrificial feast, to which Jehovah summons all the birds of the air and every beast of the field (vv. 17-20). The feast is represented as a sacrifice not in any religious sense, but simply in accordance with ancient usage, in which the slaughtering of animals was invariably a sacrificial act. The only idea expressed by the figure is that Jehovah has decreed this slaughter of Gog and his host, and that it will be so great that all ravenous beasts and birds will eat flesh to the full and drink the blood of princes of the earth to intoxication. But we turn with relief from these images of carnage and death to the moral purpose which they conceal (vv. 21-24). This is stated more distinctly here than in earlier passages of this prophecy. It will teach Israel that Jehovah is indeed their God; the lingering sense of insecurity caused by the remembrance of their former rejection will be finally taken away by this signal deliverance. And through Israel it will teach a lesson to the heathen. They will learn something of the principles on which Jehovah has dealt with His people when they contrast this great salvation with His former desertion of them. It will then fully appear that it was for their sins that they went into captivity; and so the knowledge of God's holiness and His displeasure against sin will be extended to the nations of the world.

vii. Vv. 25-29.--The closing verses do not strictly belong to the oracle on Gog. The prophet returns to the standpoint of the present, and predicts once more the restoration of Israel, which has heretofore been assumed as an accomplished fact. The connection with what precedes is, however, very close. The divine attributes, whose final manifestation to the world is reserved for the far-off day of Gog's defeat, are already about to be revealed to Israel. Jehovah's compassion for His people and His jealousy for His own name will speedily be shown in "turning the fortunes" of Israel, bringing them back from the peoples, and gathering them from the land of their enemies. The consequences of this upon the nation itself are described in more gracious terms than in any other passage. They shall forget their shame and all their trespasses when they dwell securely in their own land, none making them afraid. [204] The saving knowledge of Jehovah as their God, who led them into captivity and brought them back again, will as far as Israel is concerned be complete; and the gracious relation thus established shall no more be interrupted, because of the divine Spirit which has been poured out on the house of Israel.

II

It will be seen from this summary of the contents of the prophecy that, while it presents many features peculiar to itself, it also contains much in common with the general drift of the prophet's thinking. We must now try to form an estimate of its significance as an episode in the great drama of Providence which unfolded itself before his inspired imagination.

The ideas peculiar to the passage are for the most part such as might have been suggested to the mind of Ezekiel by the remembrance of the great Scythian invasion in the reign of Josiah. Although it is not likely that he had himself lived through that time of terror, he must have grown up whilst it was still fresh in the public recollection, and the rumour of it had apparently left upon him impressions never afterwards effaced. Several circumstances, none of them perhaps decisive by itself, conspire to show that at least in its imagery the oracle on Gog is based on the conception of an irruption of Scythian barbarians. The name of Gog may be too obscure to serve as an indication; but his location in the extreme north, the description of his army as composed mainly of cavalry armed with bow and arrows, their innumerable multitude, and the love of pillage and destruction by which they are animated, all point to the Scythians as the originals from whom the picture of Gog's host is drawn. Besides the light which it casts on the genesis of the prophecy, this fact has a certain biographical interest for the reader of Ezekiel. That the prophet's furthest vista into the future should be a reflection of his earliest memory reminds us of a common human experience. "The thoughts of youth are long, long thoughts," reaching far into manhood and old age; and the mind as it turns back upon them may often discover in them that which carries it furthest in reading the divine mysteries of life and destiny.

> *Thus while the Sun sinks down to rest*
> *Far in the regions of the west,*
> *Though to the vale no parting beam*
> *Be given, not one memorial gleam,*
> *A lingering light he fondly throws*
> *On the dear hills where first he rose.*

For it is not merely the imagery of the prophecy that reveals the influence of these early associations; the thoughts which it embodies are themselves partly the result of the prophet's meditation on questions suggested by the invasion. His youthful impressions of the descent of the northern hordes were afterwards illuminated, as we see from his own words, by the study of contemporary prophecies of Jeremiah and Zephaniah called forth by the event. From these and other predictions he learned that Jehovah had a purpose with regard to the remotest nations of the earth which yet awaited its accomplishment. That purpose, in accordance with his general conception of the ends of the divine government, could be nothing else than the manifestation of Jehovah's glory before the eyes of the world. That this involved an act of judgment was only too certain from the universal hostility of the heathen to the kingdom of God. Hence the prophet's reflections would lead directly to the expectation of a final onslaught of the powers of this world on the people of Israel, which would give occasion for a display of Jehovah's might on a grander scale than had yet been seen. And this presentiment of an impending conflict between Jehovah and the pagan world headed by the Scythian barbarians forms the kernel of the oracle against Gog.

But we must further observe that this idea, from Ezekiel's point of view, necessarily presupposes the restoration of Israel to its own land. The peoples assembled under the standard of Gog are those which have never as yet come in contact with the true God, and consequently have had no opportunity of manifesting their disposition towards Him. They have not sinned as Edom and Tyre, as Egypt and Assyria have sinned, by injuries done to Jehovah through His people. Even the Scythians themselves, although they had approached the confines of the sacred territory, do not seem to have invaded it. Nor could the opportunity present itself so long as Israel was in Exile. While Jehovah was without an earthly sanctuary or a visible emblem of His government, there was no possibility of such an infringement of His holiness on the part of the heathen as would arrest the attention of the world. The judgment of Gog, therefore, could not be conceived as a preliminary to the restoration of Israel, like that on Egypt and the nations immediately surrounding Palestine. It could only take place under a state of things in which Israel was once more "holiness to the Lord, and the firstfruits of His increase," so that "all that devoured him were counted guilty" (Jer. ii. 3). This enables us partly to understand what appears to us the most singular feature of the prophecy, the projection of the final manifestation of Jehovah into the remote future, when Israel is already in possession of all the blessings of the Messianic dispensation. It is a consequence of the extension of the prophetic horizon, so as to embrace the distant peoples that had hitherto been beyond the pale of civilisation.

There are other aspects of Ezekiel's teaching on which light is thrown by this anticipation of a world-judgment as the final scene of history. The prophet was evidently conscious of a certain inconclusiveness and want of finality in the prospect of the restoration as a justification of the ways of God to men. Although all the forces of the world's salvation were wrapped up in it, its effects were still limited and measurable, both as to their range of influence and their inherent significance. Not only did it fail to impress the more distant nations, but its own lessons were incompletely taught. He felt that it had not been made clear to the dull perceptions of the heathen why the God of Israel had ever suffered His land to be desecrated and His people to be led into captivity. Even Israel itself will not fully know all that is meant by having Jehovah for its God until the history of revelation is finished. Only in the summing up of the ages, and in the light of the last judgment, will men truly realise all that is implied in the terms God and sin and redemption. The end is needed to interpret the process; and all religious conceptions await their fulfilment in the light of eternity which is yet to break on the issues of human history.

Footnotes:

185. Cf. ch. xxxix. 23.
186. See ch. xxxviii. 11, 12.
187. Ch. xxxviii. 19-23.
188. Ch. xxxix. 23.
189. See E. Meyer, Geschichte des Alterthums, p. 558; Schrader, Cuneiform Inscriptions, etc., on this passage.
190. Meshech and Tubal are the Moschi and Tibareni of the Greek geographers, lying southeast of the Black Sea. A country or tribe Rosh has not been found.
191. Gomer (according to others, however, Cappadocia) and Togarmah (ver. 6).
192. Cush and Put (ver. 5).
193. Ver. 7. The LXX. reads "for me" instead of "unto them," giving to the word mishmar the sense of "reserve force."
194. The words of ver. 4, "I will turn thee back, and put hooks into thy jaws," are wanting in the best manuscripts of the LXX., and are perhaps better omitted. Gog does not need to be dragged forth with hooks; he comes up willingly enough, as soon as the opportunity presents itself (vv. 11, 12).
195. Isa. x. 7.
196. An actual parallel is furnished by the crowds of slave-dealers who followed the army of Antiochus Epiphanes when it set out to crush the Maccabæan insurrection in 166 b.c.
197. In ver. 14 the LXX. has "he stirred up" instead of "know," and gives a more forcible sense.
198. Zeph. i.-iii. 8; Jer. iv.-vi.
199. Cf. besides the passages already cited, Isa. x. 5-34, xvii. 12-14; Micah iv. 11-13.
200. Ver. 21. LXX.: "I will summon against him every terror."
201. hippotoxotai (mounted archers) is the term applied to them by Herodotus (iv. 46).
202. This translation, which is given by Hitzig and Cornill, is obtained by a change in the punctuation of the word rendered "passengers" in ver. 11: cf. the "mountains of Abarim," Numb. xxxiii. 47, 48; Deut. xxxii. 49.
203. "It shall stop the noses of the passengers" (ver. 11) gives no sense; and the text, as it stands, is almost untranslatable. The LXX. reads, "and they shall seal up the valley," which gives a good enough meaning, so far as it goes.
204. Ver. 26. The choice between the rendering "forget" and that of the English Version, "bear," depends on the position of a single dot in the Hebrew. In the former case "shame" must be taken in the sense of reproach (schande); in the latter it means the inward feeling of self-abasement (schaam). The forgetting of past trespasses, if that is the right reading, can only mean that they are entirely broken off and dismissed from mind; there is nothing inconsistent with passages like ch. xxxvi. 31. It must be understood that in any event the reference is to the future; "after that they have borne" is altogether wrong.

John J. Skinner

Part V - The Ideal Theocracy
Chapter XXV - The Import Of The Vision

We have now reached the last and in every way the most important section of the book of Ezekiel. The nine concluding chapters record what was evidently the crowning experience of the prophet's life. His ministry began with a vision of God; it culminates in a vision of the people of God, or rather of God in the midst of His people, reconciled to them, ruling over them, and imparting the blessings and glories of the final dispensation. Into that vision are thrown the ideals which had been gradually matured through twenty years of strenuous action and intense meditation. We have traced some of the steps by which the prophet was led towards this consummation of his work. We have seen how, under the idea of God which had been revealed to him, he was constrained to announce the destruction of that which called itself the people of Jehovah, but was in reality the means of obscuring His character and profaning His holiness (chs. iv.-xxiv.). We have seen further how the same fundamental conception led him on in his prophecies against foreign nations to predict a great clearing of the stage of history for the manifestation of Jehovah (chs. xxv.-xxxii.). And we have seen from the preceding section what are the processes by which the divine Spirit breathes new life into a dead nation and creates out of its scattered members a people worthy of the God whom the prophet has seen.

But there is still something more to accomplish before his task is finished. All through, Ezekiel holds fast the truth that Jehovah and Israel are necessarily related to each other, and that Israel is to be the medium through which alone the nature of Jehovah can be fully disclosed to mankind. It remains, therefore, to sketch the outline of a perfect theocracy--in other words, to describe the permanent forms and institutions which shall express the ideal relation between God and men. To this task the prophet addresses himself in the chapters now before us. That great New Year's Vision may be regarded as the ripe fruit of all God's training of His prophet, as it is also the part of Ezekiel's work which most directly influenced the subsequent development of religion in Israel.

It cannot be doubted, then, that these chapters are an integral part of the book, considered as a record of Ezekiel's work. But it is certainly a significant circumstance that they are separated from the body of the prophecies by an interval of thirteen years. For the greater part of that time Ezekiel's literary activity was suspended. It is probable, at all events, that the first thirty-nine chapters had been committed to writing soon after the latest date they mention, and that the oracle on Gog, which marks the extreme limit of Ezekiel's prophetic vision, was really the conclusion of an earlier form of the book. And we may be certain that, since the eventful period that followed the arrival of the fugitive from Jerusalem, no new divine communication had visited the prophet's mind. But at last, in the twenty-fifth year of the captivity, and on the first day of a new year, [205] he falls into a trance more prolonged than any he had yet passed through, and he emerged from it with a new message for his people.

In what direction were the prophet's thoughts moving as Israel passed into the midnight of her exile? That they have moved in the interval--that his standpoint is no longer quite identical with that represented in his earlier prophecies--seems to be shown by one slight modification of his previous conceptions, which has been already mentioned. [206] I refer to the position of the prince in the theocratic state. We find that the king is still the civil head of the commonwealth, but that his position is hardly reconcilable with the exalted functions assigned to the Messianic king in ch. xxxiv. The inference seems irresistible that Ezekiel's point of view has somewhat changed, so that the objects in his picture present themselves in a different perspective.

It is true that this change was effected by a vision, and it may be said that that fact forbids our regarding it as indicating a progress in Ezekiel's thoughts. But the vision of a prophet is never out of relation to his previous thinking. The prophet is always prepared for his vision; it comes to him as the answer to questions, as the solution of difficulties, whose force he has felt, and apart from which it would convey no revelation of God to his mind. It marks the point at which reflection gives place to inspiration, where the incommunicable certainty of the divine word lifts the soul into the region of spiritual and eternal truth. And hence it may help us, from our human point of view, to understand the true import of this vision, if from the answer we try to discover the questions which were of pressing interest to Ezekiel in the later part of his career.

Speaking generally, we may say that the problem that occupied the mind of Ezekiel at this time was the problem of a religious constitution. How to secure for religion its true place in public life, how to embody it in institutions which shall conserve its essential ideas and transmit them from one generation to another, how a people may best express its national responsibility to God-- these and many kindred questions are real and vital to-day amongst the nations of Christendom, and they were far more vital in the age of Ezekiel. The conception of religion as an inward spiritual power, moulding the life of the nation and of each individual member, was at least as strong in him as in any other prophet; and it had been adequately expressed in the section of his book dealing with the formation of the new Israel. But he saw that this was not for that time sufficient. The mass of the community were dependent on the educative influence of the institutions under which they lived, and there was no way of impressing on a whole people the character of Jehovah except through a system of laws and observances which should constantly exhibit it to their minds. The time was not yet come when religion could be trusted to work as a hidden leaven, transforming life from within and bringing in the kingdom of God silently by the operation of spiritual forces. Thus, while the last section insists on the moral change that must pass over Israel, and the need of a direct influence from God on the heart of the people, that which now lies before us is devoted to the religious and political arrangements by which the sanctity of the nation must be preserved.

Starting from this general notion of what the prophet sought, we can see, in the next place, that his attention must be mainly concentrated on matters belonging to public worship and ritual. Worship is the direct expression in word and act of man's attitude to God, and no public religion can maintain a higher level of spirituality than the symbolism which gives it a place in the life of the people. That fact had been abundantly illustrated by the experience of centuries before the Exile. The popular worship had always been a stronghold of false religion in Israel. The high places were the nurseries of all the corruptions against which the prophets had to contend, not simply because of the immoral elements that mingled with their worship, but because the worship itself was regulated by conceptions of the deity which were opposed to the religion of revelation. Now the idea of using ritual as a vehicle of the highest spiritual truth is certainly not peculiar to Ezekiel's vision. But it is there carried through with a thoroughness which has no parallel elsewhere except in the priestly legislation of the Pentateuch. And this bears witness to a clear perception on the part of the prophet of the value of that whole side of things for the future development of religion in Israel. No one was more deeply impressed with the evils that had flowed from a corrupt ritual in the past, and he conceives the final form of the kingdom of God to be one in which the blessings of salvation are safeguarded by a carefully regulated system of religious ordinances. It will become manifest as we proceed that he regards the Temple ritual as the very centre of theocratic life, and the highest function of the community of the true religion.

But Ezekiel was prepared for the reception of this vision, not only by the practical reforming bent of his mind, but also by a combination in his own experience of the two elements which must always enter into a conception of this nature. If we may employ philosophical language to express a very obvious distinction, we have to recognise in the vision a material and a formal element. The matter of the vision is derived from the ancient religious and political constitution of the Hebrew state. All true and lasting reformations are conservative at heart; their object never is to make a clean sweep of the past, but so to modify what is traditional as to adapt it to the needs of a new era. Now Ezekiel was a priest, and possessed all a priest's reverence for antiquity, as well as a priest's professional knowledge of ceremonial and of consuetudinary law. No man could have been better fitted than he to secure the continuity of Israel's religious life along the particular line on which it was destined to move. Accordingly we find that the new theocracy is modelled from beginning to end after the pattern of the ancient institutions which had been destroyed by the Exile. If we ask, for example, what is the meaning of some detail of the Temple building, such as the cells surrounding the main sanctuary, the obvious and sufficient answer is that these things existed in Solomon's Temple, and there was no reason for altering them. On the other hand, whenever we find the vision departing from what had been traditionally established, we may be sure that there is a reason for it, and in most cases we can see what that reason was. In such departures we recognise the working of what we have called the formal element of the vision, the moulding influence of the ideas which the system was intended to express. What these ideas were we shall consider in subsequent chapters; here it is enough to say that they were the fundamental ideas which had been communicated to Ezekiel in the course of his prophetic work, and which have found expression in various forms in other parts of his writings. That they are not peculiar to Ezekiel, but are shared by other prophets, is true, just as it is true on the other hand that the priestly conceptions which occupy so large a place in his mind were an inheritance from the whole past history of the nation. Nor was this the first time when an alliance between the ceremonialism of the priesthood and the more ethical and spiritual teaching of prophecy had proved of the utmost advantage to the religious life of Israel. [207] The unique importance of Ezekiel's vision lies in the fact that the great development of prophecy was now almost complete, and that the time was come for its results to be embodied in institutions which were in the main of a priestly character. And it was fitting that this new era of religion should be inaugurated through the agency of one who combined in his own person the conservative instincts of the priest with the originality and the spiritual intuition of the prophet.

It is not suggested for a moment that these considerations account for the inception of the vision in the prophet's mind. We are not to regard it as merely the brilliant device of an ingenious man, who was exceptionally qualified to read the signs of the times, and to discover a solution for a pressing religious problem. In order that it might accomplish the end in view, it was absolutely necessary that it should be invested with a supernatural sanction and bear the stamp of divine authority. Ezekiel himself was well aware of this, and would never have ventured to publish his vision if he had thought it all out for himself. He had to wait for the time when "the hand of the Lord was upon him," and he saw in vision the new Temple and the river of life proceeding from it, and the renovated land, and the glory of God taking up its everlasting abode in the midst of His people. Until that moment arrived he was without a message as to the form which the life of the restored Israel must assume. Nevertheless the psychological conditions of the vision were contained in those parts of the prophet's experience which have just been indicated. Processes of thought which had long occupied his mind suddenly crystallised at the touch of the divine hand, and the result was the marvellous conception of a theocratic state which was Ezekiel's greatest legacy to the faith and hopes of his countrymen.

That this vision of Ezekiel's profoundly influenced the development of post-exilic Judaism may be inferred from the fact that all the best tendencies of the restoration period were towards the realisation of the ideals which the vision sets forth with surpassing clearness. It is impossible, indeed, to say precisely how far Ezekiel's influence extended, or how far the returning exiles consciously aimed at carrying out the ideas contained in his sketch of a theocratic constitution. That they did so to some extent is inferred from a consideration of some of the arrangements established in Jerusalem soon after the return from Babylon. [208] But it is certain that from the nature of the case the actual institutions of the restored community must have differed very widely in many points from those described in the last nine chapters of Ezekiel. When we look more closely at the composition of this vision, we see that it contains features which neither then nor at any subsequent time have been historically fulfilled. The most remarkable thing about it is that it unites in one picture two characteristics which seem at first sight difficult to combine. On the one hand it bears the aspect of a rigid legislative system intended to regulate human conduct in all matters of vital moment to the religious standing of the community; on the other hand it assumes a miraculous transformation of the physical aspect of the country, a restoration of all the twelve tribes of Israel under a native king, and a return of Jehovah in visible glory to dwell in the midst of the children of Israel for ever. Now these supernatural conditions of the perfect theocracy could not be realised by any effort on the part of the people, and as a matter of fact were never literally fulfilled at all. It must have been plain to the leaders of the Return that for this reason alone the details of Ezekiel's legislation were not binding for them in the actual circumstances in which they were placed. Even in matters clearly within the province of human administration we know that they considered themselves free to modify his regulations in accordance with the requirements of the situation in which they found themselves. It does not follow from this, however, that they were ignorant of the book of Ezekiel, or that it gave them no help in the difficult task to which they addressed themselves. It furnished them with an ideal of national holiness, and the general outline of a constitution in which that ideal should be embodied; and this outline they seem to have striven to fill up in the way best adapted to the straitened and discouraging circumstances of the time.

But this throws us back on some questions of fundamental importance for the right understanding of Ezekiel's vision. Taking the vision as a whole, we have to ask whether a fulfilment of the kind just indicated was the fulfilment that the prophet himself anticipated. Did he lay stress on the legislative or the supernatural aspect of the vision--on man's agency or on God's? In other words, does he issue it as a programme to be carried out by the people as soon as the opportunity is presented by their return to the land of Canaan? or does he mean that Jehovah Himself must take the initiative by miraculously preparing the land for their reception, and taking up His abode in the finished Temple, the "place of His throne, and the place of the soles of His feet"? The answer to these questions is not difficult, if only we are careful to look at things from the prophet's point of view, and disregard the historical events in which his predictions were partly realised. It is frequently assumed that the elaborate description of the Temple buildings in chs. xl.-xlii. is intended as a guide to the builders of the second Temple, who are to make it after the fashion of that which the prophet saw on the mount. It is quite probable that in some degree it may have served that purpose; but it seems to me that this view is not in keeping with the fundamental idea of the vision. The Temple that Ezekiel saw, and the only one of which he speaks, is a house not made with hands; it is as much a part of the supernatural preparation for the future theocracy as the "very high mountain" on which it stands, or the river that flows from it to sweeten the waters of the Dead Sea. In the important passage where the prophet is commanded to exhibit the plan of the house to the children of Israel (ch. xliii. 10, 11), there is unfortunately a discrepancy between the Hebrew and Greek texts which throws some obscurity on this particular point. According to the Hebrew there can hardly be a doubt that a sketch is shown to them which is to be used as a builder's plan at the time of the Restoration. [209] But in the Septuagint, which seems on the whole to give a more correct text, the passage runs thus: "And, thou son of man, describe the house to the house of Israel (and let them be ashamed of their iniquities), and its form, and its construction: and they shall be ashamed of all that they have done. And do thou sketch the house, and its exits, and its outline; and all its ordinances and all its laws make known to them; and write it before them, that they may keep all its commandments and all its ordinances, and do them." There is nothing here to suggest that the construction of the Temple was left for human workmanship. The outline of it is shown to the people only that they may be ashamed of all their iniquities. When the arrangements of the ideal Temple are explained to them, they will see how far those of the first Temple transgressed the requirements of Jehovah's holiness, and this knowledge will produce a sense of shame for the dulness of heart which tolerated so many abuses in connection with His worship. No doubt that impression sank deep into the minds of Ezekiel's hearers, and led to certain important modifications in the structure of the Temple when it had to be built; but that is not what the prophet is thinking of. At the same time we see clearly that he is very much in earnest with the legislative part of his vision. Its laws are real laws, and are given that they may be obeyed--only they do not come into force until all the institutions of the theocracy, natural and supernatural alike, are in full working order. And apart from the doubtful question as to the erection of the Temple, that general conclusion holds good for the vision as a whole. Whilst it is pervaded throughout by the legislative spirit, the miraculous features are after all its central and essential elements. When these conditions are realised, it will be the duty of Israel to guard her sacred institutions by the most scrupulous and devoted obedience; but till then there is no kingdom of God established on earth, and therefore no system of laws to conserve a state of salvation, which can only be brought about by the direct and visible interposition of the Almighty in the sphere of nature and history.

This blending of seemingly incongruous elements reveals to us the true character of the vision with which we have to deal. It is in the strictest sense a Messianic prophecy--that is, a picture of the kingdom of God in its final state as the prophet was led to conceive it. It is common to all such representations that the human authors of them have no idea of a long historical development gradually leading up to the perfect manifestation of God's purpose with the world. The impending crisis in the affairs of the people of Israel is always regarded as the consummation of human history and the establishment of God's kingdom in the plenitude of its power and glory. In the time of Ezekiel the next step in the unfolding of the divine plan of redemption was the restoration of Israel to its own land; and in so far as his vision is a prophecy of that event, it was realised in the return of the exiles with Zerubbabel in the first year of Cyrus. But to the mind of Ezekiel this did not present itself as a mere step towards something immeasurably higher in the remote future. It is to include everything necessary for the complete and final inbringing of the Messianic dispensation, and all the powers of the world to come are to be displayed in the acts by which Jehovah brings back the scattered members of Israel to the enjoyment of blessedness in His own presence.

The thing that misleads us as to the real nature of the vision is the emphasis laid on matters which seem to us of merely temporal and earthly significance. We are apt to think that what we have before us can be nothing else than a legislative scheme to be carried out more or less fully in the new state that should arise after the Exile. The miraculous features in the vision are apt to be dismissed as mere symbolisms to which no great significance attaches. Legislating for the millennium seems to us a strange occupation for a prophet, and we are hardly prepared to credit even Ezekiel with so bold a conception. But that depends entirely on his idea of what the millennium will be. If it is to be a state of things in which religious institutions are of vital importance for the maintenance of the spiritual interests of the community of the people of God, then legislation is the natural expression for the ideals which are to be realised in it. And we must remember, too, that what we have to do with is a vision. Ezekiel is not the ultimate source of this legislation, however much it may bear the impress of his individual experience. He has seen the city of God, and all the minute and elaborate regulations with which these nine chapters are filled are but the exposition of principles that determine the character of a people amongst whom Jehovah can dwell.

At the same time we see that a separation of different aspects of the vision was inevitably effected by the teaching of history. The return from Babylon was accomplished without any of those supernatural adjuncts with which it had been invested in the rapt imagination of the prophet. No transformation of the land preceded it; no visible presence of Jehovah welcomed the exiles back to their ancient abode. They found Jerusalem in ruins, the holy and beautiful house a desolation, the land occupied by aliens, the seasons unproductive as of old. Yet in the hearts of these men there was a vision even more impressive than that of Ezekiel in his solitude. To lay the foundations of a theocratic state in the dreary, discouraging daylight of the present was an act of faith as heroic as has ever been performed in the history of religion. The building of the Temple was undertaken amidst many difficulties, the ritual was organised, the rudiments of a religious constitution appeared, and in all this we see the influence of those principles of national holiness that had been formulated by Ezekiel. But the crowning manifestation of Jehovah's glory was deferred. Prophet after prophet appeared to keep alive the hope that this Temple, poor in outward appearance as it was, would yet be the centre of a new world, and the dwelling-place of the Eternal. Centuries rolled past, and still Jehovah did not come to His Temple, and the eschatological features which had bulked so largely in Ezekiel's vision remained an unfulfilled aspiration. And when at length in the fulness of time the complete revelation of God was given, it was in a form that superseded the old economy entirely, and transformed its most stable and cherished institutions into adumbrations of a spiritual kingdom which knew no earthly Temple and had need of none.

***

This brings us to the most difficult and most important of all the questions arising in connection with Ezekiel's vision--What is its relation to the Pentateuchal Legislation? It is obvious at once that the significance of this section of the book of Ezekiel is immensely enhanced if we accept the conclusion to which the critical study of the Old Testament has been steadily driven, that in the chapters before us we have the first outline of that great conception of a theocratic constitution which attained its finished expression in the priestly regulations of the middle books of the Pentateuch. The discussion of this subject is so intricate, so far-reaching in its consequences, and ranges over so wide an historical field, that one is tempted to leave it in the hands of those who have addressed themselves to its special treatment, and to try to get on as best one may without assuming a definite attitude on one side or the other. But the student of Ezekiel cannot altogether evade it. Again and again the question will force itself on him as he seeks to ascertain the meaning of the various details of Ezekiel's legislation, How does this stand related to corresponding requirements in the Mosaic law? It is necessary, therefore, in justice to the reader of the following pages, that an attempt should be made, however imperfectly, to indicate the position which the present phase of criticism assigns to Ezekiel in the history of the Old Testament legislation.

We may begin by pointing out the kind of difficulty that is felt to arise on the supposition that Ezekiel had before him the entire body of laws contained in our present Pentateuch. We should expect in that case that the prophet would contemplate a restoration of the divine institutions established under Moses, and that his vision would reproduce with substantial fidelity the minute provisions of the law by which these institutions were to be maintained. But this is very far from being the case. It is found that while Ezekiel deals to a large extent with the subjects for which provision is made by the law, there is in no instance perfect correspondence between the enactments of the vision and those of the Pentateuch, while on some points they differ very materially from one another. How are we to account for these numerous and, on the supposition, evidently designed divergencies? It has been suggested that the law was found to be in some respects unsuitable to the state of things that would arise after the Exile, and that Ezekiel in the exercise of his prophetic authority undertook to adapt it to the conditions of a late age. The suggestion is in itself plausible, but it is not confirmed by the history. For it is agreed on all hands that the law as a whole had never been put in force for any considerable period of Israel's history previous to the Exile. On the other hand, if we suppose that Ezekiel judged its provisions unsuitable for the circumstances that would emerge after the Exile, we are confronted by the fact that where Ezekiel's legislation differs from that of the Pentateuch it is the latter and not the former that regulated the practice of the post-exilic community. So far was the law from being out of date in the age of Ezekiel that the time was only approaching when the first effort would be made to accept it in all its length and breadth as the authoritative basis of an actual theocratic polity. Unless, therefore, we are to hold that the legislation of the vision is entirely in the air, and that it takes no account whatever of practical considerations, we must feel that a certain difficulty is presented by its unexplained deviations from the carefully drawn ordinances of the Pentateuch.

But this is not all. The Pentateuch itself is not a unity. It consists of different strata of legislation which, while irreconcilable in details, are held to exhibit a continuous progress towards a clearer definition of the duties that devolve on different classes in the community, and a fuller exposition of the principles that underlay the system from the beginning. The analysis of the

The Expositor's Bible: The Book of Ezekiel

Mosaic writings into different legislative codes has resulted in a scheme which in its main outlines is now accepted by critics of all shades of opinion. The three great codes which we have to distinguish are: (1) the so-called Book of the Covenant (Exod. xx. 24-xxiii., with which may be classed the closely allied code of Exod. xxxiv. 10-28); (2) the Book of Deuteronomy; and (3) the Priestly Code (found in Exod. xxv.-xxxi., xxxv.-xl., the whole book of Leviticus, and nearly the whole of the book of Numbers). [210] Now of course the mere separation of these different documents tells us nothing, or not much, as to their relative priority or antiquity. But we possess at least a certain amount of historical and independent evidence as to the times when some of them became operative in the actual life of the nation. We know, for example, that the Book of Deuteronomy attained the force of statute law under the most solemn circumstances by a national covenant in the eighteenth year of Josiah. The distinctive feature of that book is its impressive enforcement of the principle that there is but one sanctuary at which Jehovah can be legitimately worshipped. When we compare the list of reforms carried out by Josiah, as given in the twenty-third chapter of 2 Kings, with the provisions of Deuteronomy, we see that it must have been that book and it alone that had been found in the Temple and that governed the reforming policy of the king. Before that time the law of the one sanctuary, if it was known at all, was certainly more honoured in the breach than the observance. Sacrifices were freely offered at local altars throughout the country, not merely by the ignorant common people and idolatrous kings, but by men who were the inspired religious leaders and teachers of the nation. Not only so, but this practice is sanctioned by the Book of the Covenant, which permits the erection of an altar in every place where Jehovah causes His name to be remembered, and only lays down injunctions as to the kind of altar that might be used (Exod. xx. 24-26). The evidence is thus very strong that the Book of Deuteronomy, at whatever time it may have been written, had not the force of public law until the year 621 b.c., and that down to that time the accepted and authoritative expression of the divine will for Israel was the law embraced in the Book of the Covenant.

To find similar evidence of the practical adoption of the Priestly Code we have to come down to a much later period. It is not till the year 444 b.c., in the time of Ezra and Nehemiah, that we read of the people pledging themselves by a solemn covenant to the observance of regulations which are clearly those of the finished system of Pentateuchal law (Neh. viii.-x.). It is there expressly stated that this law had not been observed in Israel up to that time (Neh. ix. 34), and in particular that the great Feast of Tabernacles had not been celebrated in accordance with the requirements of the law since the days of Joshua (Neh. viii. 17). This is quite conclusive as to actual practice in Israel; and the fact that the observance of the law was thus introduced by instalments and on occasions of epoch-making importance in the history of the community raises a strong presumption against the hypothesis that the Pentateuch was an inseparable literary unity which must be known in its entirety where it was known at all.

Now the date of Ezekiel's vision (572) lies between these two historic transactions--the inauguration of the law of Deuteronomy in 621, and that of the Priestly Code in 444; and in spite of the ideal character which belongs to the vision as a whole, it contains a system of legislation which admits of being compared point by point with the provisions of the other two codes on a variety of subjects common to all three. Some of the results of this comparison will appear as we proceed with the exposition of the chapters before us. But it will be convenient to state here the important conclusion to which a number of critics have been led by discussion of this question. It is held that Ezekiel's legislation represents on the whole a transition from the law of Deuteronomy to the more complex system of the Priestly document. The three codes exhibit a regular progression, the determining factor of which is a growing sense of the importance of the Temple worship and of the necessity for a careful regulation of the acts which express the religious standing and privileges of the community. On such matters as the feasts, the sacrifices, the distinction between priests and Levites, the Temple dues, and the provision for the maintenance of ordinances, it is found that Ezekiel lays down enactments which go beyond those of Deuteronomy and anticipate a further development in the same direction in the Levitical legislation. [211] The legislation of Ezekiel is accordingly regarded as a first step towards the codification of the ritual laws which regulated the usage of the first Temple. It is not of material consequence to know how far these laws had been already committed to writing, or how far they had been transmitted by oral tradition. The important point is that down to the time of Ezekiel the great body of ritual law had been the possession of the priests, who communicated it to the people in the shape of particular decisions as occasion demanded. Even the book of Deuteronomy, except on one or two points, such as the law of leprosy and of clean and unclean animals, does not encroach on matters of ritual, which it was the special province of the priesthood to administer. But now that the time was drawing near when the Temple and its worship were to be the very centre of the religious life of the nation, it was necessary that the essential elements of the ceremonial law should be systematised and published in a form understood of the people. The last nine chapters of Ezekiel, then, contain the first draft of such a scheme, drawn from an ancient priestly tradition which in its origin went back to the time of Moses. It is true that this was not the precise form in which the law was destined to be put in practice in the post-exilic community. But Ezekiel's legislation served its purpose when it laid down clearly, with the authority of a prophet, the fundamental ideas that underlie the conception of ritual as an aid to spiritual religion. And these ideas were not lost sight of, though it was reserved for others, working under the impulse supplied by Ezekiel, to perfect the details of the system, and to adopt the principles of the vision to the actual circumstances of the second Temple. Through what subsequent stages the work was carried we can hardly hope to determine with exactitude; but it was finished in all essential respects before the great covenant of Ezra and Nehemiah in the year 444. [212]

Let us now consider the bearing of this theory on the interpretation of Ezekiel's vision. It enables us to do justice to the unmistakable practical purpose which pervades its legislation. It frees us from the grave difficulties involved in the assumption that Ezekiel wrote with the finished Pentateuch before him. It vindicates the prophet from the suspicion of arbitrary deviations from a standard of venerable antiquity and of divine authority which was afterwards proved by experience to be suited to the requirements of that restored Israel in whose interest Ezekiel legislated. And in doing so it gives a new meaning to his claim to speak as a prophet ordaining a new system of laws with divine authority. Whilst perfectly consistent with the inspiration of the Mosaic books, it places that of Ezekiel on a surer footing than does the supposition that the whole Pentateuch was of Mosaic authorship. It involves, no doubt, that the details of the Priestly law were in a more or less fluid condition down to the time of the Exile; but it explains the otherwise unaccountable fact that the several parts of the law became operative at different times in Israel's history, and explains it in a manner that reveals the working of a divine purpose through all the ages of the national existence. It becomes possible to see that Ezekiel's legislation and that of the Levitical books are in their essence alike Mosaic, as being founded on the institutions and principles established by Moses at the beginning of the nation's history. And an altogether new interest is imparted to the former when we learn to regard it as an epoch-making contribution to the task which laid the foundation of the post-exilic theocracy--the task of codifying and consolidating the laws which expressed the character of the new nation as a holy people consecrated to the service of Jehovah, the Holy One of Israel.

Footnotes:

205. The beginning of the year is that referred to in Lev. xxv. 9, the tenth day of the seventh month (September-October). From the Exile downwards two calendars were in use, the beginning of the sacred year falling in the seventh month of the civil year. It was not necessary for Ezekiel to mention the number of the month.

206. See pp. [10]318 f.

207. Cf. Davidson, Ezekiel, pp. liv. f.

208. See Prof. W. R. Smith, The Old Testament in the Jewish Church, pp. 442 f.

209. See ver. 10, "let them measure the pattern"; ver. 11, "that they may keep the whole form thereof."

210. This last group is considered to be composed of several layers of legislation, and one of its sections is of particular interest for us because of its numerous affinities with the book of Ezekiel. It is the short code contained in Lev. xvii.-xxvi., now generally known as the Law of Holiness.

211. This argument is most fully worked out by Wellhausen in the first division of his Prolegomena zur Geschichte Israels: I., "Geschichte des Cultus."

212. It should perhaps be stated, even in so incomplete a sketch as this, that there is still some difference of opinion among critics as to Ezekiel's relation to the so-called "Law of Holiness" in Lev. xvii.-xxvi. It is agreed that this short but extremely interesting code is the earliest complete, or nearly complete, document that has been incorporated in the body of the Levitical legislation. Its affinities with Ezekiel both in thought and style are so striking that Colenso and others have maintained the theory that the author of the Law of Holiness was no other than the prophet himself. This view is now seen to be untenable; but whether the code is older or more recent than the vision of Ezekiel is still a subject of discussion among scholars. Some consider that it is an advance upon Ezekiel in the direction of the Priests' Code; while others think that the book of Ezekiel furnishes evidence that the prophet was acquainted with the Law of Holiness, and had it before him as he wrote. That he was acquainted with its laws seems certain; the question is whether he had them before him in their present written form. For fuller information on this and other points touched on in the above pages, the reader may consult Driver's Introduction and Robertson Smith's Old Testament in the Jewish Church.

Chapter XXVI - The Sanctuary. Chapters xl.-xliii

The fundamental idea of the theocracy as conceived by Ezekiel is the literal dwelling of Jehovah in the midst of His people. The Temple is in the first instance Jehovah's palace, where He manifests His gracious presence by receiving the gifts and homage of His subjects. But the enjoyment of this privilege of access to the presence of God depends on the fulfilment of certain conditions which, in the prophet's view, had been systematically violated in the arrangements that prevailed under the first Temple. Hence the vision of Ezekiel is essentially the vision of a Temple corresponding in all respects to the requirements of Jehovah's holiness, and then of Jehovah's entrance into the house so prepared for His reception. And the first step towards the realisation of the great hope of the future was to lay before the exiles a full description of this building, so that they might understand the conditions on which alone Israel could be restored to its own land.

To this task the prophet addresses himself in the first four of the chapters before us, and he executes it in a manner which, considering the great technical difficulties to be surmounted, must excite our admiration. He tells us first in a brief introduction how he was transported in prophetic ecstasy to the land of Israel, and there on the site of the old Temple, now elevated into a "very high mountain," he sees before him an imposing pile of buildings like the building of a city (ver. 2). It is the future Temple, the city itself having been removed nearly two miles to the south. At the east gate he is met by an angel, who conducts him from point to point of the buildings, calling his attention to significant structural details, and measuring each part as he goes along with a measuring-line which he carries in his hand. It is probable that the whole description would be perfectly intelligible but for the state of the text, which is defective throughout and in some places hopelessly corrupt. This is hardly surprising when we consider the technical and unfamiliar nature of the terms employed; but it has been suspected that some parts have been deliberately tampered with in order to bring them into harmony with the actual construction of the second Temple. Whether that is so or not, the description as a whole remains in its way a masterpiece of literary exposition, and a remarkable proof of the versatility of Ezekiel's accomplishments. When it is necessary to turn himself into an architectural draughtsman he discharges the duty to perfection. No one can study the detailed measurements of the buildings without being convinced that the prophet is working from a ground plan which he has himself prepared; indeed his own words leave no doubt that this was the case (see ch. xliii. 10, 11). And it is a convincing demonstration of his descriptive powers that we are able, after the labours of many generations of scholars, to reproduce this plan with a certainty which, except with regard to a few minor features, leaves little to be desired. It has been remarked as a curious fact that of the three temples mentioned in the Old Testament the only one of whose construction we can form a clear conception is the one that was never built;[213] and certainly the knowledge we have of Solomon's Temple from the first book of Kings is very incomplete compared with what we know of the Temple which Ezekiel saw only in vision.

It is impossible in this chapter to enter into all the minutiæ of the description, or even to discuss all the difficulties of interpretation which arise in connection with different parts. Full information on these points will be found in short compass in Dr. Davidson's commentary on the passage. All that can be attempted here is to convey a general idea of the arrangements of the various buildings and courts of the sanctuary, and the extreme care with which they have been thought out by the prophet. After this has been done we shall try to discover the meaning of these arrangements in so far as they differ from the model supplied by the first Temple.

I

Let the reader, then, after the manner of Euclid, draw a straight line a b, and describe thereon a square a b c d. Let him divide two adjacent sides of the square (say a b and a d) into ten equal parts, and let lines be drawn from the points of section parallel to the sides of the square in both directions. Let a side of the small squares represent a length of fifty cubits, and the whole consequently a square of five hundred cubits.[214] It will now be found that the bounding lines of Ezekiel's plan run throughout on the lines of this diagram;[215] and this fact gives a better idea than anything else of the symmetrical structure of the Temple and of the absolute accuracy of the measurements.

The sides of the large square represent of course the outer boundary of the enclosure, which is formed by a wall six cubits thick and six high. [216] Its sides are directed to the four points of the compass, and at the middle of the north, east and south sides the wall is pierced by the three gates, each with an ascent of seven steps outside. The gates, however, are not mere openings in the wall furnished with doors, but covered gateways similar to those that penetrate the thick wall of a fortified town. In this case they are large separate buildings projecting into the court to a distance of fifty cubits, and twenty-five cubits broad, exactly half the size of the Temple proper. On either side of the passage are three recesses in the wall six cubits square, which were to be used as guard-rooms by the Temple police. Each gateway terminates towards the court in a large hall called "the porch," eight cubits broad (along the line of entry) by twenty long (across): the porch of the east gate was reserved for the use of the prince; the purpose of the other two is nowhere specified.

Passing through the eastern gateway, the prophet stands in the outer court of the Temple, the place where the people assembled for worship. It seems to have been entirely destitute of buildings, with the exception of a row of thirty cells along the three walls in which the gates were. The outer margin of the court was paved with stone up to the line of the inside of the gateways (i.e., fifty cubits, less the thickness of the outer wall); and on this pavement stood the cells, the dimensions of which, however, are not given. There were, moreover, in the four corners of the court rectangular enclosures forty cubits by thirty, where the Levites were to cook the sacrifices of the people (ch. xlvi. 21-24). The purpose of the cells is nowhere specified; but there is little doubt that they were intended for those sacrificial feasts of a semi-private character which had always been a prominent feature of the Temple worship. From the edge of the pavement to the inner court was a distance of a hundred cubits; but this space was free only on three sides, the western side being occupied by buildings to be afterwards described.

The inner court was a terrace standing probably about five feet above the level of the outer, and approached by flights of eight steps at the three gates. It was reserved for the exclusive use of the priests. It had three gateways in a line with those of the outer court, and precisely similar to them, with the single exception that the porches were not, as we might have expected, towards the inside, but at the ends next to the outer court. The free space of the inner court, within the line of the gateways, was a square of a hundred cubits, corresponding to the four middle squares of the diagram. Right in the middle, so that it could be seen through the gates, was the great altar of burnt-offering, a huge stone structure rising in three terraces to a height apparently of twelve cubits, and having a breadth and length of eighteen cubits at the base. That this, rather than the Temple, should be the centre of the sanctuary, corresponds to a consciousness in Israel that the altar was the one indispensable requisite for the performance of sacrificial worship acceptable to Jehovah. Accordingly, when the first exiles returned to Jerusalem, before they were in a position to set about the erection of the Temple, they reared the altar in its place, and at once instituted the daily sacrifice and the stated order of the festivals. And even in Ezekiel's vision we shall find that the sacrificial consecration of the altar is considered as equivalent to the dedication of the whole sanctuary to the chief purpose for which it was erected. Besides the altar there were in the inner court certain other objects of special significance for the priestly and sacrificial service. By the side of the north and south gates were two cells or chambers opening towards the middle space. The purpose for which these cells were intended clearly points to a division of the priesthood (which, however, may have been temporary and not permanent) into two classes--one of which was entrusted with the service of the Temple, and the other with the service of the altar. The cell on the north, we are told, was for the priests engaged in the service of the house, and that on the south for those who officiated at the altar (ch. xl. 45, 46). There is mention also of tables on which different classes of sacrificial victims were slaughtered, and of a chamber in which the burnt-offering was washed (ch. xl. 38-43); but so obscure is the text of this passage that it cannot even be certainly determined whether these appliances were situated at the east gate or the north gate, or at each of the three gates.

The four small squares immediately adjoining the inner court on the west are occupied by the Temple proper and its adjuncts. The Temple itself stands on a solid basement six cubits above the level of the inner court, and is reached by a flight of ten steps. The breadth of the basement (north to south) is sixty cubits: this leaves a free space of twenty cubits on either side, which is really a continuation of the inner court, although it bears the special name of the gizra ("separate place"). In length the basement measures a hundred and five cubits, projecting, as we immediately see, five cubits into the inner court in front. [217] The inner space of the Temple was divided, as in Solomon's Temple, into three compartments, communicating with each other by folding-doors in the middle of the partitions that separated them. Entering by the outer door on the east, we come first to the vestibule, which is twenty cubits broad (north to south) by twelve cubits east to west. Next to this is the hall or "palace" (hêkal), twenty cubits by forty. Beyond this again is the innermost shrine of the Temple, the Most Holy Place, where the glory of the God of Israel is to take the place occupied by the ark and cherubim of the first Temple. It is a square of twenty cubits; but Ezekiel, although himself a priest, is not allowed to enter this sacred space; the angel goes in alone, and announces the measurements to the prophet, who waits without in the great hall of the Temple. The only piece of furniture mentioned in the Temple is an altar or table in the hall, immediately in front of the Most Holy Place (ch. xli. 22). The reference is no doubt to the table on which the shewbread was laid out before Jehovah (cf. Exod. xxv. 23-30). Some details are also given of the wood-carving with which the interior was decorated (ch. xli. 16-20, 25), consisting apparently of cherubs and palm trees in alternate panels. This appears to be simply a reminiscence of the ornamentation of the old Temple, and to have no direct religious significance in the mind of the prophet.

    The Temple was enclosed first by a wall six cubits thick, and then on each side except the east by an outer wall of five cubits, separated from the inner by an interval of four cubits. This intervening space was divided into three ranges of small cells rising in three stories one over another. The second and third stories were somewhat broader than the lowest, the inner wall of the house being contracted so as to allow the beams to be laid upon it without breaking into its surface. We must further suppose that the inner wall rose above the cells and the outer wall, so as to leave a clear space for the windows of the Temple. The entire length of the Temple on the outside is a hundred cubits, and the breadth fifty cubits. This leaves room for a passage of five cubits broad round the edge of the elevated platform on which the main building stood. The two doors which gave access to the cells opened on this passage, and were placed in the north and south sides of the outer wall. There was obviously no need to continue the passage round the west side of the house, and this does not appear to be contemplated.

    It will be seen that there still remains a square of a hundred cubits behind the Temple, between it and the west wall. The greater part of this was taken up by a structure vaguely designated as the "building" (binya or binyan), which is commonly supposed to have been a sort of lumber-room, although its function is not indicated. Nor does it appear whether it stood on the level of the inner court or of the outer. But while this building fills the whole breadth of the square from north to south (a hundred cubits), the other dimension (east to west) is curtailed by a space of twenty cubits left free between it and the Temple, the gizra (see p. [11]410) being thus continuous round three sides of the house.

    The most troublesome part of the description is that of two blocks of cells [218] situated north and south of the Temple building (ch. xlii. 1-14). It seems clear that they occupied the oblong spaces between the gizra north and south of the Temple and the walls of the inner court. Their length is said to be a hundred cubits, and their breadth fifty cubits. But room has to be found for a passage ten cubits broad and a hundred long, so that the measurements do not exhibit in this case Ezekiel's usual accuracy. Moreover, we are told that while their length facing the Temple was a hundred cubits, the length facing the outer court was only fifty cubits. It is extremely difficult to gain a clear idea of what the prophet meant. Smend and Davidson suppose that each block was divided longitudinally into two sections, and that the passage of ten cubits ran between them from east to west. The inner section would then be a hundred cubits in length and twenty in breadth. But the other section towards the outer court would have only half this length, the remaining fifty cubits along the edge of the inner court being protected by a wall. This is perhaps the best solution that has been proposed, but one can hardly help thinking that if Ezekiel had had such an arrangement in view he would have expressed himself more clearly. The one thing that is perfectly unambiguous is the purpose for which these cells were to be used. Certain sacrifices to which a high degree of sanctity attached were consumed by the priests, and being "most holy" things they had to be eaten in a holy place. These chambers, then, standing within the sacred enclosure of the inner court, were assigned to the priests for this purpose. [219] In them also the priests were to deposit the sacred garments in which they ministered, before leaving the inner court to mingle with the people.

II

    Such, then, are the leading features presented by Ezekiel's description of an ideal sanctuary. What are the chief impressions suggested to the mind by its perusal? The fact no doubt that surprises us most is that our attention is almost exclusively directed to the ground-plan of the buildings. It is evident that the prophet is indifferent to what seems to us the noblest element of ecclesiastical architecture, the effect of lofty spaces on the imagination of the worshipper. It is no part of his purpose to inspire devotional feeling by the aid of purely æsthetic impressions. "The height, the span, the gloom, the glory" of some venerable Gothic cathedral do not enter into his conception of a place of worship. The impressions he wishes to convey, although religious, are intellectual rather than æsthetic, and are such as could be expressed by the sharp outlines and mathematical precision of a ground-plan. Now of course the sanctuary was, to begin with, a place of sacrifice, and to a large extent its arrangements were necessarily dictated by a regard for practical convenience and utility. But leaving this on one side, it is obvious enough that the design is influenced by certain ruling principles, of which the most conspicuous are these three: separation, gradation, and symmetry. And these again symbolise three aspects of the one great idea of holiness, which the prophet desired to see embodied in the whole constitution of the Hebrew state as the guarantee of lasting fellowship between Jehovah and Israel.

In Ezekiel's teaching on the subject of holiness there is nothing that is absolutely new or peculiar to himself. That Jehovah is the one truly holy Being is the common doctrine of the prophets, and it means that He alone unites in Himself all the attributes of true Godhead. The Hebrew language does not admit of the formation of an adjective from the name for God like our word "divine," or an abstract noun corresponding to "divinity." What we denote by these terms the Hebrews expressed by the words qadôsh , "holy," and qOdesh, "holiness." All that constitutes true divinity is therefore summed up in the Old Testament idea of the holiness of God. The fundamental thought expressed by the word when applied to God appears to be the separation or contrast between the divine and the human--that in God which inspires awe and reverence on the part of man, and forbids approach to Him save under restrictions which flow from the nature of the Deity. In the light of the New Testament revelation we see that the only barrier to communion with God is sin; and hence to us holiness, both in God and man, is a purely ethical idea denoting moral purity and perfectness. But under the Old Testament access to God was hindered not only by sin, but also by natural disabilities to which no moral guilt attaches. The idea of holiness is therefore partly ethical and partly ceremonial, physical uncleanness being as really a violation of the divine holiness, as offences against the moral law. The consequences of this view appear nowhere more clearly than in the legislation of Ezekiel. His mind was penetrated with the prophetic idea of the unique divinity or holiness of Jehovah, and no one can doubt that the moral attributes of God occupied the supreme place in his conception of what true Godhead is. But along with this he has a profound sense of what the nature of Jehovah demands in the way of ceremonial purity. The divine holiness, in fact, contains a physical as well as an ethical element; and to guard against the intrusion of anything unclean into the sphere of Jehovah's worship is the chief design of the elaborate system of ritual laws laid down in the closing chapters of Ezekiel. Ultimately no doubt the whole system served a moral purpose by furnishing a safeguard against the introduction of heathen practices into the worship of Israel. But its immediate effect was to give prominence to that aspect of the idea of holiness which seems to us of least value, although it could not be dispensed with so long as the worship of God took the form of material offerings at a local sanctuary.

Now in reducing this idea to practice it is obvious that everything depends on the strict enforcement of the principle of separation that lies at the root of the Hebrew conception of holiness. The thought that underlies Ezekiel's legislation is that the holiness of Jehovah is communicated in different degrees to everything connected with His worship, and in the first instance to the Temple, which is sanctified by His presence. The sanctity of the place is of course not fully intelligible apart from the ceremonial rules which regulate the conduct of those who are permitted to enter it. Throughout the ancient world we find evidence of the existence of sacred enclosures which could only be entered by those who fulfilled certain conditions of physical purity. The conditions might be extremely simple, as when Moses was commanded to take his shoes off his feet as he stood within the holy ground on Mount Sinai. But obviously the first essential of a permanently sacred place was that it should be definitely marked off from common ground, as the sphere within which superior requirements of holiness became binding. A holy place is necessarily a place "cut off," separated from ordinary use and guarded from intrusion by supernatural sanctions. The idea of the sanctuary as a separate place was therefore perfectly familiar to the Israelites long before the time of Ezekiel, and had been exhibited in a lax and imperfect way in the construction of the first Temple. But what Ezekiel did was to carry out the idea with a thoroughness never before attempted, and in such a way as to make the whole arrangements of the sanctuary an impressive object lesson on the holiness of Jehovah.

How important this notion of separateness was to Ezekiel's conception of the sanctuary is best seen from the emphatic condemnation of the arrangement of the old Temple pronounced by Jehovah Himself on His entrance into the house: "Son of man, [hast thou seen] [220] the place of My throne, and the place of the soles of My feet, where I shall dwell in the midst of the children of Israel for ever? No longer shall the house of Israel defile My holy name, they and their kings, by their whoredom [idolatry], and by the corpses of their kings in their death; by placing their threshold alongside of My threshold, and their post beside My post, with only the wall between Me and them, and defiling My holy name by their abominations which they committed; so that I consumed them in My anger. But now they must remove their whoredom and the corpses of their kings from Me, and I will dwell amongst them for ever" (ch. xliii. 7-9). There is here a clear allusion to defects in the structure of the Temple which were inconsistent with a due recognition of the necessary separation between the holy and the profane (ch. xlii. 20). It appears that the first Temple had only one court, corresponding to the inner court of Ezekiel's vision. What answered to the outer court was simply an enclosure surrounding, not only the Temple, but also the royal palace

The Expositor's Bible: The Book of Ezekiel

and the other buildings of state. Immediately adjoining the Temple area on the south was the court in which the palace stood, so that the only division between the dwelling-place of Jehovah and the residence of the kings of Judah was the single wall separating the two courts. This of itself was derogatory to the sanctity of the Temple, according to the enhanced idea of holiness which it was Ezekiel's mission to enforce. But the prophet touches on a still more flagrant transgression of the law of holiness when he speaks of the dead bodies of the kings as being interred in the neighbourhood of the Temple. Contact with a dead body produced under all circumstances the highest degree of ceremonial uncleanness, and nothing could have been more abhorrent to Ezekiel's priestly sense of propriety than the close proximity of dead men's bones to the house in which Jehovah was to dwell. In order to guard against the recurrence of these abuses in the future it was necessary that all secular buildings should be removed to a safe distance from the Temple precincts. The "law of the house" is that "upon the top of the mountain it shall stand, and all its precincts round about shall be most holy" (ch. xliii. 12). And it is characteristic of Ezekiel that the separation is effected, not by changing the situation of the Temple, but by transporting the city bodily to the southward; so that the new sanctuary stood on the site of the old, but isolated from the contact of that in human life which was common and unclean. [221]

The effect of this teaching, however, is immensely enhanced by the principle of gradation, which is the second feature exhibited in Ezekiel's description of the sanctuary. Holiness, as a predicate of persons or things, is after all a relative idea. That which is "most holy" in relation to the profane every-day life of men may be less holy in comparison with something still more closely associated with the presence of God. Thus the whole land of Israel was holy in contrast with the world lying outside. But it was impossible to maintain the whole land in a state of ceremonial purity corresponding to the sanctity of Jehovah. The full compass of the idea could only be illustrated by a carefully graded series of sacred spaces, each of which entailed provisions of sanctity peculiar to itself. First of all an "oblation" is set apart in the middle of the tribes; and of this the central portion is assigned for the residence of the priestly families. In the midst of this, again, stands the sanctuary with its wall and precinct, dividing the holy from the profane (ch. xlii. 20). Within the wall are the two courts, of which the outer could only be trodden by circumcised Israelites and the inner only by the priests. Behind the inner court stands the Temple house, cut off from the adjoining buildings by a "separate place," and elevated on a platform, which still further guards its sanctity from profane contact. And finally the interior of the house is divided into three compartments, increasing in holiness in the order of entrance--first the porch, then the main hall, and then the Most Holy Place, where Jehovah Himself dwells. It is impossible to mistake the meaning of all this. The practical object is to secure the presence of Jehovah against the possibility of contact with those sources of impurity which are inseparably bound up with the incidents of man's natural existence on earth.[222]

Before we pass on let us return for a moment to the primary notion of separation in space as an emblem of the Old Testament conception of holiness. What is the permanent religious truth underlying this representation? We may find it in the idea conveyed by the familiar phrase "draw near to God." What we have just seen reminds us that there was a stage in the history of religion when these words could be used in the most literal sense of every act of complete worship. The worshipper actually came to the place where God was; it was impossible to realise His presence in any other way. To us the expression has only a metaphorical value; yet the metaphor is one that we cannot dispense with, for it covers a fact of spiritual experience. It may be true that with God there is no far or near, that He is omnipresent, that His eyes are in every place beholding the evil and the good. But what does that mean? Not surely that all men everywhere and at all times are equally under the influence of the divine Spirit? No; but only that God may be found in any place by the soul that is open to receive His grace and truth, that place has nothing to do with the conditions of true fellowship with Him. Translated into terms of the spiritual life, drawing near to God denotes the act of faith or prayer or consecration, through which we seek the manifestation of His love in our experience. Religion knows nothing of "action at a distance"; God is near in every place to the soul that knows Him, and distant in every place from the heart that loves darkness rather than light.

Now when the idea of access to God is thus spiritualised the conception of holiness is necessarily transformed, but it is not superseded. At every stage of revelation holiness is that "without which no man shall see the Lord." [223] In other words, it expresses the conditions that regulate all true fellowship with God. So long as worship was confined to an earthly sanctuary these conditions were so to speak materialised. They resolved themselves into a series of "carnal ordinances"--gifts and sacrifices, meats, drinks, and divers washings--that could never make the worshipper perfect as touching the conscience. These things were "imposed until a time of reformation," the "Holy Ghost this signifying, that the way into the holy place had not been made manifest while as the first tabernacle was yet standing." [224] And yet when we consider what it was that gave such vitality to that persistent sense of distance from God, of His unapproachableness, of danger in contact with Him, what it was that inspired such constant attention to ceremonial purity in

John J. Skinner

all ancient religions, we cannot but see that it was the obscure workings of the conscience, the haunting sense of moral defect cleaving to a man's common life and all his common actions. In heathenism this feeling took an entirely wrong direction; in Israel it was gradually liberated from its material associations and stood forth as an ethical fact. And when at last Christ came to reveal God as He is, He taught men to call nothing common or unclean. But He taught them at the same time that true holiness can only be attained through His atoning sacrifice, and by the indwelling of that Spirit which is the source of moral purity and perfection in all His people. These are the abiding conditions of fellowship with the Father of our spirits; and under the influence of these great Christian facts it is our duty to perfect holiness in the fear of God.

III

No sooner has the prophet completed his tour of inspection of the sacred buildings than he is conducted to the eastern gate to witness the theophany by which the Temple is consecrated to the service of the true God. "He (the angel) led me to the gate that looks eastward, and, lo, the glory of the God of Israel came from the east; its sound was as the sound of many waters, and the earth shone with its glory. The appearance which I saw was like that which I had seen when He came to destroy the city, and like the appearance which I saw by the river Kebar, and I fell on my face. And the glory of Jehovah entered the house by the gate that looks towards the east. The Spirit caught me up, and brought me to the inner court; and, behold, the glory of Jehovah filled the house. Then I heard a voice from the house speaking to me--the man was standing beside me--and saying, Son of man, hast thou seen the place of My throne, and the place of the soles of My feet, where I shall dwell in the midst of the children of Israel for ever?" (ch. xliii. 1-7).

This great scene, so simply described, is really the culmination of Ezekiel's prophecy. Its spiritual meaning is suggested by the prophet himself when he recalls the terrible act of judgment which he had seen in vision on that very spot some twenty years before (chs. ix.-xi.). The two episodes stand in clear and conscious parallelism with each other. They represent in dramatic form the sum of Ezekiel's teaching in the two periods into which his ministry was divided. On the former occasion he had witnessed the exit of Jehovah from a Temple polluted by heathen abominations and profaned by the presence of men who had disowned the knowledge of the Holy One of Israel. The prophet had read in this the death sentence of the old Hebrew state, and the truth of his vision had been established in the tale of horror and disaster which the subsequent years had unfolded. Now he has been privileged to see the return of Jehovah to a new Temple, corresponding in all respects to the requirements of His holiness; and he recognises it as the pledge of restoration and peace and all the blessings of the Messianic age. The future worshippers are still in exile bearing the chastisement of their former iniquities; but "the Lord is in His holy Temple," and the dispersed of Israel shall yet be gathered home to enter His courts with praise and thanksgiving.

To us this part of the vision symbolises, under forms derived from the Old Testament economy, the central truth of the Christian dispensation. We do no injustice to the historic import of Ezekiel's mission when we say that the dwelling of Jehovah in the midst of His people is an emblem of reconciliation between God and man, and that his elaborate system of ritual observances points towards the sanctification of human life in all its relations through spiritual communion with the Father revealed in our Lord Jesus Christ. Christian interpreters have differed widely as to the manner in which the vision is to be realised in the history of the Church; but on one point at least they are agreed, that through the veil of legal institutions the prophet saw the day of Christ. And although Ezekiel himself does not distinguish between the symbol and the reality, it is nevertheless possible for us to see, in the essential ideas of his vision, a prophecy of that eternal union between God and man which is brought to pass by the work of Christ.

Footnotes:

213. Gautier, La Mission du Prophète Ezekiel, p. 118.

214. The cubit which is the unit of measurement is said to be a handbreadth longer than the cubit in common use (ver. 5). The length of the larger cubit is variously estimated at from eighteen to twenty-two inches. If we adopt the smaller estimate, we have only to take the half of Ezekiel's dimensions to get the measurement in English yards. The other, however, is more probable. Both the Egyptians and Babylonians had a larger and a smaller cubit, their respective lengths being approximately as follows:-- Common cubit: Egypt 17.8 in., Babylon 19.5 in. Royal cubit: Egypt 20.7 in., Babylon 21.9 in. In Egypt the royal cubit exceeded the common by a handbreadth, just as in Ezekiel. It is probable in any case that the large cubit used by the angel was of the same order of magnitude as the royal cubit of Egypt and Babylon--i.e., was between twenty and a half and twenty-two inches long. Cf. Benzinger, Hebräische Archäologie, pp. 178 ff.

215. See the plan in Benzinger, Archäologie, p. 394.

216. The outer court, however, is some feet higher than the level of the ground, being entered

by an ascent of seven steps; the height of the wall inside must therefore be less by this amount than the six cubits, which is no doubt an outside measurement.

217. Smend and Stade assume that it was a hundred and ten cubits long, and extended five cubits to the west beyond the line of the square to which it belongs. This was not necessary, and it would imply that the binya behind the Temple, to be afterwards described, was without a wall on its eastern side, which is extremely improbable. (So Davidson.)

218. According to the Septuagint they were either five or fifteen in number in each block.

219. From a later passage (ch. xlvi. 19, 20) we learn that in some recess to the west of the northern block of cells there was a place where these sacrifices (the sin-, guilt-, and meal-offerings) were cooked, so that the people in the outer court might not run any risk of being brought in contact with them.

220. So in the LXX.

221. The actual building of the second Temple had of course to be carried out irrespective of the bold idealism of Ezekiel's vision. The miraculous transformation of the land had not taken place, and it was altogether impossible to build a new metropolis in the region marked out for it by the vision. The Temple had to be erected on its old site, and in the immediate neighbourhood of the city. To a certain extent, however, the requirements of the ideal sanctuary could be complied with. Since the new community had no use for royal buildings, the whole of the old Temple plateau was available for the sanctuary, and was actually devoted to this purpose. The new Temple accordingly had two courts, set apart for sacred uses; and in all probability these were laid out in a manner closely corresponding to the plan prepared by Ezekiel.

222. It is not necessary to dwell on the third feature of the Temple plan, its symmetry. Although this has not the same direct religious significance as the other two, it is nevertheless a point to which considerable importance is attached even in matters of minute detail. Solomon's Temple had, for example, only one door to the side chambers, in the wall facing the south, and this was sufficient for all practical purposes. But Ezekiel's plan provides for two such doors, one in the south and the other in the north, for no assignable reason but to make the two sides of the house exactly alike. There are just two slight deviations from a strictly symmetrical arrangement that can be discerned; one is the washing-chamber by the side of one of the gates of the inner court, and the other the space for cooking the most holy class of sacrifices near the block of cells on the north side of the Temple. With these insignificant exceptions, all the parts of the sanctuary are disposed with mathematical regularity; nothing is left to chance, regard for convenience is everywhere subordinated to the sense of proportion which expresses the ideal order and perfection of the whole.

223. Heb. xii. 14.

224. Heb. ix. 8-10.

John J. Skinner

Chapter XXVII - The Priesthood. Chapter xliv

In the last chapter we saw how the principle of holiness through separation was exhibited in the plan of a new Temple, round which the Theocracy of the future was to be constituted. We have now to consider the application of the same principle to the personnel of the Sanctuary, the priests and others who are to officiate within its courts. The connection between the two is obvious. As has been already remarked, the sanctity of the Temple is not intelligible apart from the ceremonial purity required of the persons who are permitted to enter it. The degrees of holiness pertaining to its different areas imply an ascending scale of restrictions on access to the more sacred parts. We may expect to find that in the observance of these conditions the usage of the first Temple left much to be desired from the point of view represented by Ezekiel's ideal. Where the very construction of the sanctuary involved so many departures from the strict idea of holiness it was inevitable that a corresponding laxity should prevail in the discharge of sacred functions. Temple and priesthood in fact are so related that a reform of the one implies of necessity a reform of the other. It is therefore not in itself surprising that Ezekiel's legislation should include a scheme for the reorganisation of the Temple priesthood. But these general considerations hardly prepare us for the sweeping and drastic changes contemplated in the forty-fourth chapter of the book. It requires an effort of imagination to realise the situation with which the prophet has to deal. The abuses for which he seeks a remedy and the measures which he adopts to counteract them are alike contrary to preconceived notions of the order of worship in an Israelite sanctuary. Yet there is no part of the prophet's programme which shows the character of the earnest practical reformer more clearly than this. If we might regard Ezekiel as a mere legislator we should say that the boldest task to which he set his hand was a reformation of the Temple ministry, involving the degradation of an influential class from the priestly status and privileges to which they aspired.

I

The first and most noteworthy feature of the new scheme is the distinction between priests and Levites. The passage in which this instruction is given is so important that it may be quoted here at length. It is an oracle communicated to the prophet in a peculiarly impressive manner. He has been brought into the inner court in front of the Temple, and there, in full view of the glory of God, he falls on his face, when Jehovah speaks to him as follows:--

"Son of man, give heed and see with thine eyes and hear with thine ears all that I speak to thee concerning all the ordinances and all the laws of Jehovah's house. Mark well the [rule of] entrance into the house, and all the outgoings in the sanctuary. And say to the house of rebellion, the house of Israel: Thus saith the Lord Jehovah, It is high time to desist from all your abominations, O house of Israel, in that ye bring in aliens uncircumcised in heart and uncircumcised in flesh to be in My sanctuary, profaning it, while ye offer My bread, the fat and the blood; thus ye have broken My covenant, in addition to all your [other] abominations; and ye have not kept the charge of My holy things, but have appointed them as keepers of My charge in My sanctuary. Therefore thus saith the Lord Jehovah, No alien uncircumcised in heart and flesh shall enter into My sanctuary, of all the foreigners who are amongst the Israelites. But the Levites who departed from Me when Israel went astray from Me after their idols, they shall bear their guilt, and shall minister in My sanctuary in charge at the gates of the house and as ministers of the house; they shall slay the burnt offering and the sacrifice for the people, and stand before them to minister to them. Because they ministered to them before their idols, and were to the house of Israel an occasion of guilt, therefore I lift My hand against them, saith the Lord Jehovah, and they shall bear their guilt, and shall not draw near to Me to act as priests to Me or to touch any of My holy things, the most holy things, but shall bear their shame and the abominations which they have committed. I will make them keepers of the charge of the house, for all its servile work and all that has to be done in it. But the priest-Levites, the sons of Zadok, who kept the charge of My sanctuary when the Israelites strayed from Me--they shall draw near to Me to minister to Me, and shall stand before Me to present to Me the fat and the blood, saith the Lord Jehovah. They shall enter into My sanctuary, and they shall draw near to My table to minister to Me, and shall keep My charge" (xliv. 5-16).

Now the first thing to be noticed here is that the new law of the priesthood is aimed directly against a particular abuse in the practice of the first Temple. It appears that down to the time of the

Exile uncircumcised aliens were not only admitted to the Temple, but were entrusted with certain important functions in maintaining order in the sanctuary (ver. 8). It is not expressly stated that they took any part in the performance of the worship, although this is suggested by the fact that the Levites who are installed in their place had to slay the sacrifices for the people and render other necessary services to the worshippers (ver. 11). In any case the mere presence of foreigners while sacrifice was being offered (ver. 7) was a profanation of the sanctity of the Temple which was intolerable to a strict conception of Jehovah's holiness. It is therefore of some consequence to discover who these aliens were, and how they came to be engaged in the Temple.

For a partial answer to this question, we may turn first to the memorable scene of the coronation of the young king Joash as described in the eleventh chapter of the second book of Kings (c. b.c. 837). The moving spirit in that transaction was the chief priest Jehoiada, a man who was honourably distinguished by his zeal for the purity of the national religion. But although the priest's motives were pure he could only accomplish his object by a palace revolution, carried out with the assistance of the captains of the royal bodyguard. Now from the time of David the royal guard had contained a corps of foreign mercenaries recruited from the Philistine country; and on the occasion with which we are dealing we find mention of a body of Carians, showing that the custom was kept up in the end of the ninth century. During the coronation ceremony these guards were drawn up in the most sacred part of the inner court, the space between the Temple and the altar, with the new king in their midst (ver. 11). Moreover we learn incidentally that keeping watch in the Temple was part of the regular duty of the king's bodyguard, just as much as the custody of the palace (vv. 5-7). In order to understand the full significance of this arrangement, it must be borne in mind that the Temple was in the first instance the royal sanctuary, maintained at the king's expense and subject to his authority. Hence the duty of keeping order in the Temple courts naturally devolved on the troops that attended the king's person and acted as the palace guard. So at an earlier period of the history we read that as often as the king went into the house of Jehovah, he was accompanied by the guard that kept the door of the king's house (1 Kings xiv. 27, 28).

Here, then, we have historical evidence of the admission to the sanctuary of a class of foreigners answering in all respects to the uncircumcised aliens of Ezekiel's legislation. That the practice of enlisting foreign mercenaries for the guard continued till the reign of Josiah seems to be indicated by an allusion in the book of Zephaniah, where the prophet denounces a body of men in the service of the king who observed the Philistine custom of "leaping over the threshold" (Zeph. i. 9: cf. 1 Sam. v. 5). We have only to suppose that this usage, along with the subordination of the Temple to the royal authority, persisted to the close of the monarchy, in order to explain fully the abuse which excited the indignation of our prophet. It is possible no doubt that he had in view other uncircumcised persons as well, such as the Gibeonites (Josh. ix. 27), who were employed in the menial service of the sanctuary. But we have seen enough to show at all events that pre-exilic usage tolerated a freedom of access to the sanctuary and a looseness of administration within it which would have been sacrilegious under the law of the second Temple. It need not be supposed that Ezekiel was the only one who felt this state of things to be a scandal and an injury to religion. We may believe that in this respect he only expressed the higher conscience of his order. Amongst the more devout circles of the Temple priesthood there was probably a growing conviction similar to that which animated the early Tractarian party in the Church of England, a conviction that the whole ecclesiastical system with which their spiritual interests were bound up fell short of the ideal of sanctity essential to it as a divine institution. But no scheme of reform had any chance of success so long as the palace of the kings stood hard by the Temple, with only a wall between them. The opportunity for reconstruction came with the Exile, and one of the leading principles of the reformed Temple is that here enunciated by Ezekiel, that no "alien uncircumcised in heart and uncircumcised in flesh" shall henceforth enter the sanctuary.

In order to prevent a recurrence of these abuses Ezekiel ordains that for the future the functions of the Temple guard and other menial offices shall be discharged by the Levites who had hitherto acted as priests of the idolatrous shrines throughout the kingdom (vv. 11-14). This singular enactment becomes at once intelligible when we understand the peculiar circumstances brought about by the enforcement of the Deuteronomic Law in the reformation of the year 621. Let us once more recall the fact that the chief object of that reformation was to do away with all the provincial sanctuaries and to concentrate the worship of the nation in the Temple at Jerusalem. It is obvious that by this measure the priests of the local sanctuaries were deprived of their means of livelihood. The rule that they who serve the altar shall live by the altar applied equally to the priests of the high places and to those in the Temple at Jerusalem. All the priests indeed throughout the country were members of a landless caste or tribe; the Levites had no portion or inheritance like the other tribes, but subsisted on the offerings of the worshippers at the various shrines where they ministered. Now the law of Deuteronomy recognises the principle of compensation for the vested interests that were thus abolished. Two alternatives were offered to the Levites of the high places: they might either remain in the villages or townships where they were known, or they might proceed to the central sanctuary and obtain admission to the ranks of the priesthood there. In the former case, the Lawgiver commends them earnestly, along with other destitute members of the community, to the charity of their well-to-do fellow-townsmen and neighbours. If, on the other hand, they elected to try their fortunes in the Temple at Jerusalem, he secures their full priestly status and equal rights with their brethren who regularly officiated there. On this point the legislation is quite explicit. Any Levite from any district of Israel who came of his own free will to the place which Jehovah had chosen might minister in the name of Jehovah his God, as all his brethren the Levites did who stood there before Jehovah, and have like portions to eat (Deut. xviii. 6-8). In this matter, however, the humane intention of the law was partly frustrated by the exclusiveness of the priests who were already in possession of the sacred offices in the Temple. The Levites who were brought up from the provinces to Jerusalem were allowed their proper share of the priestly dues, but were not permitted to officiate at the altar. [225] It is not probable that a large number of the provincial Levites availed themselves of this grudging provision for their maintenance. In the idolatrous reaction which set in after the death of Josiah the worship of the high places was revived, and the great body of the Levites would naturally be favourable to the re-establishment of the old order of things with which their professional interests were identified. Still, there would be a certain number who for conscientious motives attached themselves to the movement for a purer and stricter conception of the worship of Jehovah, and were willing to submit to the irksome conditions which this movement imposed on them. They might hope for a time when the generous provisions of the Deuteronomic Code would be applied to them; but their position in the meantime was both precarious and humiliating. They had to bear the doom pronounced long ago on the sinful house of Eli: "Every one that is left in thine house shall come and bow down to him (the high priest of the line of Zadok) for a piece of silver and a loaf of bread, and shall say, Thrust me, I pray thee, into one of the priests' offices, that I may eat a morsel of bread." [226]

We see thus that Ezekiel's legislation on the subject of the Levites starts from a state of things created by Josiah's reformation, and, let us remember, a state of things with which the prophet was familiar in his earlier days when he was himself a priest in the Temple. On the whole he justifies the exclusive attitude of the Temple priesthood towards the new-comers, and carries forward the application of the idea of sanctity from the point where it had been left by the law of Deuteronomy. That law recognises no sacerdotal distinctions within the ranks of the priesthood. Its regular designation of the priests of the Temple is "the priests, the Levites"; that of the provincial priests is simply "the Levites." All priests are brethren, all belong to the same tribe of Levi; and it is assumed, as we have seen, that any Levite, whatever his antecedents, is qualified for the full privileges of the priesthood in the central sanctuary if he choose to claim them. But we have also seen that the distinction emerged as a consequence of the enforcement of the fundamental law of the single sanctuary. There came to be a class of Levites in the Temple whose position was at first indeterminate. They themselves claimed the full standing of the priesthood, and they could appeal in support of their claim to the authority of the Deuteronomic legislation. But the claim was never conceded in practice, the influence of the legitimate Temple priests being strong enough to exclude them from the supreme privilege of ministering at the altar. This state of things could not continue. Either the disparity of the two orders must be effaced by the admission of the Levites to a footing of equality with the other priests, or else it must be emphasised and based on some higher principle than the jealousy of a close corporation for its traditional rights. Now such a principle is supplied by the section of Ezekiel's vision with which we are dealing. The permanent exclusion of the Levites from the priesthood is founded on the unassailable moral ground that they had forfeited their rights by their unfaithfulness to the fundamental truths of the national religion. They had been a "stumbling-block of iniquity" to the house of Israel through their disloyalty to Jehovah's cause during the long period of national apostasy, when they lent themselves to the popular inclination towards impure and idolatrous worship. For this great betrayal of their trust they must bear the guilt and shame in their degradation to the lowest offices in the service of the new sanctuary. They are to fill the place formerly occupied by uncircumcised foreigners, as keepers of the gates and servants of the house and the worshipping congregation; but they may not draw near to Jehovah in the exercise of priestly prerogatives, nor put their hands to the most holy things. The priesthood of the new Temple is finally vested in the "sons of Zadok"--i.e., the body of Levitical priests who had ministered in the Temple since its foundation by Solomon. Whatever the faults of these Zadokites had been--and Ezekiel certainly does not judge them leniently [227] --they had at least steadfastly maintained the ideal of a central sanctuary, and in comparison with the rural clergy they were doubtless a purer and better-disciplined body. The judgment is only a relative one, as all class judgments necessarily are. There must have been individual Zadokites worse than an ordinary Levite from the country, as well as individual Levites who were superior to the average Temple priest. But if it was necessary that in the future the interests of religion should be mainly confided to a priesthood, there could be no question that as a class the old priestly aristocracy of the central sanctuary were those best qualified for spiritual leadership.

In Ezekiel's vision we thus seem to find the beginning of a statutory and official distinction between priests and Levites. This fact forms one of the arguments chiefly relied on by those who hold that the book of Ezekiel precedes the introduction of the Priestly Code of the Pentateuch. Two things, indeed, appear to be clearly established. In the first place the tendency and significance of Ezekiel's legislation is adequately explained by the historical situation that existed in the generation immediately preceding the Exile. In the second place the Mosaic books, apart from Deuteronomy, had no influence on the scheme propounded in the vision. It is felt that these results are difficult to reconcile with the view that the middle books of the Pentateuch were known to the prophet as part of a divinely ordained constitution for the Israelite theocracy. We should have expected in that case that the prophet would simply have fallen back on the provisions of the earlier legislation, where the division between priests and Levites is formulated with perfect clearness and precision. Or, looking at the matter from the divine point of view, we should have expected that the revelation given to Ezekiel would endorse the principles of the revelation that had already been given. It is equally hard to suppose that any existing law should have been unknown to Ezekiel, or to suggest a reason for his ignoring it if it was known. The facts that have come before us seem thus, so far as they go, to be in favour of the theory that Ezekiel stands midway between Deuteronomy and the Priestly Code, and that the final codification and promulgation of the latter took place after his time.

It is nearer our purpose, however, to note the probable effect of these regulations on the personnel of the second Temple. In the book of Ezra we are told that in the first colony of returning exiles there were four thousand two hundred and eighty-nine priests and only seventy-four Levites.[228] One man in every ten was a priest, and the total number was probably in excess of the requirements of a fully equipped Temple. The number of Levites, on the other hand, would have been quite insufficient for the duties required of them under the new arrangements, had there not been a contingent of nearly four hundred of the old Temple servants to supply their lack of service.[229] Again, when Ezra came up from Babylon in the year 458, we find that not a single Levite volunteered to accompany him. It was only after some negotiations that about forty Levites were induced to go up with him to Jerusalem; and again they were far outnumbered by the Nethinim or Temple slaves.[230] These figures cannot possibly represent the proportionate strength of the tribe of Levi under the old monarchy. They indicate unmistakably that there was a great reluctance on the part of the Levites to share the perils and glory of the founding of the new Jerusalem. Is it not probable that the new conditions laid down by Ezekiel's legislation were the cause of this reluctance? That, in short, the prospect of being servants in a Temple where they had once claimed to be priests was not sufficiently attractive to the majority to lead them to break up their comfortable homes in exile, and take their proper place in the ranks of those who were forming the new community of Israel? And ought we not to spare a moment's admiration even at this distance of time for the public-spirited few who in self-sacrificing devotion to the cause of God willingly accepted a position which was scorned by the great mass of their tribesmen? If this was their spirit, they had their reward. Although the position of a Levite was at first a symbol of inferiority and degradation, it ultimately became one of very great honour. When the Temple service was fully organised, the Levites were a large and important order, second in dignity in the community only to the priests. Their ranks were swelled by the incorporation of the Temple musicians, as well as other functionaries; and thus the Levites are for ever associated in our minds with the magnificent service of praise which was the chief glory of the second Temple.

II

The remainder of the forty-fourth chapter lays down the rules of ceremonial holiness to be observed by the priests, the duties they have to perform towards the community, and the provision to be made for their maintenance. A few words must here suffice on each of these topics.

1. The sanctity of the priests is denoted, first of all, by the obligation to wear special linen garments when they enter the inner court, which is the sphere of their peculiar ministrations. Vestries were provided, as we have seen from the description of the Temple, between the inner and outer courts, where these garments were to be put on and off as the priests passed to and from the discharge of their sacred duties. The general idea underlying this regulation is too obvious to require explanation. It is but an application of the fundamental principle that approach to the Deity, or entrance into a place sanctified by His presence, demands a condition of ceremonial purity which cannot be maintained and must not be imitated by persons of a lower degree of religious privilege. A strange but very suggestive extension of the principle is found in the injunction to put off the garments before going into the outer court, lest the ordinary worshipper should be sanctified by chance contact with them. That both holiness and uncleanness are propagated by contagion is of the very essence of the ancient idea of sanctity; but the remarkable thing is that in some circumstances

communicated holiness is as much to be dreaded as communicated uncleanness. It is not said what would be the fate of an Israelite who should by chance touch the sacred vestments, but evidently he must be disqualified for participation in worship until he had purged himself of his illegitimate sanctity. [231]

In the next place the priests are under certain permanent obligations with regard to signs of mourning, marriage, and contact with death, which again are the mark of the peculiar sanctity of their caste. The rules as to mourning--prohibition of shaving the head and letting the hair flow dishevelled [232] --have been thought to be directed against heathen customs arising out of the worship of the dead. In marriage the priest may only take a virgin of the house of Israel or the widow of a priest. And only in the case of his nearest relatives--parent, child, brother, and unmarried sister--may he defile himself by rendering the last offices to the departed, and even these exceptions involve exclusion from the sacred office for seven days. [233]

The relations of these requirements to the corresponding parts of the Levitical law are somewhat complicated. The great point of difference is that Ezekiel knows nothing of the unique privileges and sanctity of the high priest. It might seem at first sight as if this implied a deliberate departure from the known usage of the first Temple. It is certain that there were high priests under the monarchy, and indeed we can discover the rudiments of a hierarchy in a distribution of authority between the high priest, second priest, keepers of the threshold, and chief officers of the house. [234] But the silence of Ezekiel does not necessarily mean that he contemplated any innovation on the established order of things. The historical books afford no ground for supposing that the high priest in the old Temple had a religious standing distinguished from that of his colleagues. He was primus inter pares, the president of the priestly college and the supreme authority in the internal administration of the Temple affairs, but probably nothing more. Such an office was almost necessary in the interest of order and authority, and there is nothing in Ezekiel's regulations inconsistent with its continuance. [235] On the other hand it must be admitted that his silence would be strange if he had in view the position assigned to the high priest under the law. For there the high priest is as far elevated above his colleagues as these are above the Levites. He is the concentration of all that is holy in Israel, and the sole mediator of the nearest approach to God which the symbolism of Temple worship permitted. He is bound by the strictest conditions of ceremonial sanctity, and any transgression on his part has to be atoned for by a rite similar to that required for a transgression of the whole congregation. [236] The omission of this striking figure from the pages of Ezekiel makes a comparison between his enactments concerning the priesthood and those of the law difficult and in some degree uncertain. Nevertheless there are points both of likeness and contrast which cannot escape observation. Thus the laws of this chapter on defilement by a dead body are identical with those enjoined in Lev. xxi. 1-3 (the "Law of Holiness") for ordinary priests; while the high priest is there forbidden to touch any dead body whatsoever. On the other hand Ezekiel's regulations as to priestly marriages seem as it were to strike an average between the restrictions imposed in the law on ordinary priests and those binding on the high priest. The former may marry any woman that is not violated or a harlot or a divorced wife; but the high priest is forbidden to marry any one but a virgin of his own people. Again, the priestly garments, according to Exod. xxviii. 39-42, xxxix. 27, are made partly of linen and partly of byssus (? cotton), which certainly looks like a refinement on the simpler attire prescribed by Ezekiel. But it is impossible to pursue this subject further here.

2. The duties of the priests towards the people are few, but exceedingly important. In the first place they have to instruct the people in the distinctions between the holy and the profane and between the clean and the unclean. It will not be supposed that this instruction took the form of set lectures or homilies on the principles of ceremonial religion. The verb translated "teach" in ver. 23 means to give an authoritative decision in a special case; and this had always been the form of priestly instruction in Israel. The subject of the teaching was of the utmost importance for a community whose whole life was regulated by the idea of holiness in the ceremonial sense. To preserve the land in a state of purity befitting the dwelling-place of Jehovah required the most scrupulous care on the part of all its inhabitants; and in practice difficult questions would constantly occur which could only be settled by an appeal to the superior knowledge of the priest. Hence Ezekiel contemplates a perpetuation of the old ritual Torah or direction of the priests even in the ideal state of things to which his vision looks forward. Although the people are assumed to be all righteous in heart and responsive to the will of Jehovah, yet they could not all have the professional knowledge of ritual laws which was necessary to guide them on all occasions, and errors of inadvertence were unavoidable. Jeremiah could look forward to a time when none should teach his neighbour or his brother, saying, Know Jehovah, because the religion which consists in spiritual emotions and affections becomes the independent possession of every one who is the subject of saving grace. But Ezekiel, from his point of view, could not anticipate a time when all the Lord's people should be priests; for ritual is essentially an affair of tradition and technique, and can only be

maintained by a class of experts specially trained for their office. Ritualism and sacerdotalism are natural allies; and it is not wholly accidental that the great ritualistic Churches of Christendom are those organised on the sacerdotal principle.

But, secondly, the priests have to act as judges or arbitrators in cases of disagreement between man and man (ver. 24). This again was an important department of priestly Torah in ancient Israel, the origin of which went back to the personal legislation of Moses in the wilderness. [237] Cases too hard for human judgment were referred to the decision of God at the sanctuary, and the judgment was conveyed through the agency of the priest. It is impossible to over-estimate the service thus rendered by the priesthood to the cause of religion in Israel; and Hosea bitterly complains of the defection of the priests from the Torah of their God as the source of the widespread moral corruption of his time. [238] In the book of Deuteronomy the Levitical priests of the central sanctuary are associated with the civil magistrate as a court of ultimate appeal in matters of controversy that arise within the community; and this is by no means a tribute to the superior legal acumen of the clerical mind, but a reassertion of the old principle that the priest is the mouthpiece of Jehovah's judgment. [239] That the priests should be the sole judges in Ezekiel's ideal polity was to be expected from the high position assigned to the order generally; but there is another reason for it. We have once more to keep in mind that we are dealing with the Messianic community, when the people are anxious to do the right when they know it, and only cases of honest perplexity require to be resolved. The priests' decision had never been backed up by executive authority, and in the kingdom of God no such sanction will be necessary. By this simple judicial arrangement the ethical demands of Jehovah's holiness will be made effective in the ordinary life of the community.

Finally, the priests have complete control of public worship, and are responsible for the due observance of the festivals and for the sanctification of the Sabbath (ver. 24).

3. With regard to the provisions for the support of the priesthood, the old law continues in force that the priests can hold no landed property and have no possession like the other tribes of Israel (ver. 28). It is true that a strip of land, measuring about twenty-seven square miles, was set apart for their residence; [240] but this was probably not to be cultivated, and at all events it is not reckoned as a possession yielding revenue for their maintenance. The priests' inheritance is Jehovah Himself, which means that they are to live on the offerings of the community presented to Jehovah at the sanctuary. In the practice of the first Temple this ancient rule appears to have been interpreted in a broad and liberal spirit, greatly to the advantage of the Zadokite priests. The Temple dues consisted partly of money payments by the worshippers; and at least the fines for ceremonial trespasses which took the place of the sin- and guilt-offerings were counted the lawful perquisites of the priests. [241] Ezekiel knows nothing of this system; and if it remained in force down to his time, he undoubtedly meant to abolish it. The tribute of the sanctuary is to be paid wholly in kind, and out of this the priests are to receive a stated allowance. In the first place those sacrifices which are wholly made over to the Deity, and yet are not consumed on the altar, have to be eaten by the priests in a holy place. These are the meal-offering, the sin-offering, and the guilt-offering; of which more hereafter. For precisely the same reason all that is ?erem--i.e., "devoted" irrevocably to Jehovah--becomes the possession of the priests, His representatives, except in the cases where it had to be absolutely destroyed. Besides this they have a claim to the best (an indefinite portion) of the firstfruits and "oblations" (terûmah) brought to the sanctuary in accordance with ancient custom to be consumed by the worshipper and his friends. [242]

These regulations are undoubtedly based on pre-exilic usages, and consequently leave much to be supplied from the people's knowledge of use and wont. They do not differ very greatly from the enumeration of the priestly dues in the eighteenth chapter of Deuteronomy. There, as in Ezekiel, we find that the two great sources from which the priests derive their maintenance are the sacrifices and the firstfruits. The Deuteronomic Code, however, knows nothing of the special class of sacrifices called sin- and guilt-offerings, but simply assigns to the priest certain portions of each victim, [243] except of course the burnt-offerings, which were consumed entire on the altar. The priest's share of natural produce is the "best" of corn, new wine, oil, and wool, [244] and would be selected as a matter of course from the tithe and terûmah brought to the sanctuary; so that on this point there is practically complete agreement between Ezekiel and Deuteronomy. On the other hand the differences of the Levitical legislation are considerable, and all in the direction of a fuller provision for the Temple establishment. Such an increased provision was called for by the peculiar circumstances of the second Temple. The revenue of the sanctuary obviously depended on the size and prosperity of the constituency to which it ministered. The stipulations of Deut. xviii. were no doubt sufficient for the maintenance of the priesthood in the old kingdom of Judah; and similarly those of Ezekiel's legislation would amply suffice in the ideal condition of the people and land presupposed by the vision. But neither could have been adequate for the support of a costly ritual in a small community like that which returned from Babylon where one man in ten was a priest. Accordingly we find that the arrangements made under Nehemiah for the endowment of the

Temple ministry are conformed to the extended provisions of the Priestly Code (Neh. x. 32-39).[245]

III

In conclusion, let us briefly consider the significance of this great institution of the priesthood in Ezekiel's scheme of an ideal theocracy. It would of course be an utter mistake to suppose that the prophet is merely legislating in the interests of the sacerdotal order to which he himself belonged. It was necessary for him to insist on the peculiar sanctity and privileges of the priests, and to draw a sharp line of division between them and ordinary members of the community. But he does this, not in the interest of a privileged caste within the nation, but in the interest of a religious ideal which embraced priests and people alike and had to be realised in the life of the nation as a whole. That ideal is expressed by the word "holiness," and we have already seen how the idea of holiness demanded ceremonial conditions of immediate access to Jehovah's presence which the ordinary Israelite could not observe. But "exclusion" could not possibly be the last word of a religion which seeks to bring men into fellowship with God. Access to God might be hedged about by restrictions and conditions of the most onerous kind, but access there must be if worship was to have any meaning and value for the nation or the individual. Although the worshipper might not himself lay his victim on the altar, he must at least be permitted to offer his gift and receive the assurance that it was accepted. If the priest stood between him and God, it was not merely to separate but also to mediate between them, and through the fulfilment of superior conditions of holiness to establish a communication between him and the holy Being whose face he sought. Hence the great function of the priesthood in the theocracy is to maintain the intercourse between Jehovah and Israel which was exhibited in the Temple ritual by acts of sacrificial worship.

Now it is manifest that this system of ideas rests on the representative character of the priestly office. If the principal idea symbolised in the sanctuary is that of holiness through separation, the fundamental idea of priesthood is holiness through representation. It is the holiness of Israel concentrated in the priesthood which qualifies the latter for entrance within the inner circle of the divine presence. Or perhaps it would be more correct to say that the presence of Jehovah first sanctifies the priests in an eminent degree, and then through them, though in a less degree, the whole body of the people. The idea of national solidarity was too deeply rooted in the Hebrew consciousness to admit of any other interpretation of the priesthood than this. The Israelite did not need to be told that his standing before God was secured by his membership in the religious community on whose behalf the priests ministered at the altar and before the Temple. It would not occur to him to think of his personal exclusion from the most sacred offices as a religious disability; it was enough for him to know that the nation to which he belonged was admitted to the presence of Jehovah in the persons of its representatives, and that he as an individual shared in the blessings which accrued to Israel through the privileged ministry of the priests. Thus to a Temple poet of a later age than Ezekiel's the figure of the high priest supplies a striking image of the communion of saints and the blessing of Jehovah resting on the whole people:--

> *Behold, how good and how pleasant it is*
> *That they who are brethren should also dwell together!*
> *Like the precious oil on the head,*
> *That flows down on the beard,*
> *The beard of Aaron,*
> *That flows down on the hem of his garments--*
> *Like the Hermon-dew that descends on the hills of Zion;*
> *For there hath Jehovah ordained the blessing,*
> *Life for evermore.* [246]

Footnotes:

225. 2 Kings xxiii. 9. The sense of the passage is undoubtedly that given above; but the expression "unleavened bread" as a general name for the priests' portion is peculiar. It has been proposed to read, with a change merely of the punctuation, instead of mtsvt, mtsvt = "statutory portions," as in Neh. xiii. 5.
226. 1 Sam. ii. 36.
227. Cf. ch. xxii. 26.
228. Ezra ii. 36-40.
229. Ezra ii. 58.
230. Ezra viii. 15-20.
231. On this peculiar affinity between holiness and uncleanness see the interesting argument in Robertson Smith's Religion of the Semites, pp. 427 ff. The passage Hag. ii. 12-14 does not appear to be inconsistent with what is there said. The meaning is that "very indirect contact with the

holy does not make holy, but very direct contact with the unclean makes unclean" (Wellhausen, Die Kleinen Propheten, p. 170).

232. Cf. ch. xxiv. 17; Lev. x. 6, xxi. 5, 10.

233. It is remarkable that neither here nor in Leviticus (ch. xxi. 1-3) is the priest's wife mentioned as one for whom he may defile himself at her death.

234. Cf. 2 Kings xii. 11, xxiii. 14, xxv. 18; Jer. xx. 1.

235. Hence it does not seem to me that any argument can be based on the fact that a high priest was at the head of the returning exiles either for or against the existence of the Priestly Code at that date.

236. Lev. iv. 3, 13: cf. Lev. xvi. 6.

237. Exod. xviii. 25 ff.

238. Hosea iv. 6.

239. Cf. Deut. i. 17: "judgment is God's."

240. See below, p. ^{12}493.

241. 2 Kings xii. 4-16.

242. They also receive the best of the arîsoth, a word of uncertain meaning, probably either dough or coarse meal. This offering is said to bring a blessing on the household.

243. Deut. xviii. 3.

244. Deut. xviii. 4.

245. The regulations of the Priests' Code with regard to the revenues of the Temple clergy are most comprehensively given in Numb. xviii. 8-32. The first thing that strikes us there is the distinction between the due of the priests and that of the Levites. The absence of any express provision for the latter is a somewhat remarkable feature in Ezekiel's legislation, when we consider the care with which he has defined the status and duties of the order. It is evident, however, that no complete arrangements could be made for the Temple service without some law on this point such as is contained in the passage Num. xviii. and referred to in Neh. x. 37-39; and this is closely connected with a disposition of the tithes and firstlings different from the directions of Deuteronomy, and probably also from the tacit assumption of Ezekiel. The book of Deuteronomy leaves no doubt that both the tithes of natural produce and the firstlings of the flock and herd were intended to furnish the material for sacrificial feasts at the sanctuary (cf. chs. xii. 6, 7, 11, 12, xiv. 22-27). The priest received the usual portions of the firstlings (ch. xviii. 3), and also a share of the tithe; but the rest was eaten by the worshipper and his guests. In Numb. xviii., on the other hand, all the firstlings are the property of the priest (ver. 15), and the whole of the tithes is assigned to the Levites, who in turn are required to hand over a tenth of the tithe to the priests (vv. 24-32). The portion of the priests consists of the following items: (1) The meal-offering, sin-offering, and guilt-offering (as in Ezekiel); (2) the best of oil, new wine, and corn (as in Deuteronomy) (ver. 12); (3) all the firstfruits (an advance on Ezekiel) (ver. 13); (4) every devoted thing (Ezekiel) (ver. 14); (5) all the firstlings (vv. 15-18); (6) the breast and right thigh of all ordinary private sacrifices (ver. 18: cf. Lev. vii. 31-34) (like Deuteronomy, but choicer portions); (7) the tenth of the Levites' tithe. It will be seen from this enumeration that the Temple tariff of the Priestly law includes, with some slight modification, all the requirements of Deuteronomy and Ezekiel, besides the two important additions referred to above.

246. Psalm cxxxiii.

Chapter XXVIII - Prince And People. Chapters xliv.-xlvi. passim

It was remarked in a previous lecture that the "prince" of the closing vision appears to occupy a less exalted position than the Messianic king of ch. xxxiv. or ch. xxxvii. The grounds on which this impression rests require, however, to be carefully considered, if we are not to carry away a thoroughly false conception of the theocratic state foreshadowed by Ezekiel. It must not be supposed that the prince is a personage of less than royal rank, or that his authority is overshadowed by that of a priestly caste. He is undoubtedly the civil head of the nation, owing no allegiance within his own province to any earthly superior. Nor is there any reason to doubt that he is the heir of the Davidic house and holds his office in virtue of the divine promise which secured the throne to David's descendants. It would therefore be a mistake to imagine that we have here an anticipation of the Romish theory of the subordination of the secular to the spiritual power. It may be true that in the state of things presupposed by the vision very little is left for the king to do, whilst a variety of important duties falls to the priesthood; but at all events the king is there and is supreme in his own sphere. Ezekiel does not show the road to Canossa. If the king is overshadowed, it is by the personal presence of Jehovah in the midst of His people; and that which limits his prerogative is not the sacerdotal power, but the divine constitution of the theocracy as revealed in the vision itself, under which both king and priests have their functions defined and regulated with a view to the religious ends for which the community as a whole exists.

Our purpose in the present chapter is to put together the scattered references to the duties of the prince which occur in chs. xliv.-xlvi., so as to gain as clear a picture as possible of the position of the monarchy in the theocratic state. It must be remembered, however, that the picture will necessarily be incomplete. National life in its secular aspects, with which the king is chiefly concerned, is hardly touched on in the vision. Everything being looked upon from the point of view of the Temple and its worship, there are but few allusions in which we can detect anything of the nature of a civil constitution. And these few are introduced incidentally, not for their own sake, but to explain some arrangement for securing the sanctity of the land or the community. This fact must never be lost sight of in judging of Ezekiel's conception of the monarchy. From all that appears in these pages we might conclude that the prince is a mere ornamental figurehead of the constitution, and that the few real duties assigned to him could have been equally well performed by a committee of priests or laymen elected for the purpose. But this is to forget that outside the range of subjects here touched upon there is a whole world of secular interests, of political and social action, where the king has his part to play in accordance with the precedents furnished by the best days of the ancient monarchy.

Let us glance first of all at Ezekiel's institutes of the kingdom in its more political relations. The notices here are all in the form of constitutional checks and safeguards against an arbitrary and oppressive exercise of the royal authority. They are instructive, not only as showing the interest which the prophet had in good government and his care for the rights of the subject, but also for the light they cast on certain administrative methods in force previous to the Exile.

The first point that calls for attention is the provision made for the maintenance of the prince and his court. It would seem that the revenue of the prince was to be derived mainly, if not wholly, from a portion of territory reserved as his exclusive property in the division of the country among the tribes. [247] These crown lands are situated on either side of the sacred "oblation" around the sanctuary, set apart for the use of the priests and Levites; and they extend to the sea on the west and to the Jordan Valley on the east. Out of these he is at liberty to assign a possession to his sons in perpetuity, but any estate bestowed on his courtiers reverts to the prince in the "year of liberty."[248] The object of this last regulation apparently is to prevent the formation of a new hereditary aristocracy between the royal family and the peasantry. A life peerage, so to speak, or something less, is deemed a sufficient reward for the most devoted service to the king or the state. And no doubt the certainty of a revision of all royal grants every seventh year would tend to keep some persons mindful of their duty. The whole system of royal demesnes which the king might dispose of as appanages for his younger children or his faithful retainers presents a curious resemblance to a well-known feature of feudalism in the Middle Ages; but it was never practically enforced in Israel.

Before the Exile it was evidently unknown, and after the Exile there was no king to provide for. But why does the prophet bestow so much care on a mere detail of a political system in which, as a whole, he takes so little interest? It is because of his concern for the rights of the common people against the high-handed tyranny of the king and his nobles. He recalls the bad times of the old monarchy when any man was liable to be ejected from his land for the benefit of some court favourite, or to provide a portion for a younger son of the king. The cruel evictions of the poorer peasant proprietors, which all the early prophets denounce as an outrage against humanity, and of which the story of Naboth furnished a typical example, must be rendered impossible in the new Israel; and as the king had no doubt been the principal offender in the past, the rule is firmly laid down in his case that on no pretext must he take the people's inheritance. And this, be it observed, is an application of the religious principle which underlies the constitution of the theocracy. The land is Jehovah's, and all interference with the ancient landmarks which guard the rights of private ownership is an offence against the holiness of the true divine King who has His abode amongst the tribes of Israel. This suggests developments of the idea of holiness which reach to the very foundations of social well-being. A conception of holiness which secures each man in the possession of his own vine and fig tree is at all events not open to the charge of ignoring the practical interests of common life for the sake of an unprofitable ceremonialism.

In the next place, we come across a much more startling revelation of the injustice habitually practised by the Hebrew monarchs. Just as later sovereigns were wont to meet their deficits by debasing the currency, so the kings of Judah had learned to augment their revenue by a systematic falsification of weights and measures. We know from the prophet Amos [249] that this was a common trick of the wealthy landowners who sold grain at exorbitant prices to the poor whom they had driven from their possessions. They "made the ephah small and the shekel great, and dealt falsely with balances of deceit." But it was left for Ezekiel to tell us that the same fraud was a regular part of the fiscal system of the Judæan kingdom. There is no mistaking the meaning of his accusation: "Have done, O princes of Israel, with your violent and oppressive rule; execute judgment and justice, and take away your exactions from My people, saith Jehovah God. Ye shall have just balances, and a just ephah, and a just bath." [250] That is to say, the taxes were surreptitiously increased by the use of a large shekel (for weighing out money payments) and a large bath and ephah (for measuring tribute paid in kind). And if it was impossible for the poor to protect themselves against the rapacity of private dealers, poor and rich alike were helpless when the fraud was openly practised in the king's name. This Ezekiel had seen with his own eyes, and the shameful injustice of it was so branded on his spirit that even in a vision of the last days it comes back to him as an evil to be sedulously guarded against. It was eminently a case for legislation. If there was to be such a thing as fair dealing and commercial probity in the community, the system of weights and measurement must be fixed beyond the power of the royal caprice to alter it. It was as sacred as any principle of the constitution. Accordingly he finds a place in his legislation for a corrected scale of weights and measures, restored no doubt to their original values. The ephah for dry measure and the bath for liquid measure are each fixed at the tenth part of a homer. "The shekel shall be twenty geras; [251] five shekels shall be five, and ten shekels shall be ten, and fifty shekels shall be your maneh." [252]

These regulations extend far beyond the immediate object for which they are introduced, and have both a moral and a religious bearing. They express a truth often insisted on in the Old Testament, that commercial morality is a matter in which the holiness of Jehovah is involved: "A false balance is an abomination to Jehovah, but a just weight is His delight." [253] In the Law of Holiness an ordinance very similar to Ezekiel's occurs amongst the conditions by which the precept is to be fulfilled: "Be ye holy, for I am holy." [254] It is evident that the Israelites had learned to regard with a religious abhorrence all tampering with the fixed standards of value on which the purity of commercial life depended. To overreach by lying words was a sin; but to cheat by the use of a false balance was a species of profanity comparable to a false oath in the name of Jehovah.

These rules about weights and measures required, however, to be supplemented by a fixed tariff, regulating the taxes which the prince might impose on the people. [255] It is not quite clear whether any part of the prince's own income was to be derived from taxation. The tribute is called an "oblation," and there is no doubt that it was intended principally for the support of the Temple ritual, which in any case must have been the heaviest charge on the royal exchequer. But the oblation was rendered to the prince in the first instance; and the prophet's anxiety to prevent unjust exactions springs from a fear that the king might make the Temple tax a pretext for increasing his own revenue. At all events the people's duty to contribute to the support of public ordinances according to their ability is here explicitly recognised. Compared with the provision of the Levitical law the scale of charges here proposed must be pronounced extremely moderate. The contribution of each householder varies from one-sixtieth to one-twohundredth of his income and is wholly paid in kind. [256] The proper equivalent under the second Temple of Ezekiel's "oblation" was a poll-tax of one-third of a shekel, voluntarily undertaken at the time of Nehemiah's covenant "for the service of the house of our God; for the shewbread and for the continual meal-offering, and for the continual burnt-offering, of the Sabbaths, of the new moons, for the set feasts, and for the holy things, and for the sin-offerings to make atonement for Israel, and for all the work of the house of our God." [257] In the Priestly Code this tax is fixed at half a shekel for each man. [258] But in addition to this money payment the law required a tenth of all produce of the soil and the flock to be given to the priests and Levites. In Ezekiel's legislation the tithes and firstfruits are still left for the use of the owner, who is expected to consume them in sacrificial feasts at the sanctuary. The only charge, therefore, of the nature of a fixed tribute for religious purposes is the oblation here required for the regular sacrifices which represent the stated worship rendered on behalf of the community as a whole.

This brings us now to the more important aspect of the kingly office--its religious privileges and duties. Here there are three points which require to be noticed.

1. In the first place it is the duty of the prince to supply the material of the public sacrifices offered in the name of the people. [259] Out of the tribute levied on the people for this purpose he has to furnish the altar with the stated number of victims for the daily service, the Sabbaths, and new moons, and the great yearly festivals. It is clear that some one must be charged with the responsibility of this important part of the worship, and it is significant of Ezekiel's relations to the past that the duty does not yet devolve directly on the priests. They seem to exercise no authority outside of the Temple, the king standing between them and the community as a sort of patron of the sanctuary. But the position of the prince is not simply that of an official receiver, collecting the tribute, and then handing it over to the Temple as it was required. He is the representative of the religious unity of the nation, and in this capacity he presents in person the regular sacrifices offered on behalf of the community. Thus on the day of the Passover he presents a sin-offering for himself and the people, [260] as the high priest does in the ceremonial of the Great Day of Atonement.[261] And so all the sacrifices of the stated ritual are his sacrifices, officiating as the head of the nation in its acts of common worship. In this respect the prince succeeds to the rights exercised by the kings of Judah in the ritual of the first Temple, although on a different footing. Before the Exile the king had a proprietary interest in the central sanctuary, and the expense of the stated service was defrayed as a matter of course out of the royal revenues. Part of this revenue, as we see in the case of Joash, was raised by a system of Temple dues paid by the worshippers and expended on the repairs of the house; but at a much later date than this we find Ahaz assuming absolute control over the daily sacrifices, [262] which were doubtless maintained at his expense.

Now the tendency of Ezekiel's legislation is to bring the whole community into a closer and more personal connection with the worship of the sanctuary, and to leave no part of it subject to the arbitrary will of the prince. But still the idea is preserved that the prince is the religious as well as the civil representative of the nation; and although he is deprived of all control over the performance of the ritual, he is still required to provide the public sacrifices and to offer them in the name of his people.

2. In virtue of his representative character the prince possesses certain privileges in his approaches to God in the sanctuary not accorded to ordinary worshippers. In this connection it is necessary to explain some details regulating the use of the sanctuary by the people. The outer court might be entered by prince or people either through the north or south gate, but not from the east. The eastern gate was that by which Jehovah had entered His dwelling-place, and the doors of it are for ever closed. No foot might cross its threshold. But the prince--and this is one of his peculiar rights--might enter the gateway from the court to eat his sacrificial meals. [263] It seems therefore to have served the same purpose for the prince as the thirty cells along the wall did for common worshippers. The east gate of the inner court was also shut as a rule, and was probably never used as a passage even by the priests. But on the Sabbaths and new moons it was thrown open to receive the sacrifices which the prince had to bring on these days, and it remained open till the evening. On days when the gate was open the worshipping congregation assembled at its door, while the prince entered as far as the threshold and looked on while the priests presented his offering; then he went out by the way he had entered. If on any other occasion he presented a voluntary sacrifice in his private capacity, the east gate was opened for him as before, but was shut as soon as the ceremony was over. On those occasions when the eastern gate was not opened, as at the great annual festivals, the people probably gathered round the north and south gates, from which they could see the altar; and at these seasons the prince enters and departs in the common throng of worshippers. A very peculiar regulation, for which no obvious reason appears, is that each man must leave the Temple by the gate opposite to that at which he entered; if he entered by the north, he must leave by the south, and vice versâ. [264]

Many of these arrangements were no doubt suggested by Ezekiel's acquaintance with the practice in the first Temple, and their precise object is lost to us. But one or two facts stand out clearly enough, and are very instructive as to the whole conception of Temple worship. The chief thing to be noticed is that the principal sacrifices are representative. The people are merely spectators of a transaction with God on their behalf, the efficacy of which in no way depends on their co-operation. Standing at the gates of the inner court, they see the priests performing the sacred ministrations; they bow themselves in humble reverence before the presence of the Most High; and these acts of devotion may have been of the utmost importance for the religious life of the individual Israelite. But the congregation takes no real part in the worship; it is done for them, but not by them; it is an opus operatum performed by the prince and the priests for the good of the community, and is equally necessary and equally valid whether there is a congregation present to witness it or not. Those who attend are themselves but representatives of the nation of Israel, in whose interest the ritual is kept up. But the supreme representative of the people is the king, and we note how everything is done to emphasise his peculiar dignity within the sanctuary. It was necessary perhaps to do something to compensate for the loss of distinction caused by the exclusion of the royal body-guard from the Temple. The prince is still the one conspicuous figure in the outer court. Even his private sacrificial meals are eaten in solitary state, in the eastern gateway, which is used for no other purpose. And in the great functions where the prince appears in his representative character he approaches nearer to the altar than is permitted to any other layman. He ascends the steps of the eastern gateway in the sight of the people, and passing through he presents his offerings on the verge of the inner court which none but the priests may enter. His whole position is thus one of great importance in the celebration of public ordinances. In detail his functions are no doubt determined by ancient prescriptive usages not known to us, but modified in accordance with the stricter ideal of holiness which Ezekiel's vision was intended to enforce.

3. Finally, we have to observe that the prince is rigorously excluded from properly priestly offices. It is true that in some respects his position is analogous to that of the high priest under the law. But the analogy extends only to that aspect of the high priest's functions in which he appears as the head and representative of the religious community, and ceases the moment he enters upon priestly duties. So far as the special degree of sanctity which characterises the priesthood is concerned, the prince is a layman, and as such he is jealously debarred from approaching the altar, and even from intruding into the sacred inner court where the priests minister. Now this fact has perhaps a deeper historical importance than we are apt to imagine. There is good reason to believe that in the old Temple the kings of Judah frequently officiated in person at the altar. At the time when the monarchy was established it was the rule that any man might sacrifice for himself and his household, and that the king as the representative of the nation should sacrifice on its behalf was an extension of the principle too obvious to require express sanction. Accordingly we find that both Saul and David on public occasions built altars and offered sacrifice to Jehovah. The older theory indeed seems to have been that priestly rights were inherent in the kingly office, and that the acting priests were the ministers to whom the king delegated the greater part of his priestly functions. Although the king might not appoint any one to this duty without respect to the Levitical qualification, he exercised within certain limits the right of deposing one family and installing another in the priesthood of the royal sanctuary. The house of Zadok itself owed its position to such an act of ecclesiastical authority on the part of David and Solomon.

The last occasion on which we read of a king of Judah officiating in person in the Temple is at the dedication of the new altar of Ahaz, when the king not only himself sacrificed, but gave directions to the priests as to the future observance of the ritual. The occasion was no doubt unusual, but there is not a word in the narrative to indicate that the king was committing an irregular action or exceeding the recognised prerogatives of his position. It would be unsafe, however, to conclude that this state of things continued unchanged till the close of the monarchy. After the time of Isaiah the Temple rose greatly in the religious estimation of the people, and a very probable result of this would be an increasing sense of the importance of the ministration of the official priesthood. The silence of the historical books and of Deuteronomy may not count for much in an argument on this question; but Ezekiel's own decisions lack the emphasis and solemnity with which he introduces an absolute innovation like the separation between priests and Levites in ch. xliv. It is at least possible that the later kings had gradually ceased to exercise the right of sacrifice, so that the privilege had lapsed through desuetude. Nevertheless it was a great step to have the principle affirmed as a fundamental law of the theocracy; and this Ezekiel undoubtedly does. If no other practical object were gained, it served at least to illustrate in the most emphatic way the idea of holiness, which demanded the exclusion of every layman from unhallowed contact with the most sacred emblems of Jehovah's presence.

***

It will be seen from all that has been said that the real interest of Ezekiel's treatment of the monarchy lies far apart from modern problems which might seem to have a superficial affinity with it. No lessons can fairly be deduced from it on the relations between Church and State, or the propriety of endowing and establishing the Christian religion, or the duty of rulers to maintain ordinances for the benefit of their subjects. Its importance lies in another direction. It shows the transition in Israel from a state of things in which the king is both de jure and de facto the source of power and the representative of the nation and where his religious status is the natural consequence of his civic dignity, to a very different state of things, where the forms of the ancient constitution are retained although the power has largely vanished from them. The prince now requires to have his religious duties imposed on him by an abstract political system whose sole sanction is the authority of the Deity. It is a transition which has no precise parallel anywhere else, although resemblances more or less instructive might doubtless be instanced from the history of Catholicism. Nowhere does Ezekiel's idealism appear more wonderfully blended with his equally characteristic conservatism than here. There is no real trace of the tendency attributed to the prophet to exalt the priesthood at the expense of the monarchy. The prince is after all a much more imposing personage even in the ceremonial worship than any priest. Although he lacks the priestly quality of holiness, his duties are quite as important as those of the priests, while his dignity is far greater than theirs. The considerations that enter in to limit his power and importance come from another quarter. They are such as these: first, the loss of military leadership, which is at least to be presumed in the circumstances of the Messianic kingdom; second, the welfare of the people at large; and third, the principle of holiness, whose supremacy has to be vindicated in the person of the king no less than in that of his meanest subject.

Perhaps the most remarkable thing is that the transition referred to was not actually accomplished even in the history of Israel itself. It was only in a vision that the monarchy was ever to be represented in the form which it bears here. From the time of Ezekiel no native king was ever to rule over Israel again save the priest-princes of the Asmonean dynasty, whose constitutional position was defined by their high-priestly dignity. Ezekiel's vision is therefore a preparation for the kingless state of post-exilic Judaism. The foreign potentates to whom the Jews were subject did in some instances provide materials for the Temple worship, but their local representatives were of course unqualified to fill the position assigned to the prince by the great prophet of the Exile. The community had to get along as best it could without a king, and the task was not difficult. The Temple dues were paid directly to the priests and Levites, and the function of representing the community before the altar was assigned to the High Priest. It was then indeed that the High Priesthood came to the front and blossomed out into all the magnificence of its legal position. It was not only the religious part of the prince's duties that fell to it, but a considerable share of his political importance as well. As the only hereditary institution that had survived the Exile, it naturally became the chief centre of social order in the community. By degrees the Persian and Greek kings found it expedient to deal with the Jews through the High Priest, whose authority they were bound to respect, and thus to leave him a free hand in the internal affairs of the commonwealth. The High Priesthood, in fact, was a civil as well as a priestly dignity. We can see that this great revolution would have broken the continuity of Hebrew history far more violently than it did, but for the stepping-stone furnished by the ideal "prince" of Ezekiel's vision.

Footnotes:

247. Chs. xlv. 7, 8, xlviii. 21, 22.

248. I.e., either the seventh year, as in Jer. xxxiv. 14, or the year of Jubilee, the fiftieth year (Lev. xxv. 10); more probably the former.

249. Amos viii. 5.

250. Ezek. xlv. 9, 10. In the translation of ver. 9 I have followed an emendation proposed by Cornill. The sense is not affected, but the grammatical construction seems to demand some alteration on the Massoretic text.

251. In Exod. xxx. 13, Lev. xxvii. 25, Numb. iii. 47 (Priests' Code) the shekel of twenty geras is described as the "shekel of the sanctuary," or "sacred shekel," clearly implying that another shekel was in common use.

252. Ezek. xlv. 12, according to the LXX.

253. Prov. xi. 1.

254. Lev. xix. 35, 36.

255. Ezek. xlv. 13-16.

256. The exact figures are, one part in sixty of cereal produce (wheat and barley), one share in a hundred of oil, and one animal out of every two hundred from the flock (ch. xlv. 13-15).

257. Neh. x. 32, 33; cf. Ezek. xlv. 15.

258. Exod. xxx. 11-16. Whether the third of a shekel in the book of Nehemiah is a concession to the poverty of the people, or whether the law represents an increased charge found necessary for

The Expositor's Bible: The Book of Ezekiel
the full Temple service, is a question that need not be discussed here.
    259. Ch. xlv. 17.
    260. Ch. xlv. 22.
    261. Lev. xvi. 11, 15.
    262. 2 Kings xvi. 15, 16.
    263. Ch. xliv. 1-3.
    264. See ch. xlvi. 1-12. The Syriac Version indeed makes an exception to this rule in the case of the prince. Ver. 10 reads: "But the prince in their midst shall go out by the gate by which he entered." But why the prince more than any other body should go back by the road he came, or what particular honour there was in that, is a mystery; and it is probable that the reading is an error originating in repetition of ver. 8. The real meaning of the verse seems to be that the prince must go in and out without the retinue of foreigners who used to give éclat to royal visits to the sanctuary.

John J. Skinner

Chapter XXIX - The Ritual. Chapters xlv., xlvi

It is difficult to go back in imagination to a time when sacrifice was the sole and sufficient form of every complete act of worship. [265] That the slaughter of an animal, or at least the presentation of a material offering of some sort, should ever have been considered of the essence of intercourse with the Deity may seem to us incredible in the light of the idea of God which we now possess. Yet there can be no doubt that there was a stage of religious development which recognised no true approach to God except as consummated in a sacrificial action. The word "sacrifice" itself preserves a memorial of this crude and early type of religious service. Etymologically it denotes nothing more than a sacred act. But amongst the Romans, as amongst ourselves, it was regularly applied to the offerings at the altar, which were thus marked out as the sacred actions par excellence of ancient religion. It would be impossible to explain the extraordinary persistence and vitality of the institution amongst races that had attained a relatively high degree of civilisation, unless we understand that the ideas connected with it go back to a time when sacrifice was the typical and fundamental form of primitive worship.

By the time of Ezekiel, however, the age of sacrifice in this strict and absolute sense may be said to have passed away, at least in principle. Devout Jews who had lived through the captivity in Babylon and found that Jehovah was there to them "a little of a sanctuary," [266] could not possibly fall back into the belief that their God was only to be approached and found through the ritual of the altar. And long before the Exile, the ethical teaching of the prophets had led Israel to appreciate the external rites of sacrifice at their true value.

Wherewithal shall I come before Jehovah
Or bow myself before God on high?
Shall I come before Him with burnt-offerings,
With calves of a year old?
Is Jehovah pleased with thousands of rams,
With myriads of rivers of oil?
Shall I give my firstborn as an atonement for me,
The fruit of my body as a sin-offering for my life?
He hath showed thee, O man, what is good;
And what does Jehovah require of thee,
But to do justice and to love mercy,
And to walk humbly with thy God? [267]

This great word of spiritual religion had been uttered long before Ezekiel, as a protest against the senseless multiplication of sacrifices which came in in the reign of Manasseh. Nor can we suppose that Ezekiel, with all his engrossment in matters of ritual, was insensible to the lofty teaching of his predecessors, or that his conception of God was less spiritual than theirs. As a matter of fact the worship of Israel was never afterwards wholly absorbed in the routine of the Temple ceremonies. The institution of the synagogue with its purely devotional exercises of prayer and reading of the Scriptures must have been nearly coeval with the second Temple, and prepared the way far more than the latter for the spiritual worship of the New Testament. But even the Temple worship was spiritualised by the service of praise and the marvellous development of devotional poetry which it called forth. "The emotion with which the worshipper approaches the second Temple, as recorded in the Psalter, has little to do with sacrifice, but rests rather on the fact that the whole wondrous history of Jehovah's grace to Israel is vividly and personally realised as he stands amidst the festal crowd at the ancient seat of God's throne, and adds his voice to the swelling song of praise." [268]

How then, it may be asked, are we to account for the fact that the prophet shows such intense interest in the details of a system which was already losing its religious significance? If sacrifice was no longer of the essence of worship, why should he be so careful to legislate for a scheme of ritual in which sacrifice is the prominent feature, and say nothing of the inward state of heart which alone is an acceptable offering to God? The chief reason no doubt is that the ritual elements of religion were the only matters, apart from moral duties, which admitted of being reduced to a legal system, and that the formation of such a system was demanded by the circumstances with which the prophet had to deal. The time was not yet come when the principle of a central national sanctuary could be abandoned, and if such a sanctuary was to be maintained without danger to the highest interests of religion it was necessary that its service should be regulated with a view to preserve the deposit of revealed truth that had been committed to the nation through the prophets. The essential features of the sacrificial institutions were charged with a deep religious significance, and there existed in the popular mind a great mass of sound religious impression and sentiment clustering around that central rite. To dispense with the institution of sacrifice would have rendered worship entirely impossible for the great body of the people, while to leave it unregulated was to invite a recurrence of the abuses which had been so fruitful a source of corruption in the past. Hence the object of the ritual ordinances which we are about to consider is twofold: in the first place to provide an authorised code of ritual free from everything that savoured of pagan usages, and in the second to utilise the public worship as a means of deepening and purifying the religious conceptions of those who could be influenced in no other way. Ezekiel's legislation has a special regard for the wants of the "common rude man" whose religious life needs all the help it can get from external observances. Such persons form the majority of every religious society; and to train their minds to a deeper sense of sin and a more vivid apprehension of the divine holiness proved to be the only way in which the spiritual teaching of the prophets could be made a practical power in the community at large. It is true that the highest spiritual needs were not satisfied by the legal ritual. But the irrepressible longings of the soul for nearer fellowship with God cannot be dealt with by rigid formal enactments. Ezekiel is content to leave them to the guidance of that Spirit whose saving operations will have changed the heart of Israel and made it a true people of God. The system of external observances which he foreshadows in his vision was not meant to be the life of religion, but it was, so to speak, the trellis-work which was necessary to support the delicate tendrils of spiritual piety until the time when the spirit of filial worship should be the possession of every true member of the Church of God.

Bearing these facts in mind, we may now proceed to examine the scheme of sacrificial worship contained in chapters xlv. and xlvi. Only its leading features can here be noticed, and the points most deserving of attention may be grouped under three heads: the Festivals, the Representative Service, and the Idea of Atonement.

I. The Yearly Feasts.--The most striking thing in Ezekiel's festal calendar [269] is the division of the ecclesiastical year into two precisely similar parts. Each half of the year commences with an atoning sacrifice for the purification of the sanctuary from defilement contracted during the previous half. [270] Each contains a great festival--in the one case the Passover, beginning on the fourteenth day of the first month and lasting seven days, and in the other the Feast of Tabernacles (simply called the Feast), beginning on the fifteenth day of the seventh month and also lasting for seven days. [271] The passage is chiefly devoted to a minute regulation of the public sacrifices to be offered on these occasions, other and more characteristic features of the celebration being assumed as well known from tradition.

It is difficult to see what is the precise meaning of the proposed rearrangement of the feasts in two parallel series. It may be due simply to the prophet's love of symmetry in all departments of public life, or it may have been suggested by the fact that at this time the Babylonian calendar, according to which the year begins in spring, was superimposed on the old Hebrew year commencing in the autumn. [272] At all events it involved a breach with pre-exilic tradition, and was never carried out in practice. The earlier legislation of the Pentateuch recognises a cycle of three festivals--Passover and Unleavened Bread, the Feast of Harvest or of Weeks (Pentecost), and the Feast of Ingathering or of Tabernacles. [273] In order to carry through his symmetrical division of the sacred year Ezekiel has to ignore one of these, the Feast of Pentecost, which seems to have always been counted the least important of the three. It is not to be supposed that he contemplated its abolition, for he is careful not to alter in any particular the positive regulations of Deuteronomy; only it did not fall into his scheme, and so he does not think it of sufficient importance to prescribe regular public sacrifices for it. After the Exile, however, Jewish practice was regulated by the canons of the Priestly Code, in which, along with other festivals, the ancient threefold cycle is continued, and stated sacrifices are prescribed for Pentecost, just as for the other two. [274] Similarly, the two atoning ceremonies in the beginning of the first and seventh months, [275] which are not mentioned in the older legislation, are replaced in the Priests' Code by the single Day of Atonement on the tenth day of the seventh month, whilst the beginning of the year is celebrated by the Feast of Trumpets on the first day of the same month. [276]

But although the details of Ezekiel's system thus proved to be impracticable in the circumstances of the restored Jewish community, it succeeded in the far more important object of infusing a new spirit into the celebration of the feasts, and impressing on them a different character. The ancient Hebrew festivals were all associated with joyous incidents of the agricultural year. The

Feast of Unleavened Bread marked the beginning of harvest, when "the sickle was first put into the corn." [277] At this time also the firstlings of the flock and herd were sacrificed. The seven weeks which elapse till Pentecost are the season of the cereal harvest, which is then brought to a close by the Feast of Harvest, when the goodness of Jehovah is acknowledged by the presentation of part of the produce at the sanctuary. Finally the Feast of Tabernacles celebrates the most joyous occasion of the year, the storing of the produce of the winepress and the threshing-floor. [278] The nature of the festivals is easily seen from the events with which they are thus associated. They are occasions of social mirth and festivity, and the religious rites observed are the expressions of the nation's heart-felt gratitude to Jehovah for the blessing that has rested on the labours of husbandman and shepherd throughout the year. The Passover with its memories of anxiety and escape was no doubt of a more sombre character than the others, but the joyous and festive nature of Pentecost and Tabernacles is strongly insisted on in the book of Deuteronomy. By these institutions religion was closely intertwined with the great interests of every-day life, and the fact that the sacred seasons of the Israelites' year were the occasions on which the natural joy of life was at its fullest, bears witness to the simple-minded piety which was fostered by the old Hebrew worship. There was, however, a danger that in such a state of things religion should be altogether lost sight of in the exuberance of natural hilarity and expressions of social good-will. And indeed no great height of spirituality could be nourished by a type of worship in which devotional feeling was concentrated on the expression of gratitude to God for the bountiful gifts of His providence. It was good for the childhood of the nation, but when the nation became a man it must put away childish things.

The tendency of the post-exilic ritual was to detach the sacred seasons more and more from the secular associations which had once been their chief significance. This was done partly by the addition of new festivals which had no such natural occasion, and partly by a change in the point of view from which the older celebrations were regarded. No attempt was made to obliterate the traces of the affinity with events of common life which endeared them to the hearts of the people, but increasing importance was attached to their historic significance as memorials of Jehovah's gracious dealings with the nation in the period of the Exodus. At the same time they take on more and more the character of religious symbols of the permanent relations between Jehovah and His people. The beginnings of this process can be clearly discerned in the legislation of Ezekiel. Not indeed in the direction of a historic interpretation of the feasts, for this is ignored even in the case of the Passover, where it was already firmly established in the national consciousness. But the institution of a special series of public sacrifices, which was the same for the Passover and the Feast of Tabernacles, and particularly the prominence given to the sin-offering, obviously tended to draw the mind of the people away from the passing interest of the occasion, and fix it on those standing obligations imposed by the holiness of Jehovah on which the continuance of all His bounties depended. We cannot be mistaken in thinking that one design of the new ritual was to correct the excesses of unrestrained animal enjoyment by deepening the sense of guilt and the fear of possible offences against the sanctity of the divine presence. For it was at these festivals that the prince was required to offer the atoning sacrifice for himself and the people. [279] Thus the effect of the whole system was to foster the sensitive and tremulous tone of piety which was characteristic of Judaism, in contrast to the hearty, if undisciplined, religion of the ancient Hebrew feasts.

II. The Stated Service.--In the course of this chapter we have had occasion more than once to touch on the prominence given in Ezekiel's vision to sacrifices offered in accordance with a fixed rubric in the name of the whole community. The significance of this fact may best be seen from a comparison with the sacrificial regulations of the book of Deuteronomy. These are not numerous, but they deal exclusively with private sacrifices. The person addressed is the individual householder, and the sacrifices which he is enjoined to render are for himself and his family. There is no explicit allusion in the whole book to the official sacrifices which were offered by the regular priesthood and maintained at the king's expense. In Ezekiel's scheme of Temple worship the case is exactly the reverse. Here there is no mention of private sacrifice except in the incidental notices as to the free-will offerings and the sacrificial meal of the prince, [280] while on the other hand great attention is paid to the maintenance of the regular offerings provided by the prince for the congregation. This of course does not mean that there were no statutory sacrifices in the old Temple, or that Ezekiel contemplated the cessation of private sacrifice in the new. Deuteronomy passes over the public sacrifices because they were under the jurisdiction of the king, and the people at large were not directly responsible for them; and similarly Ezekiel is silent as to private offerings because their observance was assured by all the traditions of the sanctuary. Still it is a noteworthy fact that of two codes of Temple worship, separated by only half a century, each legislates exclusively for that element of the ritual which is taken for granted by the other.

What it indicates is nothing less than a change in the ruling conception of public worship. Before the Exile the idea that Jehovah could desert His sanctuary hardly entered into the mind of the people, and certainly did not in the least affect the confidence with which they availed themselves of the privileges of worship. The Temple was there and God was present within it, and all that was necessary was that the spontaneous devotion of the worshippers should be regulated by the essential conditions of ceremonial propriety. But the destruction of the Temple had proved that the mere existence of a sanctuary was no guarantee of the favour and protection of the God who was supposed to dwell within it. Jehovah might be driven from His Temple by the presence of sin among the people, or even by a neglect of the ceremonial precautions which were necessary to guard against the profanation of His holiness. On this idea the whole edifice of the later ritual is built up, and here as in other respects Ezekiel has shown the way. In his view the validity and efficiency of the whole Temple service hangs on the due performance of the public rites which preserve the nation in a condition of sanctity and continually represent it as a holy people before God. Under cover of this representative service the individual may draw near with confidence to seek the face of his God in acts of private homage, but apart from the regular official ceremonial his worship has no reality, because he can have no assurance that Jehovah will accept his offering. His right of access to God springs from his fellowship with the religious community of Israel, and hence the indispensable presupposition of every act of worship is that the standing of the community before Jehovah be preserved intact by the rites appointed for that purpose. And, as has been already said, these rites are representative in character. Being performed on behalf of the nation, the obligation of presenting them rests with the prince in his representative capacity, and the share of the people in them is indicated by the tribute which the prince is empowered to levy for this end. In this way the ideal unity of the nation finds continual expression in the worship of the sanctuary, and the supreme interest of religion is transferred from the mere act of personal homage to the abiding conditions of acceptance with God symbolised by the stated service.

Let us now look at some details of the scheme in which this important idea is embodied. The foundation of the whole system is the daily burnt-offering--the tamîd. Under the first Temple the daily offering seems to have been a burnt-offering in the morning and a meal-offering (minhah) in the evening, [281] and this practice seems to have continued down to the time of Ezra. [282] According to the Levitical law it consists of a lamb morning and evening, accompanied on each occasion by a minhah and a libation of wine. [283] Ezekiel's ordinance occupies a middle position between these two. Here the tamîd is a lamb for a burnt-offering in the morning, along with a minhah of flour mingled with oil; and there is no provision for an evening sacrifice. [284] The presentation of this sacrifice on the altar in the morning, as the basis on which all other offerings through the day were laid, may be taken to symbolise the truth that the acceptance of all ordinary acts of worship depended on the representation of the community before God in the regular service. To the spiritual perception of a Psalmist it may have suggested the duty of commencing each day's work with an act of devotion:--

Jehovah, in the morning shalt Thou hear my voice;
In the morning will I set [my prayer] in order before Thee, and will look out. [285]

The offerings for the Sabbaths and new moons may be considered as amplifications of the daily sacrifice. They consist exclusively of burnt-offerings. On the Sabbath six lambs are presented, perhaps one for each working day of the week, together with a ram for the Sabbath itself (Smend). At the new moon feast this offering is repeated with the addition of a bullock. It may be noted here once for all that each burnt sacrifice is accompanied by a corresponding minhah, according to a fixed scale. For sin-offerings, on the other hand, no minhah seems to be appointed.

At the annual (or rather half-yearly) celebrations the sin-offering appears for the first time among the stated sacrifices. The sacrifice for the cleansing of the sanctuary at the beginning of each half of the year consists of a young bullock for a sin-offering, in addition of course to the burnt-offerings which were prescribed for the first day of the month. For the Passover and the Feast of Tabernacles the daily offering is a he-goat for a sin-offering, and seven bullocks and seven rams for a burnt-offering during the week covered by these festivals. Besides this, at Passover, and probably also at Tabernacles, the prince presents a bullock as a sin-offering for himself and the people. We have now to consider more particularly the place which this class of sacrifices occupies in the ritual.

III. Atoning Sacrifices.--It is evident, even from this short survey, that the idea of atonement holds a conspicuous place in the symbolism of Ezekiel's Temple. He is, indeed, the earliest writer (setting aside the Levitical Code) who mentions the special class of sacrifices known as sin- and guilt-offerings. Under the first Temple ceremonial offences were regularly atoned for at one time by money payments to the priests, and these fines are called by the names afterwards applied to the expiatory sacrifices. [286] It does not follow, of course, that such sacrifices were unknown before the time of Ezekiel, nor is such a conclusion probable in itself. The manner in which the prophet alludes to them rather shows that the idea was perfectly familiar to his contemporaries. But the prominence of the sin-offering in the public ritual may be safely set down as a new departure in the Temple service, as it is one of the most striking symptoms of the change that passed over the spirit of Israel's religion at the time of the Exile.

Of the elements that contributed to this change the most important was the deepened consciousness of sin that had been produced by the teaching of the prophets as verified in the terrible calamity of the Exile. We have seen how frequently Ezekiel insists on this effect of the divine judgment; how, even in the time of her pardon and restoration, he represents Israel as ashamed and confounded, not opening her mouth any more for the remembrance of all that she had done. We are therefore prepared to find that full provision is made for the expression of this abiding sense of guilt in the revised scheme of worship. This was done not by new rites invented for the purpose, but by seizing on those elements of the old ritual which represented the wiping out of iniquity, and by so remodelling the whole sacrificial system as to place these prominently in the foreground. Such elements were found chiefly in the sin-offering and guilt-offering, which occupied a subsidiary position in the old Temple, but are elevated to a place of commanding importance in the new. The precise distinction between these two kinds of sacrifice is an obscure point of the Levitical ritual which has never been perfectly cleared up. In the system of Ezekiel, however, we observe that the guilt-offering plays no part in the stated service, and must therefore have been reserved for private transgressions of the law of holiness. And in general it may be remarked that the atoning sacrifices differ from others, not in their material, but in certain features of the sacred actions to be observed with regard to them. We cannot here enter upon the details of the symbolism, but the most important fact is that the flesh of the victims is neither offered on the altar as in the burnt-offering, nor eaten by the worshippers as in the peace-offering, but belongs to the category of most holy things, and must be consumed by the priests in a holy place. In certain extreme cases, however, it has to be burned without the sanctuary. [287]

Now in the chapters before us the idea of sacrificial atonement is chiefly developed in connection with the material fabric of the sanctuary. The sanctuary may contract defilement by involuntary lapses from the stringent rules of ceremonial purity on the part of those who use it, whether priests or laymen. Such errors of inadvertence were almost unavoidable under the complicated set of formal regulations into which the fundamental idea of holiness branched out, yet they are regarded as endangering the sanctity of the Temple, and require to be carefully atoned for from time to time, lest by their accumulation the worship should be invalidated and Jehovah driven from His dwelling-place. But besides this the Temple (or at least the altar) is unfit for its sacred functions until it has undergone an initial process of purification. The principle involved still survives in the consecration of ecclesiastical buildings in Christendom, although its application had doubtless a much more serious import under the old dispensation than it can possibly have under the new.

A full account of this initial ceremony of purification is given in the end of the forty-third chapter, and a glance at the details of the ritual may be enough to impress on us the conceptions that underlie the process. It is a protracted operation, extending apparently over eight days. [288] The first and fundamental act is the offering of a sin-offering of the highest degree of sanctity, the victim being a bullock and the flesh being burned outside the sanctuary. The blood alone is sprinkled on the four horns of the altar, the four corners of the "settle," and the "border": this is the first stage in the dedication of the altar. Then for seven days a he-goat is offered for a sin-offering, the same rites being observed, and after it a burnt-offering consisting of a bullock and a ram. These sacrifices are intended only for the purification of the altar, and only on the day after their completion is the altar ready to receive ordinary public or private gifts--burnt-offerings and peace-offerings. Now four expressions are used to denote the effect of these ceremonies on the altar. The most general is "consecrate," literally "fill its hand" [289] --a phrase used originally of the installation of a priest into his office, and then applied metaphorically to consecration or initiation in general. The others are "purify," [290] "unsin," [291] (the special effect of the sin-offering) and "expiate." [292] Of these the last is the most important. It is the technical priestly term for atonement for sin, the reference being of course generally to persons. As to the fundamental meaning of the word, there has been a great deal of discussion, which has not yet led to a decisive result. The choice seems to lie between two radical ideas, either to "wipe out" or to "cover," and so render inoperative. [293] But either etymology enables us to understand the use of the word in legal terminology. It means to undo the effect of a transgression on the religious status of the offender, or, as in the case before us, to remove natural or contracted impurity from a material object. And whether this is conceived as a covering up of the fault so as to conceal it from view, or a wiping out of it, amounts in the end to the same thing. The significant fact is that the same word is applied both to persons and things. It furnishes another illustration of the intimate way in which the ideas of moral guilt and physical defect are blended in the ceremonial of the Old Testament.

The meaning of the two atoning services appointed for the beginning of the first and the seventh month is now clear. They are intended to renew periodically the holiness of the sanctuary established by the initiatory rites just described. For it is evident that no indelible character can attach to the kind of sanctity with which we are here dealing. It is apt to be lost, if not by mere lapse of time, at least by the repeated contact of frail men who with the best intentions are not always able to fulfil the conditions of a right use of sacred things. Every failure and mistake detracts from the holiness of the Temple, and even unnoticed and altogether unconscious offences would in course of time profane it if not purged away. Hence "for every one that erreth and for him that is simple"[294] atonement has to be made for the house twice a year. The ritual to be observed on these occasions bears a general resemblance to that of the inaugural ceremony, but is simpler, only a single bullock being presented for a sin-offering. On the other hand, it expressly symbolises a purification of the Temple as well as of the altar. The blood is sprinkled not only on the "settle" of the altar, but also on the doorposts of the house, and the posts of the eastern gate of the inner court.

We may now pass on to the second application made by Ezekiel of the idea of sacrificial atonement. These purifications of the sanctuary, which bulk so largely in his system, have their counterpart in atonements made directly for the faults of the people. For this purpose, as we have already seen, a sin-offering was to be presented at each of the great annual festivals by the prince, for himself and the nation which he represented. But it is important to observe that the idea of atonement is not confined to one particular class of sacrifices. It lies at the foundation of the whole system of the stated service, the purpose of which is expressly said to be "to make atonement for the house of Israel."[295] Thus while the half-yearly sin-offering afforded a special opportunity for confession of sin on the part of the people, we are to understand that the holiness of the nation was secured by the observance of every part of the prescribed ritual which regulated its intercourse with God. And since the nation is in itself imperfectly holy and stands in constant need of forgiveness, the maintenance of its sanctity by sacrificial rites was equivalent to a perpetual act of atonement. Special offences of individuals had of course to be expiated by special sacrifices, but beneath all particular transgressions lay the broad fact of human impurity and infirmity; and in the constant "covering up" of this by a divinely instituted system of religious ordinances we recognise an atoning element in the regular Temple service.

The sacrificial ritual may therefore be regarded as a barrier interposed between the natural uncleanness of the people and the awful holiness of Jehovah seated in His Temple. That men should be permitted to approach Him at all is an unspeakable privilege conferred on Israel in virtue of its covenant relation to God. But that the approach is surrounded by so many precautions and restrictions is a perpetual witness to the truth that God is of purer eyes than to behold iniquity and one with whom evil cannot dwell. If these precautions could have been always perfectly observed, it is probable that no periodical purification of the sanctuary would have been enjoined. The ordinary ritual would have sufficed to maintain the nation in a state of holiness corresponding with the requirements of Jehovah's nature. But this was impossible on account of the slowness of men's minds and their liability to err in their most sacred duties. Sin is so subtle and pervasive that it is conceived as penetrating the network of ordinances destined to intercept it, and reaching even to the dwelling-place of Jehovah Himself. It is to remove such accidental, though inevitable, violations of the majesty of God that the ritual edifice is crowned by ceremonies for the purification of the sanctuary. They are, so to speak, atonements in the second degree. Their object is to compensate for defects in the ordinary routine of worship, and to remove the arrears of guilt which had accumulated through neglect of some part of the ceremonial scheme. This idea appears quite clearly in Ezekiel's legislation, but it is far more impressively exhibited in the Levitical law, where different elements of Ezekiel's ritual are gathered up into one celebration in the Great Day of Atonement, the most solemn and imposing of the whole year.

Hence we see that the whole system of sacrificial worship is firmly knit together, being pervaded from end to end by the one principle of expiation, behind which lay the assurance of pardon and acceptance to all who approached God in the use of the appointed means of grace. Herein lay the chief value of the Temple ritual for the religious life of Israel. It served to impress on the mind of the people the great realities of sin and forgiveness, and so to create that profound consciousness of sin which has passed over, spiritualised but not weakened, into Christian experience. Thus the law proved itself a schoolmaster to bring men to Christ, in whose atoning death the evil of sin and the eternal conditions of forgiveness are once for all and perfectly revealed.

The positive truths taught or suggested by the ritual of atonement are too numerous to be considered here. It is a remarkable fact that neither in Ezekiel nor in any other part of the Old Testament is an authoritative interpretation given of the most essential features of the ritual. The people seem to have been left to explain the symbolism as best they could, and many points which are obscure and uncertain to us must have been perfectly intelligible to the least instructed amongst them. For us the only safe rule is to follow the guidance of the New Testament writers in their use of sacrificial institutions as types of the death of Christ. The investigation is too large and intricate to be attempted in this place. But it may be well in conclusion to point out one or two general principles, which ought never to be overlooked in the typical interpretation of the expiatory sacrifices of the Old Testament.

In the first place atonement is provided only for sins committed in ignorance; and moral and ceremonial offences stand precisely on the same footing in the eye of the law. In Ezekiel's system, indeed, it was only sins of inadvertence that needed to be considered. He has in view the final state of things in which the people, though not perfect nor exempt from liability to error, are wholly inclined to obey the law of Jehovah so far as their knowledge and ability extend. But even in the Levitical legislation there is no legal dispensation for guilt incurred through wanton and deliberate defiance of the law of Jehovah. To sin thus is to sin "with a high hand," [296] and such offences have to be expiated by the death of the sinner, or at least his exclusion from the religious community. And whether the precept belong to what we call the ceremonial or to the moral side of the law, the same principle holds good, although of course its application is one-sided, strictly moral transgressions being for the most part voluntary, while ritual offences may be either voluntary or inadvertent. But for wilful and high-handed departure from any precept, whether ethical or ceremonial, no atonement is provided by the law; the guilty person "falls into the hands of the living God," and forgiveness is possible only in the sphere of personal relations between man and God, into which the law does not enter.

This leads to a second consideration. Atoning sacrifices do not purchase forgiveness. That is to say, they are never regarded as exercising any influence on God, moving Him to mercy towards the sinner. They are simply the forms to which, by Jehovah's own appointment, the promise of forgiveness is attached. Hence sacrifice has not the fundamental significance in Old Testament religion that the death of Christ has in the New. The whole sacrificial system, as we see quite clearly from Ezekiel's prophecy, presupposes redemption; the people are already restored to their land and sanctified by Jehovah's presence amongst them before these institutions come into operation. The only purpose that they serve in the system of religion to which they belong is to secure that the blessings of salvation shall not be lost. Both in this vision and throughout the Old Testament the ultimate ground of confidence in God lies in historic acts of redemption in which Jehovah's sovereign grace and love to Israel are revealed. Through the sacrifices the individual was enabled to assure himself of his interest in the covenant blessings promised to his nation. They were the sacraments of his personal acceptance with Jehovah, and as such were of the highest importance for his normal religious life. But they were not and could not be the basis of the forgiveness of sins, nor did later Judaism ever fall into the error of seeking to appease the Deity by a multiplication of sacrificial gifts. When the insufficiency of the ritual system to give true peace of conscience or to bring back the outward tokens of God's favour is dwelt upon, the ancient Church falls back on the spiritual conditions of forgiveness already enunciated by the prophets.

> *Thou desirest not sacrifice that I should give it,*
> *Thou delightest not in burnt-offering.*
> *The sacrifices of God are a broken spirit:*
> *A broken and a contrite heart, O God, Thou wilt not despise.* [297]

Finally, we have learned from Ezekiel that the idea of atonement is not lodged in any particular rite, but pervades the sacrificial system as a whole. Suggestive as the ritual of the sin-offering is to the Christian conscience, it must not be isolated from other developments of the sacrificial idea or taken to embody the whole permanent meaning of the institution. There are at least two other aspects of sacrifice which are clearly expressed in the ritual legislation of the Old Testament--that of homage, chiefly symbolised by the burnt-offering, and that of communion, symbolised by the peace-offering and the sacrificial feast observed in connection with it. And although, both in Ezekiel and the Levitical law, these two elements are thrown into the shade by the idea of expiation, yet there are subtle links of affinity between all three, which will have to be traced out before we are in a position to understand the first principles of sacrificial worship. The brilliant and learned researches of the late Professor Robertson Smith have thrown a flood of light on the original rite of sacrifice and the important place which it occupies in ancient religion. [298] He has sought to explain the intricate system of the Levitical legislation as an unfolding, under varied historical influences, of different aspects of the idea of communion between God and men, which is the essence of primitive sacrifice. In particular he has shown how special atoning sacrifices arise through emphasising by appropriate symbolism the element of reconciliation which is implicitly contained in every act of religious communion with God. This at least enables us to understand how the atoning ritual with all its distinctive features yet resembles so closely that which is common to all types of sacrifice, and how the idea of expiation, although concentrated in a particular class of sacrifices, is nevertheless spread over the whole surface of the sacrificial ritual. It would be premature as well as presumptuous to attempt here to estimate the consequences of this theory for Christian theology. But it certainly seems to open up the prospect of a wider and deeper apprehension of the religious truths which are differentiated and specialised in the Old Testament dispensation, to be reunited in that great Atoning Sacrifice, in which the blood of the new covenant has been shed for many for the remission of sins.

Footnotes:

265. Smith, Religion of the Semites, pp. 196 f.
266. Ch. xi. 16.
267. Micah vi. 6-8.
268. Smith, Old Testament in Jewish Church, p. 379.
269. Ch. xlv. 18-25.
270. Vv. 18-20. In ver. 20 we should read with the LXX. "in the seventh month, on the first day of the month," etc.
271. Vv. 21-25. Some critics, as Smend and Cornill, think that in ver. 14 we should read fifteenth instead of fourteenth, to perfect the symmetry of the two halves of the year. There is no MS. authority for the proposed change.
272. Smend.
273. Exod. xxiii. 14-17 (Book of the Covenant, with which the other code--Exod. xxxiv. 18-22--agrees); Deut. xvi. 1-17.
274. Cf. Lev. xxiii. 4-44 (Law of Holiness); Numb. xxviii., xxix.
275. It is usual to speak of these ceremonies in Ezekiel as festivals. But this seems to go beyond the prophet's meaning. Only a single sacrifice, a sin-offering, is mentioned; and there is no hint of any public assemblage of the people on these days. It was the priests' business to see that the sanctuary was purified, and there was no occasion for the people to be present at the ceremony. The congregation would be the ordinary congregation at the new moon feast, which of course did not represent the whole population of the country. No doubt, as we see from the references below, the ceremony developed into a special feast after the Exile.
276. Cf. Lev. xxiii. 23-32; Numb. xxix. 1-11.
277. Cf. Deut. xvi. 9, with Lev. xxiii. 10 f., 15 t. In the one case the seven weeks to Pentecost are reckoned from the putting of the sickle into the corn, in the other from the presentation of a first sheaf of ripe corn in the Temple, which falls within the Passover week. The latter can only be regarded as a more precise determination of the former, and thus Unleavened Bread must have coincided with the beginning of barley harvest.
278. Deut. xvi. 13.
279. Ch. xlv. 22.
280. Ch. xlvi. 12: cf. xliv. 3.
281. 2 Kings xvi. 15: cf. 1 Kings xviii. 29, 36.
282. Ezra ix. 5.
283. Numb. xxviii. 3-8; Exod. xxix. 38-42.
284. Ch. xlvi. 13-15.
285. Psalm v. 3, probably used at the presentation of the morning tamîd. A more distinct recognition of the spiritual significance of the evening sacrifice is found in Psalm cxli. 2.
286. 2 Kings xii. 17.
287. Cf. ch. xliii. 21.
288. Another explanation, however, is possible, and is adopted by Smend and Davidson. Assuming that a burnt-offering was offered on the first day, and holding the whole description to be somewhat elliptical, they bring the entire process within the limits of the week. This certainly looks more satisfactory in itself. But would Ezekiel be likely to admit an ellipsis in describing so important a function? I have taken for granted above that the seven days of the double sacrifice are counted from the "second day" of ver. 22.
289. Ver. 26.
290. thr (ver. 20).
291. ht' a denominative form from ht' = sin (ver. 22).
292. kpr (ver. 26).
293. See Smith, Old Testament in Jewish Church, p. 381.
294. Ch. xlv. 20.
295. Ch. xlv. 15, 17.
296. As distinguished from sins, bsnnh, or through inadvertence. See Numb. xv. 30, 31.
297. Psalm li. 16, 17.
298. See his Burnet Lectures on the Religion of the Semites, to which, as well as to his Old Testament in the Jewish Church, the present chapter is largely indebted.

Chapter XXX - Renewal And Allotment Of The Land. Chapters xlvii., xlviii

In the first part of the forty-seventh chapter the visionary form of the revelation, which had been interrupted by the important series of communications on which we have been so long engaged, is again resumed. The prophet, once more under the direction of his angelic guide, sees a stream of water issuing from the Temple buildings and flowing eastward into the Dead Sea. [299] Afterwards he receives another series of directions relating to the boundaries of the land and its division among the twelve tribes. [300] With this the vision and the book find their appropriate close.

I

The Temple stream, to which Ezekiel's attention is now for the first time directed, is a symbol of the miraculous transformation which the land of Canaan is to undergo in order to fit it for the habitation of Jehovah's ransomed people. Anticipations of a renewal of the face of nature are a common feature of Messianic prophecy. They have their roots in the religious interpretation of the possession of the land as the chief token of the divine blessing on the nation. In the vicissitudes of agricultural or pastoral life the Israelite read the reflection of Jehovah's attitude towards Himself and His people: fertile seasons and luxuriant harvests were the sign of His favour; drought and famine were the proof that He was offended. Even at the best of times, however, the condition of Palestine left much to be desired from the husbandman's point of view, especially in the kingdom of Judah. Nature was often stern and unpropitious, the cultivation of the soil was always attended with hardship and uncertainty, large tracts of the country were given over to irreclaimable barrenness. There was always a vision of better things possible, and in the last days the prophets cherished the expectation that vision would be realised. When all causes of offence are removed from Israel and Jehovah smiles on His people, the land will blossom into supernatural fertility, the ploughman overtaking the reaper, and the treader of grapes him that soweth seed, the mountains dropping new wine and the hills melting. [301] Such idyllic pictures of universal plenty and comfort abound in the writings of the prophets, and are not wanting in the pages of Ezekiel. We have already had one in the description of the blessings of the Messianic kingdom; [302] and we shall see that in this closing vision a complete remodelling of the land is presupposed, rendering it all alike suitable for the habitation of the tribes of Israel.

The river of life is the most striking presentation of this general conception of Messianic felicity. It is one of those vivid images from Eastern life which, through the Apocalypse, have passed into the symbolism of Christian eschatology. "And he showed me a pure river of water of life, clear as crystal, proceeding out of the throne of God and of the Lamb. In the midst of the street of it, and on either side of the river, was there the tree of life, which bare twelve manner of fruits, and yielded her fruits every month: and the leaves of the tree were for the healing of the nations."[303] So writes the seer of Patmos, in words whose music charms the ear even of those to whom running water means much less than it did to a native of thirsty Palestine. But John had read of the mystic river in the pages of his favourite prophet before he saw it in vision. The close resemblance between the two pictures leaves no doubt that the origin of the conception is to be sought in Ezekiel's vision. The underlying religious truth is the same in both representations, that the presence of God is the source from which the influences flow forth that renew and purify human existence. The tree of life on each bank of the river, which yields its fruit every month and whose leaves are for healing, is a detail transferred directly from Ezekiel's imagery to fill out the description of the glorious city of God into which the nations of them that are saved are gathered.

But with all its idealism, Ezekiel's conception presents many points of contact with the actual physiography of Palestine; it is less universal and abstract in its significance than that of the Apocalypse. The first thing that might have suggested the idea to the prophet is that the Temple mount had at least one small stream, whose "soft-flowing" waters were already regarded as a symbol of the silent and unobtrusive influence of the divine presence in Israel. [304] The waters of this stream flowed eastward, but they were too scanty to have any appreciable effect on the fertility of the region through which they passed. Further, to the south-east of Jerusalem, between it and the Dead Sea, stretched the great wilderness of Judah, the most desolate and inhospitable tract in the

The Expositor's Bible: The Book of Ezekiel

whole country. There the steep declivity of the limestone range refuses to detain sufficient moisture to nourish the most meagre vegetation, although the few spots where wells are found, as at Engedi, are clothed with almost tropical luxuriance. To reclaim these barren slopes and render them fit for human industry, the Temple waters are sent eastward, making the desert to blossom as the rose. Lastly, there was the Dead Sea itself, in whose bitter waters no living thing can exist, the natural emblem of resistance to the purposes of Him who is the God of life. These different elements of the physical reality were familiar to Ezekiel, and come back to mind as he follows the course of the new Temple river, and observes the wonderful transformation which it is destined to effect. He first sees it breaking forth from the wall of the Temple at the right-hand side of the entrance, and flowing eastward through the courts by the south side of the altar. Then at the outer wall he meets it rushing from the south side of the eastern gate, and still pursuing its easterly course. At a thousand cubits from the sanctuary it is only ankle deep, but at successive distances of a thousand cubits it reaches to the knees, to the loins, and becomes finally an impassable river. The stream is of course miraculous from source to mouth. Earthly rivers do not thus broaden and deepen as they flow, except by the accession of tributaries, and tributaries are out of the question here. Thus it flows on, with its swelling volume of water, through "the eastern circuit," "down to the Arabah" (the trough of the Jordan and the Dead Sea), and reaching the sea it sweetens its waters so that they teem with fishes of all kinds like those of the Mediterranean. Its uninviting shores become the scene of a busy and thriving industry; fishermen ply their craft from Engedi to Eneglaim, [305] and the food supply of the country is materially increased. The prophet may not have been greatly concerned about this, but one characteristic detail illustrates his careful forethought in matters of practical utility. It is from the Dead Sea that Jerusalem has always obtained its supply of salt. The purification of this lake might have its drawbacks if the production of this indispensable commodity should be interfered with. Salt, besides its culinary uses, played an important part in the Temple ritual, and Ezekiel was not likely to forget it. Hence the strange but eminently practical provision that the shallows and marshes at the south end of the lake shall be exempted from the influence of the healing waters. "They are given for salt." [306]

We may venture to draw one lesson for our own instruction from this beautiful prophetic image of the blessings that flow from a pure religion. The river of God has its source high up in the mount where Jehovah dwells in inaccessible holiness, and where the white-robed priests minister ceaselessly before Him; but in its descent it seeks out the most desolate and unpromising region in the country, and turns it into a garden of the Lord. While the whole land of Israel is to be renewed and made to minister to the good of man in fellowship with God, the main stream of fertility is expended in the apparently hopeless task of reclaiming the Judæan desert and purifying the Dead Sea. It is an emblem of the earthly ministry of Him who made Himself the friend of publicans and sinners, and lavished the resources of His grace and the wealth of His affection on those who were deemed beyond ordinary possibility of salvation. It is to be feared, however, that the practice of most Churches has been too much the reverse of this. They have been tempted to confine the water of life within fairly respectable channels, amongst the prosperous and contented, the occupants of happy homes, where the advantages of religion are most likely to be appreciated. That seems to have been found the line of least resistance, and in times when spiritual life has run low it has been counted enough to keep the old ruts filled and leave the waste places and stagnant waters of our civilisation ill provided with the means of grace. Nowadays we are sometimes reminded that the Dead Sea must be drained before the gospel can have a fair chance of influencing human lives, and there may be much wisdom in the suggestion. A vast deal of social drainage may have to be accomplished before the word of God has free course. Unhealthy and impure conditions of life may be mitigated by wise legislation, temptations to vice may be removed, and vested interests that thrive on the degradation of human lives may be crushed by the strong arm of the community. But the true spirit of Christianity can neither be confined to the watercourses of religious habit, nor wait for the schemes of the social reformer. Nor will it display its powers of social salvation until it carries the energies of the Church into the lowest haunts of vice and misery with an earnest desire to seek and to save that which is lost. Ezekiel had his vision, and he believed in it. He believed in the reality of God's presence in the sanctuary and in the stream of blessings that flowed from His throne, and he believed in the possibility of reclaiming the waste places of his country for the kingdom of God. When Christians are united in like faith in the power of Christ and the abiding presence of His Spirit, we may expect to see times of refreshing from the presence of God and the whole earth filled with the knowledge of the Lord as the waters cover the sea.

II

John J. Skinner

Ezekiel's map of Palestine is marked by something of the same mathematical regularity which was exhibited in his plan of the Temple. His boundaries are like those we sometimes see on the map of a newly settled country like America or Australia--that is to say, they largely follow the meridian lines and parallels of latitude, but take advantage here and there of natural frontiers supplied by rivers and mountain ranges. This is absolutely true of the internal divisions of the land between the tribes. Here the northern and southern boundaries are straight lines running east and west over hill and dale, and terminating at the Mediterranean Sea and the Jordan Valley, which form of course the western and eastern limits. As to the external delimitation of the country it is unfortunately not possible to speak with certainty. The eastern frontier is fixed by the Jordan and the Dead Sea so far as they go, and the western is the sea. But on the north and south the lines of demarcation cannot be traced, the places mentioned being nearly all unknown. The north frontier extends from the sea to a place called Hazar-enon, said to lie on the border of Hauran. It passes the "entrance to Hamath," and has to the north not only Hamath, but also the territory of Damascus. But none of the towns through which it passes--Hethlon, Berotha, Sibraim--can be identified, and even its general direction is altogether uncertain. [307]

From Hazar-enon the eastern border stretches southward till it reaches the Jordan, and is prolonged south of the Dead Sea to a place called Tamar, also unknown. From this we proceed westwards by Kadesh till we strike the river of Egypt, the Wady el-Arish, which carries the boundary to the sea. It will be seen that Ezekiel, for reasons on which it is idle to speculate, excludes the transjordanic territory from the Holy Land. Speaking broadly, we may say that he treats Palestine as a rectangular strip of country, which he divides into transverse sections of indeterminate breadth, and then proceeds to parcel out these amongst the twelve tribes.

A similar obscurity rests on the motives which determined the disposition of the different tribes within the sacred territory. We can understand, indeed, why seven tribes are placed to the north and only five to the south of the capital and the sanctuary. Jerusalem lay much nearer the south of the land, and in the original distribution all the tribes had their settlements to the north of it except Judah and Simeon. Ezekiel's arrangement seems thus to combine a desire for symmetry with a recognition of the claims of historical and geographic reality. We can also see that to a certain extent the relative positions of the tribes correspond with those they held before the Exile, although of course the system requires that they shall lie in a regular series from north to south. Dan, Asher, and Naphtali are left in the extreme north, Manasseh and Ephraim to the south of them, while Simeon lies as of old in the south with one tribe between it and the capital. But we cannot tell why Benjamin should be placed to the south and Judah to the north of Jerusalem, why Issachar and Zebulun are transferred from the far north to the south, or why Reuben and Gad are taken from the east of the Jordan to be settled one to the north and the other to the south of the city. Some principle of arrangement there must have been in the mind of the prophet, and several have been suggested; but it is perhaps better to confess that we have lost the key to his meaning. [308]

The prophet's interest is centred on the strip of land reserved for the sanctuary and public purposes, which is subdivided and measured out with the utmost precision. It is twenty-five thousand cubits (about 8-1/3 miles) broad, and extends right across the country. The two extremities east and west are the crown lands assigned to the prince for the purposes we have already seen. In the middle a square of twenty-five thousand cubits is marked off; this is the "oblation" or sacred offering of land, in the middle of which the Temple stands. This again is subdivided into three parallel sections, as shown in the accompanying diagram. The most northerly, ten thousand cubits in breadth, is assigned to the Levites; the central portion, including the sanctuary, to the priests; and the remaining five thousand cubits is a "profane place" for the city and its common lands. The city itself is a square of four thousand five hundred cubits, situated in the middle of this southmost section of the oblation. With its free space of two hundred and fifty cubits in width belting the wall it fills the entire breadth of the section; the communal possessions flanking it on either hand, just as the prince's domain does the "oblation" as a whole. The produce of these lands is "for food to them that serve' [i.e., inhabit] the city." [309] Residence in the capital, it appears, is to be regarded as a public service. The maintenance of the civic life of Jerusalem was an object in which the whole nation was interested, a truth symbolised by naming its twelve gates after the twelve sons of Jacob. [310] Hence, also, its population is to be representative of all the tribes of Israel, and whoever comes to dwell there is to have a share in the land belonging to the city. [311] But evidently the legislation on this point is incomplete. How were the inhabitants of the capital to be chosen out of all the tribes? Would its citizenship be regarded as a privilege or as an onerous responsibility? Would it be necessary to make a selection out of a host of applications, or would special inducements have to be offered to procure a sufficient population? To these questions the vision furnishes no answer, and there is nothing to show whether Ezekiel contemplated the possibility that residence in the new city might present few attractions and many disadvantages to an agricultural community such as he had in view. It is a curious incident of the return from the

Exile that the problem of peopling Jerusalem emerged in a more serious form than Ezekiel from his ideal point of view could have foreseen. We read that "the rulers of the people dwelt at Jerusalem: the rest of the people also cast lots, to bring one of ten to dwell in Jerusalem, the holy city, and nine parts in [other] cities. And the people blessed all the men that willingly offered themselves to dwell at Jerusalem." [312] There may have been causes for this general reluctance which are unknown to us, but the principal reason was doubtless the one which has been hinted at, that the new colony lived mainly by agriculture, and the district in the immediate vicinity of the capital was not sufficiently fertile to support a large agricultural population. The new Jerusalem was at first a somewhat artificial foundation, and a city too largely developed for the resources of the community of which it was the centre. Its existence was necessary more for the protection and support of the Temple than for the ordinary ends of civilisation; and hence to dwell in it was for the majority an act of self-sacrifice by which a man was felt to deserve well of his country. And the only important difference between the actual reality and Ezekiel's ideal is that in the latter the supernatural fertility of the land and the reign of universal peace obviate the difficulties which the founders of the post-exilic theocracy had to encounter.

This seeming indifference of the prophet to the secular interests represented by the metropolis strikes us as a singular feature in his programme. It is strange that the man who was so thoughtful about the salt-pans of the Dead Sea should pass so lightly over the details of the reconstruction of a city. But we have had several intimations that this is not the department of things in which Ezekiel's hold on reality is most conspicuous. We have already remarked on the boldness of the conception which changes the site of the capital in order to guard the sanctity of the Temple. And now, when its situation and form are accurately defined, we have no sketch of municipal institutions, no hint of the purposes for which the city exists, and no glimpse of the busy and varied activities which we naturally connect with the name. If Ezekiel thought of it at all, except as existing on paper, he was probably interested in it as furnishing the representative congregation on minor occasions of public worship, such as the Sabbaths and new moons, when the whole people could not be expected to assemble. The truth is that the idea of the city in the vision is simply an abstract religious symbol, a sort of epitome and concentration of theocratic life. Like the figure of the prince in earlier chapters, it is taken from the national institutions which perished at the Exile; the outline is retained, the typical significance is enhanced, but the form is shadowy and indistinct, the colour and variety of concrete reality are absent. It was perhaps a stage through which political conceptions had to pass before their religious meaning could be apprehended. And yet the fact that the symbol of the Holy City is preserved is deeply suggestive and indeed scarcely less important in its own way than the retention of the type of the king. Ezekiel can no more think of the land without a capital than of the state without a prince. The word "city"--synonym of the fullest and most intense form of life, of life regulated by law and elevated by devotion to a common ideal, in which every worthy faculty of human nature is quickened by the close and varied intercourse of men with each other--has definitely taken its place in the vocabulary of religion. It is there, not to be superseded, but to be refined and spiritualised, until the city of God, glorified in the praises of Israel, becomes the inspiration of the loftiest thought and the most ardent longing of Christendom. And even for the perplexing problems that the Church has to face at this day there is hardly a more profitable exercise of the Christian imagination than to dream with practical intent of the consecration of civic life through the subjection of all its influences to the ends of the Redeemer's kingdom.

On the other hand we must surely recognise that this vision of a Temple and a city separated from each other--where religious and secular interests are as it were concentrated at different points, so that the one may be more effectually subordinated to the other--is not the final and perfect vision of the kingdom of God. That ideal has played a leading and influential part in the history of Christianity. It is essentially the ideal formulated in Augustine's great work on the city of God, which ruled the ecclesiastical polity of the mediæval Church. The State is an unholy institution; it is an embodiment of the power of this present evil world: the true city of God is the visible Catholic Church, and only by subjection to the Church can the State be redeemed from itself and be made a means of blessing. That theory served a providential purpose in preserving the traditions of Christianity through dark and troubled ages, and training the rude nations of Europe in purity and righteousness and reverence for that by which God makes Himself known. But the Reformation was, amongst other things, a protest against this conception of the relation of Church to State, of the sacred to the secular. By asserting the right of each believer to deal with Christ directly without the mediation of Church or priest it broke down the middle wall of partition between religion and every-day duty; it sanctified common life by showing how a man may serve God as a citizen in the family or the workshop better than in the cloister or at the altar. It made the kingdom of God to be a present power wherever there are lives transformed by love to Christ and serving their fellow-men for His sake. And if Catholicism may find some plausible support for its theory in Ezekiel and the Old Testament theocracy in general, Protestants may perhaps with better right appeal to the grander ideal represented by the new Jerusalem of the Apocalypse--the city that needs no Temple, because the Lord Himself is in her midst.

"And I John saw the holy city, new Jerusalem, coming down from God out of heaven, prepared as a bride adorned for her husband. And I heard a great voice out of heaven saying, Behold, the tabernacle of God is with men, and He will dwell with them, and they shall be His people, and God Himself shall be with them, and be their God.... And I saw no temple therein: for the Lord God Almighty and the Lamb are the temple of it. And the city had no need of the sun, neither of the moon, to shine in it: for the glory of God did lighten it, and the Lamb is the light thereof." [313]

It may be difficult for us amid the entanglements of the present to read that vision aright-- difficult to say whether it is on earth or in heaven that we are to look for the city in which there is no Temple. Worship is an essential function of the Church of Christ; and so long as we are in our earthly abode worship will require external symbols and a visible organisation. But this at least we know, that the will of God must be done on earth as it is in heaven. The true kingdom of God is within us; and His presence with men is realised, not in special religious services which stand apart from our common life, but in the constant influence of His Spirit, forming our characters after the image of Christ, and permeating all the channels of social intercourse and public action, until everything done on earth is to the glory of our Father which is in heaven. That is the ideal set forth by the coming of the holy city of God, and only in this way can we look for the fulfilment of the promise embodied in the new name of Ezekiel's city, Jehovah-shammah,--

The Lord is There.

Footnotes:

299. Ch. xlvii. 1-12.
300. Chs. xlvii. 13-xlviii. 35.
301. Amos ix. 13.
302. Ch. xxxiv. 25-29.
303. Rev. xxii. 1, 2.
304. Isa. viii. 6.
305. Engedi, "well of the kid," is at the middle of the western shore; Eneglaim, "well of two calves," is unknown, but probably lay at the north end. The eastern side is left to the Arabian nomads.
306. Ver. 11.
307. I do not myself see much objection to supposing that it leaves the sea near Tyre and proceeds about due east to Hazar-enon, which may be near the foot of Hermon, where Robinson located it. In this case the "entrance to Hamath" would be the south end of the Be?a', where one strikes north to go to Hamath. This would correspond nearly to the extent of the country actually occupied by the Hebrews under the judges and the monarchy. The statement that the territory of Damascus lies to the north presents some difficulty on any theory. It may be added that Hazar-hattikon in ver. 16 is the same as Hazar-enon; it is probably, as Cornill suggests, a scribe's error for ntsrh nvn (the locative ending being mistaken for the article).
308. Smend, for example, points out that if we count the Levites' portion as a tribal inheritance, and include Manasseh and Ephraim under the house of Joseph (as is done in the naming of the gates of the city), we have the sons of Rachel and Leah evenly distributed on either side of the "oblation." Then at the farthest distance from the Temple are the sons of Jacob's handmaids, Gad in the extreme south, and Dan, Asher, and Naphtali in the north. This is ingenious, but not in the least convincing.
309. Ver. 18.
310. Vv. 31-34. It is difficult to trace a clear connection between the positions of the gates and the geographical distribution of the tribes in the country. The fact that here Levi is counted as a tribe and Ephraim and Manasseh are united under the name of Joseph indicates perhaps that none was intended.
311. Ver. 19.
312. Neh. xi. 1, 2.
313. Rev. xxi. 2, 3, 22, 23.